AF361508

"MOORS DRESSED AS MOORS"

JAVIER IRIGOYEN-GARCÍA

"Moors Dressed as Moors"

Clothing, Social Distinction,
and Ethnicity in Early
Modern Iberia

UNIVERSITY OF TORONTO PRESS
Toronto Buffalo London

ISBN 978-1-4875-0160-0

Library and Archives Canada Cataloguing in Publication

Irigoyen-García, Javier, 1975–, author
"Moors dressed as Moors" : clothing, social distinction, and ethnicity
in early modern Iberia / Javier Irigoyen-García.

(Toronto Iberic)
Includes bibliographical references and index.
ISBN 978-1-4875-0160-0 (cloth)

1. Moriscos – Clothing – Iberian Peninsula – History – 16th century.
2. Moriscos – Clothing – Iberian Peninsula – History – 17th century.
3. Moriscos – Iberian Peninsula – Ethnic identity – History – 16th century.
4. Moriscos – Iberian Peninsula – Ethnic identity – History – 17th century.
5. Iberian Peninsula – Ethnic relations – History – 16th century. 6. Iberian
Peninsula – Ethnic relations – History – 17th century. 7. Iberian Peninsula –
Social life and customs – 16th century. 8. Iberian Peninsula – Social life
and customs – 17th century. I. Title. II. Series: Toronto Iberic

DP104.I75 2017   946'.02   C2016-908251-2

University of Toronto Press acknowledges the financial assistance to its
publishing program of the Canada Council for the Arts and the Ontario Arts
Council, an agency of the Government of Ontario.

A la memoria de Jerónimo García Servet

Contents

Acknowledgments

No book is an individual project, and this even less so. I have benefited from the intellectual exchange with many colleagues, namely Natalio Ohanna, Seth Kimmel, María del Pilar Chouza-Calo, Enrique García Santo-Tomás, D. Fairchild Ruggles, Alejandro García-Reidy, Eleonora Stoppino, Mercedes Alcalá-Galán, Marcus Keller, Juan Hernández Franco, Julio Baena, Mariselle Meléndez, Steven Hutchinson, Joyce Tolliver, José Ignacio Hualde, Eric Calderwood, L. Elena Delgado, Eduardo Ledesma, and Paula M. Carns, as well as many graduate students with whom I explored some of these themes in our seminars. I am thankful to Miguel Martínez for inviting me to present an early version of this work at the Western Mediterranean Culture Workshop at the University of Chicago, where this book took shape. A special note goes to William Childers, whose work and conversation convinced me of the need to combine archival research with critical theory. I am still in debt to Barbara Fuchs for her continued support, but also for the period I worked as a research assistant for her. This book is largely an extension of the conversations we had when she was writing *Exotic Nation*, as I kept pondering many of those issues for years until I was finally able to articulate questions I did not even know I had.

Writing in a language that is not my own is often a painful process, but it has its rewards, as it forced me to think twice about the exact meaning of every word and, more important, provided me with the opportunity to work with devoted readers. I am grateful to Teresa Greppi for her enthusiasm and careful revision of the manuscript. Without the expert eye, infinite knowledge, and generous encouragement of Linde Brocato I would not have been able to finish this book. I am extremely grateful to the staff of the Interlibrary Loan services at the

University of Illinois at Urbana-Champaign, and especially to Lesley Lee, for their diligence, professionalism, and patience in providing me with all my requests, no matter what they might be. I must also thank the University of Illinois Research Board, the Department of Spanish and Portuguese at the University of Illinois, and Silvina Montrul for their support for this project.

On the other shore of the Atlantic, there is also a plethora of archivists to whom I owe much gratitude: Soledad Nuevo Ábalos and Manuel Garrido Pérez (Archivo Municipal de Archidona), Rafael Gómez Díaz (Archivo Municipal de Talavera de la Reina), Eustaquio Jiménez Puga (Archivo Municipal de Almagro), Eugenio Villarreal Mascaraque (Archivo Municipal de Leganés), Ricardo Guerra Sancho (Cronista Oficial de Arévalo), Pepe Zumel (Archivo Municipal de Chinchón), Carlos Rodríguez (Archivo Municipal de Medina de Rioseco), Jesús Cuadros Callava (Archivo Municipal de Priego), Francisco Toro Ceballos (Archivo Municipal de Alcalá la Real), María José Calvo (Archivo Histórico Municipal de Baeza), Dolores Serrano (Archivo Municipal de Baza), Alejandro Romero (Archivo Municipal de Jaén), Rafael Gómez Díaz, César Pacheco Jiménez, and Yolanda Moreno (Archivo Municipal de Talavera de la Reina), Mariano García Ruipérez (Archivo Municipal de Toledo), Mercedes Noviembre (Biblioteca Zabálburu), María Ángeles Santos Quer (Instituto Valencia de Don Juan), and Isabel Aguirre and the staff at the Archivo General de Simancas.

My contact with archivists and local historians in Spain made me realize that I had to dedicate this book to my grandfather, Jerónimo García Servet. I grew up watching him reading manuscripts without understanding why he was consuming his delicate vision with those undecipherable characters. Three decades later, I realized much too late that he would have been an excellent interlocutor. As a dear colleague once told me, my grandfather was an "eccentric historian." That was intended as a compliment, as my grandfather, while a recognized local historian of Murcia, did not belong to academia. I am not a professional historian either, even if I saw how the historiographical research needed to build up my own argument has kept growing over the last three years. Many of the archival sources consulted in this book had already been mined by other historians and in many instances my work has consisted in retracing their steps to verify the sources and continue their work. It was sometimes a redundant task, as very often the work previously done by others was as exhaustive and accurate as it could be and I had nothing to add to their findings. But in many cases, verifying primary sources proved a necessary exercise, as it elicited very different conclusions than those made by others, either because there were paleographic errors in their readings or, more frequently, because different interpretations could be made. Yet even when we had different interpretations and approaches, my experience taught me to appreciate the efforts of previous historians, as I realized that without their previous patient and time-consuming mining of the archives I would not have been able to begin my research in the first place. By the time I decided to dedicate this book to my grandfather, I was surprised to find out that Javier Castillo Fernández was working at the Archivo General de la Región de Murcia, the same archive (albeit in a different location) in which my grandfather spent most of his life. Since Castillo Fernández's work on the Moriscos of Granada has greatly influenced my own, I felt fortunate not only in meeting him in person and receiving invaluable advice for my research, but also for this felicitous coincidence that showed me how to recuperate some sort of dialogue with my grandfather in the most serendipitous way.

Ós meus carrabouxos.

Figure 1. Anonymous. "Haist el schugo de Kainna" [Game of Canes]. *Códice de trajes*, 1r. Courtesy Biblioteca Nacional de España, RES/285.

Figure 2. Jan Cornelisz Vermeyen. "The Game of Canes" (1538). Private Collection. C.L. Stopford Sackville. Courtesy Photographic Survey, Courtauld Institute of Art.

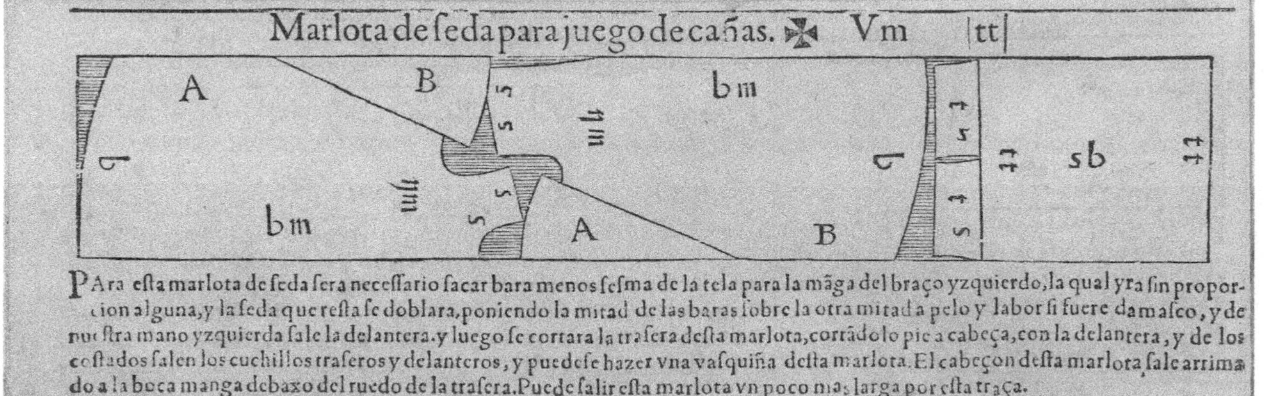

PAra esta marlota de seda sera necessario sacar bara menos sesma de la tela para la mãga del braço yzquierdo, la qual yra sin propor-
cion alguna, y la seda que resta se doblara, poniendo la mitad de las baras sobre la otra mitad a pelo y labor si fuere damasco, y de
nuestra mano yzquierda sale la delantera, y luego se cortara la trasera desta marlota, cortãdolo pie a cabeça, con la delantera, y de los
costados salen los cuchillos traseros y delanteros, y puedese hazer vna vasquiña desta marlota. El cabeçon desta marlota sale arrima-
do a la boca manga debaxo del ruedo de la trasera. Puede salir esta marlota vn poco mas larga por esta traça.

Figure 3. Juan de Alcega. Pattern for *marlota* for the game of canes. *Libro de geometría, práctica y traza* (1580), 62v. Courtesy Biblioteca Nacional de España, R/7641.

Figure 4. Anonymous. "Game of canes with the participation of Philip the Handsome in Valladolid, on July 19, 1506." Bibliothèque Royale de Belgique, Brussels. Courtesy Art Resource, NY.

Figure 5. Alfonso Sánchez Coello. *Infantes don Diego and Don Felipe* (1579). Monastery of Las Descalzas Reales, Madrid. Courtesy Art Resource, NY.

Figure 6. Jehan Lhermite. "Game of Canes in the Plaza Mayor" (1592). *Le passetemps de Jehan Lhermite*. Bibliothèque Royale de Belgique, Brussels. Cabinet des manuscrits, MSS II 1028.

Figure 7. Juan de la Corte, "Festival in the Plaza Mayor" (1623). Museo de Historia de Madrid. Courtesy Art Resource, NY.

Figure 8. Gregorio Tapia y Salcedo. "Game of Canes." *Exercicios de la gineta al príncipe Nuestro Señor Baltasar Carlos* (1643). Biblioteca Nacional de España, R/3275.

Figure 9. Stairs of the Colegios Mayores. Salamanca.

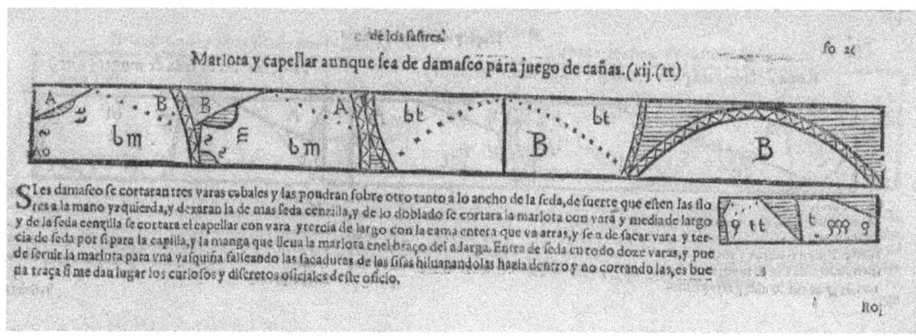

Figure 10. Diego de Freyle. Pattern for *marlota* for the game of canes. *Geometría y traça para el oficio de los sastres* (Sevilla: Fernando Díaz, 1588), 20r. Courtesy Folger Shakespeare Library.

Figure 11. Abraham van Bruyn. "Sic Hispani Taurus insectantur." *Diversarum gentium armatura equestris*. 1578. Courtesy Anne S.K. Brown Military Collection, Brown University Library.

Figure 12. Felipe de Vigarny. Baptism of the Moriscos in the Kingdom of Granada (c. 1520). Capilla Real, Catedral de Granada, Granada. Courtesy Art Resource, NY.

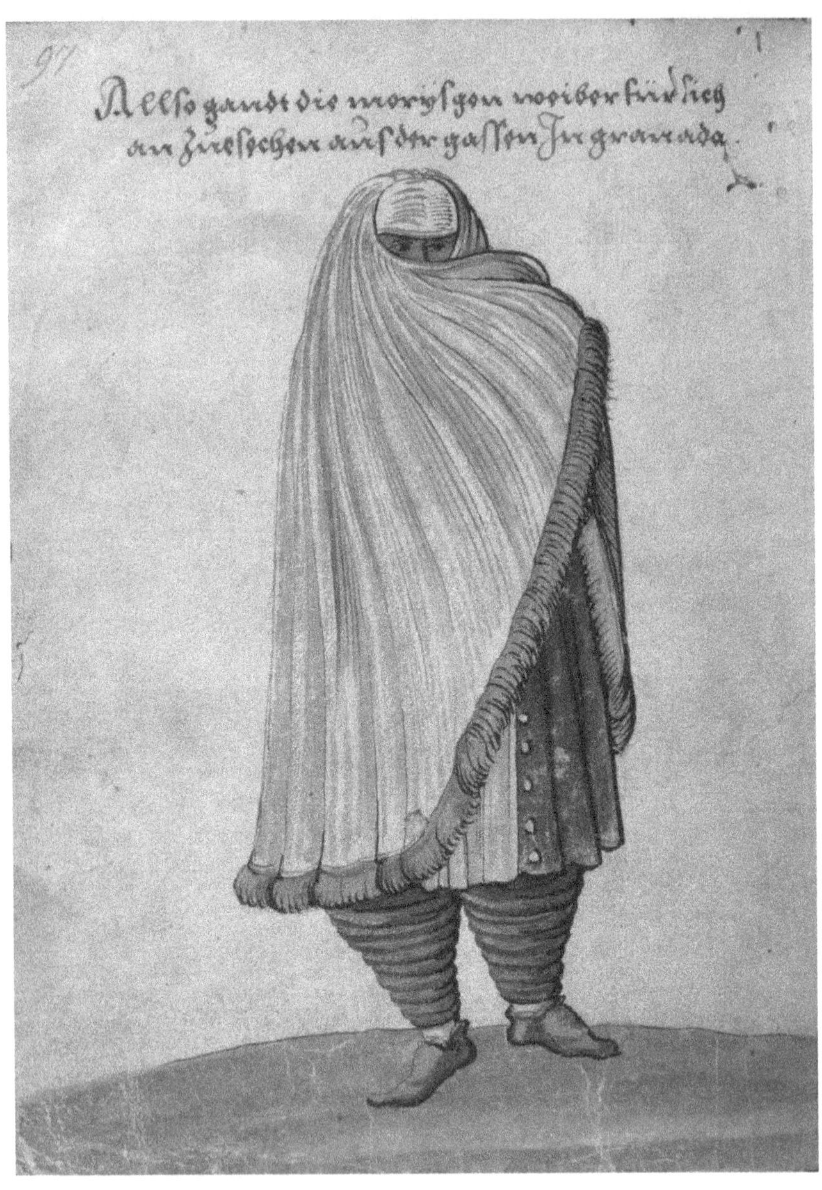

Figure 13. Christoph Weiditz. "Street-Dress of Fashionable Morisco Women in Granada." Plate 98v of *Trachtenbuch* (c. 1530–40). Hs 22474. Photograph by L. Streppelhoff. Courtesy © Germanisches Nationalmuseum.

Figure 14. Christoph Weiditz. Morisco Travelling with Wife and Child in the Kingdom of Granada. Plate 105v–6r of *Trachtenbuch* (c. 1530–40). Hs 22474. Photograph by L. Streppelhoff. Courtesy © Germanisches Nationalmuseum.

Figure 15. Christoph Weiditz. "Morisco Dance." Plate 107v–8r of *Trachtenbuch* (c. 1530–40). Hs 22474. Photograph by L. Streppelhoff. Courtesy © Germanisches Nationalmuseum.

Figure 16. Vicent Mestre. "Embarkment of the Moriscos in the port of Denia" (1613). Fundación Bancaja, Valencia.

Figure 17. Jan Cornelisz Vermeyen. "Combat of Moors" (c. 1535–37). © Musée du Louvre, dist. RMN – Grand Palais / Martine Beck-Coppola. Département des Arts Graphiques, INV 19192 recto.

Figure 18. Francisco Heylan. "Morisco Uprising in Ugíjar" (c. 1624). Engraving for Justino Antolínez de Burgos's *Historia eclesiástica de Granada*. Courtesy Museo Casa de los Tiros, Granada.

Figure 19. Francisco Heylan. "Martyrs of Mairena" (c. 1624). Engraving for Justino Antolínez de Burgos's *Historia eclesiástica de Granada*. Courtesy Museo Casa de los Tiros, Granada.

"MOORS DRESSED AS MOORS"

Introduction: "Moors Dressed as Moors"

In his *Historia del rebelión y castigo de los moriscos del reino de Granada* (1600), Luis del Mármol Carvajal recounts the 1569 rebellion of the descendants of the Muslims from the Kingdom of Granada (also known as Moriscos) and the military repression of this group and its dispersal throughout the Kingdom of Castile. As Mármol Carvajal frames the story of the uprising, its most immediate cause was a series of decrees from Philip II in 1567 banning Morisco cultural practices, including the prohibition on speaking Arabic, using bathhouses, and wearing Morisco clothing. Mármol Carvajal's work soon became one of the most authoritative historical references on the subject and his view greatly influenced subsequent historiography on the Moriscos, even to the present day.

According to Mármol Carvajal, the first episode of the uprising took place on Christmas Eve of 1568, when the rebel Morisco Farax Abenfarax led a troop of two hundred men and tried to stir up a revolt among the Moriscos of the city of Granada. In order to convince the reluctant urban Moriscos of the Albaicín, Abenfarax and his men dressed up as Turks to feign that they had the support of the Ottoman Empire, but they had no success whatsoever and ultimately had to leave Granada at dawn. Abenfarax's plan failed due to a combination of strategic, climatological, and social factors: he could not gather as many men as he intended because of unexpectedly heavy snowfall, and his attempt to stir up the Albaicín failed because the urban Moriscos did not identify with the cause of rural communities. What interests me here is that Abenfarax's plan also failed in one small but significant detail: the Turkish disguise did not fool anybody. Not only did the Moriscos not find it a convincing proof of Ottoman support, but Old Christians also saw through this instance of passing. According to Mármol Carvajal, the next day a soldier reported to the Marquis of Mondéjar, the military commander of Granada, that the rioters were "moros vestidos ... como moros" [Moors dressed ... as Moors]. Read literally, the soldier's report claimed that the Moors were trying to pass as themselves – and failed.[1]

As the context makes clear, the soldier meant that the rebels were Moriscos trying to pass as Turks. Yet the apparently naive expression "Moors dressed as Moors" lays bare a complex equivocation that reveals the ambiguous semantics of Spanish *moro*. On the one hand, and more obviously, *moro* as a synonym for Muslim could be applied to very different peoples, such as Iberian Moriscos, North Africans, or Turks. While this semantic conflation was common in early modern Iberia, it is striking to find it in Mármol Carvajal's text, precisely because he explains the etymology of the word *moro* in the introductory chapters and claims that it is only properly used when applied to North Africans.[2] Even if the conflation of such different ethnic and sartorial features under the term *moro* is attributable to the anonymous soldier, Mármol Carvajal seems to take a perverse pleasure in transcribing this equivocation without further clarification – perhaps because he does not feel that his reader would need one. Was Mármol Carvajal making fun of Abenfarax's attempt to pass? Was he mocking the anonymous soldier's simplicity? Or did he copy this passage from another source without realizing that this conflation undermined his previous scholarly exhibition on the term *moro*? On the other hand, and more relevant to my point, the expression "Moors dressed as Moors" is an equivocation because each instance of the word *moro* refers to very different meanings. In the first instance, *moro* refers to religion, as the Moriscos were thought to cling to their Muslim faith even though they were baptized Christians. Meanwhile, the second instance of *moro* refers to sartorial practices and appearances. Paradoxically, the equivocation shows that *moro* as a synonym for a Muslim was not necessarily considered to be the same as *moro* as dressed body. This book focuses on this second meaning of *moro* to analyse the complex relationship between social bodies and Moorish clothing in early modern Iberia.

In chapters 4 and 7 I will offer alternative interpretations of Abenfarax's passing by contextualizing it within the discourses of early modern sumptuary legislation and Iberian festivals. For now, it suffices to point out the kinds of questions that this passage elicits when considered within the larger frame of the War of the Alpujarras and the prohibition of "Morisco clothing" dictated by Philip II: if the Moriscos failed so miserably to dress as "Moors," why was Philip II prohibiting them from doing something they were actually not used to doing? What, then, was the connection between Moriscos and "Moorish clothing," and how did it relate to the larger context of the uses of Moorish clothing in early modern Iberia? Where did Abenfarax obtain Turkish clothing for almost two hundred men? What if those Moriscos never tried to trick anybody but instead dressed as "Turks" for a different reason that is now opaque to us? Abenfarax's passing, to which I will return throughout this book, serves as a model because it allows us to reconsider the place of Moorish clothing within early modern Iberian society, to complicate assumptions about the relationship between clothing and ethnicity, and to question the iconographic and historiographical traditions through which we have imagined the sartorial landscape of early modern Iberian society.

Legislating Appearances: Medieval to Early Modern

This book deals with the use of Moorish clothing in early modern Iberia between 1492 and the first half of the seventeenth century. It is nonetheless necessary to venture a little bit further back in time and look at the relationship between religious identity and sartorial legislation in the Middle Ages to understand how it changed in the transition to modernity. During the late Middle Ages, when Christians, Jews, and Muslims inhabited the same Iberian space, their social relations were often mediated by royal and ecclesiastical legislation aiming to create a strict sartorial separation between the different religious communities.

As early as 1215, the Fourth Lateran Council prohibited Jews and Muslims from displaying signs of social status and mandated that they wear distinctive marks on their clothing so they could be easily identified. Similar laws were passed in all the Iberian kingdoms from the thirteenth through the fifteenth century, aiming at forcing sartorial practices upon religious minorities to clearly separate them from Christians. It seems that these laws, though constantly reiterated, were only rarely implemented, and even less frequently obeyed, and crosscultural influences among all Iberian kingdoms and across religious lines were constant throughout the medieval period.[3] Yet, regardless of the actual efficacy of these laws, the underlying logic dominant in political and social discourse was that religious difference should be made visible through clothing and that non-Christians should not wear textiles and adornments that were considered signs of social distinction, namely gold, silver, and silk.[4]

The imposition of sartorial differentiation disappeared when the coexistence of the three monotheistic religions on Iberian soil was halted soon after 1492, the year that Isabel of Castile and Fernando II of Aragon conquered the Kingdom of Granada, the last Muslim territory of former al-Andalus.[5] That very same year, they ordered that Iberian Jews either convert to Christianity or go into exile. In 1497, less than a decade later, Portuguese Muslims were forced to convert to Christianity, as were those of Castile in 1501 – Muslims in the Crown of Aragon would not be forced to convert until the 1520s.

Cultural repression followed on the heels of religious conversion, as some of the cultural markers of the Moriscos, such as the Arabic language, clothing, dances, and bathhouses were perceived as an attachment to Islam. In 1526, Charles V tried to forbid Morisco cultural practices, although enforcement of the prohibition was delayed for forty years in exchange for a levy. On 1 January 1567, Pedro de Deza, the president of the Royal Chancery of Granada, publicized Philip II's decree banning Morisco cultural practices. Philip II's decree is often thought to be the cause of the uprising of the Alpujarras, which started on Christmas Eve of 1568 (with Abenfarax's assault on the Albaicín) and ended in 1571 with the dispersion of the Moriscos of Granada throughout Castile.[6] Because religious and cultural repression seem to go hand in hand, Deborah Root notes that "[t]he Edicts of Faith, which prohibited Islamic religious practices, and the royal ordinances, which prohibited Morisco customs ... reinforced each other and supported the equation of social deviance (Morisco customs) with religious deviance (heresy)."[7]

Thus, by reading the legal language at face value, we may have the impression that in the Middle Ages strict separation was enforced along religious lines, while after 1492, in line with the promotion of religious homogeneity, sartorial difference was simply banned and cultural assimilation was promoted instead. In general, it is true that the rhetoric of medieval laws focused on separation while that of early modern laws focused on assimilation and homogenization. Yet there is no dramatic shift between medieval and early modern legislation, as we can still find traces of the medieval promotion of the use of special signs after 1492.[8] Furthermore, the way legislation on the sartorial practices of the Moriscos intersected with general sumptuary laws regulating the use of luxurious textiles across class lines indicates the prevalence of the logic of separation, even if it does not manifest itself in such an explicit form.[9] Medieval laws not only mandated that Jews and Muslims living in Christian lands wear certain identifying signs; they also prohibited them from wearing certain luxury items, such as precious metals or clothing made of silk. Thus, along with the command to be visually identifiable as Jews or Muslims, those laws also aimed at the lumpenization of the two religious minorities by preventing their elite members from wearing adornments and clothing associated with a certain elite class status.

Almost every scholar working on Moriscos mentions Philip II's 1567 decree prohibiting so-called Morisco culture as the cause for the rebellion of the Alpujarras. The entire bibliography focuses on the same passage of the legal document, in which Philip II banned the Moriscos from wearing "vestido de moros" [dress of Moors].[10] What usually passes unnoticed is that this same decree also prohibited Moriscos from wearing silk, regardless of their class status. This seemingly small but significant detail entails an untenable combination of both medieval and early modern repressive measures: at the same time that the Moriscos were not allowed any cultural practice that might be remotely associated with Islam, they were prohibited as a community from wearing silk – which means that they were legally treated as if they were in fact still Muslims living under Christian rule in medieval Iberia, even if they had converted decades before.[11]

Because of the cross-cultural influences within the Iberian Peninsula, the study of Moorish clothing cannot be limited to the Moriscos. There is no shortage of studies and cataloguing of clothing in medieval and early modern Iberia.[12] Scholars are aware that there was a high degree of sartorial influence between Muslims and Christians, and that Moorish clothing had a clear ceremonial value among Christians well into the early modern period.[13] Yet the recognition of these influences has not shattered the assumption that there was a well-defined Christian culture as opposed to an Islamic one, which had established a deterministic bond between the practice of Islam (or genealogical connection with Muslim ancestors) and the use of Moorish clothing.[14] This decontextualization is quite evident in the influential work of Carmen Bernis, which has tended to separate the study of "Moorish fashions" from the properly "European" or "Spanish" ones.[15] This exoticization was exacerbated in her most recent book *El traje y los tipos sociales del Quijote*, in which the study of Moorish clothing is relegated to the last chapter, tellingly entitled "El mundo del cautivo" [The Captive's World] – since this chapter deals with Cervantes's captivity in Algiers, it further deter-ritorializes Moorish clothing as foreign and external to a proper Iberian culture.[16]

What I call throughout this book "Iberian Moorish clothing" is not the product of an occasional cultural influence from the Islamic period, but an autonomous tradition developed by Christians for centuries – at the very least from the fifteenth century until very nearly the end of the seventeenth. Over the course of that period, clothing *a la morisca* experienced its own internal evolution, hovering between the two poles of exoticness and familiarity, but firmly embedded in cultural practices the social meaning of which had little or nothing to do with its real or alleged origins. This is especially true for men's clothing. Garments *a la morisca* were part of aristocratic ceremonial clothing up to the beginning of the sixteenth century. For instance, Sancho de Aranda recounts how in 1476 his father went to the court dressed *a la morisca*.[17] Yet by the sixteenth century, probably due to larger changes in sartorial fashion in Europe, clothing *a la morisca* began to disappear from aristocratic men's wardrobes as daily-life clothing, relegated to the equestrian performance known as the game of canes.

The game of canes (Spanish *juego de cañas*; Portuguese *jogo de canas*; Catalan *joc de canyes*) was one of the most prominent urban spectacles in early modern Iberia. In the game of canes, the participants, all of them dressed as Moors, threw light spears at each other while riding horses in complex patterns to demonstrate their equestrian prowess. The conventional Moorish attire consisted of leather boots [*borceguíes*], a Moorish tunic [*marlota*], a hooded cape [*capellar*], and a turban, as well as the leather shield known as an *adarga*. All these elements can be seen clearly in an anonymous drawing from the sixteenth century (Figure 1).[18] The game of canes was closely associated with the *gineta* riding style, in which riders used shorter stirrups, which allowed them to manoeuvre the horse more easily.[19] Riders were divided into several *quadrillas* [teams], whose number could vary but always had to be even (usually four or six), and which were usually distinguished by their colours. While games of canes could be improvised, they were most commonly choreographed performances that were rehearsed in advance. A minor variant of this game was the *juego de alcancías*, in which, instead of light spears, riders threw each other hollow balls made of clay.[20] Very frequently, the game of canes was played in conjunction with bullfights, which was considered the plebeian part of the festival.[21]

The evocation of Moorishness permeated almost every aspect of the game's organization, not only clothing. Riders were supposed to hurl and shout in a distinctive way that allegedly evoked the way Moors went to war. Music was also an essential component of the game, as can be seen in the prominence of musicians in Jan Cornelisz Vermeyen's painting (Figure 2). Indeed, sources always mention the presence of musicians as a given, even if it is not clear what kind of music supposedly accompanied the celebration. Only Jaume de Oleza states, in his *Exercicio militar* (1604), that the music of the game consisted of "sones moriscos" [Moorish melodies].[22] Along with music, clothing, and equestrian style, there might be other aspects that organizers, participants, and audiences regarded as essential to the display of Moorishness that are no longer evident to us. For instance, in a game of canes held to mark the arrival of the Duke of Osuna in Archidona in 1581, Juan de Herrera was instructed to "hazer de la gente a la morisca a pie y a cauallo" [arrange the people *à la morisca* on foot and horse], by which we may understand that he was in charge of gathering the people who were going to dress as Moors and rehearse the performance in advance. Meanwhile, Francisco de Molina was designated to look for eighteen liveries that were needed for the game. There is still a third person, a certain Juan Monsalve, who was designated "para que sea morabito y haga lo tocante a la morisca" [to be *morabito* and make everything dealing with the Moorish things].[23] In Spanish, *morabito* means some kind of Islamic saint or religious leader, but in this context, the title probably meant that Juan Monsalve was designated as some kind of master of ceremonies who would be in charge of music and choreography.

A common but inaccurate interpretation that is very often found in the bibliography is the idea that impersonations of the Moors in the game of canes parallel the festivals of *moros y cristianos*, which celebrate the Christian conquest with staged mock combats between Muslims and Christians that invariably end with the victory of the latter.[24] The origin of this confusion seems to be the oft-cited definition of the game of canes offered by the Real Academia Española in 1729, which states that "Sometimes [the game of canes] is made with half of the riders dressed as Moors and the other half dressed in the Castilian way, and then this festival is called Moors and Christians."[25] This definition was made in the eighteenth century, when the currency of the game of canes had clearly declined and had evolved into different forms of equestrian performance. It therefore does not necessarily reflect how the game of canes was played when it was in all its splendour in the previous centuries.

Indeed, it is hard to find in the game of canes the confrontational value of *moros y cristianos* predicated in the Real Academia Española's definition. While the game of canes staged a mock combat that was very often conceived as a military exercise, typically all participants were dressed as Moors. It is true that confrontational uses of the game of canes reenacting encounters between Christians and Muslims did exist. An oft-cited instance of a confrontational game of canes is that celebrated in 1463 Jaén by the Constable of Castile, Miguel Lucas de Iranzo. According to his anonymous chronicle, the constable organized a carnivalesque game of canes in which half the participants dressed as Moors and half as Christians, and in which the mock battle ended with the victory of the Christian side and the baptism of the fictional Muslim king.[26] Yet cases like this were exceptional and often took place in frontier situations, which explains the introduction of the confrontational aspect.[27]

Even when mock battles pitted Christians against Moors, it does not necessarily mean that they were intended to provide a symbolic resolution for religious conflict. In a game of canes celebrated in Alcalá de Henares in 1503, riders dressed as Moors and as Christians, but there is no indication that the Christian side was supposed to defeat the Moors.[28] There is also a confrontational representation in an anonymous painting of a game of canes in Palma de Majorca.[29] Cases like these can be explained by looking at specific material constraints, rather than ideological intentions. As Jaume de Oleza observes, the game of canes was often played in Majorca with half of the participants riding in the *brida* style and half in the *gineta* style – the former being perceived as the proper European style while the latter was believed to derive from the Islamic period, and therefore closely associated with Moorish clothing. Yet, as he clarifies, the reason for this divide was that the game of canes had only recently been imported to Majorca and as a consequence it was not always possible to find enough people who were skilled in the *gineta* style.[30] To clarify, my emphasis here on the lack of a confrontational aspect in the game of canes does not aim to depict early modern Iberia as a utopian society free of ethnocentrism, but to show that the significance of Moorish clothing had little to do with theatrical impersonations and everything to do with the display of social status.

For Teófilo Ruiz, it is a "perverse contradiction" that Philip II prohibited Morisco clothing in 1567 while he used to dress in Moorish clothing with other nobles for many games of canes.[31] The present book seeks precisely to disentangle this apparent cultural chiasmus. The juxtaposition of the cultural persecution of Moriscos and the promotion of clothing *a la morisca* among Christian nobles in equestrian performances looks like an ideological contradiction to us because the underlying logic followed by Philip II and his contemporaries is completely strange to our modern sartorial codes. We tend to regard it as an ideological contradiction because we overlook how "Iberian Moorish clothing" is closely related to the sumptuary laws regulating the use of luxurious garments across social lines. As mentioned above, in 1567 Moriscos were not only prohibited from wearing "Morisco clothing," but also silk. Thus Philip II did not necessarily prohibit the Moriscos from wearing clothing *a la morisca* because it was associated with the practice of Islam, but because it was considered a sign of high social status in Iberian society. Meanwhile, Moorish clothing served Old Christians as a way of circumventing the restrictions on the use of silk imposed by sumptuary laws, which often granted exemptions precisely for chivalric performances – among them, the game of canes.[32]

Analysing the use of Moorish clothing by Old Christians and studying the sartorial practices of the Moriscos (as well as representations of them by Old Christians) are thus inextricably interwoven, not because of the alleged Islamic origins of the garments and the ensuing cultural influence, as is generally assumed, but because Moorish clothing was closely related to the discourses of nobility and class distinction that affected Moriscos and Old Christians alike. In spite of such inextricability, this book is divided in two parts for the sake of clarity. Part I (chapters 1–4) focuses on the game of canes to analyse the production and circulation of Moorish clothing among Old Christians and how it served as a marker of nobility. Part II (chapters 5–8) focuses on how sartorial legislation against the Moriscos served to hinder their full integration in Iberian society, while showing how the Moriscos were construed as a sartorially distinct community when empirical evidence indicates otherwise. Specialists in early modern Iberian studies may notice that I have inverted the order in which these two questions are traditionally presented. If I had talked about Moriscos first and about "Christian Moorish clothing" afterwards, I would have reproduced the logical syntax predicating that Moorish clothing is merely a cultural remainder of the Islamic period. The purpose of this book is to show quite the opposite, that "Moorish clothing" had a particular social value in a specific historical period (even though it likely derived from contact with Muslims during the Middle Ages) and that this historically determined social value in hegemonic Christian society conditions both the way Old Christians embodied Moorishness in relation to class identity as well as the ambivalent legal and literary representations of Moriscos.

Iberian Christian Moorish Clothing

Throughout this book I use the term "Iberia" for the Iberian Peninsula and "Iberian" when alluding to the people who inhabited the Iberian Peninsula. I am well aware that this use of Iberia is anachronistic, since in the early modern period it existed only as a learned word. Properly speaking, the inhabitants of the kingdoms of Aragon, Castile, and Portugal defined themselves as "españoles" because they inhabited a geographical space named "España" that was equivalent to what we call the Iberian Peninsula today. Aragonese, Portuguese, and Castilian subjects defined themselves as "españoles" even during the periods in which they participated in different political realms, linguistic areas, and religious communities – as this term had not yet been appropriated by a specific political institution and did not have the more restricted political meaning that it has today. Using "español," no matter how much I qualified it, could have been misinterpreted very easily (and almost unavoidably) as though I were suggesting that early modern "España" was the same political entity as it is in the present – an even greater hazard when using the English terms "Spanish" and "Spain." Hence my preference for the anachronistic "Iberia" as the lesser of two evils, which is justified for this project because the use of Moorish clothing for the game of canes was one of the many cultural practices shared by all Iberians beyond their differences.[33]

We do not know when or why Christians began playing the game of canes dressed in Moorish garb. The first documented cases, from the end of the thirteenth century, already present it as a well-established tradition requiring no comment. Therefore, any origin is possible: it might be a cultural influence borrowed from the Islamic period, a form of colonial cultural appropriation, a masquerade of victory over Islam, or a combination of all of these.[34] Even if this book does not deal with the origins of the game of canes, it does not suggest thereby that discourses on cultural origin are irrelevant. Indeed, Iberians' cultural archaeology of Moorish performances is integral to the game itself – but at the same time the narratives of cultural archaeology were very imaginative and variegated, and reflected the cultural and political anxieties of the people producing them rather than a desire to learn where this cultural practice came from.[35] Emphasis on the origin of a determined cultural practice often obscures its actual significance in a specific historical context. Therefore this book focuses only on how the use of Moorish clothing in the game of canes (whatever its origin) served as an expression of power hierarchies and social relations in the early modern period.

Considering how much emphasis is placed on the Islamic influence in early modern discourses on the games of canes, one would expect to find the involvement of Muslim people or Moriscos in the making of Moorish clothing or references to trade with North Africa. This is true only to a very limited extent. The continued use of the *gineta* riding style and its equestrian gear certainly contributed to the economic and cultural ties between the Iberian Peninsula and North Africa, since there was trade across the religious divide between both shores of the Mediterranean in spite of occasional royal and ecclesiastical prohibitions.[36] Pedro de Aguilar's *Tractado de la cavalleria de la gineta* (1570) states that Tlemcen was the origin of some of the elements used for the *gineta*, namely spurs and stirrups.[37] Similarly, Mármol Carvajal's *Primera parte de la descripción general de África* (1573) praises those elements of the games of canes, such as the *gineta* saddles, stirrups, and *adargas* manufactured in the kingdoms of Morocco and Fes.[38]

Yet, beyond these economic exchanges, the bulk of the production of Moorish clothing in early modern Iberian society was from the hands of Old Christian tailors, weavers, and embroiderers. There were certain centres specializing in the making of Moorish clothing, such as Toledo, which was the main manufacturer of silk textiles, but garments *a la morisca* were made almost everywhere. Granada was naturally an important centre for the production of Moorish clothing, since the area was the main producer of silk, but we should take into account that by 1560 most of the tailors in the city of Granada were in fact Old Christians.[39] As we shall see in chapters 5 and 6, despite some initial uncertainty on whether the prohibitions against so-called Moorish clothing were intended for the descendants of the Muslim population or for Old Christians as well, it soon became clear that royal legislation solely targeted the Moriscos and did not affect Old Christian tailors.

One useful source for verifying the importance of Moorish clothing is the series of municipal regulations overseeing the local production of clothing and garments for the game of canes – which involved several professions, not just tailors. The 1527 ordinances of Seville (reprinted in 1632) required silk embroiderers to be examined in the making of "obra morisca."[40] In 1541, one ordinance for the tailors of Granada gave instructions on how to make Moorish clothing – it is important to note that, contrary to other ordinances within the same document, this one does not address the Moriscos in particular.[41] The 1566 ordinances of tailors in Toledo directed that tailors should be examined on how to make clothing for the game of canes.[42] The ordinances on mechanical trades made in Lisbon in 1572 mandated that weavers know how to make "all the things related to the Moorish craft."[43] The Lisbon ordinances also offer very detailed information on how blacksmiths should make Moorish stirrups, how the *adargueiros* should make the shields for the games of canes, and how tanners should make the *gineta* saddles.[44] Tailoring acreditations in Madrid usually required the knowledge of how to make Moorish clothing for the game of canes.[45] In sum, as Cristóbal Suárez de Figueroa stated in his *Plaza universal de todas las artes* (1615), tailors were explicitly expected to know how to make the *marlotas*, *capellares*, and all other garments for the game of canes.[46]

The production of Moorish clothing in the Iberian Peninsula is also attested in tailoring books, which in most cases included patterns for Moorish clothing, most notably *marlotas* and *capellares* for the game of canes.[47] The first tailoring book is Juan de Alcega's *Libro de geometría, práctica y traza* (1580). It was quite successful and was reprinted in 1589. It included a detailed description of how to make *marlotas* and *aljubas* for the game of canes (Figure 3).[48] Patterns for *marlotas* and *capellares* can also be found in subsequent tailoring books from the end of the sixteenth century through the middle of the seventeenth, such as Diego de Freyle's *Geometría y traça para el oficio de los sastres* (1588), Francisco de la Rocha Burguen's *Geometría y traça perteneciente al oficio de sastres* (1618), and Martín de Andújar's *Geometría y trazas pertenecientes al oficio de sastres* (1640).[49]

In order to show the importance of "Christian Moorish clothing" in early modern Iberia, chapter 1 traces games of canes celebrated at court from the late Middle Ages to the end of the seventeenth century. By looking at festival books and pictorial representations, this chapter shows how Moorish clothing was not merely a costume for occasional masquerades, but was deeply rooted in Iberian court and aristocratic ceremonies.

While the overwhelming record of festival books describing magnificent games of canes organized by monarchs and grandees gives the impression that it was merely entertainment for the monarchy and the high nobility, they were only the tip of the iceberg of a broader cultural phenomenon. Almost every town and city in the Iberian Peninsula held games of canes with greater or lesser frequency, but vast documentation is buried in local archives. Certainly local historians have amply noted the importance of the game of canes in municipal government, but their findings are rarely put in dialogue with each other and there is no comprehensive monograph on the game of canes across the Iberian Peninsula.[50] Chapter 2 analyses the production and circulation of Moorish clothing, showing how much it cost, who could afford it, and how it was distributed. By looking at municipal archival records, I show that, precisely because the ceremonial use of Moorish clothing was supposed to be a mark of differentiation between commoners and elites, it became a privileged locus for social confrontation and for negotiating nobility, as well as a commodity that, when distributed as livery, could trigger accusations of corruption, nepotism, and wasteful spending of municipal funds.

Festival books have to be read cautiously because of their celebratory tone, but municipal records should be read with equal care, not only because of their dry language, but mostly because they tend to privilege the side of local administration. In order to overcome the shortcomings of the sources deployed in chapter 2, chapter 3 analyses how literary texts and parodies made explicit the underlying logic sustaining the currency of Moorishness. The idealization of the noble Moor from the past in ballads, narrative, and theatre is complemented by a set of parodies that construed the commoner appropriating Moorish clothing for social climbing as a Morisco. This chapter thus suggests that literary manifestations of Moorishness not only reflected debates about the place of the Moriscos in the construction of a national and cultural identity, but may be symbolic resolutions for class struggle.

Chapter 4 examines Lope de Vega's life and oeuvre as a case study for the interpretation of Moorish clothing. First I look at the afterlife of Moorish clothing once the social capital of the game of canes had faded away to suggest that the overstock of Moorish livery was likely reused as theatrical costumes. This implies that the importance of plays including Muslim characters may not come solely from interactions (confrontational or otherwise) with Islam, but also from the material conditions of theatre as a commercial enterprise. Second, I examine how Lope constructed his own public persona in relation to the social value of Moorishness. While Lope refigured himself as a gallant Moorish rider in his early poetic works in his endeavour to be recognized as noble, the last part of his career shows an increasing disengagement from aristocratic Moorishness that parallels the frustration of his social ambitions and his relations with the court.

Moorishness Is in the Eye of the Beholder

Without losing sight of the social importance of Moorish clothing in Iberian society at large, the second part of this book focuses on legal actions against the Moriscos during the sixteenth century and at the beginning of the seventeenth, as well as how Morisco bodies were ambiguously construed as a site of sartorial difference. Even though religion, language, and clothing (as well as the gamut of cultural practices that were the object of legislation) are usually grouped together, they belong to different spheres of cultural identity. Moriscos were usually represented as crypto-Muslim illiterate labourers and as Arabic speakers dressed in Moorish garb, yet it is quite rare to find individuals who fulfil such stereotypes. Furthermore, each of these markers of ethnic identity shows a different degree of visibility. Religious beliefs, which were in theory the primary object of the Inquisition, are, by their nature, hardly accessible. Language seems in principle to be more defining as a marker of ethnicity. Yet, while it is clear that for many of the Moriscos from Granada and Valencia there was a strong attachment to Arabic, many others were bilingual or Castilian monolinguals with no knowledge of Arabic, especially in Castile and Aragon.[51]

Among these cultural elements, clothing stands as the most visible trait for homogenizing Moriscos as a group and therefore it serves in theory as the perfect means of visualizing their alleged cultural difference. Yet for the external observer, clothing as a marker of ethnic identity can also deceive. Different from language and religion, clothing generates specific social meanings and strategies of interpretation that go beyond its mere materiality. The Morisco as a differently-dressed body is a ghostly signifier. On the one hand, the need to render difference visible turns Morisco bodies into the privileged location of exoticness in pictorial, religious, and literary representation. Yet, on the other hand, there was resistance to fully identifying the Moriscos with Moorishness during the period in which Moorish clothing had an essential social value in early modern Iberian society.

This book thus participates in the historiographical debate about the assimilation of the Moriscos in early modern society, aligning itself with the recent tendency in Morisco studies that emphasizes their cultural assimilation.[52] Yet when discussing the cultural assimilation of the Moriscos, we should recall that there is no stable definition of the culture they were supposed to be embracing. We often tend to forget that so-called Castilian culture was far from being homogeneous and that regional sartorial differences across the Iberian Peninsula were pronounced, determined by factors such as class status, socio-economic position, and profession. In sum, sartorial difference was everywhere and it was impossible for anyone not to dress differently from others, yet legal texts never make explicit to which of these subgroups the Moriscos should be assimilating. The other methodological problem is that cultural assimilation is hardly a traceable or quantifiable phenomenon, since the Moriscos who fully assimilated into their local communities were those who had effaced the memory of their Muslim ancestors.[53] Those "unassimilated," on the contrary, were not necessarily those individuals who were clearly identifiable because of their cultural practices, but rather those whose reputation as descendants of the Muslims overlaid their sartorial practices with unintended meanings. No matter what garments they wore, those recognized as Moriscos could always be construed as dressing as "Moors."

The particularity of Moorish/Morisco clothing is that it creates a twofold relationship between ethnicity and class status that forces us to reformulate our view of early modern clothing. By looking at how sumptuary legislation tried to establish an unequivocal link between clothing and class status, Rosalind Jones and Peter Stallybrass argue that in Renaissance Europe "clothes permeate the wearer, fashioning him or her within."[54] Hence the persistent (and mostly futile) goal of sumptuary laws that during the medieval and early modern period aimed to control the appropriation of clothing allegedly belonging to the higher classes by individuals from society's lower rungs, as this appropriation was assumed to annul the effectiveness of clothing as a transparent sign of social relations.

But class difference may not work in relation to clothing in the same way that ethnicity does. The peculiarity of early modern Iberia is that sumptuary laws restricting luxurious garments depending on class intersected with the laws regulating the sartorial practices of ethno-religious minorities during the medieval period as well as the so-called Morisco cultural difference in the sixteenth century. The ambivalent status of Moorish clothing as a mark of both social status and ethno-religious identity in early modern Iberia complicates the relationship between inner identity and exteriority attributed to clothing, since the perception of Moorish clothing as a signifying practice denoting either class or ethno-religious identity depended not only on the materiality of dress, but also on the social standing of the individual wearing it. Rephrasing Jones and Stallybrass, we can also say that, inversely, knowledge about the genealogical origins of the wearer also conditions the perception of his or her clothing in an environment in which the expression of social status is confounded by markers of ethno-religious difference.

Hersch, MacKay, and MacKendrick already point to this interpretation in a suggestive article. As they propose, the transition between the medieval laws requiring Jews and Moors to wear distinctive signs and the sixteenth-century laws mandating quite the opposite, that the descendants of Jews and Muslims assimilate their sartorial practices with Old Christians, meant an oversignification of dress depending on genealogy:

> whereas Jews were thought not to be respecting boundaries, as signified by dress, *conversos* and *moriscos* were accused of being crypto-Jews or crypto-Muslims precisely because they were alleged to cling to the dress signifiers of their previous religions. These readings of dress signs clearly indicate that such signs were not necessarily read logocentrically but that meaning was imputed to them in order to suggest signifieds which were alien to authorial intention.[55]

As a result, they raise an important question: "Is it possible that the signified was at times arrived at without any relevant signifier being present?"[56] Or, as I propose in this book, is it possible that the dress of an individual known to be a Morisco was automatically perceived to be "Morisco" independent of the clothing she or he was actually wearing? As these authors argue, this possibility is clearly articulated in the satirical poem that the Count of Paredes composed towards the end of the fifteenth century, in which he accused Juan Poeta of being a *converso* and transforming every sign of Christianity into signs of Judaism with his mere presence at church. The transformation that Juan Poeta's presence exerts upon reality includes of course the alteration of religious robes into the garments associated with a stereotypical image of Jews: "The blessed robe was turned into a coat ... The alb turned into a vest when it was touched by your finger ... the stole turned into a mantle, and the liturgical cloth [was turned into] a pointed hood."[57] Beyond this apparent supernatural transformation of signs, the poem alludes to how the social reputation of an individual affects the social practices in which he participates, and how the interpretation of a cultural object (in this case, the ethnicity of clothing) is mediated by the public image of the people who use them rather than by the object itself.

More than a hundred years later, we find a similar formulation in Francisco de Quevedo's ballad "A los moros por dinero," although in this case the instability of the imaginary of difference targets an Old Christian. Quevedo takes as his subtext a previous anonymous ballad in which Doña Urraca, complaining that her father the king is disinheriting her, announces that she will be forced to prostitute herself "to the Moors for money, and to the Christians for free."[58] In Quevedo's parodic ballad, the subject complains that prostitutes, conceived as contemporary Doña Urracas, make him a Moor when they force him to pay: "All of them call me Antón and charge me [as if my name were] Azarque, and my love notes are Qurans in our transactions. The hat that I take off looks like a turban to them, and my prose Arabic, even though I speak in plain Spanish."[59] The analogy is clearly tongue-in-cheek and does not aim to conflate Moorishness and Spanishness. Nevertheless, it reveals how easily the slippage works at the symbolic level.[60] These two poems expose in a comic tone the underlying problem when trying to establish a neat sartorial difference across ethno-religious lines: that the perception of the "ethnicity of clothing" is not only located in objects or practices themselves, but also in the context (as in Quevedo's poem) and the genealogy of the participants (as in the Count of Paredes's composition).[61]

In adopting this situational approach I do not intend to negate sartorial difference in its entirety. If I suggest that Morisco sartorial difference is spectral in the cultural imaginary it is not because I claim that there was no basis for it, but because the way differences and similarities were categorized depended on the contexts that were considered meaningful for articulating such difference. Even if some Moriscos quite probably wore some distinctive garments (especially Morisco women in rural areas by the beginning of the sixteenth century), such difference crystallized in legal discourses and visual documents as if all the Moriscos in any period, location, and context were dressed as "Moors," when in fact most of the Moriscos were indistinguishable from Old Christians living in the same communities. In many instances, as we shall see, the Moorishness of the Moriscos exists only in the eye of the beholder.

Chapter 5 focuses on the ever-changing perception and policing of the Moriscos' sartorial practices in the Kingdom of Granada from 1492 until the uprising of the Alpujarras (1568–71), as reflected in the legal documents prohibiting so-called Morisco culture, namely Charles V's decree of 1526 and Philip II's decree of 1567. I analyse the ideological motivations and assumptions underlying these legal documents and show how their conception of ethnicity is permeated by concerns about gender policing and socio-economic status. I argue that the main goal of these laws was not the repression of Morisco culture, as generally held, but the further marginalization of elite male Moriscos by precluding their access to the signs of social status available to their Old Christian counterparts. This chapter also contests the emphasis attributed by both early modern and contemporary historians to sartorial prohibition as the primary cause for the uprising of the Moriscos and shows how such historians created the myth of a sartorial revival during the uprising.

Chapter 6 analyses how the search for Morisco sartorial difference extended to the rest of the Iberian Peninsula between the War of the Alpujarras and the expulsion of the Moriscos in 1609–14. I look at several local cases in which Moriscos were construed as keeping differentiated sartorial practices, namely in Lorca (Murcia), Magacela (Badajoz), Valle de Ricote (Murcia), and Orihuela (Alicante). In many of these cases, Moriscos disputed such classification, while in others the contradictory language of the documents reveals in itself that there was no agreement on how to interpret sartorial practices. This chapter shows how the construction of the Moriscos as visually differentiated bodies became meaningful only within specific socio-economic and political contexts not necessarily related to the discourses of religious and cultural homogenization they were ostensibly implementing.

Chapter 7 looks at those instances in which the Moriscos dressed as Moors in public festivals along with Old Christians. While the musical performances known as *zambras* were allowed and even promoted by Christian authorities (in spite of intermittent prohibitions), the Moriscos' participation in games of canes and military exhibitions was usually regarded with suspicion, because those public displays afforded participants a claim to social equality. These cases show that the Moriscos probably saw in Moorish clothing not an issue of cultural identity, but an opportunity for social climbing.

In chapter 8 I turn to literature and propaganda to analyse the historical evolution of how the Moriscos were construed as theatrical bodies. Discourses on the Moriscos written at the beginning of the seventeenth century, around the eve and the aftermath of their expulsion in 1609–14, construe them as a miserably dressed expendable population. Even though the authors justifying the expulsion tried to exaggerate their alterity, they could not imagine the Moriscos dressing as "Moors" because Moorish clothing was still considered a sign of noble status. In contrast, dramatic texts written in the next decades of the seventeenth century increasingly exoticized Moriscos by representing them dressed as Moors, and this shift happened precisely as Moorish clothing was losing its social prestige in early modern Iberian society.

A Note on Terminology: Moorish or Morisco Clothing?

We should be cautious about the inherent conflation of the term "Moor" and the adjective "Moorish," and how these terms relate to the equivalent terms in Castilian, Portuguese, and Catalan. The term "Moor" is not homogeneously used across Europe, since its meaning fluctuates and acquires specific connotations depending on the semantic field in which it is used. The overlapping terminology to describe Muslims is common to medieval and early modern Europe, but there are some specificities in early modern Iberian conceptions of Muslims.[62] It is important to note that for early modern Iberians the Spanish word *moro* did not necessarily indicate a phenotypic difference, as it did in northern Europe. Even when Iberian sources refer to Moriscos as *moros*, they were merely accusing them of being crypto-Muslims, but Moriscos and Old Christians were in general phenotypically indistinguishable from each other.[63]

The most specific term, "Morisco," is also a problematic category, since this is the exo-ethnonym used by Old Christians to define those individuals who descended from Iberian Muslims, but it is rarely used as an endo-ethnonym. Some Moriscos, those who still adhered to Islam in secret, would refer to themselves as *muslimes*, while those who converted would refer to themselves simply as Christians.[64] "Morisco" alternates in early modern texts with other terms like "cristiano nuevo de moros" [New Christian from Muslim origin], to differentiate them from Old Christians, those who boasted of not having mixed their lineage with Jews, Muslims, heretics, or their descendants. This difference, like any other categorization based on lineage, was susceptible to falsification – yet it was operative in social discourse.[65]

A similar set of problems arises when we deal with how the terms *moro* and *morisco* were applied to clothing. The category of "Moorish clothing" is extremely vague and can hardly be a useful tag to describe cultural realities. It is always difficult to reconstruct the sartorial landscape and the systems of clothing categorizations used in the past, because such a project is complicated by factors such as the lack of correlation between names and images, as well as geographical, social, and temporal variation.[66] In the case of Moorish clothing, in many instances it is hard to know what exactly texts mean by terms such as Morisco, *moro*, or *a la morisca* that are used almost interchangeably. Clothing worn by a Morisco of Granada at the beginning of the sixteenth century, a Muslim in Fes, and an Iberian aristocrat playing the game of canes – to name only a few of the many instances in which the category "Moorish clothing" is applied – were probably quite different garments. To complicate things further, the expression *a la morisca* very often referred to a certain quality of dress, most usually meaning that it was lavishly decorated and with a certain kind of embroidery.

Of the problematic referentiality of these terms, María Judith Feliciano Chaves argues, "[s]artorial items commonly called 'Morisco' ... oscillated between the realms of Iberian clothing (daily wear) and costume (theatrical, performance-oriented), depending on the wearers, the circumstances and the intended audience."[67] Feliciano Chaves points out the distortion implied in using terms overcharged with religious connotations when dealing with textiles and clothing, such as "Islamic," "Muslim," or "Moorish," and proposes instead to talk about "Andalusi textiles" and of *mudejarismo* as a cultural practice that crossed religious lines.[68] The adjectives "Andalusi" and "Andalusi-derived" have evident advantages for conducting archaeological research on the influence of Andalusi textiles and clothing in medieval Iberian kingdoms, as Feliciano Chaves notes.[69] Yet I must emphasize that this is not a book of cultural archaeology of objects, but a genealogy of discourses and imaginaries. In spite of the necessary methodological caution, erasing the category "Moorish clothing" from our descriptive language would prevent us from acknowledging the way in which early modern Iberians conceptualized (and usually conflated) all these different realities under the same mystifying term. While "Moorish clothing" cannot be adopted as an accurate descriptive term, it is a legitimate (indeed necessary) object of study when dealing with cultural imaginaries. Unlike more precise terms such as "Islamic," "Muslim," "Arabic," "Berber," "Turkish," or "Andalusi derived," "Moorish" has a broader semantic range, since it does not limit itself to Islam, but rather to a whole range of cultural practices, objects, or even individuals, who may or may not be related to Islam.[70]

Nonetheless, whenever possible I try to preserve some terminological precision when describing objects. Therefore, I do not use "Moorish clothing" when dealing with Moriscos – unless I am referring to their participation in cultural practices that are defined as "Moorish" and that are common to both Moriscos and Old Christians. The aim of this book is precisely to explore the equivocation between the different meanings of the terms *moro* and *morisco* when applied to clothing, and how this ambiguity works as an ideological tool to categorize the Moriscos. In this sense, this book does not aim to provide certainties about Moorish clothing in early modern Iberia, but rather to emphasize those instances in which it is not clear which meaning of "Moorish clothing" is being used. This ideological confusion (deliberate or not) informs the debates about the legacy of the Islamic period in Iberia, forcing us to interrogate the location of Moorish dress in the early modern Iberian imaginary, and, more specifically, the gap that mediates between the imaginary attribution of so-called Moorish clothing and its actual social value.

I propose a vague definition of Moorish clothing as those garments that are identified as such by Old Christians. In spite of its imprecision, such a definition allows us to account for the strategic and situational classification of garments in the Old Christian imaginary. If we return to the passage in Mármol Carvajal that gives this book its title, we must acknowledge that the translation of his phrasing "eran moros vestidos como moros" depends on the intended objective of our analysis. If our objective is to describe the historical context in the most accurate way possible, we should translate it as "they were Moriscos dressed as Turks." However, if the purpose is precisely to analyse the ideological conflations of clothing in early modern Iberian society, as I intend to do in this book, the appropriate translation would be, literally, "they were Moors dressed as Moors."

PART ONE

"Morisma nueva de Christianos":
Iberian Christian Moorish Clothing

Entre un segundo Marte, a cuya instancia
la pluma templo en sangre de Africanos,
como podra hazer dulze consonancia
esta morisma nueva de Christianos?

[How could there be sweet agreement between a second Mars,
for whom I temper the quill with African blood,
and this rabble of new Moors from Christian origin?]

Gaspar Savariego de Santana, *La Iberiada* (1603)

1 Moors at Court

con librea encarnada azul y blanca,
capellar y marlota el cuerpo adorna,
y la cabeza con bonete turco
de toca tunezi blanca cercado,
con manga encarrusada el braço diestro,
de quien pende una toca plateada;
sereno el uello rostro, el cuerpo tiesso,
clauadas las rodillas con la silla,
rasgando el açicate el cuero duro
de la manchada hijada del cauallo;
una caña en la mano blandiendo,
con que apunta al contrario la herida
y muestra mil destrezas de la lança;
ciento y quarenta moros ban siguiendo
de dos en dos el uello jouen diestro,
christiano el coraçon y Moro el traje.

[with red, blue, and white livery; his body decorated with *capellar* and *marlota*, and on his head a Turkish beret wrapped with a white Tunisian turban; his right arm with a rolled-up sleeve with a silver band; his serene and beautiful face and his upright figure; his knees tight to the saddle, ripping the hard skin of the bloodstained side of the horse with the stirrups; handling a cane in his hand, targeting the wound of the enemy, and he shows a thousand skills of the lance; one hundred forty Moors are following in pairs the dexterous youngster, Christian in his heart and Moor in his dress.]

Anonymous ballad describing Philip III, 1595

Such detailed poetic description praises not a Muslim knight, but the monarch Philip III dressed as a Moor for a game of canes held in Madrid in 1595.[1] Since its first manifestations, the game of canes has been associated with the display of power of Iberian monarchs.

The first documented celebration of a game of canes I have been able to find was for the coronation of Juan I of Castile, held in Murcia in 1379.[2] Subsequently, we find scattered mentions of the game of canes since the beginning of the fifteenth century. The game of canes was played in honour of the young Juan II in Seville at the beginning of the fifteenth century.[3] It seems that Christian and Muslim knights played the game of canes in Saragossa for the coronation of Fernando I of Aragon in 1414.[4] An inventory of the belongings of the latter's eldest son, Alfonso V of Aragon (reigned 1416–58), includes Moorish clothing that the monarch used in the game of canes.[5] The prologue of Juan Alfonso de Baena's poetic compilation (c. 1430) mentions the game of canes as one of the entertainments worthy of nobles and monarchs.[6] Even if the cultural influence took shape in the frontier between Christian and Muslim kingdoms, by the fifteenth century it had radiated to almost the entire Iberian Peninsula, including Portugal. I allude only tangentially to Portugal in this book, but it is worth mentioning that the game of canes was a well-established courtly practice in this kingdom when King Duarte I wrote his *Livro da ensinança de bem cavalgar toda sela* (c. 1433–8), in which he gave instructions for this equestrian performance.[7] In fact, of the many equestrian treatises on the *gineta* riding style during the late Middle Ages and the seventeenth century, at least five were written by Portuguese authors.[8] Garcia de Resende's *Miscelânea* (published posthumously in 1554) claims that the *gineta* was a practice proper to Portugal which was admired, among others, by Castilians, Andalusians, and North Africans.[9] There is evidence of games of canes celebrated during the reigns of almost every Portuguese monarch, such as Afonso V (1432–81),[10] João II (1481–95),[11] Manuel I (1495–1521),[12] and Sebastião I (1554–78).[13] Significantly, the last thing the ill-fated King Sebastião did in the Peninsula before leaving for the Moroccan battle of al-Qaṣr al-Kabīr (Alcazarquivir), in which he lost his life in 1578, was to stop in Cádiz to watch the celebrated game of canes of Jerez de la Frontera.[14] Three decades later, and probably emulating King Sebastião's journey, the Portuguese soldier Juan Méndez de Vasconcelos praised the game of canes precisely as the navy passed Cádiz while en route to North Africa.[15] Méndez de Vasconcelos described the Moorish garments of the participants as "Christiana adarga, el Español turbante" [Christian *adarga*, Spanish [i.e., Iberian] turban].[16] Thus he simultaneously Christianized and Iberianized Moorish clothing in a shared cultural and political context in which "español" was still a geopolitical concept comprising all the kingdoms in the Iberian Peninsula.

Enrique IV of Castile (reigned 1454–74) has traditionally been singled out as having Moorish proclivities, mainly due to the propaganda orchestrated by his half-sister Isabel I of Castile.[17] We can certainly document Enrique IV holding games of canes in Seville in 1455 to celebrate his wedding with Maria of Portugal, in Madrid to celebrate the arrival of the French ambassador in 1459, and to welcome the count of Armagnac in 1462.[18] Yet, in spite of the maurophobic discourse used to legitimize Isabel's claim to power, the game of canes and the custom of dressing in Moorish garb remained an integral part of royal entries and court ceremonies both before and after Enrique IV's reign, which was not exceptional in this regard. Indeed, games of canes were held to celebrate Isabel's wedding with Fernando II of Aragon in 1469,[19] as well as for her entries in Seville in 1477[20] and Barcelona in 1492.[21] Fernando II's participation is recorded in games held in Burgos in 1497,[22] in Granada in 1500,[23] and in Valladolid in 1508.[24]

Monarchs of non-Iberian origin were very quickly integrated into the game of canes – which makes us wonder if the Castilian court protocol required monarchs to dress *a la morisca* as a way to legitimize their claim to rule. A game of canes was organized to welcome the Flemish Prince Philip the Handsome to Toledo in 1502, and only six days later Philip himself was already participating in another game.[25] A few years later, now crowned Philip I of Castile, he again participated in a game of canes held in Valladolid in 1506. In this instance, there is a visual record of Philip the Handsome dressing as a Moor (Figure 4).[26]

Like his father Philip the Handsome, the emperor Charles V was born in Flanders and did not visit Castile until he was a young adult in 1517. Also, like his father, being a foreigner was no excuse for not following the Iberian ritual of dressing as a Moor to participate in the game of canes. Indeed, when compared to previous Iberian monarchs, Charles V's reign represents a substantive quantitative and qualitative leap in the wealth of information that we have on this practice. The documentation of Charles V's royal entries throughout the Iberian Peninsula as well as other territories in Europe is simply impressive, likely because, as Helen Watanabe-O'Kelly remarks, the emperor was the one who "established the festival book as a genre."[27] Charles V's presence is registered in many games of canes held throughout the Iberian

Peninsula and Europe, and in many of them he participated dressed as a Moor. For instance, in 1537, Charles V, along with the grandees, gathered 120 riders dressed as "Turks" and played the game of canes in Valladolid. Among the audience were not only the ambassadors of England and Venetia, but also his own son Prince Philip (later Philip II), who was then ten years old.[28] One of these occasions, the game of canes held in Toledo in 1539, was depicted by the Flemish artist Jan Cornelisz Vermeyen (Figure 2).[29] Charles V is depicted as a background spectator, wearing the strict black that came to be identified with Iberian fashion.[30] Yet the extant visual imagery of the emperor wearing black should not make us forget that he also appeared publicly dressed in colourful Moorish clothing, like the rider of the game of canes depicted in the anonymous illustrated manuscript known as *El códice de trajes* (Figure 1).[31]

The game of canes was so central to the display of power that it was included explicitly in the regulations for the royal household. A questionnaire about court protocol written in the first half of the sixteenth century mandated that tailors should consult directly with the monarch and no one else when they had questions about appropriate Moorish clothing for the game of canes.[32] Gonzalo Fernández de Oviedo's *Libro de la cámara real del príncipe don Juan* (1548) specified that one of the duties of the "guión real" was to carry the royal banner and accompany the monarch both at war and at the game of canes so that he could be easily recognized by the other participants.[33]

The game of canes constituted an integral part of the prince's education and the transmission of power. If as a ten-year-old boy Prince Philip saw his father Charles V dressed as a "Turk" for the game of canes held in Valladolid in 1537, in 1549 in Gant it was Philip's turn to participate in the game of canes under the approving gaze of his father.[34] Much like his father, Philip II's display of power was surrounded by the organization of magnificent games of canes to celebrate weddings and royal entries, in many of which he participated as a rider dressing *a la morisca*.[35] In conjunction with his presence in games of canes during the second half of the sixteenth century, Philip II promoted them through legal action, both directly and indirectly. In 1566, he approved the ordinances of tailors in Toledo, which instructed that tailors be examined on how to make clothing for the game of canes.[36] In 1572, he issued ordinances to several cities in Castile recommending the reinvigoration of military exercises, among them the game of canes, as a way to ensure proper military training.[37] How can we reconcile Philip II's continuous promotion of the game of canes with the dictum that he is also the monarch who prohibited the Moriscos from wearing "Moorish clothing" in 1567? As argued in the introduction and analysed in detail in chapter 5, rather than seeing this as an ideological contradiction, we must consider whether Philip II prohibited the Moriscos from wearing luxurious Moorish clothing precisely to prevent them from dressing like him and the aristocrats who played the game of canes with him.

If a direct link between the use of Moorish clothing and the stigmatization of the Moriscos existed, one would expect to see a decline in the display of Moorishness during the reign of Philip III (r. 1598–1621), because he ordered their expulsion in 1609. Far from it – Philip III was no less "Moorish" than his predecessors. His father nurtured his royal Moorishness from the beginning. Towards 1579, Philip II commissioned court painter Alonso Sánchez Coello to portray the *infantes* Diego and Philip (later Philip III) as prepared for the game of canes, carrying the characteristic *adarga* in one hand, holding a cane in the other, and wearing *sayos vaqueros*, a garment of Turkish origin often used in lieu of traditional *marlotas* (Figure 5).[38] This painting was (and still is) located at the Monastery of Las Descalzas Reales in Madrid, founded by Philip II's sister, Juana of Austria, in 1559, as a place to which the women at court could retire from active life at court as widows or as nuns by vocation. Philip III held the monastery in high regard, as he was very influenced by his aunt Mary of Austria (1528–1603) and his cousin Margaret of Austria (1567–1633), both of whom retired there in 1582.[39] In at least two different games of canes held in Madrid in 1595 and 1599, Philip III, now a young man, dressed up as a Moor and paraded in front of the monastery to wave to his relatives.[40] The inhabitants of the monastery would therefore have seen Philip III in two different but complementary ways: on a quotidian basis they would see him as a child preparing for the game of canes, as shown in the painting held in the interior of the monastery; they would have seen him as a young adult on special occasions fulfilling the destiny promised in the painting, now definitely dressed as a gallant Moor in actual games of canes through the streets of Madrid.

I have already mentioned that Charles V observed the young Philip II riding in a game of canes in Gant in 1549. An almost identical scene took place five decades later, this time in Madrid in 1595, as, according to Jehan Lhermite, Philip III dressed as a Moor and played the game of canes under the approving gaze of his father Philip II, who enjoyed the spectacle despite being bedridden with gout.[41] Lhermite also includes a schematic drawing of a similar festival held at the Plaza Mayor of Valladolid in 1592 (Figure 6). The epigraph to this chapter, an anonymous ballad referring to the 1595 festival describes Philip III's Moorish clothing in vivid detail:

> with red, blue, and white livery; his body decorated with *capellar* and *marlota*, and on his head a Turkish beret wrapped with a white Tunisian turban; his right arm with a rolled-up sleeve with a silver band; his serene and beautiful face and his upright figure; his knees tight to the saddle, tearing the hard skin of the stained side of the horse with the stirrups; handling a cane in his hand, targeting the wound of the enemy, and he shows a thousand skills of the lance; one hundred forty Moors are following in pairs the dexterous youngster, Christian in his heart and Moor in his dress.[42]

The detailed description of Philip III dressing as a Moor is supplemented by the no less impressive Moorish army that accompanies him. The 140 Moors following the monarch on horse would constitute a magnificent spectacle for the audience in Madrid.

Along with the cases already mentioned, Philip III's reign is characterized by the organization of elaborate games of canes to celebrate almost any important event, such as the monarch's marriage in Valencia (1599),[43] the marriage between the Duke of Bragança and Ana de Velasco in Vila Viçosa (1603),[44] the truce with England celebrated in Valladolid (1604),[45] the birth of Prince Philip (later Philip IV) in Valladolid in 1605,[46] the intermarriage of the French and Spanish princes held in Burgos in 1615,[47] the festivals held in Lerma in 1617,[48] and the royal entry in Lisbon in 1619.[49] These are only some of the most grandiose cases recorded in printed festival books, and municipal archives show that Philip III's reign (even after the expulsion of the Moriscos) was probably the pinnacle of the game of canes.

By comparison with previous monarchs, Philip IV's reign (1621–65) constitutes the beginning of the slow decline of the game of canes. It seems that Philip III never witnessed his son playing the game of canes, as was customary with previous monarchs – most likely because Philip III died too young to replicate this ceremony. While this interruption in royal rituals does not explain the decline of the game of canes in early modern Iberia, it does symbolize the rupture initiated in the early 1620s. Certainly, the beginning of Philip IV's reign is marked by one of the most magnificent games of canes ever known, that held for Charles I of England's visit in 1623, in which Philip IV himself participated and for which there are many festival books as well as a painting by Juan de la Corte (Figure 7).[50] Yet this seems to be the swan song of the game of canes in early modern Castile.[51]

In spite of the signs of decline, the games of canes did not disappear overnight. In 1632 the Count-Duke of Olivares recommended the use of the *gineta* riding style, probably an act promoting the game of canes, since use of the *gineta* saddle was mostly restricted to this equestrian game.[52] In a similar vein, in 1638 Philip IV issued an internal instruction recommending the reinvigoration of the game of canes at court.[53] Furthermore, several seventeenth-century festival books still refer to the use of Moorish clothing in games of canes celebrated throughout the century.[54] Yet these were signs of a languishing and increasingly anachronistic equestrian culture becoming less and less frequent during Philip IV's reign, and in tandem, throughout the seventeenth century Moorish clothing increasingly lost its prestige for monarchs and grandees.[55]

The moment of inflection is represented by Gregorio Tapia y Salcedo's equestrian treatise *Exercicios de la gineta* (1643), which gives very detailed instructions on how to put on turbans, *marlotas*, and *capellares*, but refers to the use of Moorish clothing as a thing of the past.[56] The drawings included in his book, which represent riders wearing capes and hats, further suggest the abandonment of Moorish clothing (Figure 8). More important, like many modern scholars, Tapia y Salcedo conceives of the game of canes through the festivals of *moros y cristianos*: "In the game of canes it was customary that half of them appeared wearing Christian clothing, and half of them Moorish, with all the requirements of their garments."[57] His concept of the games of canes as an ideological and symbolic opposition does not correspond to how they were most typically played in the sixteenth century and the beginning of the seventeenth. This misinterpretation, which was further disseminated when the Real Academia de la Lengua based their definition of the *juego de cañas* on Tapia y Salcedo's work, has created a historiographical distortion conceiving of Moorish clothing as a mere costume for carnivalesque representations of religious confrontation, and therefore ignoring the fact that, at least until the 1620s, Moorish clothing was ceremonial dress with the clear role of social distinction.

Several hypotheses have been suggested to explain the decline of the game of canes. María José del Río Barreiro attributes it to political manipulation by the Count-Duke of Olivares of the court ceremony and the subsequent disaffection of the grandees in the 1640s.[58] Watanabe-O'Kelly observes that the ascent of the Bourbon dynasty with Philip V (1700–46) and the subsequent prevalence of French fashion gave the final blow to an already declining sartorial taste and ceremonial.[59] Similarly, Carlos Pereira notes that during the eighteenth century the Portuguese game of canes underwent a process of Europeanization and nationalization that replaced traditional Moorish costumes and shields with French fashion.[60] While these are all very plausible interpretations, they only explain the decline of Moorishness at court. The question of why the game of canes declined more broadly in early modern Iberia is connected to the question of why Iberians were so fond of dressing as Moors in the first place, a question I can only begin to address here.

One possible answer to the attraction that early modern Iberians had for Moorish clothing is based on cultural identity. Barbara Fuchs has established an insightful comparison of Iberian Moorish impersonations with Indian impersonations in the US analysed by Philip J. Deloria.[61] As Deloria shows, eighteenth-century colonialists impersonated a stereotypical image of Native Americans as a form of political protest, as this simulacrum of Native culture was used to forge a national identity and a sense of cultural and political difference vis-à-vis British colonial power.[62] This is also certainly one of the aspects of Moorishness in early modern Iberia, in which Moorish impersonations were used to create a sense of cultural uniqueness within Europe, as Fuchs demonstrates.[63] Yet bringing in the comparison with Indian impersonations in the US is also useful for underlining the differences between the two cases. To begin with, one would not imagine key political figures in the US dressing up as Indians in the same way that early modern Iberian monarchs, grandees, and local elites displayed their political legitimacy by dressing as Moors. As this chapter has shown, the games of canes organized by Iberian monarchs were not extraordinary, carnivalesque performances, but ritual exhibitions of power deeply ingrained in court protocols. Diplomatic uses of Moorishness, as important as they were, did not override the primary social function of the game of canes within the Iberian Peninsula, which sets this case apart from Indian impersonations in the fledgling United States.

The relevance of the game of canes as a social practice lies in the less well-known and probably less spectacular forms of municipal life, in which the use of Moorish clothing was one of the rites of passage to nobility, revealing itself clearly as a form of social distinction permeated with socio-economic concerns. Moorish impersonations were institutionalized political practices that reinforced aristocratic status – or, to be more precise, they reinforced the fiction of aristocratic status. Simply put, in medieval and early modern Iberia, individuals wishing to demonstrate their noble status had to dress as Moors.

2 Moorish Clothing and Nobility

As I have come to understand the situation in Spain during the sixteenth century, there were always trunks full of Moorish costumes.

Hendrik J. Horn

As we have seen in chapter 1, the game of canes was deeply ingrained in the ritual celebration of Iberian court culture. When festival books list the participants in such games of canes, they usually mention monarchs, grandees, and titled nobles, but they rarely list the names of the lesser ranks of the complexly stratified nobility, even though in many cases these equestrian performances included dozens or even hundreds of participants with heterogeneous social status. For instance, a game of canes in Toledo in 1502 included 400 riders, while for a game of canes held in Valladolid in 1527 there were 160 riders; 350 riders participated in the game of canes held in Salamanca in 1543 to celebrate Philip II's wedding with Maria Manuela of Portugal; and at a game organized by Philip III in Madrid in 1595, there were 100 riders with him, all of them dressed as Moors.[1] The social relevance of the game of canes lies precisely in those very individuals who were more than eager to be included in them but whose names were not usually mentioned in festival books.

The courtly games of canes analysed in chapter 1 were only a fraction (arguably the most spectacular) of the total number of occurences in early modern Iberia, as this equestrian performance was central to the display of social status at the municipal level as well. The celebration of the game of canes is well documented in important cities such as Seville,[2] Valladolid,[3] Toledo,[4] and obviously Madrid once the court was permanently established there in 1561. They were also routinely held at many other cities and towns throughout Old Castile,[5] La Mancha,[6] Andalusia,[7] Galicia,[8] and Murcia.[9] In the Kingdom of Aragon, the game of canes was common in Valencia[10] and some parts of Aragon,[11] while there is less evidence in Catalonia.[12] Even universities were among the promoters of the game of canes, at least in Salamanca and Alcalá de Henares. The stairway of the Colegios Mayores in Salamanca, built at the beginning of the sixteenth century, shows in the last flight of stairs a clear representation of a bullfight and turbaned riders wearing the characteristic *adarga* of the game of canes (Figure 9). It is striking to see such a profane motif crowning the moralistic iconographic program sculpted in the university stairs, which attests to the social relevance of such events in early modern Iberian society.[13]

Yet the importance of the game of canes and the subsequent use of Moorish clothing in municipal government has not been clearly related to the transient nature of nobility in Iberia. Almost the entire bibliography on the game of canes notes that it was an aristocratic performance. While this remark is largely accurate, we need to define exactly what we mean when we say "aristocratic," as we must take into account that the early modern Iberian nobility had a particular character when compared to the rest of Europe. In early modern Castile, nobles accounted for about 10 per cent of the population (with uneven regional distributions), while in Italy, Central Europe, and England they rarely made up more than 3 per cent.[14] Of course, this higher proportion of nobles does not imply that in Castile there were more wealthy aristocratic landowners than in other parts of Europe, but rather that the practices for recognizing nobility were more inclusive and incorporated municipal and administrative elites. This relative inclusivity is especially true in the case of *hidalguía*, a malleable category with very diffuse borders and therefore always in constant negotiation. This constant state of flux turned *hidalguía* into a space for social climbing, despite the emphasis on the immanent nature of aristocratic lineages emphasized in the discourses on nobility.[15]

The significance of the game of canes is very likely related to these particular Iberian categories of nobility. As Bartolomé Bennassar notes, there seems to be a correlation between the higher proportion of nobles and the ubiquity of equestrian spectacles in early modern Iberia – they, too, were far more common than in the rest of Europe.[16] There is also one important feature that makes the game of canes fit into the unique conditions of *hidalguía*: the use of Moorish clothing. While the armour used in jousts all around Europe was so expensive that it restricted the participant pool according to socio-economic standing, Moorish clothing for the game of canes was costly enough to be a sign of distinction and social status, but affordable enough to accommodate all sorts of local elites and not only titled nobles.

There were thousands and thousands of Moorish garments made for the game of canes during the sixteenth and seventeenth centuries. Yet specialists in early modern Iberian culture rarely consider how such a wealth of Moorish clothing becomes available and what the social implications of its circulation might be. The only instance of a genuine interrogation of this issue comes from a non-specialist in early modern Iberian studies. When dealing with Jan Cornelisz Vermeyen's depictions of Iberian mock battles, Hendrik Horn forms a hypothesis that is both naive and extremely insightful for the purposes of this book: "As I have come to understand the situation in Spain during the sixteenth century, there were always trunks full of Moorish costumes at hand for such special occasions."[17] In contrast to Horn, specialists in early modern Iberia either avoid the question or take it for granted, and rarely ponder the origin and distribution of those "trunks full of Moorish costumes." The Moorish garments for the game of canes were certainly not everyday clothing, but they were not "costumes" either, as Horn and many others put it.

Moorish clothing was not only a display of grandeur for monarchs and wealthy aristocrats, but was avidly consumed by those individuals who lived on the fringes of nobility as well, including both those who were eager to enter the nobility and those whose noble status could be called into question. For such individuals, although Moorish clothing was more affordable than armour, it was a very serious matter into which they invested too much energy, money, and reputation to consider it merely a festive costume, making the contents of those hypothetical "trunks" not merely a trivial wardrobe without social consequences. As this chapter shows, by analysing the circulation and consumption of Moorish clothing for the game of canes, we can observe the gap between discourses of class difference and actual social practices. In order to do so, this chapter looks at a wide array of documents (equestrian and legal treatises, as well as tailoring books and archival records) for instances that reveal the divergence between theory and practice. Especially telling are municipal proceedings (usually called *Libros de Acuerdos* or *Actas del Cabildo*), as they provide essential information on how local nobles pressed to obtain financing from public funding and therefore led to accusations of corruption and nepotism against the organization of festivals.[18]

The Game of Canes as Aristocratic Performance

Since the game of canes was considered to be an aristocratic equestrian exercise, participation in it was regarded as a sign of status. There was therefore a circular logic in the discourse about the connection between nobility and equestrian culture, predicated on a series of assumptions: that all of the participants possessed the necessary social standing and reputation to justify their inclusion in this allegedly elitist public festival, that they had the economic means to maintain a horse and arms, and that they had the minimum equestrian skill required to perform complex equestrian manoeuvres. Yet the notion that every participant met those requirements was a fiction closely related to the social fiction underlying the concept of nobility itself. Consequently, cases in which the reality did not correspond to the theory were probably the norm rather than the exception.

The strongest evidence for the social import of being invited to participate in a game of canes can be found in litigation by individuals who wanted to be recognized as noble, and who often listed participation in games of canes as proof of their claims.[19] When looking at litigations claiming *hidalguía*, we must abandon an immanent view of nobility. Naturally, litigants invariably claimed that their lineages were noble from time immemorial. Yet the fact that they litigated to be recognized as nobles indicates, at best, that their nobility was being put into question, quite probably because they had moved to a new town (nobility was based locally and was not necessarily transferable), or because in their process of social climbing they had not been yet recognized by their peers. When litigants adduced as evidence of their noble status that they were invited to participate in a game of canes, they meant that they had already been recognized as *hidalgos*. Yet, even if these arguments were administratively accepted, they were often regarded as far-fetched in early modern Iberian society. In Cristóbal Suárez de Figueroa's *El pasajero* (1617), written in dialogue form, one of the interlocutors recommends tongue-in-cheek that, in order to pass as noble, the first thing to do is buy a horse and learn how to use it. Afterwards, the candidate should purchase a public position and do everything possible to be admitted to a game of canes.[20] Even if all these steps did not necessarily occur in the order spelled out by Suárez de Figueroa, his commentary reveals, albeit in a simplified and ironic form, the procedures through which many individuals accessed nobility, as well as the central role that the game of canes played in this process of social climbing.

There were some privileges associated with *hidalguía*, such as not being imprisoned because of debts. For instance, in 1552, Rodrigo Cervantes (father of Miguel de Cervantes) claimed that he had been unlawfully imprisoned because of debts, since he was an *hidalgo*. In the trial to determine whether he could be imprisoned or not, several witnesses deposed in his favour that they had seen him and his family playing the game of canes, which served as proof of his *hidalgo* status.[21] Historians have traditionally argued that the main reason for attaining nobility was to be exempt from direct taxes. Yet the costs of legally contesting noble status could be much higher than any tax benefit derived from obtaining it, and the real goal was the ability to hold municipal offices with the concomittant control of local resources.[22]

Something similar happens with the assumption that riders had to own horses and equestrian gear. Many individuals lacked horses and equestrian equipment for the game of canes and had to borrow them for the occasion. In many cases they were aristocrats, even titled nobles, who, for different circumstances, did not have those elements at hand when they were suddenly invited to participate in a game of canes outside of their place of residence. For instance, Alonso Osorio, Marquis of Astorga, having been invited to participate in a game of canes organized by the Count of Benavente in 1565, asked another noble for the basic accroutrements to participate, such as a horse, saddle, and tack.[23] The Count of Gondomar's correspondence contains several similar requests.[24] If even titled nobles found themselves in the situation of borrowing horses for the game of canes, we can imagine that many *hidalgos* would not even be in that advantageous position.[25]

Antonio Luis Ribero parodies these kinds of borrowings in his equestrian treatise *Espejo del cavallero en ambas sillas* (1671). Ribero concludes his work with a burlesque ballad in which he presents himself trying to satisfy Charles II's sudden desire to watch a game of canes the following day. Given the amount of preparation usually involved in these performances, such a degree of improvisation is a challenge – which Ribero is willing to undertake. Most of Ribero's task consists not only in organizing other participants for the game, but also in procuring clothing, stirrups, a saddle, and a horse for himself, all of which he borrows from various donors.[26] He manages to do everything overnight.

Unfortunately for him, his efforts prove to be futile: when he shows up with his team the next day, the monarch has just left, apparently having forgotten about his own capricious demand. This is a striking scene of self-deprecation in which the author of an equestrian treatise, who signs his work as a Portuguese *fidalgo*, exposes his lack of means to participate in the same performance that he describes as worthy of nobles like him. Such burlesque self-reference is admissible because Ribero compensates it with his diligence in improvising the organization of the game and training participants overnight. In any case, Ribero's exceptional open recognition of his own poverty probably reveals, albeit tongue-in-cheek, a common situation that is silenced in the celebratory discourses on games of canes.

A related assumption when conceiving of the game of canes as an aristocratic equestrian performance is that participants not only had horses and equestrian gear, but were also well-trained and skillful riders.[27] Again, this presumed ability occurs more often in theory than in practice. The proliferation of equestrian treatises between the mid-sixteenth century and the mid-seventeenth century analysed above may in fact indicate not only the increasing relevance of aristocratic festivals, but also the existence of a flourishing market of individuals who were in need of quick equestrian training for which they had neither the time nor the resources. Many of these equestrian treatises explicitly address novices in the art, or give advice to the organizers of games of canes on how to deal with a mixture of experienced and inexperienced riders. As most of these equestrian treatises point out, the main reason for the custom of riding in pairs is to couple one skilled rider with a fledgling one, so that the former can cover the lack of dexterity of the latter.[28] This tension between the presence of inexperienced participants and the need for the festival to be gallant, explains why, as we will see in the next section, truly skillful riders were much appreciated and would be invited and even hired (regardless of their class status) as a way to compensate for the inferior abilities of the rest of participants. While the full social prestige of the game of canes was attained by showing off exceptional equestrian ability, for many of the participants it sufficed to be invited and to merely perform as decently as possible.

Rise and Decline: Urban Militias and Festivals (1560–1620)

The game of canes and aristocratic status were already closely connected during the late Middle Ages and the first half of the sixteenth century, but the game likely became more important in municipal life when Philip II tried to reform local militias in the second half of the sixteenth century.[29] After a period of deliberation and consultation with several cities in the Kingdom of Castile in 1562, Philip II issued a decree on 17 June 1563, mandating that local elites with a certain minimum wealth be listed as *caballeros de cuantía* and maintain horses and arms to participate in two annual military musters [*alardes*]. The response from the different cities and villages in Castile was not homogeneous. In many cities, especially in Murcia and Andalusia, Philip II's order was probably perceived as an intervention in the local regulation of honour and status, as the *caballería de cuantía* constituted a class from the previous frontier period that was already in the process of ennoblement. Urban elites in these places refused to participate in the mandatory *alardes* precisely because their inclusion could be interpreted as a sign of commoner status – since *hidalgos* were usually exempted from participating in military exercises.[30] In other cities, Philip II's order triggered the opposite reaction, inspiring the formation of aristocratic brotherhoods that included playing canes among their main activities.[31]

In 1572, obviously unsatisfied with the results of his previous order, Philip II issued new instructions for several cities and towns throughout Castile to ensure military training, but this time he encouraged the foundation of aristocratic brotherhoods to conduct military exercises during festivals and allowed town councils to implement excise taxes to help participants defray some of the costs.[32] The responses from the towns were again mixed, specifically contesting the mandate that town councils should contribute economically to the military training of nobles. Yet this law seems to have had an even more tangible effect, as evidenced by the fact that the regular celebration of games of canes among noble brotherhoods expanded rapidly throughout the Iberian Peninsula.[33]

As Pedro M. Cátedra suggests, these projects of reforming urban militias, independent of their actual results in improving military training, contributed to the reinvigoration of aristocratic ceremonies between the 1560s and the 1620s, as they implied a certain democratization of the concept of nobility and thus opened a door for social mobility.[34] This relative democratization probably explains why those laws promoted the game of canes over other martial exercises. In principle, the 1563 decree gave the option of riding either in the *brida* or the *gineta* style – the two riding styles associated with the armoured knight of the joust and the light chivalry of the game of canes, respectively. However, an amendment issued on 1 November 1563, prescribed the use of the *gineta* style as the only option.[35] This small but significant restriction of the riding style to be practised by the *caballeros de cuantía* actually privileged the game of canes over jousts. In contrast, the 1572 decree ordering the formation of noble brotherhoods explicitly instructed that games of canes be held along with jousts.[36] This discrepancy reveals that there was an implicit hierarchy between the two equestrian practices, with jousts being perceived as a more elevated aristocratic exercise than the game of canes. Certainly, as in the rest of Europe, jousts were part of Iberian aristocratic festivals, and they were routinely held by monarchs, grandees, and, to a lesser extent, local elites.[37] Yet jousts were much less frequent and rather exceptional when compared to the ubiquitous game of canes, even among titled nobles.[38] There is an economic basis for this imbalance. As Noel Fallows observes, even though the Moorish clothing for the game of canes was expensive, it was actually more affordable than the armour required for the traditional aristocratic performances of jousts.[39] The game of canes thus fit into the particular social stratification of early modern Iberia, as it allowed for the inclusion of more participants with lesser economic means and fewer equestrian skills.

This connection between military training and the wearing of luxurious clothing was recognized, albeit indirectly, by royal legislation. It is very telling that in a sumptuary law issued on 25 October 1563, precisely as he was trying to reinvigorate military exercises, Philip II restricted the use of brocades but allowed for the use of silk in equestrian performances during festivals.[40] Even if this law did not say so explicitly, it promoted the making of Moorish clothing (usually made of silk) for the game of canes because it provided local elites with the legal loophole to circumvent the sumptuary restrictions on silk. This sumptuary exception was maintained throughout the second half of the sixteenth century and the first decades of the seventeenth, as Philip II reissued the same law in 1590, and in 1611 Philip III issued a new sumptuary law that explicitly allowed the use of silk in the *marlotas* and *capellares* for the game of canes.[41]

The equestrian treatises that proliferated between the mid-sixteenth century and the seventeenth attest to this connection between the importance of the game of canes and the use of Moorish clothing.[42] Most of these equestrian treatises dealt with how to play the game of canes and emphasized that it should be performed in Moorish attire, among them Pedro de Aguilar's *Tractado de la caualleria de la gineta* (1572),[43] Pedro Fernández de Andrada's *De la naturaleza del caballo* (1580),[44] Juan Arias

Dávila Puertocarrero's *Discurso ... para estar a la gineta con gracia y her-mosura* (1590),[45] Diego Ramírez de Haro's *Tratado de la brida y gineta* (ms. written towards the end of the sixteenth century),[46] Jaume de Oleza's manuscript *Exercicios militares* (1604),[47] and Pedro Gallego's *Tratado da gineta* (1629).[48] Even those equestrian books that taught how to wear hats and capes for the games of canes and did not emphasize the need to dress as Moors, did not express any kind of opposition to the practice.[49] Obviously, the authors of equestrian treatises that defended the *gineta* presented the game of canes as an exercise that could prepare participants for warfare, and more specifically for the North African campaigns.[50] Yet they never explain how the alleged military ethos could be compatible with wearing Moorish clothing, which had no purpose other than the display of gallantry. The proliferation of equestrian treatises in this period suggests that there was an audience ripe for quick training in horsemanship, even though this bookish learning would not prepare their readers for war, as their authors claimed, but would only provide a few tricks to show off their equestrian dexterity the day of the festival.

This importance of the game of canes (or at least of the use of Moorish clothing) halted during the transition between the reigns of Philip III and Philip IV. In 1619, Philip III disolved the *caballería de cuantía* in Andalusia.[51] While the effectiveness of this law in dissolving the social category of the *caballeros de cuantía* was probably not immediate, it signals the desire to curtail the exorbitant expenses of festivals as well as to restrict the means of access to the nobility. It does not seem a coincidence that sumptuary laws grow stricter precisely after this period, and that the game of canes was no longer listed as an exception to the prohibition on wearing luxurious garments. Philip IV continued this tendency towards sartorial moderation at the beginning of his reign. For instance, in 1622 he forbade the embroiderers of Zamora to make livery for the game of canes.[52] In 1623, he issued another sumptuary law prohibiting the manufacture of livery for festivals, with the argument that the onerous investments in gallant clothing actually hindered the practice of horsemanship.[53]

The combination of these legal measures trying to dissociate the use of luxurious clothing from equestrian performances must have altered the raison d'être of the game of canes by the 1620s, when it began to lose its value as a display of socio-economic status and as a sign of distinction.[54] The signs of the decline in the use of Moorish clothing for the game of canes after this period are clear. After the 1620s, the publication of equestrian treatises slowed, and when they mentioned the use of Moorish clothing, they referred to it as a remnant of the past.[55] References to Moorish clothing similarly disappeared in tailoring books after Francisco de la Rocha Burguen's *Geometría y traça perteneciente al oficio de sastres* (1618) and Martín de Andújar's *Geometría y trazas* (1640).[56] An important cultural shift is that, even if large cities such as Madrid, Valladolid, and Seville continued to hold games of canes, after the 1620s several municipal councils started to face several financial and social problems in organizing them. Between the 1610s and 1620s, the councils of Berja and León had to hire riders for the game of canes, which indicates that local elites no longer perceived horsemanship as a necessary display of social status.[57] In places such as León and Guadalajara, the game of canes simply disappeared from urban ceremonies after the 1620s.[58] But until that point, there had been a very strong link between Moorish clothing and an aristocratic way of life that conditioned many aspects of early modern Iberian society.

Moorish Clothing as Livery

Along with equestrian ability and the possession of the appropriate horses and tack, the wearing of Moorish clothing was central to the outward demonstration of status. Undoubtedly, wealthy individuals had their own *marlotas*, and the inventories of Iberian monarchs and other wealthy nobles abound in Moorish clothing.[59] Some kept their Moorish clothing as a sign of identity from one game of canes to the next, such as Gaspar Mercader in Valencia, who always used an orange *marlota* embroidered with silver hearts.[60] Yet they were expensive garments that only the wealthiest could afford to own.

Very often, participants received Moorish clothing as gifts of livery from monarchs or grandees. As Jones and Stallybrass state in the case of early modern England, "Livery acted as the medium through which the social system marked bodies so as to associate them with particular institutions."[61] This use of livery as a way to associate individuals with the monarchy is clear in a game of canes celebrated in Valladolid in 1527, in which Charles V gave the nobles of the city Moorish clothing with his royal insignia.[62] This gift-giving practice continued during the sixteenth and seventeenth centuries – although the logic of marking liveries with the patron's insignia seems to disappear. For instance, the Marquis of Alcañices distributed livery for the participants in the game of canes held in Toro for the wedding of Juana of Castile and Prince

João of Portugal in 1552.[63] Prince Charles, the ill-fated son of Philip II, organized a *quadrille* in Valladolid in 1559 that cost 398 *ducados*,[64] and soon after he spent 1,367 *ducados* in attiring twenty riders for another game of canes in Toledo (about 68 *ducados* per rider).[65] An anonymous sixteenth-century festival book describing a festival in Madrid recounts how the Marquis of El Valle provided some *borceguíes* and *zaragüelles* for the participants in the game of canes so they could be sufficiently gallant.[66] In the festivals held in Lerma in 1617, the Count of Saldaña organized a game of canes and distributed *marlotas* and turbans to all the participants.[67] Cases like these are numerous, and they were quite often mentioned in festival books to emphasize the magnanimity of patrons. This distribution had to have been quite frequent, since in 1611 the lexicographer Sebastián de Covarrubias primarily defines the *capellar* and the *marlota* as livery.[68] They were therefore not daily wear, and yet their distribution was part of a durable ritual.

Patrons devoted time and effort to overseeing the Moorish clothing for games of canes. Towards the end of the sixteenth century, the tailor Francisco Zapata wrote to Diego Sarmiento de Acuña, Count of Gondomar, to inform him that he had finished the eighteen *marlotas* and *capellares* commissioned for one of the four teams for a game of canes. The tailor also estimated that making the clothing for the other three teams would amount to more than 600 *ducados* and asked for the count's confirmation before continuing his task, indirectly pointing to careful negotiations about the quality of textiles and the cost of fabrication.[69]

The distribution of livery by individual patrons was not merely an act of magnanimity, but rather a way to cement social bonds and to insert themselves into specific networks of sociability, especially when the organizer of the game of canes and the patron paying for the liveries were not the same person. In 1606, Martín Valero Franqueza, Count of Villafranca, wrote to the Count of Gondomar thanking him for the invitation to participate in a game of canes in which Philip III would participate as well and, in the same letter, indicated where to find the liveries and the headdresses.[70] There is something strange in seeing the person invited to the game of canes pointing out to the organizer where to locate the liveries, suggesting that the Count of Gondomar's invitation was not disinterested. While this is in no way explicit in the letter, it seems to suggest that, in exchange for the honour of being invited to such a visible performance at court, the Count of Villafranca felt obliged to provide the Moorish clothing, which actually implies an indirect payment for being provided with this opportunity of social advancement.

Municipal Liveries: Corruption, Nepotism, and Social Unrest

In addition to monarchs and grandees, one of the main distributors of
Moorish liveries was municipal councils in towns and cities throughout
the Kingdom of Castile. There are, however, two essential differences
between the distribution of liveries by monarchs and grandees and that
of town councils: first, patrons and recipients of municipal livery were
very often the same (or belonged to the same social networks), which
could raise suspicions of nepotism. Second, and obviously related, the
councilmen's "magnanimity" was not exercised with their own wealth,
but with the public funds they were supposed to manage. Because of the
economics of the distribution of livery when it was paid with municipal
funds, it could become a contentious issue rife with accusations of corruption and nepotism. In the instructions for municipal governments
issued in 1500 by Fernando of Aragon and Isabel of Castile, officials
were ordered not to accept clothing paid for with municipal funds nor
to use those funds to organize festivals.[71] Throughout the sixteenth century, several jurists, such as Pedro Núñez de Avendaño's *De exequendis mandatis regum Hispaniae* (1564) and Juan García de Saavedra's *De
expensis et meliorationibus* (1578), commenting on the monarchs' prohibition, criticized festival expenses and instructed that officials should
return to the council any clothing purchased with municipal funds.[72]

Nonetheless, in spite of this legal corpus of prohibitions and instructions, municipal councils continued to use public funds to provide local
aristocrats with Moorish liveries for the games of canes.[73] For Charles
V's entry in Granada in 1526 the city council gave the fabrics on which
it spent 68 *ducados* to the thirty-two riders who participated in a game
of canes.[74] This amount is relatively modest when we compare it with
later reports from the end of the sixteenth century and the beginning of
the seventeenth, quite probably because of the extraordinary inflation
of the early modern period – but also because the expenses of Charles
V's entry in Granada reflect only the cost of the textiles and do not
include the cost of tailoring them.

For the game of canes to celebrate the entry of Philip III and Margarita
of Austria in 1599, the council of Madrid spent the extravagant sum of
15,973 *ducados* on Moorish clothing for thirty-six riders, which amounts
to the exorbitant figure of 443 *ducados* per livery – out of the total sum
of 104,000 *ducados* spent on an already onerous celebration that threw
Madrid into debt for years.[75] For the entry of Philip III in Toledo in
1600, the council allocated a "maximum" of 28,000 *ducados* for the

festival – the document does not specify the cost of the forty-eight sets of livery commissioned for the game of canes.[76] *Marlotas* could be made of fabrics of very different quality: some were rather cheap costumes while others were gallant clothing, and of course, observers could see the difference. As Pinheiro da Veiga remarks for a game of canes celebrated in Valladolid in 1605: "The ordinary [*marlotas*] were counterfeit, but some nobles had them made in fine cloth of silver, which were very valuable."[77] This also indicates that, even while liveries were supposed to homogenize riders and teams, some participants counteracted the potential blurring of socio-economic hierarchies by further decorating and embellishing the garments with which they were provided.

Moorish clothing was affordable enough (when compared to armour) to allow for a more inclusive pool of wearers, but expensive enough to continue to serve as an object around which boundaries of class distinction could be articulated. In order to properly gauge the social importance of Moorish clothing, we need to examine its material value and try to establish, at least approximately, how much it cost and who could afford it. Purchasing *borceguíes*, *marlotas*, *capellares*, and turbans, often complemented with feathers and other adornments, was a significant investment, not to mention the equestrian gear, the horse, and the *adarga*. In order to offer an estimate of how much Moorish clothing could cost, I take as an example the detailed accounts of a game of canes held in Cuenca in 1604 for the entry of Philip III. Moorish livery for thirty-two riders for the game of canes cost 1,188 *ducados*, broken down as follows: fabric for the *capellares* (163 *ducados*), fabric for the liveries (472 *ducados*; since the itemized budget lists the *capellares* in the first place, we can safely assume that when the document mentions *libreas* it means *marlotas*), salary for embroiderers (90 *ducados*), salary for the *cordoneros* [fringe makers] (77 *ducados*); and finally one expense of 384 *ducados* for "hechura y recado," which could be translated as "making and storage," and which may indicate the labour of specialized tailors.[78] This amounts to a total of about 37 *ducados* for each Moorish outfit.[79]

This sounds like a small fortune, which we can only ascertain indirectly, by an approximate reconstruction of the price of this commodity by contrasting salaries and the cost of living.[80] A common practice is to look at the price of hens – which in early modern Castile were often an exchange commodity. Since the price of hens was 116 *maravedís* in New Castile in 1604, and since one *ducado* was 375 *maravedís*, each livery of the Cuenca festival costing 37 *ducados* would be equivalent to 120 hens. Juan Carlos Zofío Llorente calculates that, on average, artisans working in Madrid in the second half of the sixteenth century spent almost 2 *ducados* in monthly rent, and that the total cost of living for each month was about 6 *ducados*.[81]

If we compare the 37 *ducados* figure of the Cuenca liveries to salaries, we can clearly see how Moorish clothing was beyond the economic reach of most people. By 1604, a female cook earned about 11 *ducados* a year and a gardener about 24 *ducados* a year. Even when taking into consideration that monetary wages for many professions were usually complemented by allowances for food and lodging, Moorish clothing was clearly out of reach for these workers, since they would cost the equivalent of their entire annual earnings. These expenses were still out of reach even for more skilled workers. A master mason earned around 271 *maravedís* a day, which means that he would have needed to devote an entire month's salary to purchasing one Moorish outfit.[82] These figures show that Moorish clothing was a luxury far beyond the reach of a commoner, and that even skilled artisans and public servants had to make substantial investments in order to purchase such very expensive clothing that was probably worn only once. These excessive prices do not mean that commoners were simply resigned to not participating in games of canes, but that, in order to do so, they had to make a significant economic investment that could plunge them into debt, or that they had to procure Moorish clothing by alternative means – such as rental, an option to which I will return at the end of this chapter and in chapter 3.

The distribution of liveries created all sorts of conflicts between the different parties involved in the financing of the festival. In preparation for the arrival of Anne of Austria in Madrid in 1570, the royal council allocated funds to celebrate the entry and charged the Council of Madrid with organizing the festivals. The Council of Madrid decided to organize one *encamisada* [night masque], one *juego de alcancías*, and one game of canes, all of them requiring *marlotas* and *capellares*, and planned on distributing livery to all the participants.[83] On 8 November, the royal council prohibited the municipal government of Madrid from providing livery, declaring that each participant should buy his own.[84] It is not clear whether there was a negotiation not reflected in the proceedings or whether the municipality of Madrid found a way to circumvent the order, since they continued with the scheduled plans, and later in the same month gave very specific instructions about what liveries were to be distributed for the *juego de alcancías* and the game of canes.[85] José Manuel Cruz Valdovinos suggests that the order by the royal council not to distribute livery might reflect a budgetary issue, as the Moorish clothing for the *encamisada* amounted to 900 *ducados* and for the *juego de alcancías* to 1,500 *ducados*.[86] Yet, since the royal council's opposition stood even when the municipality of Madrid offered to pay for the livery it commissioned, it seems that the conflict was primarily about something else, perhaps about determining who should be able to participate in this festival, since the indiscriminate distribution of livery threatened to blur the hierarchies between the royal retinue and the members of the municipality; alternatively, Philip II may have been acting to counter the councilmen's plundering of public resources.

Local tensions could be triggered in the process of organizing the festival, a phenomenon exemplified in Philip III's entry in Ávila in 1600. The council of Ávila was given very short notice that Philip III would visit their city. The councilmen, anxious about favourably impressing the monarch, rushed to plan a whole program of celebrations, including a masque, a game of canes, and dances. In their improvisation, problems constantly arose. For instance, they could not procure the desired silk fabrics in Madrid because the city of Segovia had already bought them all – Philip III was visiting that city as well. Their main concern was of course how to pay for the festival. Since the city apparently had no funds available, they argued that the city's environs had to pay all the expenses. Agustín de Treviño, the environs' representative, opposed the decision, and released 2,000 *ducados* only when he was harassed and threatened with prison. Yet he kept avoiding the city councilmen and developed strategies to delay reimbursing more funds.[87] In a later session, the council protested that many workmen who participated in the preparations had not been paid, and recounted a story that in their minds further justified imprisoning Treviño. Right before the game of canes, the riders went to the town representative to claim the ornaments for their horses – which he had apparently promised to provide, but claimed he could not find. The suspicion was that he had never had them in the first place and that his promise was merely another deception. The riders rebelled, threatening not to play the game of canes and finally taking the adornments by force from somewhere else.[88] The transcriptions of the discussions in the municipal proceedings obviously side with the city councilmen and do not reveal the real reason behind Treviño's behaviour. Yet we can imagine that his opposition was not a personal decision, but probably represented the resistance of the villages surrounding Ávila to financing the livery for the urban nobility.

In many other cases, town councils granted permission to celebrate games of canes only under the explicit condition that the local nobility cover all or most of the expenses.[89] Even when there was no explicit opposition to aristocratic equestrian performances, we can glimpse an implicit tension over the distribution of livery. The municipal proceedings of Almagro indicate that for the festival of Santiago the town regularly paid for bullfights and musicians, implicitly leaving the organization and funding of games of canes to the local nobility. Suddenly, in 1585, the councilmen decided to use municipal funds to purchase livery for twelve riders in an equestrian performance.[90] Two years later, and for the same annual festival, the councilmen made it clear that noblemen would have to procure their own liveries and horses.[91] While conflict does not surface explicitly in these documents, the sequence of contradictory orders indicates the constant pressure of the nobility for the provision of livery from municipal funds, as well as resistance from other socio-economic groups.[92]

Town councils looked for creative ways to provide Moorish liveries while keeping expenses at bay. This is what happened for instance in Medina de Rioseco, where the council typically paid for bullfights while the cost of organizing games of canes was defrayed by local aristocratic brotherhoods. In 1584, when one of the nobles commissioned to organize one of the teams for the game of canes was not able to do it, the council accepted the task of replacing the missing team and paying for the liveries with municipal funds – arguably because the number of teams always had to be even and the whole game would have been cancelled otherwise.[93] We know that the council kept the liveries because three years later they were mentioned again in the municipal proceedings, when councilmen, arguing that those garments would be of no use in subsequent local festivals, decided to donate them to a monastery.[94] The argument that the liveries would be of no use is unconvincing in a place like Medina de Rioseco, where games of canes were regularly organized at least twice a year, suggesting rather that the initial retention of the liveries from the 1584 game was a conscious act to avoid creating a precedent, so that local nobles did not get used to the idea of receiving liveries purchased with municipal funds. It is clear that the town council did not have a well-thought-out plan for what to do with the liveries, since they were kept for three years until they found a way to give them to a different institution, instead of reusing them. That is precisely the solution found by the municipal council of Santiago de Compostela, which mandated in 1608 that all the people who had "marlotas de la ciudad" return them. This order indicates that, at least in some instances, liveries were no longer considered gifts but the inalienable property of the municipal council, even though recipients seem to have thought otherwise. The same document also allocated funds for repairing the *marlotas* that could be retrieved.[95] Again the next year, the council repeated the same request, ordering that new ones only be made once they knew how many *marlotas* could be recovered.[96] These intermediate formulas caused a semantic erosion of the term "livery," which now ceased to be a gift but was transformed into a momentary borrowing. The same document also reveals the limitations of such a formula, since year after year the council recognized that some *marlotas* were missing.

In other cases, instead of providing livery, town councils offered participants some kind of stipend to help defray the cost. This is, for example, what happened in Priego de Córdoba in 1601, when the council offered 200 *reales* for each team – each with four riders, which amounts to about 4.5 *ducados* per participant, a relatively modest sum compared to the other cases analysed here.[97] Such financing of individuals for purchasing their own livery created a different sort of problem, as participants might be tempted to spend less than the stipend on their outfit and thus accrue an immediate benefit from the transaction. This is the situation that can be glimpsed in the municipal proceedings of Valladolid regarding the festivals for Philip III's entry in 1600. The city council ordered the livery from a game of canes to be gathered and reconciling the 300 *ducados* spent by participants in an equestrian masque, since apparently the participants had reused old clothing instead of making new outfits as they had promised.[98]

The games of canes that were proposed but could not take place are even more revealing of the social tensions surrounding their organization, as they make explicit how Moorish clothing constituted one way in which local officials and aristocrats tried to plunder collective resources for their own benefit. For instance, the city council of Santa Fe (Granada) discussed the possibility of organizing a game of canes in 1579, but ultimately rejected the idea because of the economic burden that it would impose on municipal finances.[99] In 1575, the city of Valladolid organized a game of canes and ordered the distribution of silk textiles to several members participating in the city *quadrilla*. Yet one of the councilmen denounced the case to the Royal Chancery in Valladolid, which revoked the order and prohibited the city council from paying for livery with municipal funds.[100] In 1609, the township of Arévalo

(Ávila), proposed celebrating a game of canes with twenty-four riders, who would receive the customary liveries. The council arrived at an estimate of 2,000 *ducados*. Since the town lacked the economic resources to meet this exorbitant figure, they petitioned Philip III for permission to apply an excise tax. However, the representatives of Arévalo and its territory complained that the land was already impoverished and could not bear an additional tax, and they successfully prevented the celebration of the game of canes.[101] In 1611, the *teniente de corregidor* of Madrid prohibited the town of Leganés from celebrating its festival in honour of Saint Nicasius because of the excessive expenses in plays, dances, bullfights, and games of canes.[102] This document does not reveal who denounced the expenditures projected for the festivals of Saint Nicasius, but based on the examples provided above, we can imagine that it was triggered by local tensions. What all these cases reveal is that, while the local elite always attempted to appropriate common funds for festivals for their own benefit, commoners were able to contest such abuses by appealing to higher instances of justice.

The conflict about who paid for the liveries illustrates how dressing *a la morisca* in public festivals took place within very specific power relations and socio-economic tensions that could be openly expressed as accusations of corruption. It would be too reductive to state that the only reason people strove to participate in the game of canes was because of the clothing they could obtain as livery. After all, in many cases participants had to procure Moorish attire on their own, or, even if they received it as livery, they still had to procure a horse as well as other costly equipment. The real benefit of dressing as a Moor was the social reputation that one could attain by being seen in the performance, as public image was an essential element in being regarded as noble, which in turn allowed those individuals to be admitted to certain offices and privileges. In other words, the shining allure of Moorish clothing resided in its promise of cementing upward social mobility.

Yet, as producers, patrons, wearers, and spectators alike were aware, Moorish clothing was in itself a valuable commodity, even if it had little use outside of the specific performance of the game of canes. When Moorish clothing was distributed as livery, questions arose about where the money came from, how the beneficiaries of liveries had been selected, and what was to be the fate of those garments when the festival ended and participants returned home with an object that could be monetarily very valuable but had no use in daily life. Certainly, Moorish clothing could be reused from one game of canes to the next, but, more often than not, beneficiaries sought a more immediate gain from their liveries, either by selling them or recycling them into daily wear.

The Afterlife of Moorish Clothing

In the early modern corpus of legal treatises on municipal government, only Jerónimo Castillo de Bovadilla defended the practice of giving livery to city officials for the celebration of local festivals, in his *Política para regidores y señores de vassallos* (1597). Paradoxically, the justifications that he offered are very revealing of the criticism of this practice. First, he argued that giving livery was a custom of the land, and that with these generous gifts cities and towns were able to show their magnificence and splendour; second, he pointed out that officials could not return liveries because those garments had no value once they had been tailored for the occasion; and, finally, he noted that officials could not return their liveries to the municipal government because they had already promised to turn them into skirts for their wives.[103] Castillo de Bovadilla's overemphasis shows that he had a hard time trying to justify this practice, which was quite frequent but criticized as unethical, because it was a way in which municipal officials used their offices to appropriate public funds.

Castillo de Bovadilla also reveals an important detail that never surfaces in municipal documents: that Moorish clothing was made so that it could be easily recycled. His argument that liveries were to be transformed into daily wear was not far-fetched, but echoed a well-established practice of making livery intentionally as reusable textiles. The first two tailoring books published in the 1580s probably followed a well-established practice when they explained how to make the *marlotas* for the game of canes so they could be easily turned into skirts. Juan de Alcega's *Libro de geometría, práctica y traza* (1580) succinctly but directly remarks that "one can make a skirt out of this *marlota*" (Figure 2).[104] Diego de Freyle's *Geometría y traça para el oficio de los sastres* (1588) is even more explicit about how to sew the *marlota* so it could be easily turned into a skirt: "the *marlota* can be used to make a skirt by making fake seams, sewing them toward the interior and not finishing them" (Figure 10).[105] The early modern lexicographer Francisco del Rosal states under the entry "Marlota" that the verb *marlotar* derives from this garment, meaning "to exchange or sell clothing."[106] While I have not been able to document such a use of *marlotar* in other early modern texts, the examples offered above seem to confirm the accuracy of Francisco del Rosal's definition, as the *marlota* was understood to be a commodity with an intrinsic exchange value – a luxurious garment that, once exhibited in the public arena of the festival, was intended to be transformed into daily wear.

There is also a telling self-contradiction in Castillo de Bovadilla's argument, since he undoes his own argument that liveries had no value once they have been tailored when he reveals right away that councilmen's *marlotas* were intended to be transformed into skirts after the game of canes. As Jones and Stallybrass observe in the case of early modern England, even though livery was conceived in principle to be an inalienable gift, "[t]he notion that clothes could escape circulation was, by and large, a fantasy."[107] In contrast to the case of England, in early modern Iberia there is very little in the written record tracing the subsequent circulation of Moorish livery once the game of canes ended. One plausible option is the sale of Moorish clothing on the second-hand market.[108] Indeed, this documentary silence could be intentional, because any selling of livery would in principle be a dishonourable act revealing that the public display of gallantry exhibited during the game of canes was but a momentary posturing in which participants displayed a socio-economic standing that was, in the majority of cases, beyond their actual status.

There is yet a plausible if undocumented second option for the fate of the Moorish clothing after the festival: selling it to a clothing lender. We know that the other end of this transaction existed, since, in many cases, individual participants rented their own attire from clothing lenders, an act that further eroded the original meaning of the term "livery."[109] Some towns rented "Moorish livery" from a clothing lender for the occasion and distributed them with the understanding that participants would return them after the festival. For example, in 1622 the municipal council of Berja (Almería) procured the liveries for the game of canes from a clothing lender. This kind of rental might have been common, but has left very little documentary trace – indeed, we know of this case only because two of the participants were sued for not returning their clothing.[110] Renting livery was the less prestigious form of exhibiting oneself publicly in gallant clothing, as it indicated that the renter did not have either the economic status theoretically required to participate in the game of canes or the social position to merit the privilege of receiving it as a gift from the organizers. The renting of individual Moorish livery for the game of canes has barely left a trace, quite probably because of the smaller sums involved in such transactions, but there is abundant indirect information about this practice, which I will explore in chapter 3.

In conclusion, we can see how analysing the circulation of Moorish clothing leads us to reassess idealizing discourses on the game of canes such as festival books. In theory, the game of canes was an equestrian exercise in which nobles wearing Moorish clothing displayed a certain social status. Yet when we look at how such Moorish clothing was made and distributed before the game (and resold or recycled afterwards), we can observe the gap between discourse and practice. For many participants, the game of canes was a momentary imposture in which they pretended to show off a higher standing. Looking at the material conditions of the game of canes also sheds light on the socio-economic interests that were interwoven with the circulation of Moorish clothing, as well as the social tensions behind the selection of participants and the distribution of livery, which could be contested by those bearing the burden of the festival.

This gap between theory and practice also affects the ideologies of representation: while the explicit goal of the game of canes was to pass as Moors, in practice these individuals were primarily passing as nobles when they dressed as Moors. Certainly, the use of Moorish livery for the game of canes was not the only way councilmen exploited common resources for their own benefit. However, criticism was probably more visible and vehement when dealing with the hardly justifiable practice of distributing Moorish liveries because contestation could be more easily articulated around already existing Islamophobic discourses. The instrumentalization of Islamophobic rhetoric to solve local tensions does not surface in the documents analysed in this chapter, but is openly exposed in literary texts, as the next chapter explores.

3 Unlawful Moorishness

Pude casar mi hija
con un hombre que ha estado
para un juego de cañas convidado.

[I once had the opportunity to marry my daughter to a man
who was once invited to a game of canes]

Francisco de Quevedo, "Entremés del
marido pantasma"

las marlotas son vasquiñas
que a sus mugeres les hazen:
de los capellares, bandas,
y cuellos de los turbantes

[the *marlotas* are now tunics
that they make for their wives,
from the *capellares* [they make] sashes,
and collars from turbans]

Anonymous ballad, 1599

The social tensions involved in the circulation of Moorish clothing and its problematic association with nobility can scarcely be glimpsed in archival sources and festival books, since these documents not only share many ideological assumptions but also silences that cannot be easily unveiled. Therefore it is necessary to turn to literary texts to see how the role of Moorish clothing in Iberian society was imagined and negotiated, either because these kinds of texts offer symbolic resolutions to the ideological contradictions involved in the circulation of Moorish clothing or, on the contrary, because they satirize the game of canes by bringing to the surface underlying assumptions and denials that were not openly expressed in other discourses. Indeed, the anonymous character of many of the texts analysed here allowed the authors to reveal aspects of the circulation of Moorish clothing that are otherwise purposefully ignored or silenced.

The social belief that honour and nobility could be attained through participating in the game of canes was openly ridiculed in some literary texts. In Francisco de Quevedo's "Entremés del marido pantasma," one of the characters brags that "I once had the opportunity to marry my daughter to a man who was once invited to a game of canes."[1] What makes this comment comical is that the character tries to attain honour for her family through a pretentious concatenation of unfulfilled potentialities: she is proud of a hypothetical son-in-law who did not actually play in any game of canes, but whose having been invited is somehow an honour transferred to the entire family, in the same way that her daughter might have married that man but never actually did. This is obviously a literary exaggeration, but it is merely carrying to the point of absurdity similar arguments actually made in legal claims to nobility, which very often claimed *hidalgo* status on the basis of indirect information about ancestors having participated in games of canes in the past. For instance, in Esteban Bonifaz Escobedo's application to the military Order of Alcántara, one of the witnesses testified in favour of the family's nobility that Rodrigo Godínez, the applicant's grandfather, had been admitted to the confraternity of Santiago de los Caballeros, "in which only those who are known as nobles can be admitted, since they are required to play games of canes."[2] One can clearly see the reach of the argument in this case, in which the assumption that the candidate's ancestors might have participated in the game of canes can be used as proof of nobility for the entire lineage.

Similarly, one of the characters in Luis Vélez de Guevara's *El diablo Cojuelo* (1641) criticizes an arrogant bartender by ironically foreseeing that "before a thousand years I expect to see him playing canes for the birth of some prince."[3] This passage seems to suggest that the bartender will consolidate his own social status by participating in a game of canes, but the allusion to such an extended period of time may also be interpreted as an intuition that, as soon as his descendants continue their process of social climbing, they will construe his predecessor the bartender as a noble participating in equestrian performances instead of a man tending tables in a sordid tavern. Vélez de Guevara's work contains yet another allusion to the game of canes, exposing its central role as a platform for social promotion, when the narrator later explains how the characters arrive in Córdoba "just in time to celebrate bullfights and a game of canes, which is a positive act [*acto positivo*] that the noblemen in that city perform in the most excellent way."[4] The irony in this passage is easy to miss, as it appears to be a formulaic celebration of Córdoba's nobility. It is certainly accurate to describe the participation in the game of canes as an *acto positivo*, which is a strict legal term from litigations for nobility used to refer to the evidence that proactively demonstrated the applicant's social status. Yet idealizing discourses on the game of canes never describe it as mere procedural practice warranting nobility. By defining the game of canes solely through legal language, Vélez de Guevara reduces it to its crudest administrative function and deprives the game of its social and performative prestige.

The following pages will show that, while literary maurophilia idealizing the Moor of the past derived largely from the currency of the game of canes in early modern Iberian society, literary parodies criticized commoners appropriating Moorish clothing by construing them as Moriscos. This chapter thus argues that literary manifestations of Moorishness did not merely reflect larger debates about the Moriscos' place in the construction of a national and cultural identity, but provided a symbolic expression of class struggle as well.

Moorish Ballads, "Moriscos," and Wannabes

Social tensions surrounding the distribution and display of Moorish clothing are reflected in a wide array of literary texts in which the Moor of the past plays a prominent role, works that have been considered by scholars either as merely aesthetic divertissements or as ideological interventions in the collective imaginary of Iberian identity vis-à-vis its Islamic legacy. The first expression of this literary trend is to be found in the compilations of late-medieval ballads, many of which depict the Moor as an honourable hero.[5] The publication of the short tale of *El Abencerraje* in the early 1560s crafted the definitive model of the idealized figure of the gallant Moor in the literary imagination. In the 1580s and 1590s early modern authors composed a new cycle of ballads imitating the traditional ones. These ballads, belonging to the cycle known as the *romancero nuevo*, further promoted the idealized Moor of the past, most frequently focusing on the use of gallant Moorish clothing and centring on the game of canes. Ginés Pérez de Hita's *Historia de los vandos de los Zegríes y Abençerrages* (1595, also known as the first part of the *Guerras civiles de Granada*), as well as a plethora of Moorish tales, such as Mateo Alemán's "Historia de Ozmín y Daraja," included in the first part of his *Guzmán de Alfarache* (1599), further expanded this literary vogue.[6]

The idealized literary representation of the Moor of the past, usually branded as "maurophilia," has long puzzled literary scholars and historians, who oscillate between considering it a nostalgic expression and cultural admiration of the defeated enemy or as a refined celebration of the victory of Christianity over Islam.[7] Beyond such interpretations of the cultural identity presented in these literary texts, however, an additional factor was their immediate application to an already existing social demand for models of Moorishness embodied in the game of canes. The documented instances of games of canes predate the first extant literary manifestations of maurophilia by decades if not centuries, which suggests that these aristocratic equestrian performances informed literary creation. If anything, tales like *El Abencerraje* provided a narrative frame for the game of canes and other urban performances – and it may not be a coincidence that the diffusion of *El Abencerraje* in the early 1560s coincided with Philip II's attempt to reinvigorate urban militias and the practice of horsemanship in the Kingdom of Castile.[8] While most scholars are certainly aware of the influence that the game of canes has exerted on the literary imagination of the medieval past, they have not considered the possibility that this equestrian exercise could also be, to a large extent, the primary (if not the only) source of iconographic materials for early modern literary maurophilia. This lapse echoes that of early modern authors who take the game of canes as the primary "archaeological" tool to "reconstruct" the Islamic period, and thus inevitably project the social signification that Moorish clothing had in their own time onto that past.

What all these Moorish compositions have in common beyond their generic differences is that their construction of the noble Moor is predominantly sartorial and praises his equestrian abilities during imagined games of canes held in the no less imaginary realm of the past. For instance, in the tale of *El Abencerraje*, the first description of the Muslim knight Abindarráez presents him as a lavishly dressed rider, as the ambushed Christian soldiers gaze upon his arrival:

> they saw a gallant Moor coming toward them on a roan horse. He was of powerful build and had a beautiful face, and he looked very fine in the

saddle. He wore a crimson cloak and a damask burnoose of the same color, all embroidered in gold and silver. His right sleeve was turned back, with a beautiful lady embroidered on it, and he held a fine and sturdy lance with two points. He carried a shield and a scimitar, and wore a Tunisian head wrap with many folds that served to both adorn and protect him. So dressed, the Moor advanced with a noble air.[9]

As the narrator adds, this visual characterization of Abindarráez is supposed to leave the audience in awe, signalled by the comment that the Christian soldiers were "transported by the sight of him, almost let him through."[10]

The emphasis on clothing is even more pronounced in the ballads, in which the stories of Moorish lovers are literally woven around their garments.[11] For instance, "El más gallardo jinete," describes Arbolán "wearing a *marlota* which was half blue, half red, which are the effects that the Moor causes in the beautiful Moor Guala; a yellow *capellar*, which is the colour of despair; blue turban and linens, because of the jealousy he is feeling."[12] Similarly, in "El animoso Celín," the Muslim knight takes off his gallant clothing when he sees the Christians laying siege to the city of Baza:

> He takes off the *marlota* he was wearing, which was green, purple and white, lined with yellow, and he says: the lining will serve me because this colour suits me. I don't want the green feathers, since I have lost any hope ... I leave behind the purple turban, since, even though I have love, it is possible that she will find another one who can enjoy her company better.[13]

Ginés Pérez de Hita's *Historia de los vandos de los Zegríes y Abençerrages* (1595) further develops the predominance of the sartorial aspect by expanding the content of earlier Moorish ballads in narrative form.[14]

In opposition to this literary vogue of idealizing the Moor of the past as a gallant knight (of which I have only offered a few examples), a series of satirical ballads written in the1590s contested such idealization, often accusing the poets of Moorish ballads of being Muslims themselves.[15] These ballads are usually known in scholarship as *romances anti-moriscos* because their common strategy consists of contrasting the idealized image of the gallant Moor with the impoverished Morisco labourer, such as the anonymous "Ah mis señores poetas"[16] and Gabriel Lobo Lasso de la Vega's "Señor moro vagabundo" and "Poetas a lo moderno."[17] Because of the blatant Islamophobic language used in these compositions, most scholars have focused on how this literary corpus echoes the debates about the place of Moriscos in Iberian society.[18] Taking a different approach, Antonio Sánchez Jiménez analyses how the dialogue that some of these ballads establish among themselves indicates that they might have been composed within the space of a literary academy, thus arguing that the satirical ballads reflect only a literary discussion between poets in which the Islamophobic language is but a farcical and inconsequential rhetorical strategy.[19] My interpretation is situated somehow in the middle: I agree with Sánchez Jiménez that the primary target of these ballads is not the Morisco, yet we should not conclude that the choice of Islamophobia as a rhetorical strategy is altogether ideologically unmotivated. Rather, if we analyse how these ballads address certain aspects of the circulation of Moorish clothing that are otherwise ignored in festival books, we can see that the Islamophobic rhetoric is the signifier articulating a conflict about social mobility.

Literary scholars have long pointed out that maurophilia and maurophobia seem to be two sides of the same coin, and that they seem to have some relationship with how class difference was articulated in early modern Iberia. Yet there is a gross imbalance in the representativity that has been attributed to each discourse: Maurophilia has been recognized as a complex phenomenon with a very ambivalent interpretation as critics continue to debate whether it represents a nostalgic cultural attachment to the Islamic legacy, the glorification of the Christian victory over Islam in the Peninsula, a manifestation of aristocratic ethos, or an inconsequential aesthetic fashion. Meanwhile, maurophobic literary manifestations have been regarded unproblematically as blatant expressions of xenophobia. An oft-cited interpretation is that of Claudio Guillén (for whom so-called maurophilic texts like *El Abencerraje* do nothing to defend the place of the Moriscos in Iberian society): "the exaltation of the Moorish knight, always a nobleman, was far from being incompatible with a profound scorn for the *morisco*, who was always a plebeian."[20]

While Guillén's dictum is an insightful interpretation of the ideologies of representation of Moorish fictions in relation to class difference, he reduces it to an oversimplified opposition between the Christian noble and the Morisco peasant. But more important for my point here, Guillén also ignores that both "Moor" and "Morisco" can be literary and social tropes. If the "Moorish knight" does not refer to actual Muslims and can be used as a metaphor to represent nobility in Moorish fictions and urban performances, then, by the same token, the signifier

"Morisco" does not necessarily refer to the descendants of Iberian Muslims, but can equally be used to represent something else. That something else is not quite the plebeian, but precisely those individuals who, without being noble yet, want to be recognized as such, and could therefore be conceived in the imaginary as "wannabe Moors." Rephrasing Guillén's insight, we could say that the exaltation of the nobleman, who was conceived of as a gallant Moorish knight, was compatible with a profound scorn for the plebeian who wanted to be recognized as noble, and who was therefore construed as a debased Morisco.

Literary maurophilia and maurophobia are two sides of the same coin because the divide between the gallant Moor and the impoverished Morisco is its constitutive illusion. The stark opposition between these two forms of "Moors" – one idealized and one debased – sublimates the social tensions of early modern Iberian society and reflects them in purified form, by negating the instability of the boundary dividing those who were allegedly able to show an immanent aristocratic status through the adoption of Moorish clothing from those who were perceived as attempting to access nobility through the same practice.[21]

This critique of the pretensions of social mobility through participation in festivals is clear in one of the earlier known satires, "Ensíllenme el asno rucio" (c. 1585), attributed to Luis de Góngora. The traditional classification of this poem as *romance antimorisco* is somewhat misleading. While it is obvious that the ballad is a line-by-line parody of the maurophiliac ballad "Ensíllenme el potro rucio" attributed to Lope de Vega, it does not follow that this composition is attacking Moorishness in itself (or even Lope). "Ensíllenme el asno rucio" deals with a rustic individual intending to participate in a courtly equestrian performance in Toledo while lacking both the socio-economic means and any kind of aristocratic refinement. After listing his ridiculous dress and horse, the poem describes the rustic Galayos as "that weepy mare driver, donkey rider, who has his origin in the place where he was born and is descendant of mare drivers, some kind of men that provide for themselves without kings supplying them."[22] Because of the obvious intertextual relation with Lope's ballad, literary criticism has favoured a biographical reading of the personal and poetic confrontation between Lope and Góngora.[23] Although these aspects are valid, the emphasis on the biographical interpretation has obscured analysis of the larger social debate behind this contrafactum. Thus the line "hombres que se proveen ellos" has been traditionally read as a scatological allusion.[24] While this interpretation is probably accurate, the passage also points to more complex social issues, since it may refer as well to the fact that Galayos is not receiving livery from the king because he does not belong to the royal circle of patronage. Therefore, in his own procuring of "livery" from the mundane garments available at his house, he is unlawfully pretending to belong to the network of Toledo's social elite.

This social intervention becomes more explicit in other parodic ballads that circulated in manuscript and have received less attention because they were not included in the printed compilations. In an anonymous poetic manuscript held at the Biblioteca Nacional de España, there are several compositions focusing on how, for many individuals, procuring Moorish clothing and equestrian tack for the game of canes and other equestrian performances was a costly investment. One of the ballads describes a masque celebrated in Valladolid in 1594. It begins with the traditional narrative frame of the Moorish ballads by referring to events allegedly taking place in fifteenth-century Granada. Yet the poem itself soon dispenses with its own fictitious setting as it starts to criticize several participants whose clothing showed that they were not the wealthy aristocrats they were pretending to be: "another *quadrille* of six Moors of middling status, which had hardly horses or scimitars ... Even though their garments were patched, their look was not poorly received, since there were few expectations about those who amount to so little."[25] The ballad oscillates between both the idealizing and the satirical forms of Moors, making it clear that the perceived presence of the commoners was enough to disrupt the literary conventions of Moorishness.

Another anonymous poem included in the same manuscript, and probably referring to the same event, also emphasizes the miserable condition of some of the participants by pointing out that their socio-economic status might not be so very different from that of the audience: "Those who have no money, there they are, and they are not among us. There they are, the noblemen, devoting their braveries to Love with more feathers than money ... and after they have lunched, it is true, they have returned home and have shed their clothing in order not to wear it out."[26] In this case, the ballad points out that even nobles (it does not specify of which rank) have incurred an excessive expenditure in their Moorish clothing, which they have to carefully protect for the next performance – or maybe because they need to return it to the clothing lender.

Only a few years later, yet another anonymous ballad, beginning with the well-known verses "Mala la hubistes, franceses," questions the exuberance displayed at the festivals held in Valencia to celebrate Philip III's wedding in 1599.[27] The ballad begins with a tailor complaining about why they need to undo the *capellares* used in the game of canes, to which another tailor responds that those riders were actually wretched individuals who could participate only because they had "loaned taffeta clothes, rented horses, and borrowed reins."[28] As the second tailor states, all this Moorish clothing was to be immediately transformed into daily wear: "the *marlotas* are now skirts that they make for their wives, from the *capellares* [they make] sashes, and collars from turbans."[29] There is a certain contradiction within the ballad, as it points to two different transactions at once – logically, one could recycle a livery, but not a rented garment that had to be returned to the lender. Yet the social critique of the infatuations of Moorishness remains clear. While the first comment criticizes the arrogance of those who pretended to show a higher status through the rental of Moorish clothing and equestrian gear, the second remark moves to the debates on whether government officials should be allowed to keep the local festival clothing. The reference to how the *marlotas* would be made into skirts for the participants' wives clearly rephrases one of the arguments in Jerónimo Castillo de Bovadilla's *Política para regidores y señores de vassallos* (1597), which, as I have already analysed in chapter 2, made an ardent defence of municipal officials' right to receive liveries paid with public funds. This ballad, composed only two years later, shows that at least some of his contemporaries perceived Castillo de Bovadilla's justification of this practice as cynical.

Following the same line of argument, the anonymous sonnet "Una puerta de villa a la malicia" [A City Gate of Malice] criticizes the Madrid *regidores* wearing Moorish livery in 1599 by emphasizing their greed: "Councilmen dressed in greed / clothing of brocade, silk, and wool / welcome our sovereign Queen / by holding in her honour a thousand festivals of avarice."[30] The modern editor Benito Ruano refers to the expenses made by the council of Madrid, but does not address what seems to be the most obvious reading: that the author of the sonnet denounces the councilmen's greed because of the public funds that they have spent to dress for the festival. All these poetic compositions reflect that, even if the criticism of municipal expenditure in festivals was prevalent throughout the sixteenth century, there was a surge in social unrest in the 1590s, quite probably as a consequence of the accession to power of Philip III and the exorbitant expenses incurred in the celebrations of his wedding in 1599.

The ballad "Qué se me da a mí que el mundo" [What do I care about the world?], attributed to Lope, presents an equally contradictory critique of Moorish clothing conflating two different arguments into one. First, it exposes the corruption and exploitation of the ruling classes implicit in the distribution of livery when the poetic voice proclaims that he does not care if the courtier "wears cloth and wastes silk at the expense of the peasant."[31] But in a second instance it refers to the Moorish ballads, saying that he does not care if the Moors in Granada "play games of canes dressed in a thousand different ways, nor that they wear rented livery in their *zambras*."[32] Obviously, the object of the critique is not the Moors of Granada or their descendants, but the burdensome expenditures of public funds made by nobles and municipal officials. Like "Mala la hubistes, franceses," "Qué se me da a mí que el mundo" makes the apparently contradictory move of accusing riders of both receiving liveries paid with municipal funds and of renting them, which shows that in public opinion both practices were considered somehow analogous, as both undermined the theoretical socioeconomic standing of the participants.

The most explicit literary account of how Moorish clothing circulated in early modern Iberian society is found in Gabriel Lasso de la Vega's *Manojuelo de romances nuevos* (1601). In "Yengo a buscar una botarga" [While looking for a cheap costume] the narrator goes to the clothing lender looking for a costume for Carnival. Unfortunately for him, the clothing lender replies that the poets have already rented everything he had in order to dress their literary Moors.[33] Thus the ballad imagines an impossible transaction, in which real clothing is being used to dress literary characters. Furthermore, accusing the literary Moors of wearing rented livery undermines the exhibition of gallantry on the part of both the Moorish figures and the poets, who are here conceived as some kind of second-rate patrons.

If Lasso de la Vega signals the renting of Moorish clothing in "Yengo a buscar una botarga," he alludes to the opposite transaction of selling liveries in the ballad "Quién compra dieciséis moros" [Who'll buy sixteen Moors?]. This poem begins by asking the audience a rhetorical question: "Who buys sixteen Moors that were left over from a game of canes?"[34] The poetic voice aims at gaining as much profit as possible from selling the fictional Moors of other ballads as though they were real, making explicit the intended buyer of the Moorish clothes: "I will sell the *marlotas* of blue and silver damask ... to a man who lends costumes for the dances of the Corpus Christi, I will sell headdresses and turbans, purple tunics and sleeve."[35] The poem seems to allude to these "Moors" as if they were Moriscos, characterizing them as a debased group of labourers that the poetic voice plans on enslaving: "Until one day I will put in their hands two hoes, and they will work my vineyard, water my garden and farm, and I will sell them to row in the galleys when the money runs out."[36]

In spite of the reference to the Moriscos, they are not the most immediate object of scorn, but rather those participants of the game of canes who were on the fringes of nobility and could participate only because they received Moorish clothing as livery – probably borrowing horses and tack as well. These ballads do not say that their literary subjects *are* Moriscos, but that in their aim to pass as gallant Moors, these people are actually *like* the impoverished Moriscos as they were represented in Islamophobic discourses, and thus subject to the same treatment.[37] Such poetic compositions chastise those people who ostentatiously pretended to share the space of the spectacle with wealthy nobles and even grandees, but who after the game of canes found themselves in the miserable situation of either returning their rented clothing or having to sell their liveries to clothing lenders.

These poetic denunciations also indicate that there was a widespread awareness of how Moorish clothing was recycled into daily clothing. While the idealizing Moorish ballads focused on Moorish clothing as a gallant display of nobility in the public arena, their parodic counterparts focused on the wretched aspects of Moorish clothing production and circulation as a way to underscore how their momentary display of magnificence was but a pretence – or, in the worst of the cases, a way to appropriate common resources. In so doing, these parodic ballads do not question Moorishness itself, but rather target a very specific group of participants: those who pretend to be of the high nobility without actually having the necessary means.

The Islamophobic rhetoric of these ballads was soon picked up by other authors criticizing the use of Moorish clothing in the first decades of the seventeenth century. In the prologue to his epic poem *La Iberiada* (1603), Gaspar Savariego de Santana criticizes Moorish fashion in both literature and courtly culture, and derogatively refers to the participants in games of canes as "Morisma nueva de Christianos."[38] This expression, coined by Savariego de Santana, is a complex word game difficult to translate. Covarrubias defines the derogative term *morisma* as "multitude of Moors or sect."[39] It entails therefore a certain degree of objectification of Muslims as a mob lacking individuality. By adding the adjective *nueva* [new], Savariego de Santana plays with the expression "cristiano nuevo de moros" [literally, new Christian from Moors], a phrase alternatively used to categorize the Moriscos. The pun in Savariego de Santana lies in his reversal of the direction of the conversion, so that Christians are conceived to have converted to Islam with their adoption of Moorish clothing.

The proliferation of maurophobic discourses around the years of the expulsion of the Moriscos may suggest at first the existence of a process of cultural cleansing that, in correlation with the search for religious homogenization, tried to erase the legacy of the Islamic past.[40] Yet such a project is at most fragmentary and contradictory. Francisco Núñez de Velasco, in his *Diálogos de contención entre la milicia y la ciencia* (1614), criticized the Iberian nobility's taste for the game of canes, "regarding as greatness and gallantry the act of dressing up in the Moorish style with *marlotas*, Moorish hoods, and turbans, and the cities and court rejoicing in this dress by impersonating ... a Moorish horde."[41] Similarly, Francisco de Quevedo's satirical poem "No he de callar, por más que con el dedo" (c. 1625) maintained that the *gineta* riding style and the game of canes were Islamic influences and called instead for the restitution of jousts and tournaments.[42]

Yet we should be cautious about conflating all maurophobic discourses under the same homogenizing rubric. The critiques by Savariego de Santana and Núñez de Velasco quite probably exemplify the voice of the non-noble soldier, as they draw from a larger debate that pits the professionalization of regular armies and commoners against the display of aristocratic equestrian prowess.[43] On the contrary, Quevedo's criticism of the game of canes, which is framed as a larger critique of the Count-Duke of Olivares, Philip IV's favourite, proposes an anachronistic recuperation of cuirasses and jousts. As elaborated in chapter 2, the cost of armour limited the inclusion of participants in equestrian performances, and therefore promoted a very restrictive concept of nobility, contrary to the relatively open notion of nobility represented in the game of canes.[44]

These were isolated critiques of Moorishness, which were not backed by the overall reputation that the game of canes had in religious and humanist discourses. The infrequent ecclesiastical censorship of the game of canes focused only on the wasteful spending for public festivals and the dangers implicit in bullfights.[45] Moralists dealing with gaming justified the game of canes as a preparation for war.[46] When moralists dealt with clothing, they devoted their strongest comments to proving that the widespread use of luxurious garments was a threat to social order, women's chastity, or courtiers' virility – but do not even mention Moorish clothing as an issue.[47] Not only did these authors never criticize the use of Moorish clothing as a contradiction to Catholic identity, nobody ever seems to have even raised his voice to complain that dressing as a Moor could be incompatible with the celebration of Christian figures.[48]

Since the political agendas revealed in each of these critiques are often antithetical, they can hardly reflect a coherent social rejection of Moorish clothing. These dissonant voices calling for its elimination were probably not the cause of the decline of the game of canes, but the symptom of a latent social conflict articulated in the association between Moorish clothing, noble status, and public expenditure in festivals. Thus, instead of focusing exclusively on how maurophilic or maurophobic discourses reflect individual positions within the social debate over the place of Moriscos or the cultural legacy of the Islamic period, we must analyse how the strategy of capitalizing on Islamophobic discourses more likely represents the interests of particular social classes, in particular social contexts.[49]

The "moro gracioso" as Emblem of Class Difference

Many of the plays in which Christian characters pass as Moors on stage not only reproduce the idealizing forms of Moorishness of maurophilic tales and ballads, but very often also make explicit how class difference is encoded in the use of Moorish clothing. The gallantry of noble Christians who adopt gallant Moorish clothing is emphasized with the recurrent presence of the *gracioso*, the Old Christian commoner jester who, in contrast to aristocrats, is not fully able to dress as a Moor.[50] This conventional comic type, which echoes the debased form of Moorishness found in the parodic Moorish ballads written in the 1590s, is usually referred to in stage directions as dressing as "moro gracioso" or "moro a lo gracioso." This type was first deployed in Lope de Vega's *Los cautivos de Argel* (c. 1599), *La desdichada Estefanía* (1604), *La doncella Teodor* (c. 1608–10), and *La octava maravilla* (1609),[51] and is taken up as well in many other plays throughout the seventeenth century, such as Luis Vélez de Guevara's *Don Pedro Miago* (c. 1613),[52] Tirso de Molina's *Las quinas de Portugal* (c. 1638) and *El cobarde más valiente*,[53] Álvaro Cubillo de Aragón's *El conde de Saldaña* and *La manga de Sarracino*,[54] the collective play *La luna africana* (c. 1643),[55] and Francisco de Rojas's version of *El caballero del Febo* (1664).[56]

The most explicit passage about this sartorial characterization is probably found in Vélez de Guevara's *Don Pedro Miago* (c. 1613), in a scene in which the rustic servant Berrueco tries to blend in with the Muslim embassy. Even though he acknowledges that he cannot pretend to speak Arabic, he claims that his physical appearance is not different from that of the Moors and therefore he vows to remain silent, hoping that his looks can compensate for his lack of linguistic skills. The play focuses on passing in sartorial terms. As the stage directions announce, he appears "vestido de moro a lo gracioso" [dressed as a Moor in the jester style]. Berrueco himself explains his sartorial transformation to the audience:

> the sheet from the bedding, and my uncle's beret, which he uses to sleep when it is cold, and this ... what's its name? ... *ciegayernos* [literally, son-in-law blinder] or *almaizar* [Moorish cloak], blanket or ... What is this? Something that serves as *capellar* to my frightening figure. This *adarga* and this lance that I have taken from my master's house, suit me well today.[57]

Berrueco is not successful in his passing because the Muslim characters immediately recognize him as a Christian. Yet, precisely because Berrueco's failure to pass as a Moor is inconsequential within the plot, the mockery is in itself telling of the value of Moorish clothing for the articulation of class identity. The ridicule of the scene derives from Berrueco's aim to reuse domestic drapes as improvised versions of the lavish Moorish clothing, such as a sheet as an *almaizar* and a blanket as a *capellar*. Even though Berrueco is hesitant about the correct Arabic names, he finally says them right, which suggests that he is relatively familiar with them already. The main impediment for Berrueco in passing as a Moor is not that he is a Christian, as it seems at first glance, but that he is a rustic commoner. Thus the play emphasizes in a comic tone that passing as "Moor" is a privilege of class status only available to nobles.

A similar passage is found in Álvaro Cubillo de Aragón's *La manga de Sarracino*, in which the commoner Mendoza reveals his social status through his clumsiness in putting on a Moorish robe. As he comments, "I think I have dressed myself inside-out."[58] Moorish clothing as a sign of distinction is revealed not only in the mere possibility of owning them, but also in having the knowledge of how to embody a sartorial technology in which only the initiated (definitely not the commoners) could participate.

In some of these passages there is a clear intertextual relation to the satirical ballads analysed at the beginning of this chapter. Further, the anonymous ballad "Ese moro ganapán" [That miserable Moor] (c. 1595) denounced the Moorish clothing of the game of canes as an artificial pastiche by comparing it with both the Galician language and grafting: "that is not Arabic, but Galician, and a costume beret, tree of many grafts."[59] When in Tirso de Molina's *Las quinas de Portugal*, the jester Brito appears dressed as a ridiculous Moor, he comments on his own sartorial transformation with identical references to Galicia and grafting: "Here I am, turned into a Muslim sage from Orense [a region in Galicia], a Galician grafted onto a Moor."[60] The coincidence of the simultaneous evocation of both a stereotype of the Galician people and grafting as instances of hybridity, indicates that Tirso de Molina is referring to the so-called *anti-morisco* ballads and echoing the same social debates encoded in those compositions.

The theatrical convention of the "moro gracioso" as the expression of the commoner who cannot conform adequately to the aristocratic display of Moorishness thus produces a sense of comic relief for the social tensions encoded in the use of Moorish clothing, and early modern audiences would relate these *graciosos* to the imaginary of both nobility and Moorish clothing. Yet, while it is true that the primary function of this comic type is to convey the alleged inability of the commoner to dress as a Moor, it may also serve to undermine aristocratic gallantry. When Berrueco in Vélez de Guevara's *Don Pedro Miago* calls the *almaizar* "ciegayernos," he is not misspelling the Arabic sartorial jargon for *almaizar*. The Spanish *ciegayernos* could be translated as "sucker trap," or more literally, "something that bewilders sons-in-law," and therefore emphasizes the ability of Moorish clothing to awe audiences aiming for social advancement (such as procuring the advantageous marriage of Quevedo's "Entremés del marido pantasma"). Thus Berrueco reveals how Moorish clothing was used as a way to suspend suspicion about the wearer's reputation and real social status.

This chapter has shown that literary expressions of both maurophilia and maurophobia were conditioned by more than the ideological relations of Spanish identity vis-à-vis Islam. Satiric literary texts used the rhetoric of Islamophobic discourses to disparage those individuals who were trying to pass as nobles through participation in urban equestrian performances. Yet analysis of the content of such literary texts offers only one side of the story, since poets and playwrights themselves were not isolated from the social tensions encoded in the use of Moorish clothing that they laid out in their plots. The social status and ambitions of playwrights also left their mark in the way plays referred to the game of canes and to Moorishness in general. This trace becomes clear, above all, in the literary career of Lope de Vega, as the next chapter explores.

4 Lope's Moors: Self-Fashioning and Resentment

Porque para ser lozano
un cristiano hidalgo, es llano
que ha de tener algo moro.
[Because for a Christian noble
to be gallant, it is plain that he
must have something Moorish]

Lope de Vega, El hijo de Reduán (c. 1588–95)

yo no entiendo de caracoles,
sino de sonetos.
[I do not know about equestrian pirouettes,
but about sonnets]

Lope de Vega, Letter to the Count of Sessa, 1628

As chapter 3 demonstrated, early modern writers often lent their pens to celebrating the aristocracy's games of canes, but they also devoted their wit to denouncing and parodying those very same aristocratic equestrian exercises. Poets, playwrights, and novelists may have had a personal interest in either idealizing or scorning Moorishness, especially if their literary career was related to their own processes of social climbing. By looking at Lope de Vega's life (1562–1635) and oeuvre we can observe how fictions about the game of canes and the use of Moorish clothing may not only represent a particular vision of the society these works described, but at the same time, in a complex dynamic, are conditioned by the widespread circulation of Moorish liveries, and reflect the specific relationship that a writer might establish with his Moorish fictions in his own process of self-fashioning.

Lope de Vega cultivated the two literary genres discussed in chapter 3. While in his early career Lope was one of the main cultivators of Moorish ballads, he was also recognized as the creator of the Spanish *comedia* between the 1590s and the early seventeenth century. The bulk of his prolific production falls squarely within the period in which Moorishness was most prominent as a display of aristocratic status, during the reigns of Philip II and Philip III, which is thus also the moment of the greatest material presence for Moorish garb. The author's flirtation with the figure of the Moor as his alter ego in Moorish ballads served to construct his own public identity. As I will show, Lope de Vega's ambivalent use of Moorishness throughout his literary career reveals a desire to use his literary work to market a particular social image of himself. His unsuccessful aspirations to be recognized as noble correlates with his trajectory from maurophilia to maurophobia, which makes him an ideal case study of how those individuals on the fringes of nobility approached Moorishness as a shortcut for social promotion – in Lope's notorious case, unsuccessfully.

From Livery to Stage

Before dealing with Lope's personal investment in Moorishness, we should consider how the widespread circulation of Moorish clothing may have created the material conditions for the development of theatre as a commercial enterprise. The prevalence of Moorish themes in early modern Iberian theatre has been amply studied, but, like ballads, it has been analysed traditionally as a religious confrontation with Islam reflecting on issues such as fetishization of the *Reconquista*, social debates about the Moriscos, colonial expansion in North Africa, or military confrontation against the Ottoman Empire.[1] Yet even if the relation between theatre and Iberian attitudes vis-à-vis Islam is undeniable, the social relevance of the game of canes and the ubiquity of Moorish clothing may also have affected the development of the Iberian stage by the end of the sixteenth century. Arsenio Moreno Mendoza suggests that the sartorial representation of Muslims on stage was quite probably inspired by the ubiquitous Moorish impersonations of the game of canes.[2] If we take this interpretation a step further, we might also wonder whether the game of canes was not merely a sartorial inspiration for theatrical Muslim characters, but rather its more immediate material condition, as it created a means of making use of the abundance of Moorish clothing in early modern Iberian society.

There is evidence of a tenuous but constant synecdochal relationship between theatre and the game of canes, as both were part of public celebrations. Some sixteenth-century theatrical urban performances were inspired quite explicitly by the game of canes, for example Diego Sánchez de Badajoz's *Farsa del juego de cañas* (published in 1554)[3] and Mateo Flecha's musical interlude *Las cañas*, probably written between the 1530s and the 1540s.[4] Jean Sentaurens documents the performance of two urban ballets in Seville in 1561 and 1572 that were named after the game of canes.[5] Do these theatrical pieces merely evoke the game of canes, or were they conceived to be staged in conjunction with them? The stage directions accompanying Tomás Villacastín's *Triunpho de la fortuna*, staged in Valladolid in the 1580s, seem to indicate that a game of canes was included within the staging of the play.[6]

The interrelation between the game of canes and the development of theatre is clear in Francisco Agustín Tárrega's play *El prado de Valencia* (c. 1590). In the second act of *El prado de Valencia*, Tárrega inserts a long description of an actual game of canes held in Valencia to celebrate the wedding of Lucrecia de Moncada and Francisco de Palafoix in 1590, and depicts in every detail the Moorish garments of the participants.[7] While Moorish clothing is merely mentioned in act 2, it takes the stage in the denouement of the play. In act 3, Rodolfo and his soldiers fake a Moorish attack on the coast as part of their scheme to restore the honour of one of the female characters. As they put on their Moorish costumes, Rodolfo comments on his own attire to his soldiers: "Seeing myself in such deeds, ... I have a gut feeling that either I am a Moor from Algiers, or I am going to play the game of canes."[8] In mirroring the game of canes described in the second act, this scene reflects the cultural practices of the Valencian urban elites and their fondness for Moorishness. Yet the contrast between both passages further reveals paradoxical perceptions and imaginings about the circulation of Moorish clothing.

When Rodolfo prepares for the fake Moorish ambush for which he and his soldiers will disguise themselves as Moors, he plans to send somebody to Valencia to "bring by money and work, *marlotas*, capes, and turbans from North African Moors, yet there are still many [marlotas] made in Valencia, and not only a few."[9] Rodolfo's comment on the availability of Moorish clothing in Valencia conceives of it as having a North African origin, only to end up acknowledging that they were locally produced. Even if the play does not ultimately clarify whether the Moorish clothing used by these characters was made in Valencia or imported from North Africa, Rodolfo's hesitation collides with material reality, since Moorish clothing was regularly made in the Iberian Peninsula. Indeed, Rodolfo's ambivalence about the origins of the Moorish clothing is contradictory within the plot itself: since the participants in the game of canes described in the second act wear Moorish clothing, it is not clear why Rodolfo does not propose to reuse their garments or at least procure them from the same place. The lack of resolution at the level of the plot begs the question of what happens at the level of performance: it is quite plausible that the play was related to the wedding of Lucrecia de Moncada and Francisco de Palafoix in 1590, and therefore the game of canes described in the second act of the play refers to an actual game held for the celebration. Rodolfo's uncertainty about the origin of Moorish clothing may indicate an unwillingness to acknowledge that there is a potential transfer of Moorish clothing from the actual game of canes to the stage, which is silenced because livery was not supposed to circulate (either sold or borrowed).[10]

Literary scholars have pointed out how this play foreshadows several dramatic techniques later employed by Lope, who was in Valencia in the 1590s and got acquainted with the Valencian circle of dramatists of which Tárrega was a member.[11] Tárrega's status as precursor of Lope's dramatic innovations in his *arte nuevo* may not be unrelated to the centrality of Moorish clothing and the game of canes in the latter's dramatic work.

Among Lope de Vega's numerous works, we find a significant number of plays involving Muslim characters and therefore requiring the use of Moorish clothing, as they dealt with the romanticized Islamic period, with North African piracy and Christian captivity, such as *El Argel fingido* (1599), *Los cautivos de Argel* (1599), and *Los esclavos libres* (1600), or with the conflict with the Ottoman Empire, such as *El Grao de Valencia* (1589–90), *El rey sin reino* (c. 1597–1612), and *La nueva victoria del Marqués de Santa Cruz* (1604). In his study of Muslim characters in Lope's oeuvre, Thomas Case lists some seventy plays relating to these themes.[12] The breadth of the corpus of Lope's plays that include Muslim characters precludes a thorough analysis here, but the evidence marshalled in this study does support a general hypothesis concerning the relationship between the circulation of Moorish liveries and the stage in Lope's time. Assuming that in Lope's plays all Muslim characters (as well as Christians passing as Muslims) were characterized by the use of Moorish dress, the extravagant quantity of Moorish clothing that had to be used for staging his plays becomes evident – even if we can safely assume that some of those garments were reused in other plays with similar plots.[13]

All the scholars who have analysed the use of clothing in Lope's drama have focused on the symbolic meanings associated with the use of different garments.[14] While the symbolic aspect of clothing on stage is indeed essential for understanding drama, the production of meaning was also framed by material constraints. Imagining that Lope freely decided to write about any topic (in this case, relations with Islam) and then proposed his dramatic text to the company directors is probably an anachronistic and romantic view of early modern theatrical production. If we foreground the role of company directors instead, a quite plausible motivation might be prompting requests that playwrights write about certain topics precisely because they needed to capitalize on their investment in props and clothing, in this case their stock of Moorish garb. As a parallel case, documentation indicates that Lope included the appearance of lions in some of his plays only to make use of the lion skins that were readily available in the company's assests and properties.[15] Since Lope was well aware of the material conditions of the theatre, it is safe to assume that he would not have required costumes as expensive as Moorish clothing without being certain that the material conditions had already been met for the staging of such plays. Thus, instead of assuming that costumes were sought once the play was written, as is often the case now, we should consider the opposite possibility: that the overstock of Moorish clothing may have conditioned the prevalence of certain plots in which actors could wear those recycled liveries.

Nor was Lope ignorant of the commercial aspects of theatre, and thus understood its economic relationship with the circulation of clothing in general, and Moorish garb in particular. To begin with, he was intimately familiar with the production of clothing, since his father Félix de Vega was an embroiderer, as were two of his brothers-in-law, Luis de Rosicler and Juan de Vega.[16] There is also evidence that during his many sojourns in Toledo – which was in fact one of the main centres of silk textile production for the Moorish clothing for the game of canes – he met several people who were simultaneously theatre agents and clothing brokers.[17] One of those people was the illiterate Agustín Castellanos, also known as "El poeta sastre" [The Tailor Poet], who was involved in the garment-lending trade.[18] The other was Pedro Gaspar de Porres, who staged some of Lope's plays, and who was also involved in both the clothing trade and the organization of plays and urban spectacles.[19]

There is ample evidence for the presence of Moorish clothing in theatre company inventories in early modern Iberia.[20] In some cases, we find company directors buying textiles, which indicates that wealthier theatre companies could commission specific new garments.[21] However, in most cases, theatre companies could not afford to own such expensive costumes, and resorted to renting them from the *alquiladores de hatos* (clothing lenders), whose inventories abounded in Moorish clothing.[22] Clothing traders loaned Moorish clothing not only to theatre companies, but also to local authorities who wanted to organize games of canes.[23] There are, however, some limitations on the data that can be harvested from the study of commercial contracts. They certainly reflect how theatre companies pawned their costumes, how costumes circulated among clothing lenders, and how they bequeathed them in their wills, but these documents do not shed light on the origin of the majority of all that Moorish clothing that was stocked by clothing lenders and theatre companies.

Given the chronological coincidence in time between the peak of the game of canes as the central social performance and the development of theatre in early modern Iberia in the last decades of the sixteenth century, as well as the close relationship between clothing traders and theatre companies, it seems very likely that clothing lenders and theatre companies sought leftover Moorish livery, as well as other kinds of costumes. Theatre companies in early modern England acted as brokers for clothing, serving as one of the venues through which livery was recycled.[24] In the case of early modern Iberia, there seems to be no trace of such transactions in extant documentation. One possible reason for this lack is that small quotidian transactions made in cash are not usually reflected in commercial contracts.[25] Individual piecemeal purchases of Moorish liveries on the second-hand market probably did not require the intervention of notaries, resulting in only circumstantial evidence of what must have been very common but has left no paper trail.

Indirect evidence is, however, found, for example in the post-mortem inventory of the clothing lender Gabriel Núñez made in 1610, in which we find a large number of garments usually conceived of as Moorish, such as *marlotas*, *capellares*, and *sayos vaqueros*.[26] Of these, only a few are accompanied by the expression "de juego de cañas."[27] Because of the ambiguity of the preposition *de* in Spanish, it is hard to interpret whether these garments came *from* a game of canes or were intended *for* them. In the valuation of Núñez's estate, these second-hand garments were valued at a much lower price than the Moorish clothing typically made for the game of canes. As seen in chapter 2, the set of Moorish clothing for a game of canes held in Cuenca in 1604 amounted to about 37 *ducados* per participant; by contrast, the *marlotas* and *capellares* in Gabriel Núñez's inventory were valued at an average of 2 *ducados*.[28] Of course, these figures cannot be compared on an equal basis, since there is no easily interpretable indication of quality of the Moorish clothing listed in such archival sources, nor can we establish how much Moorish clothing depreciated on the second-hand market, since I have found no documentation comparing the prices of the same garment when it was bought new and then later sold on the second-hand market.

Another potential, if equally inconclusive sign of the relationship between the game of canes and the second-hand market, can be found in a contract between Pedro de Ávila and the jeweller Juan Bautista García drafted in 1633. The contract stipulates that Ávila could not lend nor buy "libreas de cañas," since that would be his partner's task.[29] As in the previous case, the wording is confusing, and it is not clear whether Pedro de Ávila had to refrain from buying clothing *for* these festivals or from purchasing it *from* these events. It is also possible that the document alludes to both forms of transactions, since any used livery purchased on the second-hand market could later be loaned to other festival organizers. Arguably, for lending clothing to be a profitable trade, brokers needed to diversify their activities and to be able to act as both buyers and sellers by purchasing liveries when they knew the participants would no longer use them and by making them when necessary and lending them out to theatre companies or municipal governments.

Also revealing about such transactions are the literary parodies of Moorish ballads analysed in the previous chapter. As we have seen, Gabriel Lasso de la Vega's *Manojuelo de romances nuevos* (1601) includes compositions addressing the circulation of Moorish clothing in a very explicit way. In "Yengo a buscar una botarga," the poetic voice goes to the clothing lender looking for a dress for Carnival.[30] Meanwhile, in "Quién compra dieciséis moros" [Who buys sixteen Moors?], the poetic voice intends to strip his purchased Moors and sell their Moorish clothing from the game of canes to the clothing lender.[31] By juxtaposing "Quién compra dieciséis moros" and "Yendo a buscar una botarga," we find the poetic voice situated on both sides of transactions in the Moorish clothing trade, both as a frustrated costume buyer and as a potential vendor who in both cases turns to the *alquilador de hatos*, who served as the intermediary for livery reuse by theatre companies and other public performances.

Thus Lasso de la Vega's ballads and other indirect evidence indicate that the transfer of Moorish clothing from games of canes to the stock of clothing lenders and company directors must have been common by the end of the sixteenth century, providing costumes-in-hand to inspire the creation of characters. The widespread availability of Moorish clothing may well have served as one of the material conditions for Lope's development of the *comedia nueva* and the emergence of theatre as a mass urban spectacle. This possibility would imply that, instead of merely reflecting a particular Iberian obsession with Islam, the ubiquity of Muslim characters on stage could have been conditioned by the necessity to make use of the abundance of Moorish clothing derived from the game of canes. While I do not aim to deny the active participation of playwrights in public debates over the legacy of the Islamic period, by looking at material conditions we can also consider whether the prevalence of Moorish themes on stage might also have been conditioned by the particularities of the second-hand clothing market, as clothing lenders and company directors occupied a central role in redistributing the fund of Moorish liveries from the game of canes and made them available for reuse on stage. It would of course be too reductive to state that Lope was inspired to write so many plays with Muslim characters merely because of his continuous contact with the materiality of Moorish clothing, yet he must have been well informed of the ins and outs of clothing production and circulation in Iberian society, and he would be aware that this materiality had to be taken into account in order for drama to be a profitable enterprise.

When Miguel de Cervantes praised the theatre before Lope de Vega's success in the prologue to his *Ocho comedias y ocho entremeses* (1616), he claimed that "during that time there was no stage machinery or challenges between Moors and Christians."[32] Cervantes's remembrance was probably idealizing the simplicity of the pre-Lopean stage, since the transfer of clothing and props from Moorish spectacles to the stage seems to have been taking place at least since the 1560s. But his opinion reflects a general perception at the beginning of the seventeenth century that identified the use of gallant Moorish clothing on stage as one of the features of the *comedia nueva*. Such an opinion is not without foundation, since, as we have seen, among Lope de Vega's vast body of work there is a large number of plays that include Muslim characters and therefore require the use of Moorish clothing. There is also a wealth of Muslim characters in the work of other seventeenth-century playwrights, such as Luis Vélez de Guevara, Álvaro Cubillo de Aragón, and Tirso de Molina, to name only a few.[33]

Luis Vélez de Guevara's *Don Pedro Miago* (c. 1613) is a historical play set in the reign of Alfonso VI of Castile. It presents a group of Muslim ambassadors coming to Valladolid to escort Zaida, the daughter of the Muslim King of Seville, who will convert to Christianity and marry Alfonso VI. The story is thus the perfect excuse to stage gallant encounters between Christians and Moors and to fantasize about a shared equestrian and sartorial culture. The cultural affinity between Muslims and Christians is clear when Pedro Miago offers the Moor Galván garments and horses for the game of canes as a present.[34] As the rustic characters discuss the game of canes that will take place to celebrate the wedding, the common sartorial culture becomes increasingly more evident:

> MINGO: Are Moors and Christians playing with the same clothing?
> BERRUECO: I suspect they are, Mingo, and that Moors and Christians are
> riding in pairs.[35]

While the game of canes announced by Mingo and Berrueco could not be staged, in the final scene the entire troupe appears dressed for the game of canes.[36] The play does not clarify whether the "same clothing" that Muslims and Christians will both wear for the game of canes is the same kind of clothing that Muslim characters are already wearing (and therefore, Christians will assimilate to the clothing of their visitors) or whether it would be a different kind of clothing (and therefore both Muslim and Christian characters will change their clothing for the equestrian performance). Nor should we assume that all Moorish clothing is the same. At least one particular feature differentiates the Moorish garb used in the game of canes. While the right arm was visible and threw the reed, the left arm was not visible because it embraced the *adarga* (shield). Thus the left *manga* (sleeve) was left plain, while the right *manga* was richly embroidered. The cost of staging a scene with an entire troupe of actors dressed as Moors with lavish *mangas* would depend entirely on the source of the costumes. New ones would require a significant investment and reduce net profits for the theatre company, and the play would need to be a success and to be staged several times to recoup the cost.[37] Or, as this chapter has suggested, costumes sourced from available second-hand Moorish livery were bought up by costume lenders after games of canes and rented out – or even bought by the theatre company for its own use and to increase the net profits by reducing production costs.

Another play in which the game of canes takes an essential role is *La manga de Sarracino*, by Álvaro Cubillo de Aragón (1597–1661).[38] Adolf Schaeffer suggests that Cubillo de Aragón wrote this play at the beginning of his literary career in the 1620s or 1630s, as it reflects the influence of Lope de Vega.[39] While it presents itself as a historical play, the plot actually derives from the Moorish ballad "En el cuarto de Comares" [In the Comares Room], in which the Moorish princess Galiana makes her beloved Sarracino a sleeve for a game of canes: "At the Comares palace [i.e. the Alhambra], the beautiful Galiana, with knowledge and skill, makes a rich sleeve for the strong Sarracino, who plays canes for her."[40] Cubillo de Aragón's *La manga de Sarracino*, like the ballad, is centred around the act of making this Moorish garment, repeatedly referring to how Galiana embroiders the gallant sleeve for Sarracino.[41] Cubillo de Aragón also introduces Christian characters into the plot that he weaves around the original story of Galiana and Sarracino, as the noble Diego Girón and his squire Mendoza are taken captive in the medieval Muslim Kingdom of Toledo. When the Moors, Muslim King Abenámar and noble Sarracino, recognize Diego Girón's nobility, they invite him to participate in a game of canes. Act 3 begins with "sounds of games of canes," to indicate the celebration of the proposed performance off stage. Immediately after that, Abenámar and Sarracino appear on stage chasing Diego Girón and Mendoza, all of them wearing the garb for the game of canes. The equestrian spectacle that was allegedly the common denominator between noble Muslims and Christians turns into the trigger of violence, because the Muslim characters cannot accept that Christians have demonstrated a superior dexterity in the game.[42]

A later play that attests to the intricacy of theatre and courtly Moorishness is *La luna africana*, which was composed in collaboration among nine different playwrights for a festival in Philip IV's court around 1643.[43] Act 1 features a long description of the opulent festivals in the Nasrid court largely borrowed from Ginés Pérez de Hita's *Guerras civiles de Granada* but which also seems to echo an actual Moorish festival that had been held at the Castilian court by the time of its composition.[44] If the play does echo a real festival *a la morisca*, the inclusion of both Christian and Muslim characters dressed as Moors in act 3 may well indicate reuse of the Moorish garb used in the actual festivals.[45]

These are only a few examples of the many early modern plays in which the use of Moorish clothing may indicate a connection between the stage and the circulation of liveries. Theatre not only represents the productions and circulation of clothing in early modern Iberian society, but quite probably contributed to that circulation through the recycling of liveries in their search for profit. Yet theatre professionals as individuals were not alien to the cultural relevance of Moorish clothing. On the one hand, actors were social bodies who could use the stage as a space of exception to circumvent the constraints of sumptuary legislation by wearing Moorish clothing.[46] On the other hand, literary texts more broadly explicitly refer to and critique how Moorish clothing served as a sign of social mobility, a process in which authors and actors themselves might be involved.

Moorish Disguise and Social Ambitions

The game of canes was not merely a source of inspiration, either material or ideological, for early modern literature. Playwrights and poets were not indifferent to how the circulation and consumption of Moorish clothing produced social meaning and prompted social desires and fantasies. If we analyse the evolution in the uses of Moorishness in Lope's oeuvre we can see that he established an emotional attachment to it early on that evolved throughout his life. Indeed, there is a striking divide between his earlier and later works that parallels the ups and downs of his social ambitions.

The beginning of Lope's literary career is marked by the composition of a series of Moorish ballads between 1581 and 1588. Some of these Moorish ballads were indeed very successful, such as "Mira Zaide que te aviso" [Look, Zaide, that I warn you] or "Sale la estrella de Venus" [Venus's star rises], both of which circulated widely both orally and in print.[47] Literary scholars have traditionally favoured a biographical interpretation of these ballads, in particular those included in the cycle of Gazul, which has been identified as one of the alter egos Lope used to convey his sentimental misfortunes. Even though there is a high degree of speculation in the way these ballads have been identified, interpreted, and grouped according to a peculiarly romanticized version of Lope's biography, it is undeniable that they are the first manifestations of Lope's attempt to construct a public persona for himself.[48]

María Goyri de Menéndez Pidal notes that the unifying feature of the Gazul ballads is the focus on the preparation and participation in a game of canes.[49] In "Límpiame la jacerina" [Clean my doublet], the jealous Gazul prepares to leave for Jerez to kill his beloved's fiancé.

The bulk of the ballad does not focus on the sentiment, but on how Gazul gives instructions to his squire about how to prepare his gallant Moorish clothing.[50] In "En el tiempo que Celinda" [Meanwhile Celinda], Celinda makes Gazul new Moorish clothing for the game of canes in Gelves, and again the focus falls on the description of the garments.[51] "De los trofeos de amor" [On Love's trophies], a continuation of the previous ballad, depicts Gazul lavishly dressed for the game of canes in Gelves. In this case the identification with Lope is clear in the insignia on Gazul's *adarga*: "he brings his own *adarga,* in which there is a phoenix burning in lively flames and turning to ashes."[52] The ballad "Por la plaza de Sanlúcar" [In Sanlúcar's square] also portrays Gazul's garments for the game of canes: "Through the square of Sanlúcar comes the brave Gazul, dressed in white, purple, and green. The Moor wants to leave to play a game of canes at Gelves, since the commander of the fortress is hosting a festival to celebrate the truce between the Kings."[53] Independent of whether the characters' love stories in these ballads actually refer to their author's personal life or not, it is clear that Lope projects himself as a gallant Moor into a poetic world in which the game of canes is the central motif around which he weaves different characters and situations.

Drawing on Stephen Greenblatt's concept of self-fashioning, several scholars have looked at how Lope tried to create a certain public image of himself in his works, and have pointed out that, although he made a living in the theatre, he presented himself as a cultivator of more prestigious genres such as epic poetry or pastoral novels.[54] The recognition of this polarization between economic profit represented by theatre and social prestige represented by high literary genres has placed the earlier Moorish ballads in a kind of limbo in the study of Lope's literary production and, as a result, they have been conceived of as a mere divertissement or a pseudo-biographical vehicle. Yet these poetic compositions can also be analysed by considering Greenblatt's invitation to look at "larger networks of meaning in which both the author and his work participate."[55] The fact that in his earlier years Lope repeatedly projects himself in the public literary arena as a fictitious character worthy of participating in this equestrian exercise is not an inconsequential fantasy, but may have contributed to creating a social reputation in the early stages of his career, given the social prestige associated with the impersonation of Moors in the game of canes. This literary mask turns into a sham when we take into account that Lope, the son of an embroiderer, was probably never invited to a game of canes. Seen in this light,

Lope's impersonation of literary Moors was not merely a poetic venue to convey his lack of sentimental fulfilment or a fanciful recreation of the frontier past, but a compensatory fantasy that was moulded upon the parameters of social advancement in his own time.

There is indeed evidence that Lope's contemporaries perceived the pretentiousness underlying his projection of his own public persona into the Moorish ballads. Although Lope was not the only author of these kinds of compositions, he was widely acknowledged as one of their main cultivators, and thus the anti-Moorish ballads often targeted him.[56] Looking solely at the Islamophobic language used in such attacks, Francisco Márquez Villanueva suggests that anti-Moorish ballads accused Lope of being a Morisco.[57] Yet there is no evidence that Lope's "blood purity" was questioned outside the farcical poetic arena, in which almost anything could be said without affecting the legal standing of poets.[58] What motivates Lope's enemies to compare him with a Morisco while criticizing his Moorish ballads is that cultivating Moorish themes and equating himself with gallant Moors was a pretence to project a noble status that was perceived as no less fictitious and obnoxious than his literary masks.

While Lope articulated his Moorish ballads around sartorial aspects of Moorishness, the satires against him focused on the incongruity between the humble socio-economic status they allege for their maurophiliac author and the decadence of Moorish clothing. Lasso de la Vega's "Yendo a comprar una botarga," concludes by chastising not the fictional Moors, but the poets themselves and their abuse of fictional Moorish clothing, which was outlandishly expensive in real life: "since dressing with a *feather/quill* costs them little or nothing, with their words and quill they toss seams that are gone with the wind."[59] The anonymous "Toquen aprisa a rebato" [Quick, sound the alarm], which also targets Lope, is even more explicit when attacking the economic means of Moorish-ballad poets, since it challenges the poet to produce in the real world even a cheap beret: "He who made costly liveries for Adalifes and Azarques should try to produce a beret for himself, and he will see how much it costs him."[60] Within the same line of thought, the ballad "Triste pisa y afligido" [Sad and sorrowful he walks] says that Zulema "does not wear on his *marlota* embroidered ciphers, nor letters on the field of his *adarga* ... because he is a foolish Moor and did not have one of those poets (who nowadays are also tailors) whose quills are scissors."[61] The analogy between the act of composing poetry and making clothing might hint at Lope's friend Agustín Castellanos, known as "el poeta sastre," but also to Lope himself, whose entire family were embroiderers. This is probably the trade his enemies thought he was meant to take up. One of the harshest anti-Moorish ballads, "Ah mis señores poetas" [Oh sir poets], similarly focuses on clothing when it orders the literary Moors to return the Moorish clothing to the person from whom they borrowed it: "I have had enough about Gazul and Celindaja, who should return those *marlotas* from whomever they borrowed them."[62] In this case, the focus on borrowing the gallant clothing reveals that the literary Moor as well as the person behind the poet/patron mask lacked the necessary funds to purchase his own Moorish clothing.

These series of satires were not without response. "Por qué, señores poetas" (c. 1592) [Why, sir poets?], attributed to Lope, defends the idea that the Moors from the past were "españoles," and that satires somehow missed their target, since celebrating their deeds constituted a fetishistic reminder of the victory of Christians over Muslims.[63] Most relevant here is that the author responds in kind to the accusations of sartorial posturing: "If this sad slanderer is in need of clothing, you could freely give him your *marlotas* so he shuts up, and thus this miserable beggar will understand that they [the *marlotas*] are blazons of Spain, won with fire and blood, and not borrowed, as he says."[64] The explicit addressees are those poets who remain silent instead of defending Moorish ballads, and the poetic voice turns to this audience to collect clothing for the grumbling poet of "Ah señores poetas." Thus, "Por qué, señores poetas" responds by pointing out that the composers of satirical Moorish ballads were not aristocrats either and that the coveted Moorish clothing was also absent from their wardrobes – which implies that even they would like to own such livery, along with the social prestige that was associated with it. Yet "Por qué, señores poetas" somehow misses the point of the accusation of borrowing clothing in "Ah mis señores poetas," which literally accuses the poets of dressing their Moors with someone else's wardrobe. Thus "Por qué, señores poetas," deflects the individual accusation about the poverty of poets by turning it into a larger debate of collective cultural identity, obscuring the material aspects of possessing such attire.

The poetic exchange seems to have ceased abruptly in the late 1590s, and, in fact, Lope stopped composing Moorish ballads at that point. They were still successful, and were still widely reprinted, recited, and glossed. Yet it seems that Lope himself realized that he had rushed into presenting himself as a gallant Moorish knight before having cemented his social position – and before having ever been invited to participate in an actual game of canes. Indeed, it is possible that this precipitous public exposure in the literary arena actually inhibited Lope's chances of ever being invited to a game of canes, given that he had been branded publicly as the epitome of those individuals who were unlawfully seeking Moorishness even as they were unsuited to litigate for nobility.

Resented Moorishness

While the biographical element is less evident in Lope's theatre, there is indeed a certain continuity between the earlier composition of Moorish ballads and his plays with Moorish themes, which most frequently expanded anecdotes from the ballads, such as *Los hechos de Garcilaso de la Vega y el moro Tarfe* (c. 1577–83), *El hijo de Reduán* (c. 1588–95), *El remedio en la desdicha* (c. 1596–1602), *El cerco de Santa Fe* (c. 1598), *Los palacios de Galiana* (1599), *El hidalgo Bencerraje* (c. 1605–6), *El primer Fajardo* (c. 1610–12), and *El bastardo Mudarra* (1612).[65] The exalted connection between Moorishness and nobility is still evident in *El hijo de Reduán* (c. 1588–95), in which one of the characters states that "for a Christian noble to be gallant, it is obvious that he must have something Moorish."[66] Although this declaration occurs in a historical play about the Nasrid Kingdom of Granada, it would be evident to early modern Iberian audiences that it was hinting at how Moorishness was constitutive of aristocratic status in Old Christian society.

The chronology of the plays dealing with Muslim characters suggests that Lope stopped including Muslim characters (and therefore, Moorish clothing, we might safely assume) after the mid-1610s.[67] David Castillejo reads this sudden interruption in the composition of plays including Muslim characters as a consequence of the expulsion of the Moriscos in 1609.[68] This is a plausible interpretation only without the evidence brought forward in the present analysis, which has clearly shown that there was no ideological incentive to abandon Moorish themes after the expulsion of the Moriscos. Indeed, the voices linking actual Moriscos with the gallant Moors were rather a minority, as we shall see in chapter 8.[69]

Thus an alternative explanation is required for Lope's abandonment of Moorish themes. It is evident that he showed an increasing disaffection for Moorishness, first in abandoning Moorish ballads and then in ceasing to write plays with Muslim characters. This increasing disaffection towards Moorishness seems related to the changes in his self-fashioning and his frustrated social ambitions. Lope never completely renounced the patronage of the nobility nor his self-fashioning as noble, and consequently kept a certain detachment from his true economic activity as playwright, as it was not considered a proper lucrative activity within an aristocratic way of life. Yet by 1609 Lope had started to refer to his dramatic production as a source of social prestige, precisely when he began referring to the game of canes in an increasingly derogatory and cutting manner.[70]

As stated previously, there is no indication that Lope was ever invited to participate in a game of canes. However, he was present at many aristocratic festivals that included exuberant games of canes. He even wrote poetic descriptions of many of those festivals, such as *Fiestas de Denia* (1599), which describes Philip III's wedding in Valencia, and *La descripción de la tapada*, dealing with the festivals in Vila Viçosa for the wedding of Teodósio II in 1603. In 1605, the city of Toledo commissioned Lope to produce the festival book for the celebrations held in honour of Philip IV's birth.[71] He also inserted descriptions of royal festivals in several of his plays, such as *La burgalesa de Lerma* (1613), *Lo que pasa en una tarde* (1617), and *No son todos ruiseñores* (1635).[72] In addition to these festivals, Lope's presence is also attested to in the festivals held in Burgos in 1615 to celebrate the intermarriage of the Spanish and French princes.[73]

In spite of his attendance at many courtly spectacles throughout the Iberian Peninsula, it does not seem that Lope received any substantial benefit from celebrating these festivals with his pen. Scholars have noted that the court never responded to his claims to be designated as royal chronicler or to be recognized as "poeta laureado."[74] It is also well known that Lope sought to be recognized as noble, a project in which he was equally unsuccessful and which probably relates directly to his attempts to approach the court.[75] After all, being invited to one of the many games of canes at which he was present would have been an excellent proof if he had wanted to litigate for nobility. However, in all these courtly spectacles, Lope seems to have remained part of the audience, even if a relatively privileged and very solicited witness.

Even worse, Lope's only documented participation in a courtly equestrian performance would have actually disqualified him in any litigation for nobility. In 1599, during the wedding of Philip III in Valencia, the Marquis of Sarria (later Count of Lemos) organized a *quadrille* of masked riders dressed as Turks. Lope was not among them, but appeared instead as a carnivalesque figure preceding the parade on a mule (and not a horse) and wearing a ridiculous costume made of dead animals, such as rabbits, partridges, and hens. Dressed in this attire, he recited some verses for the monarch.[76] Thus Lope's only recorded participation in an equestrian performance figures him as a jester, not as a gallant rider – and certainly not as the lavish Gazul into whom he had earlier projected himself in his Moorish ballads.[77] As it turns out, no matter how much Iberian aristocrats admired Lope, they never considered him an equal who could ride along them dressed as a Moor in the game of canes.

Lope's resentment about his unfulfilled social and professional ambitions runs parallel to the gradual disappearance of Moorish clothing from his plays and his increasingly caustic representations of courtly spectacles and the game of canes. The first evidence of this can be found in the play *Los cautivos de Argel* (1599), which was probably composed soon after the wedding of Philip III in Valencia, to which it makes a strikingly oblique reference.[78] The stage directions of the first scene present Francisco as "a Morisco from the Kingdom of Valencia, in their customary attire."[79] Through his participation in piratical acts against the coast of Valencia, Francisco is promoted to leadership among North African Muslims and marches with honours in a parade in Algiers. The stage directions at the end of the first act emphasize how Francisco changes his appearance as a result of his successful career as a pirate: "As many Moors as possible should appear marching, and behind them, if at all possible on horse, on foot otherwise; that Morisco Francisco, as a very gallant Moor."[80]

Los cautivos de Argel makes a distinction between the clothing of local Moriscos of Valencia and North African Muslims, likely a theatrical convention that should not be taken as ethnographically accurate – as we shall see in chapter 6, historical sources do not allude to distinct attire for the male Moriscos of Valencia. The insistence here on the presence of the horse on stage clearly suggests that the clothing of "gallant Moor" should be reinforced with all the signs of nobility as they were found in the iconography of the game of canes. Therefore, what the early modern audience would have "seen" on stage is the social ascension of Francisco, coded in the transition from local Morisco peasant to gallant Moor on horse, the sign of nobility par excellence. Thus, while the content of the play condemns Francisco for his religious apostasy and for his acts of piracy (for which he is finally executed), his passing is visually presented as the social climbing that the Morisco could not make while in the Iberian Peninsula. As I will examine in the second part of this book, part of the repression of the Morisco community was that, unlike their Old Christian peers, they were not allowed to exhibit elite status by dressing as gallant Moors, a sign of nobility.

Obviously, Lope would not identify with a treacherous Morisco pirate. Yet he shared with his character Francisco the same boundaries of social climbing, which were marked by limited access to Moorish clothing. The fictional Francisco had to be exiled to North Africa and to openly embrace Islam in order to be able to adopt Moorish clothing as a sign of social promotion, while Lope had to exile himself to the fictional space of ballads to fashion himself as the gallant Moorish rider he could not become in his lived social reality. We can indeed relate *Los cautivos de Argel* to Lope's frustrating experience as a jester in Philip III's wedding in Valencia, to which the play explicitly refers. At the end of act 3, one Christian captive in Algiers comments on the news coming from the other shore of the Mediterranean about the festivals organized by the Duque of Lerma in Denia:

> Oh, King of Algiers, the Marquis [of Lerma] has made him [Philip III] such great festivals that they were seen from here; and it is no wonder that they have crossed the sea, since the fireworks were shown in the crystals of the sea, which serves as a mirror that shows our own image.[81]

The mirroring sea separating Denia from Algiers can be seen as emphasis on the sartorial analogy between the North African Muslims and Turks on the one hand and, on the other, the Iberian aristocrats dressing as Moors to play the game of canes.[82] The specular nature of the play further reinforces the analogy between Francisco and Lope, but does not leave Lope in a very favourable position. While Lope could only participate in the aristocratic exercises in Valencia as a jester for the monarch's amusement, on the other shore of the Mediterranean the fictional Morisco Francisco achieved the right to ride a horse dressed as a gallant Moor (even if he is ultimately to be executed within the plot), a privilege that Lope could never enjoy in early modern Iberia.

When other poets mocked his pretensions to be perceived as a gallant Moorish rider, Lope began to develop a caustic attitude towards the game of canes. In *La burgalesa de Lerma*, one of the characters describes the festivals that took place in Lerma in 1613 and notes that the usual Moorish clothing was replaced by a more "Christian" livery: "Note that the liveries were not Moorish invention, but Christian and modern, and the *marlotas* and *capellares* were now cloaks and *vaqueros*."[83] Taken at face value, this comment would confirm a desire for cultural purification and "Christianization" of this equestrian spectacle. Yet there is also evidence that the Christianization of the game of canes occurs only in the a posteriori poetic recreation. Before writing *La burgalesa de Lerma*, Lope described the same game of canes in a letter to the Duke of Sessa, in which he merely commented that "The game of canes is done with *vaqueros* and capes without gold; they say that with the garments for hunting, with silver harnesses over colourful leather; the novelty pleases me; I do not understand about the rest of it."[84] In spite of the character's commentary in *La burgalesa de Lerma*, neither the Duke of Lerma nor Philip III renounced the courtly uses of Moorishness after they decreed the expulsion of the Moriscos. Another element that complicates the interpretation of this passage in *La burgalesa de Lerma* is that the *sayo vaquero* is conceived to be the "Christian" opposite of the *marlota*, when in fact the *sayo vaquero* was a garment of Turkish or eastern European origin, which was clearly perceived as Moorish, at least during the sixteenth century – even as its exoticness was partially lost as it was more and more integrated in quotidian fashions.[85]

A similarly complex conceptualization of Moorish clothing is found in one of Lope's latest Moorish plays. *La envidia de la nobleza*, set in the Nasrid Kingdom of Granada and dealing with the story of the Abencerrajes. Morley and Bruerton date this play between 1613 and 1618 based on the versification.[86] In principle, the plot makes this play similar to the Moorish plays with which Lope began his dramatic career in the 1590s. However, in line with *La burgalesa de Lerma*, *La envidia de la nobleza* provides an indirect critique of the Iberian Moorish clothing of the game of canes. At some point, the Moor Hamete accuses his enemies the Abencerrajes of being effeminate because of the eccentricity of their attire: "Their *golillas*, their dresses, their curly hair; their white hands, which are full of make up and, in order not to see them harmed, they barely touch the swords's pommels."[87] This consciously anachronistic description of the fifteenth-century Moors from the Kingdom of Granada clearly alludes to the concept of the *lindo*, the caricature of the effeminate courtier in Lope's own time.[88]

The anachronism is even more pointed if we take into account that Lope himself explicitly criticized the improper use of clothing on stage (and specifically the use of collars for Muslim characters). In his *Arte nuevo de hacer comedias* (1609), one of the inaccuracies seen on stage that Lope denounced was precisely "staging a Turk with a Christian collar."[89] This commentary, which is usually read as a denunciation of the sartorial practices in theatrical craft, might actually be hinting at the Moorish clothing for the game of canes. Visual evidence indicates that the combination of Moorish clothing with the use of ruff collars that were in fashion among elites was not an eccentricity of playwrights, but a common sartorial practice of aristocrats to mark their class status. Thus they created a sartorial pastiche evident in both Abraham van Bruyn's engraving depicting a rider of the game of canes, made around 1578 (Figure 11), and Juan de la Corte's painting of the 1623 game of canes in Madrid's Plaza Mayor (Figure 7). Hamete's comment in *La envidia de la nobleza* also echoes the anonymous ballad "Ese moro ganapán" (c. 1595), which denounced Moorish attire used in the game of canes as an artificial pastiche.[90] If Turks on stage were an anachronistic sartorial pastiche, as Lope claims in his *Arte nuevo*, it is not (or not merely) because theatre directors did not care about sartorial realism, but because actors were imitating the Moorish clothing that courtiers used in the game of canes – if they were not in fact reusing the very same Moorish garments previously worn by courtiers and nobles of lesser rank. The difference between the ballad "Ese moro ganapán" and *La envidia de la nobleza* is that Lope, instead of reverting to maurophobic discourse to criticize Iberian Moorish clothing in fashion in the 1610s, resorts to the anachronistic voice of a medieval Muslim character in order to convey an identical anti-aristocratic message.

Lope's resentment towards aristocratic equestrian performances is more clearly expressed in *Amor secreto hasta celos* (1614). In this historical play set in the medieval period, the servant Fabio (whose name is one of Lope's well-known literary aliases), passes as his master Don Juan while in the court of Sancho of Castile. When offered the opportunity to participate in a game of canes, he rejects the invitation and argues that "this is something for Moors, already very old-fashioned and boring. In the time of the Moor Muza … it was something pleasant, but now it is rather bothersome, with either the turban or the hood."[91] Fabio's commentary that the game of canes is old-fashioned is striking regardless of the temporal perspective we adopt to read this passage. On the one hand, as we have seen throughout these pages, the game of canes was anything but old-fashioned in Lope's own time. On the other hand, the audience would find it an even more inaccurate description of the vague medieval time in which the play is set, since ballads, plays, and Moorish fictions made them imagine an Iberian past in which the game of canes was the common diplomatic encounter between Christians and Muslims. Lope's audience would have interpreted it as a comical outburst, a mere pretext from Fabio because his non-aristocratic identity would be exposed by his lack of equestrian training. Yet if we read this passage within Lope's biography, his theatrical alter ego's rejection of one of the most desirable ways to enhance one's social reputation in early modern Castile seems to be a fictive compensation for not having been invited to participate in them.

Another depiction of a real game of canes is found in *Lo que pasa en una tarde*, which describes the festivals organized by the Duke of Lerma for Philip III in 1617. The *gracioso* Tomé recounts how some brave *hidalgo* named Colindres excelled in the game of canes and the bullfight. Tomé concludes his description by adding that Colindres will not have any trouble with debtors because of his participation in the festival, since his clothing was provided to him as livery:

> I can only assure you that this ostentation and spending has not been at his expense, but at his masters's. Don't be afraid that the bailiff will ever take the ten percent of seizing his possessions because of so many fabrics and satins, and no tailor will complain for the making of so many garments.[92]

This passage alludes to those individuals who participated in the game of canes pretending to show a socio-economic position that was beyond their limits and as a result incurred excessive debt.[93] But Lope takes the opportunity to criticize as well the arbitrariness of the social policing implicit in the selection of participants, which chose individuals like this fictional lackey while discarding others like Lope.

In Lope's novella *La desdicha por la honra* (1624), the main character Felisardo is a good Christian Spaniard who suddenly finds out while in Sicily that his own parents are Moriscos and meets them in Constantinople after they are expelled by Philip III. The reluctant assumption of his new identity in the Ottoman Empire is accompanied by a sartorial transformation construed in the fiction as a return to his alleged cultural and genealogical roots: "He was wearing his gallant clothing and turban, and since he was dark-skinned and tall and had a big mustache, the clothing suited him as if he were born to it."[94] While in Constantinople, some Christian captives organize the staging of a play (actually one by Lope), and Felisardo briefly dresses as a Christian in order to play one of the roles. The narrator falls into a telling contradiction when he says that the Christian clothing is Felisardo's "true" dress and the trigger of his memory: "Felisardo played his role outstandingly, and seeing himself in his true dress he cried true tears, moved by just memories and regretful for unjust offenses."[95] Performing the identity of a Christian causes him to convert back to Christianity and renounce Islam, leading to his martyrdom.

The immediately obvious eschatological opposition between Christianity and Islam obscures the underlying social opposition embedded in Moorishness that is a constant in Lope's oeuvre. In addition to the inclusion of one of Lope's plays, the novella contains other references to its author. The name of the character Felisardo is a combination of Lope's middle name (Félix) and his well-known poetic alter ego Belisardo. Thus, by the 1620s, Lope projects himself once again, as he did in *Los cautivos de Argel* and *La villana de Getafe*, into the fictional figure of a Morisco. But this time, Felisardo's salvation (and martyrdom) comes first through theatre, and only later through conversion to Christianity. This movement from conversion to Islam signalled by the adoption of Turkish garb, and conversion to Christianity through theatrical performance, parallels Lope's shift between the futile (at least for him) adoption of Moorishness as a means to attain nobility and the embrace of theatre as a profitable career trajectory.

This opposition between courtly Moorishness and literary career is further evinced in a letter to the Duke of Sessa of 1628, in which Lope comments on a game of canes held at court. Apparently, some people in the audience considered it of poor quality, but Lope refuses to give his own opinion, arguing that "I do not know about pirouettes, but about sonnets."[96] This is a disdainful denial rather than a confession of ignorance. Lope knew a lot about games of canes, which he described many times in his panegyric works and in the ballads in which he depicted himself as a gallant rider. He claims not to know in the final stage of his career because by then he has been completely convinced that aristocratic Moorishness was a dead end for his social ambitions, and has focused instead on his poetic ability as a source of social prestige.

All these instances should not be read necessarily as a rejection of Moorishness as a whole – even as Lope stopped writing Moorish plays in the 1620s, he continued to edit old ones for publication in the *Partes*. The contemptuous and ambiguous references to the game of canes and Moorish clothing in Lope's last period may reflect not only the frustration of his social ambitions, but the general situation of his entire social class and the competition among the numerous individuals pressing to enter the nobility. There are many other writers who, like Lope, remained spectators of equestrian performances in which they were not included. Their inclusion in networks of patronage explains why they praised these games of canes and the aristocratic figures that participated in them, but this inclusion is limited, since they were never invited to participate in the spectacle they were asked to praise. If we go beyond the obvious maurophobic rhetoric of satirical scorn of the game of canes and literary Moorishness, both in ballads and theatre, we can observe that they exude a surreptitious resentment and feeling of exclusion not immediately related to religious confrontation with Islam. The position of poets as privileged witnesses who were at the same time excluded from participation, made them well aware of how Moorish clothing in the game of canes was central to a certain distribution of wealth and honour in which the higher nobility (as well as local elites in the process of ennobling themselves) used local and royal economic resources to cement their own social ties, to the disadvantage of the social stratum to which many of these writers usually belonged.[97] Thus, rather than deploying an essentially religious critique, they might well be capitalizing on maurophobic discourses to criticize an aristocratic practice of Moorishness, which was perceived as one of the barriers to their own social promotion.[98]

Since Moorish clothing encodes issues of class difference, aristocratic identity, and the distribution of wealth, the specific case of Lope de Vega reveals that literary and performative uses of maurophilia or maurophobia also served to articulate the social relations between performers and audiences, between patrons and writers, and between sponsors and riders in the game of canes. Thus it further confirms that Moorish clothing was primarily an issue of class distinction within early modern Iberian society – and that maurophobic discourses were intentional instrumentalizations of issues of cultural legacy. Yet it is also clear that there has to be some kind of connection between the currency of Moorish clothing in early modern society, the debates on the cultural legacy from the Islamic period, and the presence of a large population of Muslim descent. In analysing this sartorial currency, I have intentionally left aside an exploration of these connections, mainly because I am here working under the assumption that the primary value of Moorish clothing as a marker of social class in early modern Iberian society conditioned how Moriscos were imagined and how their bodies were policed in sartorial legislations aimed against them, to which we turn in the second part of this book.

PART TWO

Moorishness in the Eye of the Beholder: Moriscos as Dressed Bodies

En contraste con el traje cristiano, sometido a una moda cambiante y en continua transformación de la Baja Edad Media, el de los musulmanes se caracteriza por su estabilidad. Podían pasar siglos sin que cambiasen la forma de sus vestidos.

[in contrast to Christian dress, subject to always changing fashions and in continued transformation since the low Middle Ages, that of Muslims was characterized by its stability. Centuries could pass without the pattern of their attire ever changing.]

Carmen Bernis

European-focused history … imagines its 'Others' as 'uncontaminated,' without history … The Other is imagined as eternally itself …, subject to the mobile and restless observation of the European observer: the Other is changeless, outside of fashion.

Ann Rosalind Jones and Peter Stallybrass

5 Policing Moriscos in Sixteenth-Century Granada

While the first part of this book analyses how Moorish clothing was deeply embedded in the construction of class identity among Old Christians, it has yet to explore how the social distinction attributed to Moorish clothing affected the way Christians conceived of and regulated the sartorial practices of Moriscos, the descendants of Iberian Muslims. The issue is much more complex than has usually been held, since their alleged sartorial difference was not as evident as our historical imagination has tended to postulate. As in the case of Old Christians, legislation about Morisco clothing intersects with issues of class identity, gender policing, and cultural racialization in subtle and nuanced ways. Furthermore, and even when *morisco* and *moro* are used almost interchangeably to refer to both the Moorish clothing of the game of canes and the allegedly traditional clothing of some Morisco communities, they were not necessarily the same, in spite of the confusing overlap in the language used to define them.

Both nobles playing canes and Moriscos were very often construed as dressing as *moros*, yet *moro* did not mean the same in both cases: while in the case of the Moriscos dressing as *moro* meant wearing certain regional garments that identified them as Muslims in Christian eyes, in the case of the participants in the game of canes, *moro* implied a certain sartorial extravagance. Morisco clothing and Moorish clothing were never fully equated in the Christian Iberian imaginary, since participants in the game of canes were either described as dressing as *moros* or wearing clothing *a la morisca* – but they were never described as dressing as Moriscos. To complicate this further, Moriscos throughout the Iberian Peninsula never dressed homogeneously – in the same way that sartorial practices among Old Christians were not homogeneous.

In most cases, the sartorial practices of Moriscos and Old Christians living in the same local community were the same, yet Moriscos could always be perceived as dressing as "Moors."

In this chapter, I look at the sixteenth-century legal texts on the Moriscos of the Kingdom of Granada to analyse how they police but also construct Moriscos' alleged sartorial difference from the rest of Iberian society. Legal action against the sartorial practices of the Moriscos of Granada cannot be properly understood without at the same time considering the value of social distinction that Moorish clothing had in early modern Iberian society. In the second part of this chapter, I analyse what I call "the myth of the Morisco sartorial revival," the subsequent reinterpretation that takes place in early modern historiographical works that, in the aftermath of the uprising of the Alpujarras and well into the seventeenth century, pushed the construction of Morisco sartorial difference within the early modern historical imagination even further. Contrary to what the historiographical image of the Moriscos might suggest, the full equivalence of the Moriscos with the figure of the Moor as an exotically dressed body took place only after the expulsion of the Moriscos, precisely when Moorish clothing started to lose its social relevance around the middle of the seventeenth century.

While the decrees by Charles V in 1526 and Philip II in 1567 constitute the hallmarks of the process of cultural cleansing, there were in fact myriad royal, ecclesiastical, and local ordinances that targeted "Morisco clothing," from the beginning of the sixteenth century until the expulsion of the Moriscos in 1609.[1] Scholars have usually described these laws as repetitive, as if they were merely reinstating previous legal measures. In spite of their apparent redundancy, the introduction of variants reveals that there is a process of adaptive "strategic reformulation" that capitalizes on the authority of earlier legal texts while adapting them to specific and evolving historical and political contexts.[2] To be sure, the complex interrelation between a legal discourse capable of reformulating itself and an always changing historical reality still remains to be studied. The power of law to create rather than only reflect reality has been disregarded, leading to an essentialized interpretation of Morisco clothing that distorts its actual social dimensions.

Canonical scholarship on the Moriscos is predicated on their sartorial essentialization. For instance, Antonio Gallego y Burín and Alfonso Gámir Sandoval posit an immutable Morisco community when they state that, in spite of prohibitions, "the Moriscos kept using many garments of their clothing right up to the moment of their definitive expulsion in 1609."[3] Comments like this abound in the bibliography about Morisco sartorial practices. For Louis Cardaillac, "the Morisco … through his clothing, was connected with a glorious past as well as with his Maghribian brothers. It was for him one of the signs of identity to which he was very attached."[4] And for Carmen Bernis, "in contrast to Christian dress, subject to always changing fashions and in continued transformation since the late Middle Ages, that of Muslims was characterized by its stability. Centuries could pass without the pattern of their attire ever changing."[5] Thus, for these scholars, the dress of Moriscos is equated to an equally immutable image of the Muslim and establishes a perfect, uninterrupted continuity both in time and space.

These comments exemplify what Jones and Stallybrass identify as one tendency of the European-focused history of colonialism which "imagines its 'Others' as 'uncontaminated,' without history … The Other is imagined as eternally itself …, subject to the mobile and restless observation of the European observer: the Other is changeless, outside of fashion."[6] This selective colonial gaze is prevalent in scholarship about Moriscos which denies them the possibility of similar processes of cultural absorption and change.[7] This chapter argues on the contrary, that, when we analyse in detail what is prohibited and when, we can see that the more similar the Moriscos were to Old Christians, the more legislation regulating sartorial practices stereotyped them as an essentially distinct community. In an effort to counteract crystallized linguistic expressions, I will avoid addressing the question as the Moriscos assimilating to Castilian culture; if such a thing as "Castilian culture" ever existed outside of the collective imaginary, the Moriscos were already part of it. Even though sartorial legislation invariably refers to "Morisco clothing" as a self-evident category, the notion is both ideologically fraught and imprecise, and will be complicated in these pages, since these legal texts did not refer to observable realities, but to perceptions of cultural identity that were influenced by gender, social, and genealogical factors.

Policing Morisco Bodies, 1498–1565

The legislation on Morisco sartorial practices began in 1499, very soon after the fall of Granada (1492), when the Catholic monarchs issued a general decree trying to prevent commoners from wearing silk, reinstating previous prohibitions in the Kingdom of Castile. The particularity in this case is that they introduced an exemption for the Muslims of Granada: "Since the Moors in this Kingdom of Granada cannot ride horses ... we allow that ... they could wear clothing made of silk as they were accustomed to do."[8] The exemption of the Muslims of Granada is presented as a compensation for a previous prohibition of using horses – this prohibition would of course have had a military justification, but as the document acknowledges, the ban on equestrian practices had social implications as well, since riding a horse was a sign of social status.[9] These kinds of concessions based on cultural grounds were not as exceptional as they might seem – for instance, the inhabitants of Asturias, Guipuzkoa, and Biscay were also permitted to wear certain adornments and silk in 1501.[10] Strikingly, this first legal text addressing the sartorial practices of the Moriscos is usually ignored in scholarship, quite probably because it does not fit into the teleological narrative of increasing cultural repression through which we tend to interpret these documents.[11] Yet it reveals that the issue of "Morisco clothing" was closely intertwined with the larger frame of sumptuary regulation and that the importance of silk as a sign of class status may be more relevant than traditionally thought for understanding how "Morisco clothing" was articulated in legal language.

The first proclamations against the use of "Morisco clothing" appeared soon after this concession of permission for the Muslim inhabitants of Granada to wear silk. In 1498, Hernando de Talavera, archbishop of Granada, had instructed Old Christian settlers not to engage in Morisco customs, among them dressing as "Moors."[12] By 1500, Hernando de Talavera issued another letter to the Moriscos of the Albaicín in Granada recommending that they adopt "Christian" clothing:

> so that your relations with Old Christians be without scandal and so that they do not believe that you are still attached to the sect of Mohammad in your heart, it is necessary that you adapt in everything and by every means to the good and honest behavior of good and honest Christians in dress, footwear, and adornment.[13]

It is important to note that Talavera is not merely asking Moriscos to dress like any other Christians, but to dress like "good and honest Christians." This is not a rhetorical nuance. Talavera was also the author of a moralizing treatise entitled *De la demasía en el vestir y comer* (written in 1477 and published in Granada in 1496). His moralist thought was in line with the sumptuary laws of his own time, as he denounced the excesses in clothing by commoners because they not only manifested a sinful attitude but also threatened to blur social distinctions.[14] Thus, in his 1500 letter to the Moriscos, written precisely after they had successfully convinced the monarchs that they should not be prohibited from wearing silk, Talavera uses his religious authority over the Moriscos to ask them to conform as a group to the same standards of sartorial modesty that he had been preaching to Christians in his moralist treatise – quite probably to no avail. That is, Talavera was not merely requesting that the Moriscos dress as Christians, but to dress as Christian commoners who knew their place in society and did not try to trespass class boundaries through the adoption of luxurious clothing, entreating the Moriscos to willingly accept what was for many of them a downward social and cultural assimilation by following his model of sartorial modesty.

Hernando de Talavera's recommendation does not seem to have had legal force, but it may have paved the way for subsequent decrees. Indeed, we must infer that there are some gaps in the extant documentation from this period. In a 1500 letter by Fernando of Aragon and Isabel of Castile, the Moriscos of Tabernas were conceded several rights, among them "that until they have worn out the garments that they now have, they should not be forced to wear different ones."[15] A similar letter was issued to the *mudéjares* in Murcia, stating that all new clothing should be "like that of other Christians in our kingdoms, so there is no difference from that of Old Christians," implicitly permitting the use of any garment that was already made until it was replaced with a new one.[16] These concessions suggest that some law may have been passed before 1500 prohibiting Morisco clothing, although we only have the indirect information in this document. An alternative interpretation is that when these documents referred to "Morisco clothing" they actually meant clothing *a la morisca*, and that therefore these local cases simply capitalized on the 1499 permission to wear silk.

In 1511, a royal decree by Juana I of Castile reiterated that the Moriscos "should not make Morisco garments, nor wear any except those that had already been made."[17] The new decree, whose existence suggests that the previous law was not obeyed, provoked a very significant response: the next year, the representative of the tailors of Granada petitioned the municipal township for clarification, asking what kinds of clothing they should be making instead, so they could abide by the royal decree.[18] The town council replied by giving more specific instructions:

> that the aforementioned tailors can make hoods for slashed tunics and four spans long for men, and doublets in the Castilian style and hose for

men, and *ropones*, which they call *cotas*, and every kind of men's clothing, except *marlotas*; and that they do not cut or make any clothing in the Morisco style [a la morisca] for women.[19]

The petition is in itself telling, indicating how, even if Morisco tailors were eager to obey the law, they experienced trouble interpreting what exactly was being prohibited under the label *a la morisca*. If, nineteen years after the fall of the Nasrid Kingdom of Granada, the experts in the profession were confused and could not clearly understand what was meant by "Morisco clothing" (or by the no less vague term "Castilian clothing"), we can only imagine how much greater was the confusion for the rest of the population, Moriscos and Old Christians alike.

Furthermore, it was unclear who the target of prohibitions was, whether consumers or producers, the inhabitants of the Kingdom of Granada or all subjects in Castile, Moriscos only or Old Christians as well. Consequently, the demand for Morisco clothing soon found a legal loophole to the 1511 prohibition, as shown by the need to issue a new decree on 12 February 1512, prohibiting both Old Christian and *converso* tailors from making Morisco clothing.[20] This new decree directed at both Old Christians and *conversos* shows that genealogy and ethnic belonging were not the definitive factor in the production and circulation of so-called Morisco clothing.[21] Indeed, we have to conclude that the succession of amendments was intended for Moriscos as consumers, since the overwhelming consumption of clothing *a la morisca* by aristocrats dressing for the game of canes clearly demonstrates that production of "Moorish clothing" never ceased, not in 1513 or with successive bans that, unlike this one, targeted specific consumers rather than production.

The 1513 decree also targeted Morisco women in particular, prohibiting them from wearing *almalafas* and ordering them to wear "cloth cloaks and their faces unveiled, as the Old Christian women wear."[22] An illustration of what the *almalafa* may have looked like can be found in the relief representing the baptism of the Moriscas in the alterpiece of the Royal Chapel in Granada (Figure 12). The altarpiece was designed by Felipe de Vigarny (or Bigarny), between 1520 and 1522, and reflects the mass baptism of the Moriscos imposed by Cardinal Francisco Jiménez de Cisneros in 1499.[23] Yet it is probably an intervention in the political debates during the 1510s. There is also an engraving by the German traveller Christoph Weiditz, who found Morisco women an exotic object for his drawings (Figure 13). The prohibition of the *almalafa* was in fact an issue of policing all female sartorial behaviour, as it was soon followed by another decree that included Christian women as well.[24]

A good measure for gauging the confusing situation after these early-sixteenth-century decrees is the correspondence of the II Count of Tendilla, Íñigo López de Mendoza (1440–1515), who was the military governor of the Kingdom of Granada. At first he denied the existence of such a sartorial difference between Morisco and Castilian clothing. On 18 August 1513, the Count of Tendilla wrote that "all women wear Castilian dress, and whoever says the opposite is lying," and suggested that the initiators of the rumor were trying to extract a levy from the Moriscos.[25] While in this letter he referred to the Moriscas in the city of Granada, in a letter to Fernando II of Aragon recommending against the implementation of the decree, he points out that Old Christian women in Castile used their cloaks to cover their faces in the same way that Moriscas did with their *almalafas*, and that therefore this garment was not related to the practice of Islam. Yet he implicitly recognized that "Castilian" cloaks and *almalafas* were different garments, even if their function was the same.[26]

The Count of Tendilla abandoned his initial strategy of denying cultural difference and soon after wrote another letter to the monarch proposing that he not enforce the prohibition in exchange for a fine – part of which, incidentally, would serve to pay for the wedding of his own daughter.[27] This change in his opinion on the matter reveals the count's cynical position. When he presented himself as the protector of the Moriscos, he was in fact playing a political game in which he situated himself as the intermediary between them and the monarchy, and for the intermediary to play a relevant role, cultural difference must exist.[28] Of course, other members of the Morisco elite challenged his mediating role. On 20 December 1513, the Count of Tendilla complained that several Morisco leaders, namely Miguel de León and Hernando de Morales El Fistelí, were conspiring to displace him in negotiations with the monarch.[29]

In a letter of 14 February 1515, the Count of Tendilla claimed that the Morisco tailors had asked him (instead of Miguel de León) to take care of the *servicio* that they would pay in exchange for keeping their cultural practices.[30] In another, of 13 May 1515, he complained that the Morisco Miguel de León was instructing the tailors of *almalafas* to continue making them.[31] It seems from the tailors' petition that the Moriscos were willing to abide by the law, but were prevented from doing so by the constant interference of the political conflict between the Count of Tendilla and Miguel de León. In the meantime, the Count of Tendilla recanted his own words and claimed that he had never proposed the idea that the prohibition be lifted in exchange for a levy.[32] Finally, on 24 November 1515, Fernando of Aragon declared that the Moriscos were allowed to keep using their traditional clothing, but tied this concession to the negotiation of the special taxes paid by the Morisco community – just as the Count of Tendilla had proposed.[33]

The inconsistencies of his ambivalent position indicate what is really at stake. Even as the count was trying to use his position as intermediary to extract an economic advantage for himself, he kept suggesting that new converts to Christianity should not be banned from wearing certain clothing.[34] On 12 May 1514, in a letter to the Commander of Castile, he complained about the prohibition of Morisco clothing: "Sir, why does His Majesty ban Morisco clothing? ... Because we, sir, until the arrival to Spain of Enrique the Bastard, what attire did we have but the Morisco? ... Did kings stop being Christian and holy because of that? No, for God's sake!"[35] Yet this letter was never sent. Maybe the Count of Tendilla wrote it as a moment's relief but then thought that his outburst was politically problematic. But maybe he realized that his heated argument actually missed the point of the decree, which was never intended to prohibit the use of Moorish clothing by aristocrats but only to specifically target Moriscos.

The dearth of documentation suggests that the situation stalled for more than a decade, until the first systematic attempt to classify and prohibit Morisco customs took shape with the 1526 decree made by Charles V at a meeting in the Royal Chapel at Granada. This decree covered almost every aspect of Morisco "difference" that would become an issue until the expulsion of the Moriscos: the use of the Arabic language, bathhouses, musical instruments, burials, and any practice perceived as being related to Islam.[36] Regarding clothing, this decree mandated that neither Moriscas nor Old Christian women wear *almalafas*, but cloaks and hats instead.[37] It is important to note that there is no reference to Morisco men, as traditionally suggested by the way this decree has been summarized.[38] Most evidence suggests that by the first half of the sixteenth century there was no difference between Morisco and Old Christian men in their sartorial practices.[39] According to Francisco Núñez Muley's appeal to Philip II in 1567, by the 1520s Morisco men were already dressing in the "Castilian manner."[40] The Venetian ambassador Andrea Navagero, who visited Granada as part of Charles V's retinue, left a vivid description of the exotic clothing of Morisco women, but was completely silent about Morisco men.[41] The drawings made by the German traveller Christoph Weiditz in his *Trachtenbuch* after his travel in Castile and Aragon in 1529 also seem to confirm this situation. In one plate he depicts a Morisco couple travelling, and while the Morisca seems to be wearing some kind of *almalafa*, there is nothing distinctive in the Morisco man's attire (Figure 14).[42] The implementation of Charles V's decree was postponed in exchange for a levy – exactly as the II Count of Tendilla had proposed to do only a decade earlier. In spite of the lack of enforcement, the emperor's decree was consistently recalled as a precedent, and subsequent legal texts referred to it as a source of authority and jurisprudence – even when they introduced their own regulations.

The 1554 Synod of Guadix reinstates previous recommendations to abolish Morisco dress, but also includes interesting new information. First, it represents the adoption of "Christian clothing" and the abandonment of Morisco attire as a nonlinear process, in which some Moriscos, after initially adopting Old Christian garb, later abandoned it.[43] It also recognizes, as do previous laws, that Old Christian women also wore Morisco clothing, although in this case it singles out only those who were married to Moriscos.[44] It finally mandates that "both men and women ... do not dare to wear Morisco clothing, and most notably that they should abandon their veils, *marlotas*, and headdresses, wearing instead cloaks, tunics, and headdresses in the same way that Old Christian women do."[45] This order includes both male and female Moriscos in a strange way: the sentence begins by addressing all the Moriscos, both male and female, only to end up asking them to dress like Old Christian women. This semantic lapse, as we shall see, recurs in subsequent legislation, and is indicative of the efforts to create a sartorial legislation that embraces all the Moriscos as a community, while sartorial difference was observable only in a subset of them. Like Charles V's decree, the recommendations of the 1554 Synod were not implemented, but they further contributed to the legal formulation of (real or imaginary) Morisco sartorial practices.

In 1565, the archbishop Pedro Guerrero organized a meeting of the Church Council of Granada to deal with the implementation there of the edict of Trent and with restructuring the provincial chapters. The Council failed because of the conflict between Guerrero and Philip II, who tried to control any reform project and insisted on asserting royal authority over the Council; the king finally let the document die without either rejecting or approving it.[46] Among many other projected reforms, the Council dealt with the issue of Moriscos. Unfortunately, there is a gap in the Council proceedings, which cross-reference a chapter about Moriscos that is missing in the extant document.[47] In the scattered observations about the Moriscos that can be found in other sections, the Council still acknowledges that the use of "Morisco clothing" could not be easily reduced to ethno-religious boundaries, as it also prohibited Old Christians from wearing Morisco clothing.[48] It is difficult to extrapolate from this short instruction whether the masculine form in *christianos nueuos* and *christianos viejos* was used in its general grammatical sense comprising both genders and therefore once again policing only the use of *almalafas* by women, or whether it is meant to comprise male Morisco clothing as well.

While the original chapter on the Moriscos is missing from the extant document, Pedro Guerrero offers a summary in a letter addressed to Philip II in 1565. After reviewing the prohibitions of Queen Juana and Charles V against the *almalafas*, Guerrero instructs the monarch to prohibit the production of new Morisco clothing, letting the Moriscos wear out their old garments. Guerrero clearly frames the legislation of Morisco clothing as an issue of social distinction:

> it could be ordered that those [masculine] who marry from now on dress like Old Christians, and those others [feminine] who go in Morisco dress, they [masculine] or their women or servants [masculine], no matter how principal and noble [masculine] they are, during the time that their already-made clothing lasts, they may not be councilors, nor sheriffs, nor enjoy the privilege of wearing weapons, nor that of *hidalguía* [nobility], and that they may be summoned to attend mass and doctrine, to encourage them [masculine] in this way to leave behind their clothing before it is worn out.[49]

As had happened with the 1554 Synod of Guadix, Pedro Guerrero's recommendation vacillates with respect to the gender of the Moriscos, making it unclear whether it refers to Morisco women, men, or both. Guerrero seems to try to clarify it when he alludes to "they or their women," which might mean that when these documents say "Morisco" they are actually not counting individuals but households, and that therefore, even if only some of the members in the family were dressing in a way identified as Morisco (viz. women), then the entire family was considered to be dressing in such a way. The other revealing datum is that Guerrero linked the concession of social privileges to sartorial assimilation – oblivious to the inherent contradiction that councilmen all over Castile dressed *a la morisca* to prove their nobility. By proposing to prevent these Moriscos from accessing municipal positions and noble status, Guerrero indirectly acknowledged that this kind of social mobility was a matter of concern. As we shall see, Guerrero's suggestion to associate privilege and sartorial practices was appropriated by Philip II's decree, although in a very different way.

Philip II's response to Pedro Guerrero on 24 October 1565, acknowledged receipt of the Council recommendations and indicated that the monarch was about to gather a special council to study the best course of action regarding Morisco customs. This council would consult "what was decided in the council of 1526 and in that of 1539, and what has been ordered in several decrees and laws and other particular provisions, as well as what you propose and note in your letter."[50] Thus Philip II suggested that the new decision would merely reinstate the previous legislation, taking into account Pedro Guerrero's recommendations. Yet, as we shall see, the final decree made its own contribution to the legal policing of Morisco bodies.

According to early modern historian Luis Mármol Carvajal, the participants in the Junta of Madrid were: Diego de Espinosa, the general inquisitor and bishop of Sigüenza; the Duke of Alba; Antonio de Toledo, the prior of the Order of Saint John; Bernardo de Bolea, the vice-chancellor of Aragon; Gregorio Gallo, the bishop of Orihuela; Pedro de Deza, from the Council of the Inquisition; and the judges Menchaca and Doctor Velasco, representatives of the royal council.[51] It is difficult to determine how prepared this committee was to decide on the cultural practices of the Moriscos of Granada only on the basis of the legislation on the matter passed several decades before. The Marquis of Mondéjar, someone who obviously knew the situation better (although he also had his own interests) complained about not having been included in this council. There were, however, reasons to exclude the Marquis of Mondéjar, who was in open confrontation with Pedro de Deza.[52]

There are no extant proceedings of this council, which would allow us to glimpse how cultural difference was discussed between its members, and we have only indirect information about their work. In one letter from Diego de Espinosa to Pedro de Deza on 6 August 1566, he announced that they were about to reach a decision and that the order would be sent to him as soon as it was signed. On 21 August Espinosa instructed Deza to implement the monarch's edict on clothing, which is presented as already definitive.[53] In spite of Espinosa's encouragement, the implementation of this and other measures that were issued throughout 1566 was delayed until the next year. On 18 November, Philip II let Pedro de Deza decide when and how to implement the decrees.[54]

Philip II's Decree of 1 January 1567

According to Mármol Carvajal, Pedro de Deza had Philip II's decree printed and publicized it as the definitive prohibition of Morisco cultural practices in the city of Granada on 1 January 1567, in all likelihood to coincide with the anniversary of the Christian taking of Granada and to make a more dramatic connection between the decree and the celebration of the victory over Islam.[55] Given the centrality of this decree, analysis of the exact wording is essential, even though the original document prepared by the 1566 Junta of Madrid is still missing. In its absence, the closest version to the original is the one printed and publicized by Pedro de Deza in Granada.[56] The document contains five decrees, each prohibiting, respectively, the use of Morisco clothing, dances and celebrations, bathhouses, slaves, and Arabic. The decree prohibiting clothing figures prominently in first place, and is the longest in the document. It reviews previous prohibitions by the Catholic monarchs, Juana I of Castile, and Charles V. It suggests that previous legislation has not been obeyed and mandates the implementation of Juana I's decrees.[57] However, in spite of its apparent repetition of the language of the previous documents, this new law ignores some fundamental aspects of the complex cultural reality of Granada that had been acknowledged in the previous legislation and introduced highly significant variations which further essentialized Morisco sartorial practices. The decree mandated that

> none of the said newly converted in the aforementioned Kingdom of Granada nor their descendants can make nor tailor veiled gowns [*almalafas*], Moorish tunics [*marlotas*], hose, or any other sort of clothing such as they used to wear during the time of the Moors, and that new dresses be made like those that the Old Christian women wear, that is, cloaks and tunics.[58]

The document begins by addressing the "Moriscos" in the masculine form ("los nuevamente convertidos"), which in Spanish comprises both male and female Moriscos. But within the same sentence, it ends up requiring its addressee (heretofore in the masculine plural), to dress like "Old Christian women." It is striking to observe that Philip II's decree commits exactly the same grammatical error found in both the 1554 Synod of Guadix and the 1565 Church Council of Granada. The persistence of this grammatical lapse in the legal documents suggests that, rather than being the unintended result of poor wording, it targeted households and not individuals, as was evident in the 1565 letter by Pedro Guerrero. Some contemporary reports, which were more aware of the circumstances in which the decree was applied, were in a better position to read through its confusing language and understood that it was intended only for Morisco women, since there was no difference between Morisco and Old Christian men.[59]

Nonetheless, and quite probably originating in the grammatical lapse analysed above, both early modern and contemporary historiography has assumed that the law referred to both male and female Moriscos. This is quite evident in the influential summary offered by Mármol Carvajal which stated that: "With respect to clothing, it was ordered that the Moriscos not make any new *marlotas*, veiled gowns [*almalafas*], hose [*calzas*], or any other sort of dress such as those that they wore during the Muslim period; and that all the clothing that they produce in the future be like that worn by Christians."[60] It is important to note that most of the modern bibliography on the Moriscos of Granada cites Mármol Carvajal.[61] Yet his summary erases the gender ambiguity of the decree and initiates the historiographical distortion suggesting that the prohibition of Moriscos wearing "ropa de moros" was intended for both men and women.

There is another generally overlooked detail that goes beyond the logic of cultural and religious repression: Philip II's decree, contrary to previous legislation, referred not only to clothing labelled as "Morisco," but also to its fabric. In the second paragraph, the 1567 decree mandates that "the aforementioned *almalafas* and *marlotas*, and any other garments made of silk or having any adornment made of silk, can be worn for only one year, and those that are not made of silk or have any adornment made of silk can be worn for two years."[62] While the document begins by listing recognizable names of "Morisco" garments, such as the *almalafa* and the *marlota*, it finally prohibits *any* garment made of silk. Even if it did not say so explicitly, it was implicit that any "Christian"/"Castilian" clothing made of silk, for both males and females, would also be included in the prohibition. Allowing any clothing made of silk to be worn for only one year, yet those made of any other fabric for two, indicates that the wearing of luxurious fabric (and not merely the use of garments labelled as "Morisco") was one of the primary goals of the law.

In this way, the edict creates an equivocal conflation between ethnicity, social class, and the right to wear luxurious garments. By capitalizing on the ambiguity of the adjective *morisco* when it was applied to clothing, meaning either lavish or Moorish, the decree postulated that any Morisco wearing the sumptuary signs attributed to members of the higher class could be construed as if he or she was affirming a distinct cultural and religious identity. If Hernando de Talavera instructed the Moriscos to dress like "good and honest Christians" in 1500, by which he meant that they not engage in luxurious practices, Philip II's decree further mandated a downward sartorial assimilation of the Moriscos by requesting that all of them dress like Old Christian commoners.[63]

This emphasis on silk suggests that the decree was connected to the sumptuary laws that tried to prevent the use of luxurious garments by commoners in the early modern period. Philip II had recently issued another decree in 1563 granting that "our subjects and natives in our Kingdoms could wear any kind of silk in their clothing" (even though there were several restrictions).[64] Laid side by side with this legislation on the use of silk throughout Castile, the 1567 decree addressed the Moriscos as if they were not considered lawful subjects, since only they were universally prohibited from wearing silk, without any consideration for context or status.

This entails a surreptitious retrieval of the medieval legislation prohibiting Muslims and Jews from wearing silk.[65] In the sixteenth century, those condemned by the Inquisition were considered to be ineligible (*inhábiles*) for certain offices and honours, among them, the wearing of silk.[66] By prohibiting Moriscos from wearing luxurious items and thus negating the class distinctions that also existed within the Morisco community, Philip II's decree implicitly advocated that all Moriscos be considered as members either of the same lower social class (regardless of their actual socio-economic standing), or of the same group of heretics who had been condemned by the Inquisition as *inhábiles* (even if they were never formally condemned by the Inquisition).[67] Therefore, while prohibiting Moriscos from wearing silk and "Morisco clothing" was presented as an act of cultural and religious assimilation, it was even more a means of hindering a full and fully stratified assimilation into Old Christian society, by precluding wealthy Moriscos from participating in Castilian signs of sartorial distinction, such as the use of silk and Moorish garb. The reason wealthy Moriscos may have been offended by the law is not because it aimed at erasing "their" culture, but because it levelled and displaced them as a community under the same legal category of commoners and heretics.[68]

Thus the 1567 decree made two simultaneous but disparate interventions in both social reality and the collective imaginary. On the one hand, the applicability of the law would prevent Moriscos from accessing luxurious garments as a sign of social distinction, thus adding to the other measures that targeted them as a marginalized group, such as the prohibition of carrying weapons, the prohibition from having slaves, and differentiated taxation. On the other hand, the letter of the law conveyed the distorted image that all Moriscos, both male and female, were easily recognizable in their sartorial practices. The decree obviates that Old Christians also participated in several of the sartorial practices being prohibited. By addressing the Moriscos as those who made and consumed clothing *a la morisca*, it elided the fact that Old Christians were also involved in this trade.[69] The emphasis on a largely exaggerated sartorial difference distinguished from Old Christians helped to stretch the fictive visibility of a Morisco identity. Seen in this light, the 1567 decree is not so much an intervention in the actual sartorial practices of the Moriscos but in the collective imaginary about them, as it constitutes an invitation to "see" a largely non-existent difference which has been gladly assumed by both early modern and contemporary historians.

No less important than the close analysis of the decree's wording is the evaluation of its impact. Evidence about its enforcement as well as the reactions against it is both scarce and contradictory. According to Mármol Carvajal,

> having printed the new decree, the president [of the Royal Chancery of Granada] Pedro de Deza ... ordered that it be publicized in the city of Granada and the other cities in that kingdom, on January 1st of the year 1567. That day all the justices of the Royal Chancery, as well as those of the royal representative in Granada, gathered with great solemnity of drums, trumpets, sackbuts, musicians, and flutes, and announced it in the squares and public spaces of the city and the Albaicín neighbourhood.[70]

Yet, even if Mármol Carvajal presents himself as a privileged witness of the uprising, he did not arrive in Granada until the spring of 1569.[71] Therefore he could not have known firsthand how the decree was publicized or how the Moriscos reacted.

In a letter written on 12 January 1567, Pedro de Deza reported to Philip II on the implementation of the decrees, informing him that the decrees had been publicized in the city of Granada on 1 January and that he had sent copies to the *corregidores* in other cities in the Kingdom of Granada, who responded confirming that the Moriscas immediately started to dress like Old Christian women. Regarding the reactions in the city of Granada, Deza says that the Moriscas adopted Castilian clothing rather willingly, because they thought they would be more respected for wearing it. Indeed, as Deza frames it, Morisco men themselves encouraged their wives to adopt Castilian clothing because in this way the Moriscas would be allowed to continue to cover their faces – as many other Old Christian women did.[72]

Thus, according to Deza's report, the decree on clothing did not inspire heated reactions from the Moriscos. Certainly we should be cautious about Deza's account, since he was obviously interested in presenting himself as a dexterous politician. Yet there might be some truth in his report, as he also acknowledges in the same letter how other measures were not so well received. Regarding the demolition of bathhouses, he relates that Moriscos and Old Christians alike complained. What seems to have really concerned the Moriscos was the ban on speaking Arabic, since they did not deem that three years was a feasible period of time to master Castilian.[73]

While there is no reason to doubt Pedro de Deza and Mármol Carvajal as to how the decree was publicized in the city of Granada, there is very little trace of its actual dissemination. Mármol Carvajal states that by the end of 1567, when the first part of the decree prohibiting wearing silk was supposed to be applied, the president of the Chancery, Pedro de Deza, and the archbishop of Granada, Pedro Guerrero, ordered local churches to remind the Moriscos about it during New Year's Eve Mass for 1567–8.[74] That Pedro de Deza decided to disseminate a series of decrees made by the civil authorities through the ecclesiastical structure may or may not be a common confounding of jurisdiction in the early modern period, but it still leaves unresolved who would be in charge of enforcing these prohibitions. We should therefore wonder whether Mármol Carvajal and subsequent historians may have exaggerated the social impact of the decree, and whether it was resisted or simply ignored by municipal governments.[75]

Francisco Núñez Muley: The Genesis of "the Morisco Voice" and its Historiographical Reverberation

Arguably the most obvious way to assess the impact of Philip II's decree would be to look at the Moriscos' reaction. The best-known Morisco response (and almost the only one) is the memorandum in defence of Morisco customs written by Francisco Núñez Muley, a Morisco noble of Granada, in 1567. Trying to separate culture from religion and addressing Pedro de Deza, Núñez Muley devoted the first portion of his memorandum entirely to clothing, focusing on the economic loss that it would entail for the kingdom and pointing out that Morisco men (and to some extent women) were already dressing in the Castilian manner. He also argued that even those garments specific to Moriscos should be considered only as regional variants within the Iberian landscape, since they were indeed very different from the clothing used by Muslims in North Africa and Turkey. He also reported that Morisco clothing was usually bequeathed in dowries but had only ritual uses, such as weddings, or even an economic value as a source of ready cash, as they could be pawned in time of necessity.

This document has received well-deserved critical attention because of the way Núñez Muley differentiates between religious and cultural practices.[76] Yet, as important as Núñez Muley's memorandum is for our understanding of this period, we should be cautious about identifying him as representative of the entire Morisco community of Granada, since he may have written at such length about the sartorial issue not just as a Morisco, but as a wealthy noble who saw himself at risk of being deprived of the signs of status typical of early modern Iberia.[77] While the force of Núñez Muley's memorandum is undeniable, we must also examine its shortcomings. It is especially striking that he was not able to articulate that the prohibition of wearing silk textiles could not be justified on cultural grounds (since other Christians were allowed to wear them), and thus could only be interpreted as a collective punishment that contradicted the general sumptuary laws of the 1560s. He merely complained that "for the luxurious things we have only been granted permission for one year."[78] Núñez Muley not only failed to elaborate on this flagrant contradiction in the prohibition, and to point out that the decree was introducing new conditions while claiming to be merely reinstating previous laws, he also failed to allude to the 1499 licence for all Muslim inhabitants in Granada to wear silk, which would have provided him with an excellent legal precedent to counteract the arguments of Philip II's decree.

Kenneth Garrad suggests in his edition of Núñez Muley's memorandum that the Morisco noble was probably repeating the same arguments he had used to negotiate with Queen Juana in 1513 and Charles V in 1526.[79] That would mean that, as an elderly man, he was probably reusing the same materials from four decades earlier. There is also a second element that explains the way his memorandum is structured. Núñez Muley was responding closely to the historical explanation that served as a prologue for the printed decree – a detail that has been overlooked because the original document of the decree has rarely been consulted, only subsequent versions, which omit the prologue. Thus Núñez Muley debated the cultural identity of the Moriscos by following the rhetorical and historiographical frame moulded by the members of the 1566 Junta of Madrid – who, in turn, were influenced by previous laws written many decades before them that did not necessarily reflect the current sartorial landscape of Granada in the 1560s.

The romanticization of Núñez Muley's appeal can be further deconstructed when we take into account that he was not merely writing his memorandum on behalf of the Morisco community, but was acting in the service of the Marquis of Mondéjar. As has been discovered only recently, on 30 July 1567 Francisco Núñez Muley petitioned the Marquis of Mondéjar for a stipend of 100 *ducados* for the expenses he had incurred in gathering the materials for his memorandum.[80] We can indeed reconstruct a political pattern when we take into account that the other possible source for a Morisco voice would be Alonso del Castillo, who transcribed a letter for the Marquis of Mondéjar that the Granadan Islamic leader Aben Daud addressed to his fellow Muslims in North Africa to complain about the prohibition of their traditional clothing and language.[81] As L.P. Harvey points out, the circumstances under which the letter was allegedly found and translated, together with the fact that Castillo is well-known for his forgeries, makes this a very unreliable source for demonstrating how the Moriscos reacted to Philip II's decree.[82] What both the documents issued by Alonso del Castillo and Francisco Núñez Muley have in common, however, is that their complaints against the prohibition were mediated and commissioned by the Marquis of Mondéjar, who, like his predecessor five decades before, based his political authority on defending (if not creating or at least exaggerating) the "cultural identity" of Moriscos in order to cement his own political space as a mediator between them and the monarchy.[83]

Núñez Muley's text has not only become canonical for modern historiography, but was already being used and glossed by early modern authors. Even if his original text was not published until the twentieth century, it was consulted by early modern historians and was further disseminated through the extensive summary provided by

Mármol Carvajal in his *Historia del rebelión y castigo de los moriscos del Reino de Granada* (1600).[84] Yet Núñez Muley's voice was progressively dramatized and deflected to different Morisco characters, real or apocryphal. Antonio de Fuenmayor's *Vida y hechos de Pío V* (1595) tells of a Morisco named Cárdenas who debates with his peers opposing the rebellion and proposes to abide by Philip II's decree in order to keep the Islamic faith in secret: "Consider, for God's sake, how it is less harmful to change language and dress, since neither the Morisco voice [i.e., Arabic language] made you Moors, nor do you strip your heart with your clothing."[85] This apocryphal speech is clearly based on Núñez Muley's memorandum. Similarly, Ginés Pérez de Hita's second part of the *Guerras civiles de Granada* (1619) also includes an apocryphal Morisco speech complaining about Philip II's decree and igniting the revolt, which in this case is attributed to Fernándo de Válor's uncle Abenchoar.[86]

Diego Hurtado de Mendoza's *Guerra de Granada* (written shortly after the events but not published until 1627) has the Morisco leader Fernando de Válor complain to his fellow Moriscos about Philip II's decree:

> They order us to give up our clothing and to dress in the Castilian style; but they dress among themselves the Germans in one way, the French in another, the Greeks in another, friars in yet another, boys however they want, old people to their own taste. Every nation, every profession, every estate has its own style of dress and they are Christians; but we are Moors because we dress in the Morisco style, as if we carried our religion in our clothing and not in our hearts.[87]

The similarities between Fernando de Válor's alleged speech with Núñez Muley's memorandum reveals the apocryphal nature of this passage, since Hurtado de Mendoza could not have heard Fernando de Válor's words. While this displacement of Núñez Muley's speech onto other characters is common to many of the historiographies on the war of the Alpujarras, the absence of the noble Morisco is telling in the case of Hurtado de Mendoza's work. Hurtado de Mendoza was under the patronage of his relative the Marquis of Mondéjar and had access to the documents in the Alhambra, so he clearly read Núñez Muley's memorandum and was probably aware that the Marquis of Mondéjar commissioned its writing. But it is precisely this intimate knowledge of Mendoza's role that may explain the elision of Núñez Muley in his text.

The attribution of the speech to Fernando de Válor in Hurtado de Mendoza's work, rather than an instance of ignorance or confusion, seems to be an intentional strategy to obscure the memorandum's link to the Marquis of Mondéjar and his active participation in the creation of that alleged Morisco discourse.

In the posterity of this sleight of hand, Morisco laments over the loss of "their" sartorial identity have become a historiographical commonplace, a free-floating speech attributed in each case to a different Morisco character. Most of these passages, as Harvey points out, are apocryphal orations concocted by Old Christian historians, all of them based on Núñez Muley's appeal.[88] Jaime Bleda's *Corónica de los moros de España* (1618) is emblematic of the subsequent historiographical distortion and amplification of the episode as it duplicates the Morisco's laments over their loss of language and dress after the 1567 prohibition. First Bleda transcribes Mármol Carvajal's summary of Francisco Núñez Muley's memorandum.[89] But a few pages later he reproduces an almost identical speech attributed to Fernando de Válor – this time following Hurtado de Mendoza's work, which, as we have seen, in turn echoed Núñez Muley's memorandum without citing it.[90] The effect of Bleda's merging of historical sources is that the Morisco lament over Philip II's decree becomes a textual echo, a ritual litany whose historiographical value lays in its repetition. In this way, a legal response commissioned by the Marquis of Mondéjar for political reasons becomes in its textual reproduction and reverberation the lament of an entire community.

The War of the Alpujarras and the Myth of Sartorial Revival

We must finally consider Philip II's decree within the usual process of early modern sumptuary laws, which were cyclically issued even if they were rarely effective. Saúl Martínez Bermejo suggests that, in spite of the apparent inefficacy of sartorial laws, which were rarely implemented, their lack of application should not be interpreted as a failure but rather as an inherent part of their function, since "the procedure for 'moderating' the law allowed the king to maintain his authority even if the actual implementation of the measures never took place."[91] Scholarship on the Moriscos has emphasized the failure of the appeals to Pedro de Deza and Philip II to not enforce the prohibition, and this failure has been interpreted as a proof of how the monarch was firm this time in his intention to uproot "Morisco customs." Thus even a circumspect historian like Julio Caro Baroja dramatically proclaims that "the will to wipe out once and for all an entire social structure, an entire culture, was clear and there was nothing to do against it. Nothing, but war."[92] Yet what differentiates the way Philip II's decree regarding Morisco customs is interpreted in comparison to other sartorial laws is not the monarch's determination, but the fact that the uprising of the Alpujarras and the subsequent expulsion disrupted the normal process through which such legislation was normally negotiated, as it usually took several years to rectify and grant exceptions after the law was first issued. We can only wonder what would have happened with Philip II's decree if the War of the Alpujarras had not prevented its natural evolution, but we should question the deterministic relation of causality that has been established traditionally between Philip II's ban of Morisco customs in 1567 and the uprising of the Moriscos on Christmas Eve of 1568, known as the War of the Alpujarras.[93]

The historiographical emphasis on religious and cultural identity has obscured the complex socio-economic reasons behind the Morisco uprising and has imposed a particular historical simplification and causality. For instance, Perez Zagorin accepts such a reductive explanatory model when, in his comparative historical study of social unrest and rebellions in early modern Europe he explores the complex socio-economic causes behind each case but sets apart the uprising of the Alpujarras, since he considers it "perhaps the most extreme case in which religion lay at the heart of a provincial conflict."[94] Zagorin's opinion is conditioned by the dominant historiographical paradigm attributing the Morisco revolt to the prohibition of cultural practices. Yet there are some historians who have proposed alternative political and socio-economic interpretations.

Granada's political situation in the 1560s was quite turbulent, not only between Moriscos and Old Christians, as later accounts tend to emphasize, but also between the different institutions ruled by Old Christians. On the one hand, there was a constant conflict between the Chancery of Granada and the nobility, most notably the marquises of Mondéjar. While the Mendozas had had military control over the kingdom since the fall of Granada in 1492, from the 1540s the Chancery tried to extend its area of influence through the incorporation of criminal and legal causes traditionally excercised by the Mendozas. In order to avoid direct confrontation with the Mendozas, the Chancery undermined the base of their power: their allegedly good relations with the Moriscos. The conflict was exacerbated when Pedro de Deza, who had a personal confrontation with Luis Hurtado de Mendoza, was named president of the Chancery.[95] According to Gabriel Rodríguez de Ardila's *Historia de los condes de Tendilla* (a manuscript from the first half of the seventeenth century), Pedro de Deza promoted the prohibition of Morisco cultural practices as a way to undermine the authority of the Marquis of Mondéjar.[96] Even if Rodríguez de Ardila was obviously partial to the Mendoza family, and we should be cautious in solely blaming Pedro de Deza for the uprising of the Moriscos, it is clear that the president of the Chancery's actions were instrumental in igniting an already volatile situation. Rafael Benítez Sánchez-Blanco suggests that the interest of the provincial church of Granada, the Chancery, and the monarchy in legislating culture might have been an indirect way of extending their jurisdiction and exerting their authority at the expense of the Inquisition,[97] even if inquisitorial persecution does not seem to play a significant role in this debate, since the Inquisition rarely considered aspects like clothing.[98]

While the previous explanations focus on the possible political intentions of the Christian authorities and institutions, other socio-economic interpretations try to explain why the Moriscos rebelled precisely when they did. Kenneth Garrad has suggested that the revolt may have been directly related to the decay of the silk trade on which the Morisco economy depended.[99] According to Lorenzo Cara Barrionuevo, the revolt could have been caused by the pressure from Old Christian livestock owners in appropriating arable lands.[100] Javier Castillo Fernández, who criticizes the pre-eminence of culture over economics in contemporary historical analysis of the Moriscos, points out that one of the usually ignored reasons for the uprising is a 1567 royal instruction to gather new taxes from some integrated Moriscos who had been exempt until then.[101]

The view through which cultural identity takes the place of economic and political turmoil was already crafted by early modern Christian historians, who named the prohibition of Morisco customs as the immediate and only cause for the uprising of the Alpujarras.[102] One consequence of this logic is the assumption that there was a revival of so-called Morisco culture during the rebellion, and that Moriscos took advantage of the chaotic situation to recover "their" traditions. Julio Caro Baroja, following the same historical sources that I analyse here, speculates that "when the uprising spread, there must have been some sort of restoration of Islamic clothing."[103] Caro Baroja is rigorous enough to acknowledge his speculation as such, but subsequent historians have taken such hypotheses as well-established facts. For instance,

Juan Martínez Ruiz turns Caro Baroja's speculation into fact and asserts that "we have evidence that the Morisco uprising was accompanied by some sort of restoration of Islamic clothing."[104] Both Caro Baroja and Martínez Ruiz, in order to support their assertion of a Morisco cultural revival during the uprising, cite the same four passages in Mármol Carvajal's book that seem to prove their point.[105] Strikingly, when we go over those passages, it turns out that they can be used to demonstrate quite the opposite, that Moriscos did not have a deep attachment to so-called Morisco clothing.

The first passage refers to how el Habaquí was seized by his Morisco rival Aben Aboo. Mármol Carvajal says that el Habaquí could have escaped "if his own clothing had not betrayed him; because ... those who were looking for him spied the red caftan that he was wearing and the white turban on his head."[106] The second instance is a very similar sartorial description of the Morisco leader Aben Humeya as he appears encouraging his men on the war front: "Aben Humeya rode very flamboyantly on a white horse in front of everybody wearing a red Moorish hooded tunic and a Turkish turban on his head."[107] These two references may somehow support the assumption that there was a sartorial revival during the revolt.[108] Yet the use of Turkish clothing has little to do with recuperating some alleged "Morisco" culture, and it is more likely that either Morisco leaders were aligning themselves with the Ottoman Empire they were unsuccessfully entreating for help, or that they were fashioning their political legitimacy through the aesthetics (and even the garments) of the game of canes as it was practised by his Old Christian counterparts – as I will further detail in chapter 7. Indeed, while Moriscos appropriated Moorish/Turkish clothing for military demonstrations, they were at the same time trying to conform to the 1567 decree regarding women's clothing. In 1570, el Habaquí saved Alonso Xabalí (who had been sent as a spy by Juan of Austria) when he learned that he was a tailor and made him make "faldellines."[109] The *faldellín* was precisely one of the garments recommended by Pedro de Deza to the Moriscos to replace the traditional *almalafas*.[110]

The third passage from Mármol Carvajal cited by Caro Baroja and Martínez Ruiz does not even refer to the Moriscos, which they seem to imply when they talk about the "revival of Morisco culture," but to Luis Hurtado de Mendoza (1543–1604), V Count of Tendilla, who welcomed the arrival of Juan of Austria to Granada with a game of canes that included two hundred riders, half of them dressed *a la morisca*.[111]

The episode has struck several scholars for different reasons. For Joseph Pérez, taking into account the recent ban on Morisco clothing, "one must see in the count's attitude either irresponsibility or provocation."[112] However, while I agree with such critics about the apparent ideological contradiction of dressing *a la morisca* to repress a people who have just been prohibited from doing it, it should be emphasized that Philip II never intended to ban the use of Moorish clothing by Old Christians. Max Harris observes that the Count of Tendilla participated on the Moorish side, and notes that quite probably he wore the same Moorish costume that he had already used in other Moorish ceremonies in Granada.[113] Thus – based on the evidence presented in the first part of this book – one plausible explanation for the sartorial divide in this game of canes is that the Count of Tendilla and his soldiers had the Moorish clothing at hand, stored from previous celebrations, while Juan of Austria's troops had just arrived and had neither the means nor the time to procure their own Moorish clothing – such attire is not the kind of baggage one takes to the battlefront. This would thus not be a festival of *moros y cristianos*, but a game of canes in which one of the sides lacked the "appropriate" gear.

The fourth passage from Mármol Carvajal's text is precisely the one with which this book begins. It describes the moment when the Morisco leader Abenfarax, trying to engage the inhabitants of the city of Granada in the uprising, "made his companions take off their hats and caps, and put on red Turkish-style caps, with white turbans, in order to look like Turks."[114] Abenfarax had no success at all in his intent, and had to leave Granada at dawn. Nobody in the city of Granada, be he Morisco or Old Christian, fell for the ruse, and immediately realized that Abenfarax and his men were just a bunch of Moriscos trying to pass as Ottoman troops.[115] The next day, as already analysed, an anonymous soldier informed the Marquis of Mondéjar that the rioters were "Moors dressed … as Moors."[116] The pun (intended or not) reveals that, if Moriscos failed to pass as "Moors," it is because by 1568 they did not in fact dress like "Moors" were supposed to dress. Indeed, if Abenfarax were making a statement of cultural affirmation, it would be one that nobody would have understood to be a call for a Morisco cultural revival, since he adopted the sartorial practices of a different Muslim people living on the opposite Mediterranean shore – certainly, not truly traditional Morisco clothing, if the remains of such a sartorial tradition even existed for Morisco men by 1568.

These scenes of people dressing as Moors alleged as proof of the hypothetical cultural revival are in fact clear instances of passing, not acts of cultural affirmation. At most, they encapsulate the inconsistencies of the discourses about Morisco sartorial difference. The persistent misinterpretation of these passages exemplifies a critical anxiety to fill a gap in the visual imaginary about the Moriscos. Even if some Morisco communities and social groups (most probably women in the rural areas) may have exhibited some particular sartorial practices, such sartorial and cultural differences have been decontextualized and exaggerated in the legal and historiographical imaginary (both early modern and present day). In turn, this distortion has served to conceal the complex socio-economic causes triggering the uprising.

As this chapter has shown, when we re-contextualize "Morisco clothing" within a larger frame of sumptuary legislation and de-centre the analysis of its prohibition from a purely ethno-religious explanatory model, we can see that the application of the 1567 decree did not seek to assimilate Moriscos to Old Christian culture, but rather to stigmatize and homogenize them by both emphasizing a largely imaginary stereotype that was progressively divorced from cultural reality and by precluding their full and fully stratified participation in a shared ceremonial "Moorish culture" as sign of social distinction. The policing of Morisco bodies in sixteenth-century legal documents, in spite of its essentialized conception of ethno-religious difference, was heavily influenced by other social practices of class distinction embedded in the larger context of Iberian society – or with moralizing discourses on sartorial decency, in the case of Morisco women. Meanwhile, the subsequent historiographical works composed after the uprising of the Alpujarras have "Moorified" the male Moriscos in the historical imagination by simplifying historical events and cleansing them of the complex socio-economic circumstances underlying the revolt, dissolving the ambiguities surrounding the difference between Moorish and Morisco clothing, and creating an insurmountable sartorial cliff between Old Christian and Morisco bodies.

This "Moorification" of the Moriscos was not uniquely circumscribed within the Kingdom of Granada. As the Granada's Moriscos were expelled and relocated throughout the Kingdom of Castile, the prohibitions that were intended for them in Granada were supposed to be applicable as well in their new locations. Furthermore, the legal logic of searching for Morisco sartorial difference extended to other *mudéjar* communities in the kingdoms of Castile and Aragon, despite the fact that they had rarely been considered to be dressing differently. The requirement to assimilate to Castilian culture was unevenly promoted, mainly because, as the next chapter explores, the notion of Castilian/Spanish sartorial identity barely existed before its opposition to so-called Morisco clothing.

6 Searching for the Iberian Moorish Morisco

el ábito y traxe y calçado no se puede dezir de moros, ny es de moros. Puédese dezir ques traxe del rreyno y prouinçia, como en todos los rreynos de Castilla y los otros rreynos y prouinçias tienen los traxes diferentes unos de otros, y todos cristianos; y ansí el dicho áuito y traxe deste rreyno es muy diferente de los traxes de los moros de aliende y Berbería ... de manera que no se puede afundar ni dezir que el traxe de los nueuamente conuertidos es traxe de moros.[1]

[the style of dress, clothing, and footwear of the natives cannot be said to be that of Muslims, nor is it that of Muslims. It can more rightly be said to be clothing that corresponds to a particular Kingdom and province. All the kingdoms of Castile, and all the other kingdoms and provinces, have their own styles of dress that is different from the others, and yet they are all Christians. In like manner, the style of dress and clothing of this kingdom is very different from the clothing of the Moroccan and Barbary Muslims ... It follows that one cannot establish or state that the clothing of the new converts is that of Muslims]

Francisco Núñez Muley, Memorandum to Philip II

After the War of the Alpujarras, the royal administration lost interest in the sartorial issue, which grew increasingly irrelevant. An ordinance sent to the city of Jaén in 1569 dealing with the first deportation of Moriscos from Granada still insisted on the repression of Morisco cultural practices, including clothing.[2] A subsequent 1572 royal edict on how to proceed with the Moriscos expelled from Granada refers to the 1567 decree, but when it spells out many of the aspects being prohibited, such as the use of Arabic, it does not even mention clothing.[3] Between the uprising of the Alpujarras and the definitive expulsion of the Moriscos forty years later, the court continued to debate their fate, but left cultural practices aside. It seems that Philip II's 1567 decree was conceived of as the last word on the matter. Even if there was no effort to enforce the 1567 decree, it exacerbated the search for the alleged visibility of Morisco bodies throughout the Iberian Peninsula, as local authorities made their own ad hoc interpretations.

Local historians have pointed out that there seems to be no sartorial difference between Old Christians and *mudéjares* in the kingdoms of Castile and Aragon.[4] Yet there are several localized instances in which the Moriscos were suddenly perceived as dressing differently.

Because of the vagueness of the sartorial prohibitions against Moriscos, the investigation of what should be identified as Morisco clothing was left to the local civil and religious authorities, who defined cultural purity on an ad hoc basis and were often influenced by local power relations.[5] As stated in the introduction, the perception of "ethnicity" is not solely located in the objects and cultural practices themselves, but also in the context of use and the genealogy of their users. Such a situational approach has been done regarding the examination of Moriscos' religiosity. As noted previously, regarding religious orthodoxy Root suggests that "the indeterminability of faith apparent in the Inquisition's inability to determine dissimilarity, and its effort to circumvent this by continually increasing its demands for proof of orthodoxy, meant the definition of orthodoxy would migrate to genealogy."[6] This "migration of definition" of religious orthodoxy from inner beliefs and ritual practices to genealogy can be applied as well to the cultural realm. As argued in the introduction to this book, Moorishness is in the eye of the beholder, meaning that the same sartorial practices provoked different reactions in authorities depending on whether the wearers were Old Christians or Moriscos. Similarly, James Tueller points out that accusations of religious heterodoxy towards the Moriscos rarely took into account that even Christian religious practices were not homogeneous within Spain, and in many cases this diversity may explain some of the alleged perceptions of heterodoxy.[7] Thus Tueller concludes that "[i]t could also well be that the Moriscos were held to a very specific standard of Christian behavior and knowledge that in relation to other Christians was much higher."[8] Again, something similar could be said about cultural practices, and more specifically about sartorial uses, whose perceived difference may be due to a selective gaze that focused on the genealogy of a specific subgroup rather than the local community as a whole.

When early modern authors repeat like a mantra that Moriscos should dress like Old Christians, they never specify to which type of Old Christian clothing they are referring or which Old Christians should serve as models for cultural reference. Indeed, sartorial variants among Old Christians were plentiful. On the one hand, there was a high degree of regional sartorial diversity in the Iberian Peninsula.[9] Francisco Núñez Muley's memorandum, which contested Philip II's ban, already attributed the perceived difference of the so-called Morisco clothing of the Moriscos of Granada to regional variation, construing it as a local custom marked by its difference from the Islamic Mediterranean:

> the style of dress, clothing, and footwear of the natives cannot be said to be that of Muslims ... It can more rightly be said to be clothing that corresponds to a particular Kingdom and province. All the kingdoms of Castile, and all the other kingdoms and provinces, have their own styles of dress different from the others, and yet they are all Christians. Likewise, the style of dress and clothing of this kingdom is very different from the clothing of the Moroccan and Barbary Muslims ... It follows that one cannot establish or state that the clothing of the new converts is that of Muslims.[10]

Thus, Núñez Muley emphasized that the underlying ethnocentric concept of "Castilianness" was no more precise than the cover discourse of Christianity, when he pointed to the sartorial heterogeneity of Castile. If this point was valid for Granada, it was even more so for the rest of the Iberian Peninsula, in which Moriscos had been living side by side with Old Christians for centuries.

On the other hand, clothing diverged dramatically depending on the social class of the wearer. Therefore, while differences between Old Christians were considered merely regional or dependent on social class, any particularities of Morisco communities were decontextualized, generalized, and scrutinized by homogenizing them through the lenses of ethnicity and religious difference. Rephrasing Tueller, we could say that Moriscos were held to a very specific standard of Castilianness that was much more rigorous than that for other Castilians.

A more balanced and common truism is that some Moriscos were better integrated than others. All statements on Moriscos dressing differently are based on a fundamental decontextualization in terms of both local and class differences; yet the opposite proposition, that Moriscos dressed like Old Christians, is equally misleading unless we establish specific terms for the comparison. We should therefore discard such a dichotomy and formulate a more precise proposition that there was no sartorial difference between Old Christians and Moriscos living within the same local communities and belonging to the same profession and social class. An example of such a decontextualized comparison between the categories of Old Christian and Morisco clothing is found in a comment made by the Marquis of San Germán, who stated in 1609, "I consider the Moriscos in Andalusia to be very rich, and that in their dress and language they are much more similar to us than those in the Kingdom of Valencia."[11] In principle, this statement would prove that the Moriscos of Andalusia were more fully assimilated than the Moriscos of Valencia. Yet who was this "us" with which the Marquis of San Germán established the comparison? Was he speaking as a noble, as a Castilian, or as an Old Christian? Did he mean that the Moriscos of Andalusia dressed more similarly to Old Christians in Castile? And if so, were Old Christians in Valencia different from Old Christians in Castile as well? Was the Castilian marquis interpreting the local sartorial variations of Valencia as belonging exclusively to the Moriscos? While none of these questions are resolved in the document containing his comment, it seems that the Marquis of San Germán establishes similarity based on socio-economic status, since the Andalusian Moriscos being wealthier made them more similar to the socio-economic class to which he himself belonged.

Moriscos themselves actually argued that they were sartorially assimilated to Old Christians in a variety of cases. By the end of the sixteenth century, Moriscos litigating to be recognized as Old Christians included among their claims that they had never dressed in the Morisco style.[12] In 1583, when the Old Christians of Abanilla litigated with the Moriscos for the control of municipal offices, one of the defendants of the Moriscos deposed that "their behavior, dress, last will and testament, and every way of living match those of Old Christians."[13] Similarly, questionnaires for those Moriscos trying to stay in the Iberian Peninsula during the expulsion process usually included a question about their sartorial practices as proof of their assimilation with Old Christians.[14] We should be equally cautious about their declarations, since their opinions may not be less ideologically motivated than that of Old Christians. After all, said Moriscos were merely echoing the argument of sartorial assimilation without actually providing concrete evidence of their sartorial Castilianness or Christianity. My point here is rather to emphasize that their claims of sartorial assimilation were either rejected or accepted based on political circumstances or their ability to navigate the legal system, but never through a bona fide examination of their sartorial practices.

"Vile and Low People" (Lorca 1583)

As suggested in chapter 5, sartorial legislation against the Moriscos was constantly influenced by sumptuary laws, and the 1567 decree against the Moriscos wearing any garment made of silk did not target the wearing of "Morisco" traditional clothing (as is usually assumed), but was surreptitiously excluding them from the privilege of wearing luxurious garments. While I believe my analysis of the analogies between both discourses amply supports this interpretation, there is at least one legal case in which it is evident that just such a reading was made by early modern justices when applying sumptuary restrictions to the Moriscos.

In 1583, Jerónimo García, the *alguacil mayor* of Lorca (Murcia), entered the house of the Morisco butcher Miguel de Viamonte, where the latter's son, Diego de Viamonte, and María Muñoz were celebrating after they had been married in the church, and arrested both of them because the groom was wearing silk clothing and jewellery. The judge of the case, Dr Pedro de Zarandona, summarizes the case as "they being labourers cutting meat [i. e. butchers] and low and vile people, wear silk clothing against what has been stipulated in laws and decrees."[15] Zarandona's framing already contains the position of the prosecutor (and somehow announces his final sentencing against the Moriscos), as it does not specify what concrete law María Muñoz was supposed to be breaking by wearing silk garments: Was it the 1567 decree against "Morisco clothing"? Was it the general sumptuary laws prohibiting commoners from wearing luxurious clothing? Or was it both?

The defence attorney Andrés Jiménez tried to demonstrate that María Muñoz abided by both Philip II's 1567 decree against Morisco clothing and the usual sumptuary laws when he replied that their garments "were not only tailored ... conforming to that used by Old Christians and principal people, but conforming as well the Royal legislation of his Majesty."[16] Yet Jiménez made a grave mistake in his argumentation, which Jerónimo García did not miss the opportunity of magnifying in his response:

> because the other side acknowledges that those garments ... are the same used by principal people in this city, which are prohibited by law

> in these kingdoms to the other side, since she is the wife and daughter-in-law of butchers, which is the vilest profession in the world; besides, the aforementioned Diego de Viamonte and the aforementioned María Muñoz, who were Moriscos of those who rebelled against God and the Royal Majesty, and because of that they were disqualified [inhábiles] to wear silk clothing and other kinds of luxurious garments without explicit licence from his Majesty.[17]

Even if Jerónimo García shows an evident malfeasance against Diego de Viamonte and María de Muñoz, he is right in pointing to the weakest point of Viamonte's defence. García grasps Viamonte's comparison with the "gente principal" as the opportunity to emphasize that the Moriscos transgressed the broader sumptuary laws because they belonged to a lesser social category, both as butchers and as Moriscos.

Andrés Jiménez, probably aware of his mistake, dropped any reference to "gente principal" and rearticulated the defence by pointing out that "about the clothing and garments of the Moriscos from the Kingdom of Granada, his Majesty's laws and decrees only mandate that they use their clothing conforming to that of the Old Christians and that they not wear clothing tailored *a la morisca*."[18] He therefore insists on including the testimony of tailor examiners, who confirm that the clothing was not against the law.[19] But Jiménez could only offer a vague paraphrase of Philip II's 1567 decree against "Morisco clothing," because if he had cited the text closely, he would have found that it included a sentence prohibiting Moriscos from wearing "any clothing made of silk."[20]

Yet Jerónimo García did not lose his prey and insisted on reiterating the defence's previous slip that María Muñoz was dressing as "gente principal," as if the charge was about transgressing social boundaries – and the defendants' ethnicity the aggravating circumstance. Consequently, García asked his witnesses to confirm that Diego de Viamonte and María Muñoz were considered "vile" people as they belonged to the Moriscos deported from the Kingdom of Granada.[21]

In the defence's round of witnesses (in which he was careful to include three tailors), Andrés Jiménez made them focus on the defendants' young age, which was a proof that they could not possibly have participated in the Morisco uprising of 1569. But he also sharpened his line of argument by having his witnesses acknowledge that it was common in Lorca and other places for "miserable people" to borrow luxurious clothing for their weddings.[22] He thus tried to move his defence strategy to point out that, even if the defendants did not belong to the social groups allowed to wear luxurious clothing in everyday life, they behaved like any other Old Christian commoners when they borrowed lavish garments only momentarily for that important day.

Dr Zarandona's sentencing sided with Jerónimo García. He ordered the clothing to be confiscated (even if it did not belong to the accused) and made the Moriscos pay the trial costs.[23] As Zarandona does not justify his sentencing, there is no way of knowing whether he found Jiménez's defence unconvincing or whether he was already inclined to favour García's prosecution from the start. There was a tense relationship between Moriscos and Old Christians in Lorca, as it was a city located right on the frontier of the Kingdom of Granada and many deported Moriscos tried to stay there, hoping to one day return to their previous homeland.[24] This social tension may explain the harsh application of sumptuary laws to the Morisco couple, but the case makes clear how Philip II's 1567 decree could be read by any prosecutor in the Kingdom of Castile as a prohibition of Moriscos wearing luxurious clothing.

Andrés Jiménez appealed to the Royal Chancery of Granada, which finally ordered the *corregidor* of Lorca to liberate Diego de Viamonte and María Muñoz and return them their confiscated goods.[25] Even though this case ends relatively favourably for the Moriscos, the interference between the 1567 decree against "Morisco clothing" and the larger frame of early modern sumptuary laws is telling. The prosecutor Jerónimo García felt at ease moving between two different legal codes because the 1567 decree against the Moriscos already confounded culture and social privilege. Even Viamonte's defenders did not try to present him and his wife as individuals worthy of wearing silk, but only remarked that there were exceptional circumstances in which every commoner in the Kingdom of Castile could bypass sumptuary restrictions for weddings – especially when they were merely borrowing such luxurious garments for the event. Therefore, the defendants' side did not contradict García's reading that the 1567 decree against "Morisco customs" was indeed a sumptuary law targeting all Moriscos as unworthy of wearing luxurious clothing. Their silence amounts to an implicit acquiescence with García's main argument (or at least shows the defence's inability to refute it), which indicates that this was a common or at least a possible reading.

Such a reading was also in agreement with moralist thought on Morisco clothing. As seen in chapter 5, when Hernando de Talavera ordered the Moriscos of Granada to dress like "good and honest Christians," he was actually trying to impose on them the codes of sartorial modesty that he was unable to impose on his fellow Old Christians. Similarly, and writing shortly after this case in Lorca, Pedro Guerra de Lorca defends the prohibition of Arabic language and Morisco clothing in his *Cathecheses mystagogicae pro aduenis ex secta Mahometana* (1586) [Cathecisms of Instruction for those Coming from the Mohammedan Sect].[26] In comparison with other sources, Guerra de Lorca gives very detailed descriptions of what kind of clothing said Moriscos allegedly wore. However, its descriptive value is undermined by his desire to construe their clothing as both a way of performing their Islamic rituals and of giving in more easily to their sexual appetites.

His polemical position is clearly revealed when he deals with the alternative Christian garments that Moriscos should wear instead. This time his writing becomes extremely metaphorical. First, he praises those Moriscos who "swearing the words in baptism, have renounced Satan and his works and have put on the white garments of Christ"; later, he comments that the goal of the decrees prohibiting Morisco clothing was to "take off the old wolf skin together with the Muhammadan religion and put on the sheep skin."[27] Obviously, no one would read "garments of Christ" or "sheep skin" as accurate technical descriptions of how Old Christians dressed in early modern Iberia. As Cándida Ferrero Hernández points out, Guerra de Lorca conceives that, while Muslims used clothing as a form of distinction, Christians merely wore clothing out of necessity.[28] It would be hard to find any society in the history of humankind for which wearing clothing was only a matter of necessity, but early modern Iberia was most certainly not that unique society. Thus the clothing of the Moriscos – even if we assume that some of them had distinctive clothing – is not pitted against the heterogeneous sartorial reality of early modern Iberia, but against a vague idealization of sartorial modesty that was nowhere to be found in Iberian society.

Situational Approaches: Magacela and Ricote

One of the most telling cases of the arbitrariness of local interpretations of "Morisco" clothing is the trial against the Moriscos in Magacela (Extremadura) that took place near the end of the sixteenth century. When Fray Alonso Flórez, Prior of Magacela, initiated a campaign against the local Moriscos in 1595, he claimed, among other charges, that

> because it is evident in our eyes that the women of this town wear clothing
> and dresses in the style of the Arabic women, even though they have

been reprimanded by us in the pulpit and elsewhere and we have fined them for wearing the aforementioned dresses unless they wear the same clothing worn by women in the other neighbouring places of this Priorate of Magacela, and because there is no reason that there should be memory of such dresses where they are so abhorred. Therefore, we order that no women in this town, of any status or quality, wear the old dresses, but that they wear them like the other women in neighbouring places.[29]

Even if several witnesses confirmed the prior's opinion, their statements are too similar, suggesting that they had been prepared and agreed upon in advance.[30]

The Morisco response did not deny per se the sartorial difference alleged by the prior and his witnesses. During the trial, Alonso Delgado Calderón, councilman of Magacela, requested on 22 November 1595, that the ordinance issued by the pior be lifted, arguing that:

wearing shorter or longer dress is custom of the land, and not rite or ceremony; hence you will deduce that all the rich and principal men's wives in the aforementioned town wear long and lavish tunics, as they can, and that it is no wonder that the poor people's wives wear shorter dresses, since you know that the poor in this town are poorer than in other towns, because there is no trade in which the peasant can make his living.[31]

Delgado Calderón did not question difference, but disagreed with the prior on how to interpret it, arguing instead that the observable difference that the Prior of Magacela attributed to ethno-religious identity could in fact be explained by the socio-economic status of the Morisco community. Fernando Ballesteros, acting as representative of the township of Magacela, requested the trial's nullification on 2 July 1597, alleging that the prior had an economic interest in his accusation, and that all the inhabitants of the town were in fact Old Christians.[32] There is no further documentation on the issue and there is no way of knowing what the royal administration finally decided about how to proceed with the Moriscos of Magacela, who were included in the general expulsion in 1611, sixteen years later.[33]

Since we only have the words of Alonso Flórez and Delgado Calderón, it is impossible to determine whose perception of the Morisco sartorial practices was more accurate.[34] Yet the case of Magacela is emblematic of how sartorial difference could be enunciated and contested, and it clearly indicates how the materiality and the visuality of sartorial practices were not absolute, but mediated by discourse, and therefore subject to negotiation and interpretation.

A situational approach as we have seen for Magacela, although not common, was adopted by other early modern authors as well. Like Magacela, the Valley of Ricote in Murcia was a land densely populated by Moriscos.[35] In spite of their early conversion to Christianity and their integration with the Old Christians, occasional conflict arose. In 1611, Philip III ordered the expulsion of the *mudéjares* from Murcia, who had been exempted in previous decrees. The enforcement of the order was delayed due to local opposition, which claimed that the Moriscos of Murcia had been Christian for generations and therefore should not be included in the general expulsion. In January of 1610, Luis Fajardo wrote to the monarch arguing that in many villages the Moriscos of Murcia could not be differentiated in their clothing from the Old Christians, but he set apart the Moriscos of the Ricote Valley, who formed compact communities.[36] In 1611, Fajardo argued that the Moriscos of the Ricote Valley still kept their old clothing.[37]

In 1612, Fray Luis de Pereda was sent to investigate the situation. Even if Philip III eventually confirmed the expulsion of the Moriscos of the Valley of Ricote in 1614, Pereda's report is still very useful because he spells out very clearly his methodology for investigating difference by raising questions in a different way. He elaborated an incisive report that underlined that the Moriscos of Murcia were not different from Old Christians, and that voices clamouring for their expulsion were generally motivated by material interest or personal animosity.[38] Pereda nullified several of the depositions against them when it was clear that certain individuals testified in agreement.[39] He was therefore aware that the perception of the Moriscos had more to do with the creation and dissemination of public opinion than with the actual observable features as a separate community.

As Pereda makes clear in an appendix to his report, one of his guiding questions was "whether … in their dress and clothing they are similar to the other Moriscos or whether they are regarded as different from them."[40] Yet his only allusion to clothing is found at the beginning of the report, when he summarizes that, according to all witnesses "no one has ever dressed in the Morisco style."[41] He concludes that the Moriscos of Murcia differed in everything from the Moriscos of Granada, Valencia, and Aragon, but also that there was no observable difference between them and Old Christians living in the same area.[42] While the references to clothing are scant, we can infer that he adopted the same situational approach that he followed for his linguistic characterization of the Moriscos. According to Pereda, the only difference to which some witnesses alluded was the Moriscos' particular accent. However, Pereda is quick to add the testimony of other witnesses, who inform him that such an accent is a linguistic particularity that is not specific to the Moriscos, but general across the social spectrum in Murcia.[43]

The issue here is not whether these Moriscos had a particular accent (which from the perspective of the outside reporter would prove that they lived as a separate community), but whether they had the same accent as the rest of the Old Christians in Murcia (which would prove that they were well integrated in their local community). Pereda's anecdotal style, by means of which he makes sense of the Moriscos' accent, proves that he was aware of the discretional observation of difference that was usually applied to determine the "assimilation" of Morisco communities. Pereda's approach entailed a relational methodology substantially different from that of most of his contemporaries: instead of asking whether the Moriscos looked different without specifying the terms for the comparison, he inquired about perceptions of similarities within very specific local contexts. Later he contrasted those opinions with his own observations of both the Moriscos and their local environment. Thus he implicitly recognized the variability of cultural differences among different local communities and circumvented the biased sartorial perception of Morisco bodies. Even if Delgado Calderón's defence of the Moriscos of Magacela and Pereda's report about assimilation of the Moriscos of Murcia did not influence the authorities' decision to expel them, their relational approach serves as contrast to the contemporary decontextualized essentialization of other gazes that were looking for the Morisco difference.

Now You See It, Now You Don't: The Intermittent Sartorial Difference of the Moriscos of Orihuela

There is some uncertainty and contradictory information about the sartorial practices of the Moriscos in the Kingdom of Valencia, one of the areas most densely populated by Moriscos. For instance, Juan Luis de Rojas states in his *Relaciones de algunos sucesos postreros de Berbería, salida de los Moriscos de España y entrega de Larache* (1613) that the Moriscos of Valencia remained in the land "dressing almost in our way."[44] The author does not clarify the *almost* that qualifies the sartorial similarity or specificity of the Valencian Moriscos, and such indeterminacy suggests that their alleged sartorial difference is invisible to some and extremely evident to others.

In 1528, after the forced conversion of the Moriscos in the Crown of Aragon, Charles V conceded several privileges to the Moriscos of Valencia, among them the use of their traditional clothing for ten years: "since the aforementioned Moors have Morisco attire, which is very different from Christian clothing, most notably for women, and for them it would be very inconvenient to change it."[45] In the instructions issued by Antonio Ramírez de Haro, bishop of Ciudad Rodrigo, in 1540 (reprinted in 1566 and 1594), he ordered the Moriscos, both male and female, not to dress as Moors.[46] However, as Rafael Benítez Sánchez-Blanco suggests, it is not clear whether these instructions were modelled after the decrees of Granada, thus including issues that might not have been relevant for Valencia.[47]

By the late 1580s, Philip II had organized a Junta in Madrid to deal with the evangelization of the Moriscos of Valencia. Juan de Ribera, archbishop of Valencia, made a list of the alleged cultural traces that Moriscos preserved from their old religion, among which he suggested that "it should be mandated that New Christians could not be tailors, and that Old Christians could only make clothing in our way, and if deemed convenient to take away their clothing, it would be better to decree a short term [for the change]." Yet he concludes that "there is not much to worry about this issue, since this is not one of the things in which they are resistant."[48] Ribera's opinion is significant because he was not precisely a defender of the Moriscos, since he had already proposed their expulsion in 1582 and would be one of the most ardent promoters of such measures in subsequent years.[49] The issue is taken up again on 28 August 1587, by the Junta of Madrid, which, following Ribera's opinion, did not find the issue of clothing an urgent matter and explicitly stated that the sartorial difference between Old Christians and Moriscos was minimal:

> Morisco clothing is not used by men, at least not as it was used in the past, rather they dress in the same way as the other people in the Kingdom of Valencia, except that they wear their tunics in a certain way and with longer skirts, and the same with cloaks. But this will be very easy to remedy, by instructing the tailors in places with new converts that they should not differentiate their dress and clothing from that of the Old Christians; and about women, only a few of them use Morisco dress, and it would be solved by denying them some of the jewels that they wear and the use of henna to dye their nails and arms, and that they not wear turbans.[50]

Another Junta of 1591 ratified the decisions made by the Juntas of Madrid and Valencia, and concluded that "their clothing was not very different from that used in the kingdom, although [it was resolved] that tailors should be advised not to make them clothing in the Morisco way, but only clothing and dress in the way used in the kingdom."[51] While this document emphasizes that the Moriscos of the Kingdom of Valencia did not dress differently than Old Christians, it repeats the mandate that Old Christian tailors did not make Morisco clothing. Yet in this case it introduces a small but significant specification: while in 1587 the archbishop of Valencia suggested that tailors not make Morisco clothing *at all*, the Juntas of 1587 and 1591 recommend that tailors not make Morisco clothing *for* the Moriscos. Arguably, this small variant in the wording of the document would allow Old Christian tailors to keep making clothing *a la morisca* for Old Christians.

It is important to note that these texts were working documents that never made it into a formal legal edict, in contrast to Philip II's 1567 decree prohibiting Morisco customs. Indeed, the next draft of the document made by these Juntas retakes all the religious, cultural, and economic aspects under discussion but suddenly drops the issue of clothing, arguably because it was simply regarded as irrelevant.[52] The interpretation to be gleaned from the debates of the Juntas of Madrid and Valencia in the late 1580s and early 1590s is twofold: on the one hand, it seems to confirm that Moriscos were not perceived as dressing differently from Old Christians in the Kingdom of Valencia; on the other hand, and more important, it reveals that the legal tradition regarding the Moriscos had crystallized by accumulation throughout the sixteenth century. Previous legislation thus conditions the discussion of the same issues even when dealing with very different Morisco communities throughout the Iberian Peninsula and even when these issues might not be relevant to all of them.

Yet, even if the Juntas of 1587 and 1591 concluded that the Moriscos of the Kingdom of Valencia did not dress differently, there was a marginal note about the Moriscos of Orihuela – which I have purposely left aside in my previous exposition:

> the regent in Valencia reported ... that in the bishopric of Orihuela there were many women who wore short *almalafas* and twisted hoses and other things of Moorish dress, ... it has been resolved that those garments should be taken from those who wore them, since it is so recognizable a Moorish dress. And it is understood that they only wear this clothing in the bishopric of Orihuela.[53]

Was Orihuela unique within the Kingdom of Valencia?[54] The Moriscos of the bishopric of Orihuela comprised about 30 per cent of the population and in some places formed compact communities. However, this demographic situation was not different from adjacent areas in Valencia and Murcia, in which the Moriscos were not conceived of as dressing differently from Old Christians. While we cannot conclusively discard the possibility that the Moriscas in this area did indeed wear distinct attire, we should consider how the isolated insistence on the alleged visibility of their difference could have been conditioned by the political circumstances under which the bishopric of Orihuela was created.

The bishopric of Orihuela was created in 1564, when it was separated out from the bishopric of Cartagena after a litigation that had lasted for centuries. Against the resistance of the authorities of Murcia, the supporters of the partition soon found that the most productive argument for their cause was to claim that such ecclesiastical administrative restructuring would allow for better control of the Moriscos in the area of Orihuela.[55] In response to this argument, the supporters of Cartagena's continued authority argued that they had been actively controlling the Moriscos in the south of Valencia. To prove this, they referred to the 1555 visit there of Esteban de Almeida, bishop of Cartagena when Orihuela still comprised part of the bishopric of Cartagena, and his issuance of several ordinances for the Moriscos, including the prohibition of wearing clothing *a la morisca* and the order to dress like Old Christians instead.[56] It is hard to gauge the real repercussions of these ordinances (if there were any), since we know of their existence only because they were copied in the litigation made by the bishopric of Cartagena to prevent the secession of Orihuela. Thus, both Cartagena and Orihuela built their arguments on their respective effective vigilance over the Moriscos, even if the real issue at stake was control of the ecclesiastical revenue between the kingdoms of Valencia and Murcia.

Philip II finally conceded to Orihuela's demands in 1564, but the newly designated bishop of Orihuela, Gregorio Gallo, could not take office until 1566. We might even wonder if the participants in these negotiations between Murcia and Orihuela learned how to make strategic use of the rhetoric of controlling Morisco bodies in order to redesign unruly political landscapes. It does not seem to be a coincidence that most of the supporters of Orihuela's claim (Gregorio Gallo, the Duke of Alba, Bernardo de Bolea, and Judge Velasco) were also included in the Junta of Madrid of 1566 that prepared the edict prohibiting Morisco cultural practices in Granada.

Even as the defenders of the bishopric of Orihuela's creation clamoured so vehemently for the need to control the Moriscos in their area, no real action seems to have taken place for decades after they reached their objective of gaining independence from Cartagena – or they were at least not immediately concerned about clothing. The bishop of Orihuela, Tomás Dassio Albats, published some ordinances on the Moriscos around 1580 that do not include any reference to clothing.[57] Yet, as we have seen, in 1587 the Junta of Madrid suddenly received a report on the Moriscos of Orihuela dressing differently. In 1595, the next bishop of Orihuela, Josep Esteve (or José Esteban, as he used to Castilianize his name), wrote to Philip II confirming the alleged sartorial differentiation of the Moriscas in his diocese but at the same time contextualized and diminished its significance:

> removing their dress is a very easy matter, and essential so that they forget their barbarous customs, and thus, it would be necessary to ban them from taking clothing *a la morisca* from their parents and wearing it with the ceremony and solemnity they use in their weddings, and that in their letters of marriage they do not mention Morisco style clothing or jewelry, nor that they bequeath in their wills clothing with the aforementioned name and dress.[58]

Thus Josep Esteve acknowledged that the use of clothing *a la morisca* among the Moriscos was limited to a few specific ritual instances such as weddings. He even suggested that the polemic was a nominal issue, since what he finally proposed was to prevent the Moriscos from certain speech acts about garments in specific contexts, and not just the clothing itself. Esteve's relatively compromising approach to clothing did not show any sympathy for the Moriscos, since he ended up recommending their expulsion should these and other proposed measures failed.[59]

In spite of his initial position on the subject, five years later Josep Esteve suddenly started to worry about the sartorial difference of the Moriscos in his diocese. He sent a letter to a council convened on 5 January 1600, warning that, according to some reports, many women in Petrel and Elda, who had previously abandoned Morisco dress, were now wearing it again.[60] Morisco clothing was thus conceived as an endemic disease that could be momentarily controlled but was prone to reappear as soon as religious and civil authorities lost their grip on the

Moriscos. This time Esteve took a peculiar approach, requesting that the Moriscos in several places in his diocese sign notarized agreements promising to transform their garments by either enlarging or narrowing them.[61] In the 1600 Synod of Orihuela and in a letter addressed to Rome in 1601, Esteve stated that he had successfully convinced the Moriscos to abandon their traditional clothing.[62] The sudden switch between the denunciation of sartorial difference and the triumphal statements about its fast and effective repression, along with the insistence on producing an administrative paper trail, suggest that Josep Esteve was strategically using Morisco bodies to cement his own political persona.

Josep Esteve died in 1603, but the logic of capitalizing on the sartorial difference of the Moriscos of Orihuela had already taken on a life of its own. Even if Esteve stated that the Moriscos of Orihuela had been assimilated, only a few years later another document reported otherwise, but also suggested new and unexpected developments. In 1606, the next bishop of Orihuela, Andrés Balaguer, reported to Philip III that, during his pastoral visit to the Moriscos, he found out about his predecessor making them promise to abandon their traditional clothing in 1600: "All the New Christians renounced clothing and jewelry made in the Morisco style, swearing before public notaries to conform in everything and by everything with the virtuous clothing of Old Christians."[63] However, Balaguer adds, even though the Moriscos initially adopted Old Christian garb, this vigilance relaxed after Josep Esteve's death and, since then "they have invented and invent everyday new clothing, [which is] not entirely like the old, but very different from the use of Old Christians, notably women, [who] try to differentiate themselves as much as they can from Old Christian women."[64] Balaguer's letter reveals close but biased scrutiny of the sartorial practices of Morisco communities: any innovation in dress is considered not in tandem with the natural change in fashion characteristic of early modern Iberian society, but as another proof of an almost biological attachment to Islam. It illustrates the hermeneutical loop by which Morisco sartorial practices are viewed through the immanent, ahistorical perception of Moorish clothing, but at the same time, any innovation is interpreted as a divergence from an equally static concept of Christian clothing.

This extremely intermittent perceptibility of the ethnic sartorial difference of the Moriscos of Orihuela may be dictated by the circumstances under which this bishopric was formed and how it sought to maintain its jurisdiction, as analysed above. As Antonio Carrasco Rodríguez points out, all references to the Moriscos as an issue were made by the ecclesiastical authorities of Orihuela only in the documents that were addressed directly to the monarch, while in their internal documents they rarely considered the Moriscos their most urgent matter.[65] Thus, since the newly formed bishopric of Orihuela was created with the justification of controlling its own Morisco population, they were in a difficult balancing act, between construing the Moriscos as an obstinate community in religious and cultural terms and simultaneously demonstrating that their pastoral power could repress such resistance and bring the Moriscos into the fold. The way the sartorial difference of the Moriscos of Orihuela is imagined, forgotten, and re-imagined between the end of the sixteenth century and the beginning of the seventeenth suggests that the alleged visibility of Morisco bodies becomes meaningful only within the very specific political and local context of the formation of its bishopric.

As this chapter demonstrates, the alleged sartorial difference of the Moriscos needs to be contextualized within both the larger frame of social discourses like sumptuary laws and the circumstances of the socio-political dynamic of each locale. Otherwise, we run the risk of abstracting local conflicts involving Moriscos and Old Christians as manifestations of a cultural and religious conflict, without considering that there might be other reasons for some of the instances in which the Moriscos are seen as dressing differently. As David Nirenberg argues, xenophobia alone does not explain outbreaks of ethno-religious violence and exclusion, but certain material conditions need to be met in order for xenophobic discourse to be politically meaningful and to encompass racial and ethnocentric policies.[66] The case of Lorca reveals how Philip II's 1567 decree against Morisco customs was indeed read as a ban stripping from them the right to wear luxurious clothing, while the cases of Magacela and Murcia illustrate how being "seen" as dressing as "Morisco" could disqualify one local group from participating in local government or from defending their right to be exempted from the expulsion of 1609–14. Meanwhile, the case of Orihuela reveals how Morisco difference was manipulated to justify the administrative ecclesiastical restructuring of the newly created diocese, to build an authority not only over Moriscos, but also and primarily vis-à-vis the royal court and ecclesiastical institutions. These disparate instances of social and political instrumentalization of the alleged sartorial difference of the Moriscos show that the perception of Morisco bodies as essentially different is not merely a product of xenophobia (although it is also undoubtedly that), but that their sartorial difference, real or imagined, was relevant because it could be employed as well to satisfy a wide variety of social needs.

7 Moriscos Performing as Moors

The sartorial equivalence between Moriscos and Old Christians is most visible in public performances in which Moriscos dressed up as Moors. Such a formulation may sound paradoxical within the persistent paradigm of imagining Moriscos in Moorish garb, yet the documented instances of Moriscos passing as Moors indicate that they did not wear Moorish clothing on a daily basis – or at the very least that Moorish clothing was not the same as "Morisco" dress, even if legal texts used the ambiguous phrase *hábito de moros* which could comprise both the Moorish costumes worn in the game of canes and those garments that might be identified as being specific to Moriscos. More important, these instances prove that Moriscos may have perceived in Moorish clothing not an element of cultural identity, as traditionally argued, but an opportunity for social advancement – that is, they conceived of Moorish clothing the same way as their Old Christian counterparts.

Inventorying Morisco Wardrobes

One of the richest sources for the analysis of so-called Morisco clothing has been the study of inventories found in Morisco wardrobes, dowries, wills, and sequestered goods. While the historiographical value of these documents is undeniable, their analysis should be reassessed. The model for such approaches is the influential article by Juan Martínez Ruiz, who, by studying the inventories of property sequestered from the Moriscos between 1549 and 1568, arrived at the conclusion that Pérez de Hita's literary description of the Moorish knights in fifteenth-century Granada perfectly matched the garments actually worn by sixteenth-century Moriscos.[1] Even if subsequent historians analysing inventories have been careful not to make such an extreme claim, they have nonetheless used them to demonstrate the alleged sartorial difference between Moriscos and Old Christians.[2] There is, however, a series of methodological issues with these approaches.

First, there has been no comparison with inventories of Old Christian wardrobes. Indeed, it would be nearly impossible to compare the proportion of "Morisco" clothing among Moriscos and Old Christians. Most of the inventories of Morisco clothing were made under dramatic and exceptional circumstances, in which an entire community was being persecuted, and, as in the case of Granada, suddenly deported and expropriated of their households. Therefore, objects that would not normally surface in documentation do so very suddenly. There is simply no parallel event in which the properties of an entire Old Christian community were suddenly brought to light, but only piecemeal documentation in the form of notarial inventories in which this or that family passed on their wealth through dowry or final will.[3]

My second objection is terminological. Very often, scholars assume that clothing labelled as "Morisco" and clothing owned or made by Moriscos are equivalent. However, as we have seen throughout, when the adjective "Morisco" was applied to clothing, it referred to a certain quality of garments, and does not necessarily imply that they belonged to Moriscos or that they were made by them. Even if we accept the premise that Moriscos had more garments labelled as "Morisco" than Old Christians did in their wardrobes, the fact that their clothing was found in inventories of Old Christian individuals reveals that they were coveted objects in Iberian society at large. For instance, in 1569 Christian soldiers entered a house in Lanjarón and discovered a storage area full of Morisco clothing. Witness Jerónimo de León describes how the soldiers fought among themselves about how to divide the loot.[4]

This cultural attraction is also evident during the expulsion of 1609–14. Damián Fonseca recounts in his *Relación de la expulsión de los Moriscos del reino de Valencia* (1612) that, during their final expulsion, the Moriscos of Valencia, unable to take their belongings with them, had to sell off clothing *a la morisca* very cheaply before they could embark.[5] Since Fonseca never tries to emphasize a sartorial difference in the Moriscos, we can assume that in this context *a la morisca* does not necessarily mean a particular Morisco dress, but only that it was lavish clothing. More important, he acknowledges that these garments *a la morisca* were to be transferred to Old Christian ownership without contradicting the logic of cultural and genealogical cleansing that lies behind the expulsion. If clothing made *a la morisca* were perceived per se as an unmistakable attachment to Islamism, it would not be an object of Old Christian desire.

The last and most important methodological objection is that, even when the study of these inventories proves beyond doubt that some Moriscos stored clothing labelled as "Morisco," it does not automatically mean that "Morisco clothing" was the same as the Moriscos' daily wear. As Ulinka Rublack points out, while inventories are excellent sources for understanding how clothing was registered as property, they usually offer very limited information on how clothing was actually used.[6] In many instances, the clothing found in inventories was not stored to be worn, but was, rather, conceived of as a form of capital, as luxurious clothing was often kept as such.[7] Núñez Muley indicated this specific use when he noted in his memorandum that by 1567 the Moriscos (at least men, and many women as well) were dressing in the Castilian manner, with one exception that in his opinion did not count as cultural difference because it was not daily wear: "Here I am not speaking of garments that are worn for weddings and celebrations, because those are kept stored for such occasions, and they are passed down for three or four generations so that they might be enjoyed and made use of at those times, or so that they might be sold or pawned should the need arise."[8] The bishop of Orihuela, Josep Esteve, confirms Núñez Muley's observation when he writes in 1595 informing Philip II that the daily wear of the Moriscas in his diocese was not really an issue, but only those garments that were bequeathed in dowries and last wills.[9]

Núñez Muley also reveals that those garments labelled "Morisco" were not conceived of as daily wear by the Moriscos. In spite of all the alleged significance of clothing in all kinds of documents produced by the monarchy and the Church, the Inquisition did not persecute the use of specific daily clothing as an Islamic practice, but only when they were related to specific rituals, such as as weddings and funerals or changing clothing on Fridays instead of Sunday, regardless of the specific garments used.[10] Thus Moriscos wore both Castilian and "Morisco" clothing (as far as such a divide is even possible) for different occasions, much like their Old Christian counterparts differentiated between daily wear and clothing *a la morisca*. The existence of "Morisco" clothing in the inventories of Moriscos is not necessarily proof that they were crypto-Muslims – nor does its absence make them Christian believers – but could be read instead as a sign of their profound integration into

Iberian society. Moriscos and Old Christians might have differed only in the specific ritual contexts in which they wore them.

To further emphasize the potential similarity between both communities, we should consider that, besides the ritual uses Núñez Muley and Josep Esteve mention, the Moriscos may have stored Morisco clothing for performative purposes in public festivals –and that therefore Moriscos treated "Morisco clothing" as some sort of costume. In spite of the intermittent prohibitions against "Morisco clothing" analysed herein, local authorities constantly encouraged Moriscos to participate in Moorish garb in a wide range of public performances. As I will show in this chapter, however, there were very clear limits on the kinds of Moorishness they were allowed to perform. Most often, they were invited to act as musicians in Moorish garb, but one can find them as well in military demonstrations requiring the use of Moorish clothing – they were mentioned only rarely as participating in the most prestigious form of the game of canes.

These limits, real or imaginary, become clear in two texts referring to the Moriscos. Pedro Aznar Cardona, when describing the festivals of the Moriscos in his apologetic treatise *Expulsión justificada de los Moriscos Españoles* (1612), holds that they were

> above all very fond (and hence they commonly had bagpipes, rattles, and flutes) of ballets, dances ... and all kinds of bestial entertainments, in which with unruly noise and yelling, the young villagers used to go shouting in the streets. They bragged about being good dancers ... and their songs, and bullfights, and other similar performances that are proper to commoners.[11]

While Aznar Cardona's polemical approach does not allow us to consider his an objective description of what the usual entertainment among the Moriscos was, this passage is quite telling of the cultural and social space reserved for them in the Iberian imaginary. Contrary to the game of canes, which was regarded as ceremonial space for the display of aristocratic status, dances and bullfights were considered the space of commoners.[12] Implicit in Aznar Cardona's text is the image of a rustic community unsuitable for Moorish aristocratic culture.

The inability to imagine the Moriscos as participating in the most aristocratic forms of Moorishness is found even in texts considered to be more sympathetic towards them. This is the case of the second part of Ginés Pérez de Hita's *Guerras civiles de Granada* (1619), which recounts the Morisco festivals organized by Aben Humeya in Purchena during the War of the Alpujarras. Pérez de Hita, who obviously could not have been in Purchena with the rebellious Moriscos, does not make clear what his sources are for this scene, which is likely a product of hearsay or his own imagination. After having Aben Humeya outline all the sports, music, and dances to be held during the celebrations, the narrator focuses on what the Moriscos could not do: "and all these diverse games were ordered by the little king, because they had no means to organize bullfights and they had neither horses nor equestrian gear for the game of canes."[13]

Precisely because such poetic interludes were common early modern historiographical conventions, there is something striking in the remark about the festival's scarcity, especially when we take into account that in the first part of the *Guerras civiles de Granada*, Pérez de Hita had recounted the celebration of grandiose games of canes at length in the fifteenth-century Nasrid Kingdom. Arguably, mentioning the lack of horses in this case further emphasizes the precarious situation of the rebellious Moriscos. While this artificial passage is hardly useful for reconstructing the culture of the Moriscos, it is very indicative of how Old Christians imagined Morisco cultural difference and the place of Moorishness within it. By introducing such a realistic note in a passage that is probably fictional in its entirety, Pérez de Hita kept any potential similarity between the rebellious Moriscos and Old Christian nobles at bay. As shown in the first part of this book, in the early modern Iberian imaginary, the Old Christian nobility inhabited Moorishness as an equestrian aristocratic exercise. Meanwhile, the Moriscos were only allowed to imitate Moors in other types of performances that were associated with commoners. This imaginary corresponded largely to reality, as the Moriscos were theoretically prohibited from engaging in military performances. Yet there is evidence that the Moriscos tried to achieve some degree of social recognition through the adoption of Moorishness in public performances as a loophole through which to resist their increasing social marginalization.

The *Zambra* as Folkloric Performance

The most common and least polemical opportunity for the Moriscos to participate in public exhibitions of Moorishness was when they engaged in dance and music performances known as *zambras*.[14] While references to *zambras* are ubiquitous in festival books, legal documents, and literary texts, there are no detailed descriptions of this musical performance. At best, we have two well-known visual documents reproducing what seems to be the *zambra*: Christoph Weiditz's drawing of Morisco performers from Granada circa 1529 (Figure 15) and Vicent Mestre's painting of the expulsion of the Moriscos through the port of Denia in 1613, which specifically includes a detail of Morisco musicians and dancers (Figure 16).

Zambras were not perceived to be the most immediate concern by religious and royal authorities at the beginning of the sixteenth century. They were not included in Charles V's attempt to prohibit Morisco cultural practices, and in the 1530s, Queen Isabel of Portugal defended the use of *zambras* against the archbishop of Granada, Gaspar de Ávalos, as long as they did not include references to Islam.[15] The 1554 Synod of Guadix merely recommended supervision of Morisco dances and music without necessarily forbidding them,[16] and *zambras* were only formally prohibited with Philip II's decree in 1567, which banned them regardless of their content.[17] During the 1570s, several Moriscos appeared in the *autos de fe* accused of dancing and singing in Arabic, most often for wedding celebrations.[18]

In spite of sporadic persecution against the celebration of *zambras* when they were performed as part of certain rituals, such as weddings, Morisco musicians were routinely hired by Christian authorities to perform publicly throughout the Iberian Peninsula, both before and after the uprising of the Alpujarras. *Zambras* were included in many religious and civil festivals in the Kingdom of Granada during the sixteenth century, as documented for Baza in 1495 and 1524, Málaga in 1535, and Huéscar in 1563.[19] Between the 1570s and the early seventeenth century, the Moriscos deported from Granada were often hired to organize ballets for Corpus Christi throughout Castile.[20] In preparation for the entry of Philip III in 1600, the Council of Valladolid ordered both *mudéjares* and the Moriscos exiled from Granada to perform "a dance as sumptuous and pleasing as possible."[21]

In many instances, the *zambras* were intended as a complement for the game of canes, as happened in Baza (Granada) during the 1520s and 1530s,[22] in Mazarrón (Murcia) in 1572,[23] and in Mula (Murcia) in 1601.[24] There is much less information about the music for the game of canes because both festival books and municipal records focused on clothing as the central element of the organization, while the presence of musicians was usually acknowledged only in passing. Maurophile literature indirectly confirms the connection between the game of canes and *zambras* in Moorish performances organized by Old Christians, since they are often mentioned together in the fanciful recreations of fifteenth-century Granada, most notably in the Moorish ballads composed at the end of the sixteenth century and in the first part of Ginés Pérez de Hita's *Guerras civiles de Granada* (1595).[25] Thus the satirical ballad "Tanta Zaida y Adalifa" (c. 1593) asks Parnassus to ban *zambras*,[26] and Gabriel Lobo Lasso de la Vega's "Poetas a lo moderno" (1601) chastises the composers of Moorish ballads as "inventores de las zambras" [cultivators of *zambras*].[27]

However, it is not clear whether the *zambra* required specific clothing. In a 1535 lawsuit we find references to a Morisco of Serón (Almería) usually playing *zambras* dressed in ridiculous festive garments.[28] In many other cases, the Moriscos were described as wearing Moorish clothing, as can be seen clearly in a performance taking place in Valladolid in 1601, in which the Marquis of Mondéjar organized a parade with "forty Moriscos on foot in Moorish dress, with rattles and tambourines and a cart with lutes and other instruments, and he went to the Palace with them and in the square they performed the *zambra* in the Morisco style, which was pleasant to many people."[29] The Belgian traveller Barthélemy Joly states that, during his stay in Gandía in 1604, the Abbot of the Cistercian Order requested that the Moriscos dance "à la morisque," and he describes how they performed with their instruments and colourful clothing and adornments.[30] In nearby Aspe (Alicante), one private letter written in 1609 praises the local festival of Corpus Christi, singling out the gallantry of the clothing with which the Moriscos used to perform.[31]

Even if we should not be too deterministic in relating mentions of the *zambras* and Moriscos – not all *zambreros* were necessarily Moriscos – there is evidence that organizers of urban festivals often looked for professionalized Morisco performers to participate as musicians.[32] All these instances show how Moriscos were regularly asked to perform a certain specific form of Moorishness. Contrary to the game of canes, in which Christians were almost the sole practitioners from at least the fall of Granada in 1492, the *zambra* was the "Moorish" performance to which Moriscos were usually confined. We can imagine that, when asked to perform, Moriscos quite probably catered to the expectations of Old Christian patrons, adopting the techniques of Moorishness as crafted by the Christian literary and ceremonial imagination. At the very least, we must acknowledge that the garments Moriscos used to perform could not be their daily wear, a common sous-entendu in the scholarship, which often uses the descriptions of Morisco performances to analyse everyday sartorial practices. This biased ethnographic approach conflating performative contexts with daily life may also underlie the perception of Moriscos' clothing as exotic, colourful, and full of adornments that permeates early modern texts. As their most visible social presence came through these Moorish performances, passing observers may have been led to believe that their performative garb corresponded to their actual quotidian sartorial practices – or, even if aware of the difference, the interests of such observers might have been served by conflating both contexts.[33] Such implicit equivalence constitutes a methodological error that is tantamount to saying that, based on the documents analysed in the first part of this book, Old Christians dressed as Moors on a daily basis – indeed, if we compare the documented instances in which both Old Christians and Moriscos dressed up as Moors, we must conclude that Moorishness was by far more an attribute of the former rather than the latter. Yet this professionalization of Morisco musicians also shows the difficult position of Moriscos within early modern Iberian society, as their participation in urban festivals increased the social visibility of their community but also reinforced the Old Christian imaginary of cultural difference.

Military Exhibitions

While the participation of the Moriscos in games of canes was regarded with suspicion and their only acceptable inclusion in urban festivals was as musicians and dancers, there were other instances in which Moriscos managed to participate in military demonstrations – most commonly known as *alardes* but also *escaramuzas* or *zuizas*. Theoretically, Moriscos were persistently forbidden from carrying arms, yet many of them throughout the Iberian Peninsula participated in military demonstrations and enlisted in the army.[34]

In the first part of this book, I focused on the use of Moorish clothing for the game of canes and looked into other kinds of military exercises only tangentially. Yet many military performances often required the use of Moorish clothing as well. While the game of canes was a proper festival (even if usually justified as a martial exercise), the *alardes* were primarily intended as military exercises, and yet the boundaries between the formal military exercise and the public festival were not always clear. Arguably, both organizers and participants understood that Moorishness and military exercise complemented each other as signs of social standing. This explains why, in many instances, both sides of mock battles dressed up as Moors, as in Jan Cornelisz Vermeyen's drawing of a military exercise that, as Horn suggests, was probably held in Barcelona in 1535 in preparation for Charles V's campaign in Tunis (Figure 17).[35] In principle, the centrality of the cavalry links this visual document to the game of canes – in fact Vermeyen reused some of its elements for his composition of the game of canes in Toledo (Figure 2). Yet the presence of cannons and infantry points to a different kind of performance in which proper military choreography figures more prominently.[36]

Even when military exercises prescribed the formation of two sides, one of Christians and the other of Moors, they rarely scripted a symbolic resolution to stage the victory of Christianity over Islam (which is indeed the main feature of *moros y cristianos*). For instance, the arrival of Isabel of Valois and Philip II in Toledo in 1560 was celebrated with a mock battle between Christians and Moors which, like Vermeyen's painting, included both cavalry and infantry. While the choreography of the two confronting armies was carefully prepared, the organizers did not seem to have a plan for how to end it, and the battle was only dismantled when the monarch gave the order to dispel the squads, precisely when the participants "were so enraged with each other ... that if it had not been stopped, it would have become serious."[37] Even though we may be tempted to read this performance through the paradigm of the confrontational *moros y cristianos*, the lack of resolution indicates that the rationale of the spectacle derived from the performance itself, and not from any ideological victory over Islam that it could convey – even if many of the participants would have subscribed to such a denouement. Sebastián de Horozco also refers to this mock battle, but only says that some participants were more gallant than others, not that participants on one side were dressed as Moors.[38] Therefore, where one observer saw a confrontation between Moors and Christians, another witness perceived only different degrees of gallantry.

In 1561, only one year after the entry of Isabel of Valois and Philip II in Toledo, the V Count of Tendilla organized a similar military performance on the banks of the Genil River in Granada to celebrate his own appointment as commander of the Alhambra. Yet in this case all the participants were dressed as Moors. Just before dawn on the day of Saint John, 400 riders, 1,000 harquebusiers, and 400 Moriscos gathered for a mock battle. According to the description by Gabriel Rodríguez de Ardila, the Moriscos, wearing *zaragüelles* [baggy trousers], white shirts, red berets, and turbans, were followed by musicians wearing silk *marlotas* and twelve men riding in the *gineta* style. Finally, the Count of Tendilla arrived on horseback with his riders, all of them wearing lavish Moorish clothing.[39] The spectacle then ended with a mock battle:

> At dawn, the two sides appeared, and as Don Luis passed by on his horse, the Moriscos began to enter through the two bridges, with lines of harquebusiers, and they started a very brave and lively skirmish, as if it was for real, many of them on both sides pretending to be killed. And after a while, the horsemen began entering through the docks, the brave Don Luis in front of them ... and when the skirmish started anew, four hundred horsemen came together, a thing that has never been seen in that city, and so joyful that everybody admired it, and thus the skirmish of infantry and horsemen lasted for a long time.[40]

While the description can be confusing, when Rodríguez de Ardila says that the Moriscos began to enter through the two bridges and skirmish between them, it is clear that both Moriscos and Old Christians, both dressed as Moors, participated on both sides of the mock battle.[41] There is no reference to religious confrontation in this description, but a celebration of military prowess in which the only, albeit significant, difference between Moriscos and Old Christians is that the former participated on foot while the latter did so on horse.

This difference is confirmed by similar military musters with Morisco participation in nearby Baza. In 1525, the Moriscos of the neighbouring villages were asked to participate in the festival of Saint John. The festival included, as usual, a game of canes but the Moriscos were to serve as infantry and were explicitly told to carry fake weapons for some kind of mock battle.[42] Again in 1556, to celebrate Philip II's accession to the throne, the city of Baza organized a military parade in which the Moriscos were ordered to participate, in this case carrying real weaponry, which they could only borrow for the occasion and had to return afterwards.[43] These two cases help to contextualize the military muster organized by the Count of Tendilla in the city of Granada, as it confirms that the Moriscos were routinely asked to serve as infantry (never on horse), and that the permission to carry weapons was limited to the occasion.

If we put these performances into dialogue with other *alardes*, such as those of Barcelona in 1535 or Toledo in 1560, we can see that the Moriscos and Old Christians in Granada were not doing anything different from what was customary in the rest of Iberia, and that the use of Moorish clothing did not clearly reflect the divide between Christian colonizers and the descendants of Muslim inhabitants. What these cases reveal is a concern about the Moriscos carrying weapons in military skirmishes, which was usually framed as a security issue, but which also actually involved a certain recognition of status. As we saw in chapter 2, when Philip II tried to reinvigorate the formation of local militias in 1562 he encountered mixed responses from Castilian towns and cities, because the measure interfered with how social distinction, nobility, and military prowess were articulated locally. Some of the negative responses advising against implementing the measure came from places in Extremadura and the Kingdom of Granada, complaining that the formation of local militias would pose a security risk because Moriscos were the majority of the population.[44]

This larger cultural context sheds new light on the scene of the uprising of the Alpujarras in which Abenfarax and his men dressed up as Turks on Christmas Eve of 1567. The way Mármol Carvajal presents it, the rebelling Moriscos were trying to pass as Turks in an attempt to convince the inhabitants of the Albaicín to revolt. Such an interpretation assumes Abenfarax to be a rather naive strategist, since it is difficult to believe that he and his men were truly convinced that they could trick anybody into believing that they were Ottoman troops. It is highly unlikely that, in the chaos of the uprising, Abenfarax and his men would have had the time and resources to either make "Turkish" clothing or even less likely that they could procure "real" Ottoman garments.[45] It is much more likely that they procured already-available performative garments, perhaps coming from other military parades such as the one held by the Marquis of Mondéjar in 1561.[46] With this combination of weapons and Moorish clothing, it seems rather that Abenfarax was imitating the *alardes* common throughout the Iberian Peninsula, in which the display of arms and gallant garb reinforced each other as signs of military prowess and class status. In this way, Abenfarax could have been trying to capitalize on the combination of Moorish clothing and carrying arms as signs of social distinction that were forbidden to the Moriscos. Seen in this light, Abenfarax's intervention was an attempt to make explicit the inherent contradiction of Philip II's edict, which compelled the Moriscos to assimilate to an undefined concept of Castilianness while prohibiting them the ceremonial use of Moorish clothing so central to Castilian power and social promotion.[47]

It is the case that neither the prohibitions of enlisting the Moriscos in local militias nor the repression of the Alpujarras rebellion (and the subsequent reinstatement of prohibitions on clothing and arms) barred Moriscos from participating in martial exhibitions dressed as Moors. Rather, they were constantly invited (even forced) to do so until their expulsion between 1609 and 1614, in contexts that were eminently festive, but that involved the use of arms and therefore could potentially open the door for honourable recognition.

In 1586, the town council of Priego de Córdoba organized its customary annual festival in honour of the Virgin of Cabeza. That year they decided to make as gallant a festival as possible, since the town had had certain legal privileges recognized, and they expected the presence of the Marquis of Priego. Along with the usual bullfight and game of canes, the council proposed the organization of two companies, one of Christians and one of Moors.[48] Yet, when the town council reassumed preparations on August 25, there were some modifications of the original plan of organizing a festival of *moros y cristianos*, which turned instead into a *zuiza*, as they ordered

> to enlist all horsemen, both noblemen and *de cuantías*, as well as any other people with horses ... so that as many as possible appear dressed *a la morisca* with lances and *adargas*. And because many of them will probably be youngsters, we order that, once it is known who is participating, they carry reeds with fake silver spearheads ... and also that they take with them the New Christians of the neighbourhood, and forty well-adorned girls wearing Morisco clothing with their *almalafas*, along with thirty boys between eight and ten years, and those should be dressed *a la morisca*.[49]

This short passage encapsulates many of the issues about Moorish clothing, public performance, and social status with which this book has dealt so far. To begin with, while the mention of the horses points to the planned game of canes, the vagueness about the number of participants suggests a different kind of exercise more similar to a military muster – contrary to the game of canes, which was usually a choreographic equestrian exercise with a set number of teams with even numbers of riders. There is no mention of a Christian squad, unless we assume that those who could not get clothing *a la morisca* would be assigned to the Christian side. If such was the case, the wealthiest participants would take the Moorish side, while the Christians would be played by the least wealthy of them. In these circumstances, taking part in either side in the performance would not be interpreted primarily as a statement of religious identity, but rather as a sign of socio-economic status.

Furthermore, even if the organizers were still preparing for *moros y cristianos*, there is no clear sartorial division in the festival paralleling the local divide between Old and New Christians.[50] The inclusion of Moriscos is no less intriguing. The Morisco girls were asked to dress in Morisco clothing [en abito de moriscas] wearing their *almalafas*, but the Morisco boys were asked to dress *a la morisca*, not "en hábito de moriscos." The linguistic nuance further reveals that the discussion about Morisco clothing was focused on specific female garments, while the general term *a la morisca* was understood as a common fashion in early modern Iberia.

What the document does not specify is the place of adult male Moriscos in the festival. Maybe they were assigned the role of mere spectators. But there is also the possibility that they were included among the riders who would be assigned fake weapons. I have translated *jente nueba* as "youngsters," which seems to be the most obvious meaning. Yet we may wonder whether, within this context, this expression could be referring instead to the *cristianos nuevos*, as the order to use fake lances is reminiscent of the 1525 Baza festival in which the Moriscos were ordered to use similar mock weaponry. We might even imagine that the Moriscos who had permission to bear weapons would carry real lances. Even if none of these questions are resolved by the document, this speculation is not gratuitous, as there is evidence that the Moriscos of Priego were listed as *caballeros de cuantía* and were therefore included in military musters.[51]

This is exactly what was happening in nearby places about the same time. Also in 1586, a report to Philip II denounced that the Moriscos were listed as *caballeros de cuantía* in *alardes* in Córdoba and Baeza.[52] In response to these reports, the Crown said that the initial enlisting of the Moriscos as *caballeros de cuantía* was not a matter of concern, since those who did not have licence to carry arms would be automatically excluded from participating in military musters – but it is elusive about what happened with those Moriscos who did have licences to carry weapons.[53]

Another detailed account of the participation of Moriscos in mock battles can be found in the Manchegan town of Manzanares in 1600. This case is documented because some anonymous *hidalgos* denounced the Moriscos from Granada for carrying swords and firearms during a carnivalesque military skirmish which the document, like the document from Priego de Córdoba, calls a *zuiza*. During the subsequent investigation, it was revealed that the Moriscos, wary of the legislation prohibiting them from carrying arms, were reluctant to participate at first, even though the town council threatened them with a fine if they refused. Finally the bailiffs granted them oral permission to carry arms – in so doing, they overstepped royal authority, and because of that the prosecuting attorney held local authorities responsible for the infraction rather than the Moriscos. For several weeks before the actual festival, the Moriscos rehearsed around the town with swords, halberds, and a few harquebuses. On the day of the festival they dressed as Moors, carrying a flag with five crescents and playing musical instruments;[54] one of the witnesses describes the Moriscos' performance as "playing their flutes in the Morisco style and with their drums making noise and showing joy, raising their arms up and acting like Moors."[55] The Moriscos held bystanders captives in a castle, only liberating them after they paid a ransom that would be used for the reconstruction of the altarpiece in honour of the Virgin Mary.

By reading this document through the paradigm of *moros y cristianos*, Miguel Fernando Gómez Vozmediano assumes that the Moriscos played the role of the Moors while the local Old Christians played the role of the Christians.[56] Yet, as William Childers points out, there is not a single reference in the document to the existence of an opposing army, and therefore this *zuiza* does not fit into the confrontational pattern of *moros y cristianos*.[57] Rather, there are indications that both Moriscos and Old Christians dressed as Moors for the festival, since the captain of the *zuiza* was the Old Christian Melchor Díaz and, as one of the witnesses says in passing, there was another group of about a dozen Old Christians wearing the same flag with crescents and similar musical instruments (and, we should assume, the same Moorish costumes).[58] The reason not to focus on the Old Christian participants is that the legal prosecution was clearly caused by the distribution of real weaponry among the Moriscos, and not by the act of dressing as Moors. One of the arguments used by Juan Gutiérrez de Villegas to exonerate the Moriscos in his final report, was that they participated regularly in similar military exhibitions, which never resulted in any kind of scandal, thus revealing that this was not an isolated occurrence.[59]

In the case of Manzanares, like most of the cases analysed in this section, Old Christians added a surplus of fetishistic entertainment to the festival by having the Moriscos play the role of the Moors. As Childers suggests, Old Christians would have liked "to watch them imitate the Moors they knew about from reading *El Abencerraje* and Pérez de Hita, or from listening to Morisco ballads that were at the height of their popularity in that moment."[60] But it is important to examine the other side as well and question what Moriscos took from impersonating Moors. Since there was not a direct and uninterrupted cultural bond between Moriscos and the theatrical Moors of the past, we must conclude that the Moriscos reenacted the figure of the Moor crafted by Old Christians, which by 1600 was equally mythical for both groups. There is no indication of the origin of the Moorish costumes, and therefore we must assume that they would wear customary Moorish attire created for such occasions.

Most important, in all such cases, passing as Moors becomes a potentially empowering action for Moriscos, which explains why they were eager to engage in a cultural practice that could easily be construed as a mockery of their own cultural legacy. Certainly, it might be the case that passing as Moors allowed the Moriscos to establish a cultural attachment to the more prestigious medieval Muslim knights of Granada.[61] Or that this is a form of strategic essentialism, in which a subaltern group adopts its own stereotype created by the hegemonic group to increase its social visibility. Regardless, we should also consider the possibility that passing as a Moor in local festivals had a more immediate, empowering, and practical benefit than the vague promises of cultural and genealogical affinities. After all, dressing as a Moor in public festivals was a sign of cultural assimilation into Christian Iberian society rather than an expression of attachment to Islam. Festive impersonations of the Moor were conceived of as moments of exception in which the prohibition against Moriscos carrying arms was momentarily lifted by local authorities, thus providing Moriscos with a legal loophole that they could use later as a precedent in legal cases when they sought social recognition.[62]

Moriscos Participating in Games of Canes

Whatever the opportunities for social promotion available to Moriscos via inclusion in military musters, hierarchies between *caballeros de cuantía* and *hidalgos* were still maintained in many towns, which more than likely tried to structure them as if these social differences corresponded to the participation in either infantry or horsemanship. The most desirable form of Moorishness would still be participation in a game of canes, but there are very scant references to Moriscos participating in public festivals as horsemen. In the analysis of the game of canes made in the first part of this book, I left aside the Moorish performances celebrated in the Kingdom of Granada (which in the sixteenth century also comprised the provinces of Almería and Málaga) between its incorporation into the Crown of Castile in 1492 and the uprising of the Moriscos in 1568, as well as in other Iberian communities in which there were significant Morisco populations. In the case of the Kingdom of Granada, there are almost no sixteenth-century festival books describing lavish games of canes, but we can find scattered references to games of canes held before 1568 in the municipal proceedings of Almuñécar, Baza, Málaga, Vera, Antequera, and Motril.[63] In other cases, we have only indirect information that games of canes were regularly held. For instance, in 1510, the townships of Montejaque and Benaoján (Málaga) mourned the death of García Álvarez de Toledo at the Battle of Djerba, and, among other measures, ordered that for a period of three months people not wear silk or play games of canes, showing that they were common practices.[64]

In the city of Granada, the presence of the game of canes is recorded from the very beginning of Christian rule, and is documented in the municipal proceedings for 1517, 1526, and 1566.[65] There are also other sources referring to the celebration of games of canes: the German traveller Hieronymus Münzer describes one game organized by the Count of Mondéjar in 1494.[66] According to Francisco Bermúdez de Pedraza, in 1500 Fernando of Aragon organized a game of canes for Isabel of Castile to cheer her up;[67] and the celebration of exuberant games of canes for the entry of Charles V in 1526 is well documented in the accounts of foreign visitors.[68]

In most of these cases, there is no indication as to whether Moriscos participated in these games of canes, whether the games were reserved for Old Christian settlers, or for the local elites, independent of whether they were Old Christians or Moriscos. According to José Ángel Tapia Garrido, the game of canes was a common practice on the frontier between Castile and Nasrid Granada during the late Middle Ages, and therefore, "the Christians who came ... after the conquest ... did not have to learn it, since they knew and practiced it as well as the Moors."[69] It is indeed more probable that the game of canes was maintained as a cultural appropriation by Christian colonizers, and not by the native population of the Kingdom of Granada, since most of the Nasrid nobility either left for North Africa or was removed from Granada.[70] As we have seen, a 1499 decree reveals that the Muslim inhabitants of Granada had been prohibited from riding horses.[71] Thus the scarce information on the games of canes celebrated in the Kingdom of Granada seems to indicate that equestrian Moorishness was, ironically, one of the cultural means through which Christian colonizers demonstrated their superior social position in the Kingdom of Granada.

In the rest of the Iberian Peninsula, Morisco participation in Moorish equestrian performances was usually regarded with suspicion. In Aragon, an inquisitorial trial in 1549 refers to how the Moriscos celebrated the expected arrival of Turks by marching at night dressed *a la morisca* – in what seems to be an *encamisada* [night masque]. Another inquisitorial process from Aragon also alludes to how in 1558 the Moriscos celebrated the presence of the Ottoman navy by playing games of canes dressed as Moors.[72] While Louis Cardaillac strikingly suggests that Moriscos would have preserved such Moorish clothing from times immemorial, Gregorio Colás Latorre questions the connection established by the Inquisition between the Morisco celebrations and the Ottoman advances, as he points out that the game of canes was a purely Christian game and therefore the Inquisition (as well as modern scholars) were overreading Morisco festivals and decontextualizing them from the larger frame of Iberian festivals.[73]

The way Moriscos were conceived of in relation to Moorish performances is not entirely applicable to descendants of the Nasrid nobility who maintained their social status as they integrated into Castilian court society. Take for instance the case of Juan de Granada, who, along with Charles V and other Iberian nobles, dressed as a Moor to participate in a game of canes held in Milan in 1549.[74] Similarly, Francisco Fernández El-Zegrí, who was a councilman of the city of Granada, was made responsible for forming a quadrille for the game of canes organized by the city council in 1566.[75] But since the noble status of these individuals was never questioned, they are not representative of the Morisco population. The real issue is neither this group of well-established nobles nor the impoverished Morisco peasants, but the intermediate ranks of the Morisco elite, who, like their Old Christian counterparts, had embarked on a process of social ascent through access to *hidalguía* and the control of municipal resources.[76] These Moriscos, while not legally blocked from accessing *hidalguía*, found additional legal, social, and economic obstacles in their way in comparison with their Old Christian counterparts, as they were deprived of many of the signs through which status was traditionally exhibited, such as riding horses, carrying weapons, and (from 1567) wearing silk textiles – the three basic elements of the game of canes.

Like Old Christian commoners who wished to climb the social ladder, many Moriscos knew how to navigate the loopholes of the legal system. I have not been able to document the participation of any individual *qua Morisco* in a game of canes other than the descendants of the Nasrid nobility, but this absence probably means that they were able to participate precisely because they had succeeded in erasing the memory of their Muslim ancestry. Paradoxically, as Moorish clothing was a sign of class status, those Moriscos who managed to erase their ancestry in the collective memory could mark their integration into Old Christian society by dressing as Moors for the game of canes and thus further cement their social climbing.

The Morisco participation in Moorish performances analysed in this chapter look like expressions of Islamic cultural identity only when we consider them in isolation. However, as we situate these cases within the larger context of Iberian Moorishness, what we see instead is an issue of class struggle in which the adoption of Moorishness becomes a way to resist institutional lumpenization based on ancestry. A narrative of cultural archaeology, which insists on the Andalusi origins of Moorishness, conceals the real social value of Moorish clothing in early modern Iberia as well as the implicit hierarchies within its practices. Moriscos were pushed to adopt only the low forms of Moorishness known as *zambras*, which for many turned into a professional career. In spite of legal and inquisitorial associations of *zambras* with Islam and their persecution in the domestic sphere, local authorities did not consider them threatening cultural expressions, as long as they were performed under the vigilance of Old Christian authorities and within certain parameters of urban ceremony.

Meanwhile, Moriscos were barred from accessing the more prestigious form of Moorishness in the game of canes – not because of the potential military threat that they would pose and even less because of their alleged connection with the practice of Islam, but because horsemanship, luxurious textiles, and the right to carry weapons were considered privileges marking social advancement. Between the folkloric *zambras* and the aristocratic game of canes existed an array of martial exhibitions combining elements of public festival and military training to varying degrees, and in which dressing as a Moor could constitute a moment of exception allowing Moriscos to carry arms and therefore to become like their Old Christian counterparts. Thus Moriscos and Old Christians alike probably saw in Moorish clothing not so much an icon of cultural identity but a signifier encoding a complex process of social validation. What would be particular to Moriscos in relation to Moorish clothing is that, in exchange for temporarily adopting a carnivalesque version of their alleged sartorial legacy, Moorish impersonations provided them with a loophole through which to evade certain legal restrictions that otherwise prohibited them from performing such social roles.

8 Moriscos as Theatrical Bodies

Quédense atrás los miserables daños
que padeció de España el suelo hermoso ...
Y el mal que resultó de los engaños
del padre de la Cava cauteloso,
por cuyos pensamientos arrogantes
España vio marlotas y turbantes.
[Left behind shall be all the harm
that Spain's soil suffered ...
and the evil that resulted from the treachery
of the mischievous father of the Cava,
because of his arrogant thoughts
Spain saw *marlotas* and turbans.]

Gaspar Aguilar. *Expulsión de los moros de España*

In order to appreciate how representations of Morisco bodies are historically determined, it is necessary to examine the construction of the stereotype of Moriscos as an unassimilable community that had to be excised from the nation, as well as to consider how this stereotype fluctuated in literary works composed during the sixteenth and seventeenth centuries. This chapter shows that such fluctuation parallels the ebbs and flows in the appreciation of Moorish clothing in Iberian society. During the sixteenth century and in the years preceding their expulsion, Moriscos were most commonly characterized in literary texts by the use of an Arabized jargon, and, contrary to legal and religious texts, presented as poorly dressed bodies. This is partly because the Moriscos were indeed a marginalized group, but also because the early modern literary imagination probably reflected the downward assimilation proposed by legal actions against the Moriscos throughout the sixteenth century. On the eve of the expulsion, the theatrical stereotype of the "gracioso Morisco" combined the Arabized jargon of sixteenth-century theatre with the literary representations of the commoner who tried to transcend class boundaries by appropriating Moorish clothing as a sign of aristocratic status. It is only after their expulsion between 1609 and 1614, and more precisely only after the 1620s and only gradually at best, that Moriscos started to be fully imagined and staged with Moorish clothing. This shift occurred due to a combination of interrelated factors: the decline of the game of canes and the subsequent dissociation of Moorish clothing from aristocratic status, but also as an entailment of the influence of the myth of the sartorial revival crafted in the historiographical works on the uprising of the Alpujarras published in the 1620s. Even when seventeenth-century plays (the best-known among them Calderón de la Barca's *Amar después de la muerte*), along with the historiographical works already analysed in chapter 5, had constructed the image of the Morisco as a Moorish-dressed body, such an image was not a stable icon of difference as in previous decades.

Moriscos as Poorly Dressed Bodies

The dissemination of the Morisco stereotype in the last decades of the sixteenth century contrasted with the peak of literary and ceremonial maurophilia, which represented and enacted the idealized figure of the gallant Moor as a model of courtly and aristocratic etiquette. As seen in chapter 3, by the end of the sixteenth century composers of Moorish ballads were attacked by a series of satirical ballads that emphasized how the "real" Morisco could not compare to the figure of the idealized Moor. These parodies, most of them anonymous, focused on what they found to be sartorial incongruities. Thus the ballad "Ese moro ganapán" recounts how a poor Morisco is overwhelmed by the weight of all the clothing that the poet has put on him,[1] and Muza complains using the same terms in "Colérico sale Muza"[2] and "Valga al diablo tantos moros."[3] "Triste pisa y afligido" describes Zulema with the gallant Moorish clothing he could not possibly wear.[4] "Toquen aprisa a rebato" and "Lleve el diablo el potro rucio" also make parodic references to the Moriscos playing canes under the name of the Moors from the past.[5] "¡Ah, mis señores poetas!" claims that the gallant clothing of these fictional Moors cannot belong to the Moriscos and contrasts the rich garments of the idealized Moors with the stereotype of the impoverished rustic Morisco:

> Arbolán comes from plowing the whole day in exchange for a little bit of flour and a little bit of money, and the criminal poet pretends that the next morning he is riding in the *gineta* style and dressing in green with silver flowers ... Muza is baking his doughnuts and the other [poet] says "make room," because brave Muza is leading a team for the game of canes.[6]

"¡Ah! Mis señores poetas" thus claims that it does not make sense to represent the Moriscos participating in the game of canes, since they are for the most part labourers and doughnut bakers. This image of the Moriscos as an impoverished group is no less stereotypical than their construction as a homogeneous group of Moorish-dressed bodies.

As I argued in chapters 3 and 4, the primary target of those ballads was not the Moriscos, but those individuals who wanted to display a higher social status by figuring themselves as gallant Moors participating in the game of canes. Yet the use of Islamophobic discourse to criticize social conflicts among Christians was meaningful precisely because satiric poets borrowed their language from an already existing image of the Moriscos as an impoverished people, which these ballads also continued to perpetuate. Actually, both discourses of social exclusion reinforce each other: for the same reason that those ballads construed the commoners as Moriscos (as I argued in chapter 3), it is clear that they also construed the Moriscos as commoners (as I argue here).

Yet, while these ballads minutely list all the lavish Moorish garments that the Moriscos were not supposed to wear because of their miserable status, they are silent about the humble clothing they were supposed to be wearing instead. Thus these literary texts leave unresolved whether the Moriscos should be imagined as looking like any other Old Christian commoner or whether there was supposed to be something distinctive about their clothing. At best, this silence confirms (at least on the level of the social imaginary) the success of the downward assimilation postulated in legal actions against Moriscos. If, by the end of the sixteenth century, the Moriscos are construed simply as poorly dressed bodies, how were they supposed to be differentiated from Old Christian commoners?

In tune with the representation of Moriscos in the satirical ballads written by the end of the sixteenth century, apologetic treatises commending their expulsion in the 1610s characterized them as poorly dressed. For instance, Pedro Aznar Cardona's *Expulsión justificada de los Moriscos Españoles* (1612), describes the Moriscos as

> ridiculous in their clothing, dressing most of them with light linen hose, or any other petty thing, like sailors, and with little clothing of very little value, and very badly dressed on purpose, and women in the same way, with a colourful dress and only one tunic of yellow, green, or blue lining, and they were always light and unburdened, with very few clothes, almost wearing nothing but a shirt.[7]

The same ideologies of representation lay in the series of canvases commissioned by Philip III to celebrate the expulsion, in which the Moriscos are represented as poorly dressed bodies. Take, for instance, Vicent Mestre's painting of the expulsion of the Moriscos through the port of Denia (Figure 16). As Jesús Villalmanzo Cameno shows, the canvas depicts the Moriscos as poorly dressed, while the Old Christians are depicted wearing lavish clothing.[8] By not representing Moriscos as "Moors," the author (or the commissioners) advocates a certain notion of pictorial realism but also creates a new sartorial differentiation between Old Christians and Moriscos which is now imagined as corresponding neatly to class division.[9]

Representing Moriscos as commoners could make the expulsion more acceptable by obscuring the socio-economic integration of many Moriscos and presenting them as an expendable population. Yet this semi-solution did not satisfy the ideological requirement of imagining them as differently dressed bodies. Thus, some authors opt to have it both ways and try to solve this apparent ideological contradiction by focusing on the allegedly deceptive nature of Moriscos as a people. Gaspar Aguilar's epic poem *Expulsión de los moros de España* (1610), written to glorify the expulsion decreed by Philip III, is emblematic of this tension. Aguilar, much like Aznar Cardona, initially describes the Moriscos as poorly dressed bodies, "with shrugged serge trousers and tunics that were brown a while ago," sarcastically labelling their clothing as "rich lavish gowns."[10] However, in other passages he relies on the image of the Morisco dressed in Moorish garb, especially when he presents the expulsion as the completion of ethno-religious cleansing.[11] According to Aguilar, the expulsion did not merely eliminate Morisco bodies from the Iberian Peninsula, but would undo all the cultural influences of the Islamic period, among them the use of Moorish clothing: "Left behind shall be all the harm that Spain's soil suffered ...

and the evil that resulted from the treachery of the mischievous father of the Cava; because of his arrogant thoughts Spain saw *marlotas* and turbans."[12] Aguilar forms a direct connection between the presence of Islam in the Iberian Peninsula and the use of Moorish clothing with this allusion to the legend of the loss of Spain, according to which Count Don Julian, enraged because the Visigoth King Roderic had raped his daughter (La Cava), allowed the first Muslim army to enter the Iberian Peninsula. His text therefore implies that ethnic cleansing will further result in cultural cleansing, as sartorial influence is conceived as an undesirable contagion: "Thus by divine will, the relation with Moors, their language, treachery, cruelty, shape, and dress, disappeared from people's minds."[13] Aguilar's poem imagines that this sartorial cleansing would be carried out by the Moriscos themselves, as it describes how they retrieve the Moorish clothing that they had kept hidden: "they try on *marlotas* and turbans; like some boys, inclined to be and look like actors, who, before the play, dress in the costume that they have prepared."[14] By explicitly comparing the Moriscos "recuperating" their Moorish clothing with the rehearsal of actors, Gaspar Aguilar underscores the theatricality of Moorish garb for the Moriscos.[15]

Gaspar Aguilar's contradictory position about the location of Moorish clothing in early modern Iberian culture is rather striking if we consider both his biography and his literary works. On the one hand, his father was a *pasamanero*, a kind of tailor specialized in the manufacturing of gallant adornments, and he was well connected to a network of tailors in Valencia.[16] On the other hand, he was well connected to the nobility of Valencia and their fondness for the game of canes, and he described them dressing up as Moors for many occasions, such as the wedding of Philip III in Valencia in 1599 and the beatification of Saint Luis Beltrán in 1609.[17] Many of these nobles belonged, like Aguilar, to the literary circle of Valencia, the *Academia de los nocturnos*. Yet Aguilar was not one of them, because his socio-professional origins raised sharp barriers between him and such nobles.[18] As in the case of Lope, analysed in chapter 4, there is no evidence that Aguilar ever participated in any of the games of canes that he witnessed and immortalized with his pen. Therefore, Gaspar Aguilar knew perfectly well who the actual producers and consumers of Moorish clothing were, even though he attributes its use exclusively to the Moriscos in his epic poem. We may then wonder if the unrealistic prophecy that he makes in his epic poem about Moorish clothing disappearing from Iberia with the expulsion of the Moriscos reveals a subtle resentment towards his peers and patrons, and whether the utopia that he evokes as resulting from the expulsion contains a fantasy of a more egalitarian society.

If in Gaspar Aguilar's work the alleged revival of sartorial identity by Moriscos is construed as a theatrical rehearsal, Moriscos were also conceived of as theatrical figures when they were regarded as unassimilable bodies. According to Marcos de Guadalajara y Xavier, Juan de Ribera wrote to Philip III complaining that those Moriscos who were fully assimilated in dress and language were the most dangerous, since clergymen could not control them.[19] In a similar vein, Aznar Cardona states that Old Christians were in greater danger when the Moriscos assimilated than when they were "Moros sin disfrace" [Moors without disguise], implying that after their assimilation they were just Muslims disguised as Christians.[20] This theatrical terminology trapped the imagined bodies of the Moriscos in a hermeneutical loop that denaturalizes their relation to clothing: Christian clothing was considered to be a subterfuge for their crypto-Islamic practices, as those "assimilated" were accused of merely disguising their apostasy.[21] At the same time, Moorish clothing, which by then existed only as a ritual gallant costume for the display of class status, was equally conceived to be inappropriate for Moriscos as a lesser, lumped-together ethnic group. It is this tension between the need to construe them as exotic bodies and the reluctance to imbue them with the sartorial signs associated with nobility that explains the unstable representation of the Moriscos from the second half of the sixteenth century through the beginning of the seventeenth.

"Moriscos ridículos" on Stage

Paradoxically, even when Moriscos were construed as theatrical bodies in the discourses about them, they rarely appeared on stage before the expulsion of 1609–14, and when they did appear, it was only as secondary characters. In the pre-Lopean theatre, Moriscos were characterized by the use of a debased jargon, but nothing is said about their clothing.[22] None of the sixteenth-century plays that include Moriscos makes any sign that they should be characterized by the use of a specific theatrical costume, but they do painstakingly recreate the conventional Morisco jargon very minutely, as in the anonymous *Farsa del Sacramento llamada de los lenguajes* [*Farse of the Sacrament, also Called Farse of Languages*], Diego Sánchez de Badajoz's *Farsa de la Yglesia* (published posthumously in 1554), Luis Hurtado de Toledo and Michael de Carvajal's *Cortes de la muerte* [*The Parliament of Death*] (published in 1557), and Lope de Rueda's *Comedia Armelina* (published posthumously in 1567).[23] The absence of sartorial characterization seems to indicate that the Morisco stereotype during most of the sixteenth century was primarily based on speech rather than sartorial appearance – although it would be difficult to reach a conclusive interpretation, since pre-Lopean theatre does not usually give detailed sartorial information in stage directions.

In later plays, the overwhelming presence of Muslim characters (be they North Africans, Turks, or Iberian Moors from the frontier past) contrasts with the almost absolute absence of Moriscos on stage – the cases previously discussed in this chapter are indeed scant by comparison. As Thomas Case observes à propos Lope de Vega's work, "unlike the Moors, the Moriscos as a group were not dramatizable."[24] Here I will argue that the Moriscos were not "dramatizable" precisely because they had already been construed as theatrical figures. This interpretation is not as paradoxical as it sounds: if both Moorish and Christian clothing was considered costumes in the collective imaginary about the Moriscos, it means that there was no proper attire that could signify unmistakably their presence *qua* Moriscos on stage.

One possible solution to the undramatizability of Moriscos' inbetweenness was to imagine specific Morisco clothing that could at the same time be different from Moorish clothing. We can clearly find the enunciation of this possibility in Lope's *Los cautivos de Argel* (1599), which in the first scene presents the Morisco Francisco as "morisco del Reino de Valencia, en su hábito, como ellos andan" [a Morisco from the Kingdom of Valencia, in their costumary attire], while in contrast, at the end of the first act the same character appears in Algiers "muy galán, de moro" [as a gallant Moor].[25] The distinction between the clothing of local Moriscos of Valencia and North African Muslims is probably not intended as an accurate ethnographical description of these two groups, but as an effort to create a sartorial category "proper" to Moriscos that could be opposed to the clothing of both gallant "Moors" and Old Christian commoners. Yet the intermediate solution of *Los cautivos de Argel*, which constitutes an exception within the corpus, does not seem to have crystallized into a theatrical convention, either because it violated the economy of character types available in the sartorial repertoires of theatre companies, or because it postulated a sartorial nuance too subtle for early modern audiences.

Furthermore, Francisco in *Los cautivos de Argel* is also an exception because he is not characterized by the debased jargon typical of Morisco characters at that time, which continued to be used in the years immediately following the expulsion. For instance, in Luis Vélez de Guevara's short play "Baile de los moriscos" [Dance of the Moriscos] (published 1615), when several Moriscos debate the order of expulsion, they speak the traditional debased jargon, while the stage directions succinctly remark that they should appear "en hábito de morisco."[26] This brief comment in the stage direction unfortunately does not allow us to analyse the actual materialization of Morisco clothing, which seems to be left to the discretion of the company director, but we should not discard the possibility that any attire would be read as "Morisco" once the characters were recognized as such because of their speech.

There are other theatrical pieces composed around the expulsion that are more revealing of what kind of clothing the theatrical Morisco was supposed to wear. Antonio Mira de Amescua's *Máscara de la expulsión de los moriscos* [*Masque of the Expulsion of the Moriscos*] was staged at the festivals organized by the Duke of Lerma in 1617 to defend his position as Philip III's favourite and justify the expulsion of the Moriscos. Mira de Amescua's ballet is no longer extant, but there is a description by Pedro de Herrera detailing the sartorial characterization in it. First, one group of Christian peasants danced with rustic clothing to celebrate the expulsion, and after them appeared

> another group of musicians dressed as Moors, wearing turbans, *marlotas*, and *capellares*; and two dancers in the same costume made of taffeta, gauze, and embroideries, with many plumes and sashes, all of which were dashing and costly. With them, two Moorish ladies were also dressed splendidly in the African fashion. The four of them danced the *zambra*.[27]

The actors playing the Moriscos engaged in dancing, outlining in their movements their love affairs, until another Morisco appeared on stage and asked them to leave their sentimental troubles behind and prepare for the expulsion. Lucas Marchante-Aragón notes how the play opposed "rustic people" and Moriscos in order to create a model of national cultural identity.[28] Yet the play is also revealing of the complex dialectics of cultural imagination and the underlying contradictory location of Moorish clothing in early modern Iberian society, because the sartorial contrast is established not only between the Old Christian peasant and the Morisco, but also between the Morisco dancers and the Morisco who serves as spokesperson of all Moriscos as a people. The dancers of the *zambra* were dressed in lavish Moorish clothing, with turbans, *marlotas*, and *capellares*, that is, with gallant clothing very similar to that used by aristocrats during the game of canes.[29] In contrast to these performers, the Morisco spokesperson was represented as a "ridiculous Moor, because of his clothing, personal countenance, and the Arabizing accent of his speech."[30] This ballet functioned primarily as a courtly performance which emphasized the magnificence of the patron, rather than as a representation of the Morisco people. Meanwhile, the Morisco spokesperson, the only character really intended to represent them, is characterized as a liminal figure, not quite rustic, but also clearly marked as different from the gallant Moorish dancers.

Yet Mira de Amescua's use of the in-between figure of the "moro ridículo," who stands between the gallant Moor and the rustic commoner, is not specific to Moriscos, as it seems to have been used first to characterize Old Christian commoners. As seen in chapter 3, during the 1590s a series of parodic ballads appeared, disparaging the commoners who tried to encroach on class prerogatives through the appropriation of Moorish clothing in the game of canes. It is probably from these ballads that the theatrical type of the "moro gracioso" emerged to epitomize the Christian commoner's clumsy investment in Moorish clothing. This type is first found in many plays by Lope de Vega, such as *Los cautivos de Argel*, which, based on the reference to Philip III's wedding and the mention of the Duke of Lerma as Marquis of Denia, can be dated towards 1599;[31] *La desdichada Estefanía*, for which there is an autograph copy of the manuscript signed by Lope and dated 1604;[32] *La doncella Teodor*, which has been dated between 1608 and 1610;[33] and *La octava maravilla*, probably composed towards 1609.[34]

In the meantime, Moriscos continued to be characterized mainly by the use of a debased jargon – while at the sartorial level they were merely characterized as poorly dressed bodies. The first literary references to the Moriscos dressing in a debased version of Moorish clothing appear only in plays by Vélez de Guevara and Mira de Amescua in the years following the end of the expulsion in 1614 – and even then these plays still required the use of Morisco jargon in order to unmistakably identify the Moriscos on stage.[35] Since the use of the expression "moro gracioso" referring to the Old Christian commoner predates by almost two decades those plays in which the Morisco began to be labelled with this term, the sartorial image of the Morisco as a "moro gracioso" was in all likelihood moulded upon the mockery of an Old Christian commoner who tried to imitate a noble by dressing as a Moor. Thus, by the first decades of the seventeenth century, the relationship between the Moriscos and Moorish clothing can only be imagined as derivative, filtered through the larger context of the circulation of Moorish clothing within early modern Iberian society.

The derivative nature of the theatrical figure of the Morisco is made clear in the only play dealing with the expulsion and including the Moriscos as a community. The anonymous *Los moriscos de Hornachos* is a propaganda piece that conveys a negatively stereotyped image of the Moriscos as rude assassins, blasphemers, and thieves. The only extant manuscript of this play is dated 1647, but Jean-Marc Pelorson suggests that it had been written by the time of the expulsion.[36] At the very opening of the play, the Moriscos, dressed as Moors ("vestidos todos de moros"), are celebrating a wedding when one of them announces that he is going to sing a Moorish ballad composed by a Christian, which he explicitly states.[37] Taking into account the apologetic nature of the play, which aimed to represent the unassimilability of the Moriscos and justify their eventual expulsion, the emphasis on the poem's Christian authorship seems odd. Certainly, the Christian authorship serves to underline the rusticity of these Moriscos, since they would be unable to write Moorish ballads by themselves and would have to rely on Christians to celebrate the deeds of their Muslim ancestors. If even this blatant propaganda needs to imagine the Moriscos dressing as Moors as a passing that actually rehearses Christian Moorishness doubled in the ballad by Christians, it means that even during the expulsion, the cultural imaginary associates "Moorish culture" with class status rather than having to do with the Moriscos in and of themselves.

The Post-expulsion Moorification of the Morisco

The equation of Moriscos with Moorish clothing as their "proper" theatrical costume was consolidated in the Iberian imaginary only gradually and several years after their expulsion from 1609–14, due to the influence of the historiographical works on the uprising of the Alpujarras and the decreasing prestige of Moorish clothing in Iberian society. There were only a few literary works representing the uprising of the Alpujarras by the end of the sixteenth century, arguably because it was not a pleasant subject and writers preferred to focus on the idealized frontier encounters of the Middle Ages.[38] Most of the literary renditions of the War of the Alpujarras were composed by seventeenth-century playwrights who had no actual contact with the events they fictionalize, contrary to most of the historians they take as their primary source. Historical distance allows them to conflate the representation of sixteenth-century Moriscos with that of medieval Moors, and therefore with the sartorial imagery of the game of canes. Their dramatic simplification of historical events and the dissemination of their works to broader audiences cemented how the War of the Alpujarras was imagined in subsequent generations.[39]

In the years following the uprising of the Alpujarras, the historians analysed in chapter 5 composed their works, which circulated in manuscript form, and only made it into print in the seventeenth century.[40] Therefore, their editorial life began at least three decades after the uprising of the Alpujarras, in the years preceding and following the general expulsion of the Moriscos from 1609 to 1614. From then on, these authors' texts resonated through subsequent historiographical works that further contributed to the creation of a visual imaginary of the Moriscos of Granada by crafting a homogeneous visual image of Moriscos conceived as Moors and by attributing the uprising to their cultural resistance, prompted by precisely the threat to their alleged sartorial identity.

One illustrative example of this is the manuscript of the history of Granada of Justino Antolínez de Burgos.[41] By 1611, Antolínez de Burgos had finished his *Historia eclesiástica de Granada*, which he tried to publish in subsequent years, until he was deterred from the project when Francisco Bermúdez de Pedraza was about to publish his own homonymous *Historia eclesiástica de Granada* (1638). Antolínez de Burgos, following Mármol Carvajal, identified Philip II's 1567 prohibition of Morisco customs as the main cause for the uprising of the Alpujarras.[42] What makes this work relevant to my argument here is not Antolínez de Burgos's text itself, but the engravings he had commissioned from Francisco Heylan some time before 1624 to accompany the work in its second stage of composition. In one engraving illustrating the alleged martyrdom of Old Christians at the hands of Moriscos during the War of the Alpujarras, the Moriscos are clearly characterized as Moors (or more likely Turks) riding horses, which recalls the imagery of the game of canes (Figure 18). In order to ensure that both Morisco men and women are construed as sartorially different, a second engraving also includes an audience of Morisco women wearing the *almalafas* in the background (Figure 19). These images, along with Weiditz's, have often been disseminated in the scholarship and used to decorate all sorts of publications about Moriscos, which rarely question how these representations have served to imagine Morisco bodies as essentially different.[43]

The earliest documented staging of the War of the Alpujarras dates from the 1620s.[44] In the picaresque novel *Alonso, mozo de muchos amos* (1626), Jerónimo Alcalá Yáñez refers to how Christian captives in Algiers staged a play on the uprising of the Alpujarras entitled *La rebelión de Granada, y castigo por el prudentísimo rey don Felipe Segundo* – obviously echoing Luis de Mármol Carvajal's *Historia del rebelión y castigo de los Moriscos del reino de Granada* (1600). As the narrator and main character observes, the costumes used to portray the role of the Moriscos were provided by their North African Muslim captors: "the costumes were excellent, since we already had *capellares*, *marlotas*, and turbans at home."[45] This would seem to indicate that plays about the Moriscos staged in the 1620s conflated any sartorial differences among Christians playing the game of canes, North African Muslims, and Moriscos. We should be cautious about the information provided by this work of fiction, since we do not know whether this passage alludes to a real play no longer extant, or whether it is just a plot device that fantasizes about how a group of captives might use the expulsion of the Moriscos to represent a symbolic victory over their Muslim captors. Yet this text makes plain the shift taking place in the representation of the Moriscos by its own time and their increasing visual Moorification.

The first extant play on the uprising of the Alpujarras is Diego Jiménez de Enciso's *Juan Latino*, which was published in 1652 but was probably composed around the same time of Alcalá Yáñez's work.[46] As its title indicates, this play deals with the historic Juan Latino, a sixteenth-century black intellectual who rose from being a slave to being integrated into the academic circles of the city of Granada. Jiménez de Enciso, when romanticizing and dramatizing the little biographical information known, set the War of the Alpujarras as the historical background in which the character evolves and displays his apocryphal military skills. The play presents Philip II's prohibition of Morisco cultural practices as the cause of the rebellion. The Duke of Sessa announces to the Morisco noble Fernando de Válor that Philip II mandates "that they [the Moriscos] should not wear *almalafas*, nor *marlotas*, nor any dress that is not according to our custom. And that they are conceded two years to wear out their clothing, and they order the Moriscas not to cover their faces."[47] As in other literary renditions, this passage offers a simplification of the decree that evades the grammatical nonsense of Philip II's prohibition and rephrases it to indicate that the prohibition included male Moriscos as well, who are now imagined through the clothing of the gallant Moor. Furthermore, it elides the reference to the prohibition of silk, which the audience would probably interpret as a measure having nothing to do with religious identity and more to do with controlling access to signs of status.

In a later passage, Fernando de Válor replicates the decree by echoing Núñez Muley's memorandum, probably following Mármol Carvajal:

> It is an inhuman thing to order us to abandon the language in which we were born and the clothing we wear in three years! ... The poor people, how will they buy new attire? Or, why should they feel bad about theirs? Egyptians, Armenians, and Suabians are Christians, and they wear this dress.[48]

The cultural revival is implicit in Válor's promise that "if there was a small King who gave up the kingdom, there will be a great Válor who will restore it."[49] Later on, several Moriscos bring the attire for Fernando de Válor's coronation, as they appear "with one platter, and on it the clothing of the celebrated Moor, and a turban with a crown, a large piece of cloth, and a scepter."[50] His coronation is therefore visualized as the ceremonial adoption of Moorish clothing as if there were a natural continuation between fifteenth-century Nasrid ceremonies and sixteenth-century Morisco culture.

Undoubtedly, the best-known play on the War of the Alpujarras is Pedro Calderón de la Barca's *Amar después de la muerte* [*To Love After Death*] (c. 1633).[51] This play was composed about fifty years after the events of the War of the Alpujarras, and two decades after the expulsion of the Moriscos, by a young dramatist who had not even been born when the uprising occurred and who had probably never had much contact with real Moriscos. As Anne Cruz suggests, the trigger for the composition of the play might have been Philip IV's convocation of a contest held in 1627 to depict the expulsion of the Moriscos, won by a now-lost painting of Diego Velázquez.[52] Alexander Parker locates the play in 1630s court politics, between the defenders of the return of the Moriscos or even as an intervention regarding the relaxation of the blood purity statutes.[53] Similarly, Rafael Carrasco, Juan Carlos Bayo, and Margaret Olsen expand Parker's insight on the political climate of the 1630s, arguing that many Moriscos were still litigating to claim their place in Spain in spite of the expulsion.[54] Thomas Case proposes that the play might recondition the debate on the Leaden Books, the documents unearthed in Granada between 1588 and 1600 claiming that the city was founded by Christian Arabs, since the discussion about their authenticity was reinvigorated in the 1630s.[55] Most of these scholars cite in passing how Calderón reflects the prohibition of Morisco customs, an element that they seem to take for granted. Only Mina García Soormally devotes close attention to the play's exploration of instances of cultural permeability, while Diane Sieber and Hannaa' Walzer analyse how Calderón's play interrogates the racial and cultural identification supposed to underlie the uprising.[56]

From the very opening of the play, clothing is used to stage Morisco difference, as the Moriscos hold a private gathering in Cadí's house to perform a *zambra*, and the stage directions instruct that "all the Moriscos appear ... dressed in the Morisco style, with *casaquillas* and *calzoncillos*, and the Moriscas with white *jubones*."[57] It seems that the representational conventions for Moriscos on stage had changed, since the garments mentioned as "Morisco" by Calderón (*casaquillas* and *calzoncillos*) were neither those used to construct Morisco sartorial identity a few decades before nor the traditional Moorish clothing for the game of canes. Brent Devos also observes that these sartorial indications in the stage directions do not strictly conform to the conventions of representing Muslim characters, and he suggests that the play construes the Moriscos as slaves.[58] While it is not clear what *casaquilla* means for Calderón by the 1630s, it seems to point to the *sayo vaquero* rather than to the *marlota*, and therefore is more related to the Turkish-Italian Moorishness of the courtly game of canes of the seventeenth century than to the "traditional" Iberian representation of Moorish clothing.

Calderón also offers his own reading of Philip II's prohibition. In *Amar después de la muerte*, the conventional lament over the prohibition of Morisco customs is attributed to Juan Malec:

> The conditions, some old and some new, that were written with more emphasis, were then that no one from the African nation ... could make celebrations, organize *zambras*, wear silk, be present in bathhouses, nor could Arabic be heard spoken in any house, but the Castilian language.[59]

Again, the information seems to be taken from Mármol Carvajal.[60] Yet, in contrast to many other historians and playwrights, Calderón includes in his summary the prohibition on wearing silk, which he could connect to the sumptuary laws still prevalent in his own time.

Later, the noble Don Juan de Mendoza recounts that the first act taken by the Morisco leader Fernando de Válor was the alleged revival of Morisco customs which is constructed as perfectly mirroring Philip II's decree:

> Once he was crowned, the first thing that Válor mandated, in order to contradict our decrees in everything, was ... that nobody should be called by a Christian name, nor make any Christian ceremony ... that no one should speak but the Arabic language, and wear Moorish dress, and keep but the sect of Muhammad.[61]

Juan de Mendoza's account acknowledges the creative power of royal legislation to produce the cultural difference that it represses. By stating that the alleged revival of Morisco culture happens "to contradict our decrees in everything," Juan de Mendoza implies that Moriscos did not merely "reconstruct" an uninterrupted cultural tradition kept from the Nasrid period, but that their resilience is mediated by the definition of Morisco culture created by Christian legal texts. This idea thus recognizes the importance of Philip II's decree in imagining the Moriscos as differently-dressed bodies.

Amar después de la muerte also rewrites the story of Álvaro Tuzaní, who during the Christian siege of Galera dressed up as a Christian and infiltrated the Christian camp to avenge the death of his beloved Maleha, as described in the second part of Ginés Pérez de Hita's *Guerras civiles de Granada*.[62] Most critics have underlined how the inclusion of this sentimental story in both Pérez de Hita and Calderón's version works as a symbol of integration as it focuses on the ability of the protagonist Tuzaní to perfectly pass as a Christian. Yet his ability is presented as an exception. Indeed, Pérez de Hita's text enunciates the passing only to negate it. When Tuzaní's identity is discovered, he states that "I put on this Christian clothing because I am so."[63] In other words, Pérez de Hita presents Tuzaní as a Christian passing as Christian whereas Mármol Carvajal presents Abenfarax's men as Moors passing as Moors.

By contrast, Tuzaní's sartorial transformation in Calderón is clearly presented as the adoption of an identity that is not his. First Álvaro Tuzaní and Clara appear dressed "en traje de moros" [in dress of Moors].[64] Later on, Álvaro goes to the Christian camp with his servant Alcuzcuz. When Alcuzcuz is afraid that he will be identified as Morisco, Álvaro tells him that now that they are dressed as Christians, it is impossible that they will be recognized: "How can they recognize you if you come so well disguised? And since we have changed the clothing that we wear, we can pass as Christians among them without suspicion, because we no longer look like Moriscos in any way."[65] The commoner Morisco Alcuzcuz has a more accurate grasp of reality than his noble master, since he is aware of how his own accent when speaking Spanish prevents him from fully passing as an Old Christian: "You can easily pass as one of them, since you speak the language well and look like a Spaniard; but me, how will I avoid punishment, since I do not know how to pronounce [Spanish] and I have never worn this clothing?"[66] This dialogue not only reinforces the difference between the assimilated bilingual noble Morisco and the not-quite-assimilated Arabic-speaking commoner, but also evinces the Morisco aristocrat's detachment from the social reality of the commoner Morisco, since he orders Alcuzcuz to perform a passing that is beyond Alcuzcuz's abilities.[67] As Margaret Greer states regarding this passage, "Calderón makes the gulf that separates noble from commoner wider than that which divides Christians from *moriscos*," and if Alcuzcuz can eventually pass as a Christian it is not because of his own ability, but because, travelling as a squire, nobody pays attention to him.[68] Calderón also further advances the symbolic expulsion of the Moriscos from the refiguring of Spanish identity when he has Tuzaní and Alcuzcuz "look like Spaniards." Whereas the Moriscos had been considered "españoles" even by the apologists of the expulsion, by the middle of the seventeenth century Spanishness was being refigured as a more restrictive concept of national identity, from which the Moriscos were excluded – and the displacing of Moorish clothing to the margins of Spanishness is part of this process.

Even if Calderón's *Amar después de la muerte* construes Moriscos as a foreign body and stages a strict visual difference between Old Christians and Moriscos, it still shows traces of the complex place of Moorish clothing in the Iberian social imaginary. After Calderón's *Amar después de la muerte*, the other plays dealing with the War of the Alpujarras further crystallize the representation of sartorial difference, which becomes a theatrical convention that does not receive much thought from playwrights. Miguel González de Cunedo's *A un traidor dos alevosos* (1653), contrary to other literary accounts, focuses not on the Marquis of Mondéjar, but on the Marquis of Vélez. This is hardly surprising since the author states at the beginning that, like the Marquis of Vélez, he is also from Murcia. The play makes only scant references to clothing, as it merely begins with "los que pudieren de moros" [as many as Moors as possible].[69] Only when the Alfaquí converts to Christianity at the end, do the stage directions say that he appears "de Christiano" to underline his religious conversion.[70]

González de Cunedo relies on the convention of sartorial difference, but mostly presents it in the stage directions as an assumption whose dramatic possibilities are not explored any further. The play does not even provide justification for the Morisco uprising, since it omits Philip II's prohibition. We can only glimpse the Morisco reaction when a peasant reports to the Marquis of Vélez that the wealthiest Moriscos have gathered in Fernando de Válor's house, changing their names, and that they crowned Válor king during these ceremonies.[71] Similarly, in *El rollo de Ézija* (c. 1672), attributed to Pedro Calderón de la Barca, the rebellion of the Moriscos is barely the background of the story, there is no mention of the prohibition of Morisco customs, and the Moriscos only appear on stage in Moorish garb in the final scene.[72] Even if these two plays do not provide much food for analysis with their unproblematic and succinct association of Moriscos with Moorish clothing, they further attest to the increasing normalization of such identification by the second half of the seventeenth century.

It is only by the late seventeenth century that we find another play offering an in-depth reflection on Moorish clothing in relation to Moriscos. Antonio Fajardo y Acevedo's *Origen de Nuestra Señora de las Angustias y rebelión de los moriscos* (1675), composed a century after the uprising of the Alpujarras and six decades after the general expulsion, further develops an extreme eschatological pattern in which ethno-religious identity is staged through sartorial difference. Thus, while Christians and Spaniards are synonyms, the Moriscos appeal to Africa as the base of their identity.[73] Like many of his predecessors, Fajardo y Acevedo clearly follows Mármol Carvajal's *Historia del rebelión y castigo de los moriscos del reino de Granada* (1600) while simplifying his historiographical account in very significant ways. The main Morisco characters are Farax Abenfarax and Fernando de Válor (Aben Humeya), who initially compete for control over the rebellion until they make a pact to share their power. Fernando de Válor dies as a Christian dressed as such.[74] Meanwhile, Abenfarax is explicitly cast as an incarnation of Evil, and his main goal is not the uprising itself, but rather the desecration of the Virgin of Las Angustias – probably because Fajardo y Acevedo composes his play to celebrate the new church built in homage to this image between 1663 and 1671.[75]

The most relevant of the historical manipulations of the play is that Fajardo y Acevedo conflates the historical figures of Farax Abenfarax

and Francisco Núñez Muley in his fiction. The play begins with
Abenfarax delivering the conventional speech complaining about
Philip II's decree to convince his fellow Moriscos to revolt, saying
that Philip II "has put with his law a heavy and crude yoke upon all
of you."[76] He alludes to Fernando and Isabel's peace treaty with the
Muslims of Granada in 1492, and how the pacts were soon broken
with the forced conversion of 1501: "having contradicted what had
been agreed and established, they make us deny the religion of the
true prophet, and abandon our clothing, the language of our elders,
and our dances and celebrations."[77] He even mentions one of Núñez
Muley's economic arguments against the decree, as included in Mármol Carvajal's summary: "Wishing to change our clothing aims to
impoverish us, because our adornments are worth more than three
million. Four hundred thousand people must dress anew, how much
will this cost us?"[78] Abenfarax promises then the restoration of the
Kingdom of Granada to Islam, as well as the cultural revival that
allegedly ensued with the uprising.[79]

The play continues with Farax Abenfarax's aim to provoke the revolt
of the Albaicín district in the city of Granada on Christmas Eve, including the scheme involving his soldiers dressing up as Turks found in
Mármol Carvajal's account: "Shall they come with turbans in the Turkish style, so that, in case they are discovered by chance, the suspicion
will be make it more challenging, as they believe that the great Lord
favours our aim."[80] The way Fajardo y Acevedo presents it, Abenfarax
is not successful in his aim because of his dissension with Fernando
de Válor and the intervention of the Marquis of Mondéjar. Thus the
playwright diverges from the information provided by Mármol Carvajal, who stated that in fact Abenfarax failed in his impersonation of
the Turks and the Moriscos of the Albaicín decided not to join him.[81]
It is also telling that Fajardo y Acevedo puts "turbans" where Mármol
Carvajal was referring to red berets, a small but significant detail that
further illustrates the historically situated and ever-changing sartorial
representation of the Moriscos.

Fajardo y Acevedo's play also reflects on the recycling of textiles.
María laments all the excesses and sacrileges committed by the rebellious Moriscos in Huécija, when they desecrated its church and took
religious robes to put them on, "making clothing from religious tunics
to increase the mockery."[82] This passage reflects similar accounts of sartorial recycling of religious robes into Moorish clothing found in the
accounts of the uprising of the Alpujarras. The *Memorial a la reina acerca*

de las muertes que en odio de la fe y Religión Christiana dieron los moriscos (1671), by Diego Escolano Ledesma, archbishop of Granada, tells that the Moriscos desecrated the churches, among other offences, "by tearing the Ornaments and the Sacred robes, putting them on in mockery and scorn."[83] The play offers a symbolic resolution to this alleged affront, as María reports the sacrilegious acts to Juan of Austria and he promises to avenge them in sartorial terms: "from *almaizares* and turbans we will make rich table cloths."[84] He thus proposes to close a cycle of sartorial transformation, which in the play is clearly started by the Moriscos' profanation of churches and desecration of liturgical textiles, by threatening in turn to return their Moorish clothing to Christian use.

Naturally, Fajardo y Acevedo is careful to omit those events contradicting his eschatological frame. Thus the play describes how the Marquis of Mondéjar and the Count of Tendilla welcomed Juan of Austria when he arrived in Granada, but it does not mention that the Count of Tendilla and his men dressed up as Moors for an improvised game of canes.[85] Yet, after emphasizing Morisco sartorial identity as a sign of difference, the play ends with the Marquis of Mondéjar announcing to Juan of Austria that Philip II is going to hold the parliament in Córdoba, where they are preparing to celebrate the victory over the Moriscos with a game of canes.[86] Again, the victory over Islam is celebrated with a Moorish cultural practice in which participants will likely dress up as Moors, and in this fiction, as the audience could predict, they will actually wear the garments of the defeated.

There are several reasons why seventeenth-century playwrights preferred to focus on the War of the Alpujarras instead of the expulsion of 1609–14. The main reason for this preference likely comes from the theme itself. The uprising of the Alpujarras was full of dramatic possibilities that historical distance helped to decant, with clear heroic figures, such as the Marquis of Mondéjar, Juan of Austria, or Fernando de Válor, around which stories of passion and vengeance could be easily articulated. Yet, along with the dramatic potentiality, the War of the Alpujarras provided the potentiality to stage sartorial difference. Since the historiographical and legal texts on which these plays were based identified Philip II's decree as the cause of the uprising, the distorted interpretation of this legal document became the referent for representing Moriscos as a visually differentiated community. By contrast, the expulsion of a baptized anonymous community lacked any potential dramatic qualities, as there were no significant episodes of armed resistance or prominent figures to serve as powerful dramatic characters.

And, more important for my point, there were no references to clothing in the decrees of expulsion or in the apologetic treatises defending the measure, and therefore there was very meager empirical evidence to substantiate the staging of sartorial difference.

There is also another reason why it is important to contrast the myriad ballads, epic poems, and apologetic texts written about Moriscos between the end of the sixteenth century and the beginning of the seventeenth on the one hand, and, on the other, seventeenth-century plays focusing on the uprising of the Alpujarras. The former were anxious to create the stereotype of Moriscos as an expendable rustic population at a time when dressing as a Moor was a sign of nobility. Meanwhile, seventeenth-century plays were written in most cases by playwrights who had never seen an actual Morisco, and at a time when dressing in Moorish garb was losing its prestige, especially in the second half of the seventeenth century. It is only then, when Moorish clothing was no longer perceived as a sign of class status and did not clearly articulate relations of power, that it lost its value as ceremonial clothing and became instead an exotic costume. The plays written after the 1620s decanted their historiographical sources to offer a simplified account of the past that overlooked the uncertainties about the sartorial practices of the Moriscos, most notably for men. Instead, they compensated for the vagueness of historical sources by staging Moriscos as unmistakably Moorish-dressed bodies. The intervention of these plays is to be taken seriously, since they have contributed retroactively to the interpretation of literary and historical documents created before them and have subsequently cemented the visual exoticization and Moorification of Moriscos in the historical imagination well into the present. This is why the ideological intervention of seventeenth-century plays looks more familiar and recognizable to us than that of the apologists of the expulsion or writers dealing with the Moriscos before their expulsion or shortly afterwards. It is precisely this inherited sense of familiarity that makes it so urgent to trace its genealogy and show how and when it was crafted.

Conclusions

This book has looked at the circulation of Moorish clothing in early modern Iberia to show that it was essential for both the display of class difference and the formation of a cultural imaginary about nobility, which in turn influenced the perception of Moriscos and Muslims. *"Moors Dressed as Moors"* has asked new questions about the social meaning of Moorish clothing, attempting to detach these questions from the traditional discourse of cultural archaeology focusing on the relations between the Iberian Peninsula and Islam. During the course of my research these questions kept branching out, and therefore many of them have barely been addressed, either because of the limitations of space or a lack of documents, not to mention human limitations. I hope this book has shown at least that Moorish clothing was not merely a costume without social consequences in early modern Iberia, but a commodity with a multiplicity of meanings among which social distinction figures large, and that it is useful for other scholars to pursue these other lines of inquiry.

One potential area of exploration is how the geographical extension of the game of canes within the Iberian Peninsula articulated notions of local or national identity. Looking at the editorial history of equestrian treatises, Noel Fallows suggests that, while the game of canes was at first popular in Andalusia, it was accepted all over the Iberian Peninsula only as late as 1600.[1] My own research shows that the game of canes was not originally limited to Andalusia, but Fallows is right in pointing out that it was not as common in certain areas of northern Iberia. For instance, I have not found any evidence of games of canes being held in the Basque country, Cantabria, and Asturias – all included in the Kingdom of Castile – and Navarre. One characteristic of these areas is the higher proportion of *hidalgos* in comparison with the rest of the Kingdom of Castile, a correlation that might condition the lack of interest in the game of canes as a performance of social advancement.[2] If we look at the northeast of the Iberian Peninsula, the case of the territories comprising the Crown of Aragon seems equally peculiar. While the game of canes is well documented in Saragossa and Barcelona, I initially expected to find more instances, given the importance of these two cities. According to María Carmen Marín, in Saragossa jousts were favoured over games of canes both because this city manufactured armour and because of the leading role of the Brotherhood of St George.[3] While I have not found any explicit opposition to the game of canes in Barcelona, Agustí Durán i Sanpere's study of the aristocratic festivals in this city conveys the impression that jousts and tournaments were also favoured there.[4] The case of the Balearic Islands reinforces Fallows's intuition about the geographical spread of the games of canes towards the 1600s. The entry of Charles V in Majorca in 1541 does not register any game of canes, and Jaume de Oleza seems to suggest in his *Exercicio militar* (1604) that it was introduced on the island towards the beginning of the seventeenth century.[5] It might well be the case that concepts of *infanzonía* in the Crown of Aragon were not entirely equivalent to the Castilian *hidalguía* in regard to its interaction with equestrian performances. I also wonder whether it was perceived at some point as a "Castilian" cultural influence that interfered in the complex articulations of Aragonese and Catalan political and cultural identity.

These are only some hypotheses that attempt to explain the uneven distribution of the game of canes throughout the Iberian Peninsula, based on the extensive but not exhaustive evidence I have examined. I am well aware that in this book I have barely scratched the surface of the game of canes as a local event, and archives all over the Iberian Peninsula abound with dusty files that might further confirm or correct some of the interpretations made throughout these pages, requiring paleographic and archivistic skills, not to mention time, patience, and financial resources.

Another aspect I have intentionally left out of this book is the international dimension of Iberian Moorishness beyond the Iberian Peninsula. On the one hand, the Iberian empires (Portugal, Castile, and Aragon) took the game of canes with them as one of the colonial ceremonies that they exported to Africa, America, and Asia. When the game of canes was transposed to those territories, it necessarily changed its meaning as a sign of social status, as it was inserted into a different set of social and racial relations.[6] It must have taken on new meanings as well when it was used as a diplomatic performance in other places in Europe, such as London and Flanders, as well as in Italy and the Mediterranean basin.[7] Gabriel Guarino shows that the game of canes was well integrated into Neapolitan urban life in the early modern period (in fact, I would add, much more well integrated than in certain other places in Iberia, such as Majorca and northern mountainous regions in Castile), which he interprets as a way to reinforce the Spanish hold over Italy and a reaction against French equestrian courtly culture.[8]

On the other hand, Iberian Moorish clothing was not impervious to cultural influences coming from outside the Iberian Peninsula. The most obvious and widely recognized is North African influence, but there were other European models of Moorish clothing that had an effect on how Iberians lived their own brand of Moorishness – for instance, the introduction of Turkish garments, as differentiated from traditional Moorish clothing.[9] For the sake of clarity, I have used the category of Moorish clothing as if it were homogeneous. Yet clothing *a la morisca* very likely evolved over the course of the centuries, and early modern wearers probably differentiated between a certain concept of traditional Moorish clothing as opposed to other garments labelled as "Turkish." How this flux of cultural influences altered the perceived "Moorishness" of the game of canes is beyond the scope of this book, but it could well have influenced the codes of social distinction by introducing novelties to hierarchize aristocratic taste.

With regard to the sartorial characterization of the Moriscos in the historical imagination, this book has only reached the second half of the seventeenth century to show when the moment of inflection took place. Yet the visual Moorification of the Moriscos has continued and has been mostly exacerbated in both popular and academic imagination well into the present. Further study here would explore how subsequent visual representations of Moriscos have been historically determined by the different political contexts in which they were produced, for instance how nineteenth-century historical paintings of the expulsion related to both nation building and the colonial campaign in North Africa, or how recent debates on immigration reshape popular memory about Moriscos, including a whole range of cultural expressions, from urban performances of *moros y cristianos* to the use of Moorish clothing in the historical novel, theatre, and film.

The post-expulsion Moorification of the Moriscos runs parallel to the de-Moorification of early modern Iberian Christian society in historical imagination. In contrast to the overwhelming representation of

Moriscos in Moorish garb, the game of canes is conspicuously absent from historical representation, and monarchs such as Charles V and Philip II are always represented as hieratic figures wearing black. Our historical imagination is not able to assimilate these solemn monarchs dressed in colourful Moorish garb while throwing canes from horseback. Popular historical imagination and academic production interact with each other more often than we would like to admit. In most academic works, the use of Moorish clothing is acknowledged as a mere curiosity, an anecdotal and temporary cultural influence from the Islamic period. Even if a film director tried to reflect the practice of the game of canes, the message would be unavoidably misunderstood as a carnivalesque performance, since the ceremonial use of Moorish clothing to display class status is not part of our current sartorial culture.

My intention is not to engage in the usual chastising of the misrepresentations found in historical fictions. Such a critique would not only be futile, it would distract us from an analysis of their ideological instrumentalization of history. My point is rather that, by contrasting the visual interventions of these historical representations, we are in a better position to scrutinize the assumptions and misconceptions about early modern society that this book has sought to counteract.

Notes

Introduction: "Moors Dressed as Moors"

1 Mármol Carvajal, *Historia*, 193. All translations are mine unless otherwise noted. For a thorough analysis of this author, see Castillo Fernández, *Entre Granada y el Magreb*. In this book I use "passing" as the deliberate impersonation of a different identity. For an analysis of passing in early modern Spanish society and literature, see Fuchs, *Passing for Spain*, and Lee, *The Anxiety of Sameness*.

2 Mármol Carvajal, *Historia*, 104–5.

3 On sumptuary legislation against Jews and Muslims in medieval Castile, see González Arce, *Apariencia y poder*, 170–7. For the application of such decrees in fifteenth-century Talavera, see María Yolanda Moreno Moreno, "Los mudéjares de Talavera," 408–10. For Portugal, see Lopes de Barros, "Body, Baths, and Cloth," 9–11; and Lopes de Barros *Tempos e espaços*, 189–98. Many of the medieval documents in Castile and Aragon have been compiled by Carrasco Manchado, *De la convivencia a la exclusión*, 91–222. The Nasrid Kingdom of Granada was equally influenced by Castilian fashion during the Middle Ages, and similar anxieties existed there regarding the lack of differentiation between Muslims, Christians, and Jews, Marín ("Signos visuales," 143–52).

4 On the concept of social distinction, see Bourdieu, *Distinction*.

5 Whenever possible, I will avoid using the term *Reconquista*. While this is not the space to discuss whether this is a valid concept to describe the expansion of Iberian Christian kingdoms during the Middle Ages, it is important to note that the term itself is anachronistic, as it was coined within the context of nineteenth-century Spanish nationalism (Ríos Saloma, *La Reconquista*, 25–39).

6 For the history of the Moriscos, see, among others, Caro Baroja, *Los moriscos*; Domínguez Ortiz and Vincent, *Historia de los moriscos*; Coleman, *Creating Christian Granada*; Harvey, *Muslims of Spain*; Perry, *The Handless Maiden*; Barrios Aguilera, *La convivencia negada*; Carrasco, *Deportados en nombre de Dios*; Carr, *Blood and Faith*; and Catlos, *Muslims of Medieval Latin Christendom*, 281–308.

7 Root, "Speaking Christian," 126. While I agree with Root about the way civil and religious legislation intersected, there was not a perfect synchronicity between them – for instance, the Inquisition did not persecute quotidian sartorial practices unless they were related to specific ritual contexts such as weddings or burials (Barrios Aguilera, *La convivencia negada*, 260).

8 In 1497, some *mudéjares* were tried in Córdoba for not wearing the required distinctive sign, Aranda Doncel, *Los moriscos*, 44. In 1525, the Muslims of Valencia were ordered to wear white crescents on their clothing – even as they were being compelled to convert within the same document (Pardo Molero, *La guerra de Espadán*, 122).

9 On the sumptuary legislation in early modern Iberia, see Pérez Martín, "El derecho y el vestido," 273–8; Álvarez-Ossorio Alvariño, "Rango y apariencia," 277; Puerta Escribano, "Reyes, moda y legislación," 65–9; and Puerta Escribano, "Las leyes suntuarias"; Astor Landete, *Valencia*, 83–97; Crespo, "Trajar as aparências," 104–5; Profeti, "Storia di O"; Rodríguez Cacho, "Pecar en el vestir"; and Martínez Bermejo, "Beyond Luxury," 99–100.

10 *Recopilación de las leyes*, 152r–3r.

11 This contradictory legal status parallels the way Moriscos were supposed to be baptized Christians but were taxed as if they were still Muslims. On the differential taxation of the Moriscos, see Galán Sánchez, "'Herejes consentidos'," and Galán Sánchez, "El dinero del rey."

12 The study of early modern clothing has usually taken the form of glossaries, which, while undoubtedly useful as an initial approach to the subject, inevitably present it in an essentialized way that rarely considers spatial and temporal variations. For glossaries of medieval and early modern Iberian clothing, see Bernis, *Indumentaria medieval española*; Bernis, *Trajes y modas*; and Bernis, *Indumentaria española*; Anderson, *Hispanic Costume*; Puerta Escribano, *La segunda piel*, 95–290; Astor Landete, *Valencia*, 111–259; Tejeda Fernández, *Glosario*; Maranges i Prat, *La indumentària*; Soláns Soteras, *La moda*; Crespo, "Trajar as aparências"; and Colomer and Descalzo, eds., *Vestir a la española*. For specific works on Iberian Moorish

clothing, see Bernis, "Modas moriscas"; Arié, "Acerca del traje"; and Martínez Ruiz, "La indumentaria."

13 Feliciano Chaves, "Mudejarismo," 149–53; Díaz Rodríguez, "Sotanas a la morisca," 34–7.

14 Notable exceptions to this paradigm are Feliciano Chaves, "Mudejarismo," 127–86; and Fuchs, *Exotic Nation*, 62–72.

15 Bernis, *Trajes y modas*, 2:19–24; Bernis, *Indumentaria española*, 28–31. Anderson follows in the same vein, *Hispanic Costume*, 92–7. For a critique of this paradigm, see Feliciano Chaves, "Mudejarismo," 138–40.

16 Bernis, *El traje y los tipos*, 451–501. Similarly, Puerta Escribano addresses Moorish fashion only when writing about foreign influences in Spanish culture, *La segunda piel*, 70 and 91.

17 Toro Ceballos, *El discurso genealógico*, 127.

18 On the *marlota*, see Ricard, "Espagnol et portugais"; and Bernis, *El traje y los tipos*, 466–7. I give the most common terminology in Spanish because this book focuses mainly on the kingdom of Castile. The terminology for Moorish clothing in Portuguese and Catalan is sometimes different.

19 The term *gineta*, as well as the Spanish *jinete* probably derive from the Moroccan Berber tribe of the *cenete* (Zanāta), which came to the Iberian Peninsula in the thirteenth century, although the word does not appear in Spanish until the fourteenth century, Maíllo Salgado, "Jinete," 106–7. On the role of the *gineta* style and its opposition to other riding styles in early modern Iberia, see Clare, "Les deux façons."

20 In many cases, both games were interchangeable. For instance, in 1605 the municipal council of Mula organized a game of canes to celebrate the birth of Philip IV, AMMu, Libro de Actas Capitulares, 1599–1610, 3 May 1605, 233r–4r. Yet the final account of the expenses record a *juego de alcancías* instead, 13 June 1605, 239v–40r. Amigo Vázquez suggests that the *juego de alcancías* was more affordable and therefore perceived as more plebeian than the *juego de cañas*, ¡*A la plaza!* 252–5.

21 On the game of canes, see Fuchs, *Exotic Nation*, 89–91 and 101–2; Puddu, "'Toros y cañas'"; Fallows, *Jousting*, 267–304; and Ruiz, *A King Travels*, 212–20. For Portugal, see Pereira, *Naissance*, 354–7.

22 Oleza, *Exercicio militar*, 43v.

23 Archivo Municipal de Archidona, Actas del Cabildo 4, July 8 1581 and 17 July 1581. I am grateful to Manuel Garrido Pérez and Soledad Nuevo Ábalos for looking for this document in the archive and providing me with a copy. This festival has also been analysed by Rodríguez Marín, *Luis Barahona de Soto*, 185–6; and Conejo Ramilo, *Historia de Archidona*, 253–4.

24 On the festivals of *moros y cristianos*, see Salvà i Ballester, *Bosqueig històric*; Carrasco Urgoiti, *El moro retador*, 67–90; Harris, *Aztecs*, 31–63; Brisset Martín, "Fiestas hispanas"; Flores Arroyuelo, *De la aventura*; and González Hernández, *Moros y cristianos*.

25 "Algunas veces se hace vestidos la mitad de los Caballeros a la Morisca y la otra mitad a la Castellana, y entonces se llama esta fiesta Moros y Cristianos," *Diccionario de la lengua castellana*, 2:128. In turn, the RAE definition is based for the most part in Gregorio Tapia y Salcedo's equestrian treatise *Ejercicios de la gineta*, 35 and 84. Salcedo y Tapia published his work in 1643, at a time when Moorish clothing was already losing its currency, and therefore does not necessarily reflect the significance that it had several decades earlier.

26 *Relación de los hechos*, 85–7. This passage is analysed among others by Harris, *Aztecs*, 54–60; Ruiz, *A King Travels*, 255–6; and Devaney, *Enemies in the Plaza*, 92–6.

27 Similar confrontational uses of games of canes in the sixteenth century are usually found on the Mediterranean coast, in locations which were frequently raided by Muslim corsairs, such as Alcalá de los Gazules or Vélez-Málaga. See, respectively, Alenda y Mira, *Relaciones*, 1:82–3; and Vázquez Rengifo, *Grandezas*, 109–16.

28 Sandoval, *Historia*, 1:23.

29 Llompart i Moragues, "Festes i devocions," 96; and Llompart i Moragues, "Imágenes de una cultura caballeresca." Both articles show full colour reproductions of the painting, which is held in a private collection.

30 Oleza, *Exercicio militar*, 12r.

31 Ruiz, *A King Travels*, 215. Fuchs wonders in similar terms whether this is "a perverse nostalgia for remnants of Islamic Spain," *Passing for Spain*, 6.

32 Such as one law issued by Philip II in 1590, *Premática de los vestidos*, 85r–v, and another one by Philip III in 1611, *Pragmática y nueva orden*, 3r–v.

33 I focus on the Kingdom of Castile because of my own disciplinary boundaries and because I am more knowledgeable about archival research there, but whenever possible, I refer as well to the kingdoms of Portugal and Aragon.

34 Benito suggests that this is a form of cultural appropriation in which hegemonic society selects inocous elements from the subaltern culture, "La ubicua presencia."

35 On the discourses about the origins of the game of canes, see Irigoyen-García, "The Game of Canes."

36 The purchase of equestrian and military garments from Islamic lands was common at least after the beginning of the fifteenth century, when

the Castilians traded with the Nasrid Kingdom of Granada in order to arm their own Moorish troops, Echevarría Arsuaga, *Caballeros en la frontera*, 116–17. On the importation of clothing from North Africa to the Iberian Peninsula, see Blanes Andrés, *Valencia y el Magreb*, 126–8; Salvador Esteban, "Datos sobre el comercio," 122; and Rumeu de Armas, *Cádiz*, 22–4 and 54–5.

37 Aguilar, *Tractado*, 25r. See also Suárez Montañés, *Historia del maestre*, 123; and Pinto Pacheco, *Tratado*, 140. At the beginning of the sixteenth century, the King of Tlemcen extended a peace treaty with Castile, offering to pay a tribute which included *adargas*, *albornoces*, and Tunisian turbans, Szmolka Clares, "Estudio," cvi. While the treaty was not accepted, probably because it was not strategic at that moment, it is significant that such an offer was made in the first place, which indicates that the King of Tlemcen was aware of Castilian demand for Moorish clothing.

38 Mármol Carvajal, *Primera parte*, 2:67r and 2:89v. On the emphasis given by Mármol Carvajal to the economic potential of Africa within colonial expansion, see Martínez-Góngora, "El discurso africanista."

39 López de Coca Castañer, "La seda," 40–1.

40 *Recopilación de las ordenanzas de la muy noble y muy leal cibdad de Sevilla*, 188v. For similar ordinances, see Córdoba de la Llave, "Algunas consideraciones," 346–52; *Recopilación de las ordenanzas del Concejo de Jerez de la Frontera*, 264–8; and *Ordenanzas del concejo de Alcalá la Real*, 203 and 237.

41 *Ordenanzas que los muy ilustres*, 148r.

42 *Ordenanzas para el buen régimen*, 199. Most of the extant tailors' acreditations in Toledo for the period between 1597 and 1624 acknowledge that applicants were able to make clothing for the game of canes, AMT, caja 6056 and caja 6057.

43 "todas as cousas tocantes a obra mourisca," *Livro dos regimentos*, 157.

44 *Livro dos regimentos*, 63, 88–91, and 92–3.

45 As seen in Francisco de la Rocha Burguen's licence, granted in 1615 and included at the beginning of his *Geometría y traça*, n.p. Even though Moorish clothing was profusely produced in Madrid, I was only able to find one later tailoring acreditation (AHPM, Diego de Cepeda, Protocolo 3858, 1r–1v, 13 January 1643).

46 *Plaza universal*, 225v.

47 For an overview of tailoring books in early modern Spain, see Mendía, "Libros españoles de sastrería"; Miller, "Aspects' of Men's Dress," 5–21; and, more recently, Puerta Escribano, "Los tratados del arte del vestir," 46–59; and Puerta Escribano, *La segunda piel*, 38–46. For a comparison of

one of the few extant *marlotas* with the patterns found in tailoring books, see Fernández-Puertas, "Vestimenta," 425–43.

48 Alcega, *Libro de geometría*, 62v–63r.

49 Freyle, *Geometría y traça*, 20r; Rocha Burguen, *Geometría y traça*, 134–5; and Andújar, *Geometría y trazas*, 37. Moorish clothing for the game of canes is mentioned as well in a manuscript tailoring book dated in the seventeenth century and currently held at the Museo de Santa Cruz in Toledo (Susana Cortés Hernández and Estrella Ocaña Rodríguez, "Manuscrito de sastrería," 357). The description of garments for the game of canes is absent only in Baltasar Sagovia's *Llibre de geometria del offici de sastres* (1617).

50 Étienvre has already pointed out the need for a comprehensive analysis of the game of canes that would take into consideration the abundant archival documentation (*Márgenes literarios*, 196n14).

51 As the lexicographer Sebastián de Covarrubias states in 1611, the Moriscos who spoke perfect Castilian could not be differentiated from Old Christians, *Tesoro*, "ladino," 747, and "tagarinos," 950. On the linguistic practices among the Moriscos, see Vincent, *El río morisco*, 105–18.

52 See Dadson, *Tolerance and Coexistence*, 225–43; Castillo Fernández, "La asimilación de los moriscos granadinos"; Tapia Sánchez, "Los moriscos de Castilla la Vieja"; and Colás Latorre, "Los moriscos aragoneses."

53 Harvey states, "nobody on either side had reason to record the activities of the assimilated," *Muslims of Spain*, 250. Similarly, William Childers coins the term "disappearing Moriscos" to account for the phenomenon of Moriscos who were successful in claiming not to be known as such, "Disappearing Moriscos," 58–9.

54 Jones and Stallybrass, *Renaissance Clothing*, 2.

55 Hersch, MacKay, and MacKendrick, "The Semiology of Dress," 106.

56 Ibid., 109.

57 "La vestimenta bendita / en tavardo se bolvió … / Fízo-se el alva gramaya / tocada de vuestro dedo … / Tornóse el estola chía, / y el amito, capirote" (*Cancionero de obras de burlas provocantes a risa*, 72–3).

58 "a los moros por dineros y a los cristianos de gracia," for the medieval ballad, see Díaz-Mas, *Romancero*, 30.

59 "Todas me llaman Antón, / todas me cobran Azarque, / y son, al daca y al pido, / mis billetes Alcoranes. / El sombrero que les quito / se les antoja turbante, / y mi prosa, algarabía, / por más español que hable" (Quevedo, *Poesía original completa*, 981).

60 The comic element works in Quevedo's poem because he selects those cultural elements that clearly emphasize difference, since hats and turbans are two distinctive garments that can hardly be confused – while he

ignores that there is a whole gamut of garments whose classification as Moorish/Morisco or Christian/Castilian might be arbitrary.

61 This relational and situational approach has been employed in the field of religious practices. Root notes, regarding religious orthodoxy, that "the indeterminability of faith apparent in the Inquisition's inability to determine dissimulation, and its effort to circumvent this by continually increasing its demands for proof of orthodoxy, meant the definition of orthodoxy would migrate to genealogy," "Speaking Christian," 130. Redondo has analysed how the religious practices of Old Christians were no less heterodox than those of *conversos* or Moriscos ("La religion populaire espagnole").

62 See Harvey, *Muslims of Spain*, 2–6; Brann, "The Moors?"; and Barbour, "The Significance of the Word *Maurus*."

63 Vincent, "¿Qué aspecto físico tenían los moriscos?"; López-Baralt, "La estética del cuerpo," 335–7; Fuchs, "The Spanish Race," 94–5.

64 On the terminology of *moro*/*morisco* in early modern Castile and Aragon, see Harvey, *Muslims of Spain*, 2–6; Carrasco Urgoiti, "Apuntes," 187–9; and Colás Latorre, "Los moriscos aragoneses," 149–51. In Portuguese, the equivalent term *mourisco* is somewhat different: when applied to individuals, it referred to recent converts of North African origin, as the Muslims from Portugal were expelled in 1497, Boucharb, *Os pseudo-mouriscos*, 5–27. Throughout this book, I use "Morisco" only with the meaning used in modern Spanish, since I only deal with the conceptualization of Muslims from Iberian origin.

65 We must take into consideration the existence of categories like "cristianos viejos de moros" [literally, Old Christians from Moors], studied by Childers, "Disappearing Moriscos," 54–6; Tueller, *Good and Faithful Christians*, 85–88; and Carrasco, "*Limpieza*."

66 Bass and Wunder, "The Veiled Ladies," 106; and Bernis, *El traje y los tipos*, 465.

67 Feliciano Chaves, "Mudejarismo," 134.

68 "Muslim Shrouds," 105–6.

69 For the influence of Andalusi textiles in medieval Iberia, see Constable, *Trade and Traders*, 173–81.

70 On the tropological uses of Moorishness [*lo moro*], see González Alcantud, *Lo moro*, 115.

1 Moors at Court

1 "Relación a la fiesta que la mañana de San Juan hizo S. A. del Principe nuestro señor, año 1595," BNE Ms.18644/32, 8r.

2 AMM, Acuerdos Capitulares 6, 1379–1380, 15v. Already cited by Capel Sánchez, *La vida lúdica*, 274.

3 *Crónica de Juan II de Castilla*, 408; and Romero Abao, "Las fiestas de Sevilla," 158.

4 Blancas, *Coronaciones*, 98–9.

5 González Hurtebise, "Inventario," 179 and 188.

6 Cancionero de Juan Alfonso de Baena, 6.

7 Duarte, *Livro da ensinança*, 6 and 73.

8 Balenchana, "Introducción," lxvi–lxxi; and Pereira, *Naissance*.

9 Resende, *Livro das obras*, 570.

10 Meneses, *Chrónica*, 61.

11 Resende, *Livro das obras*, 354–5.

12 Góis, *Chrónica*, 4:199.

13 Marchi, *Narratione particolare*, 82–3; and Cascão, *Uma jornada*, 105, 109, 113, and 115.

14 Sancho de Sopranis, *Juegos*, 24–5.

15 Méndez de Vasconcelos, *Liga deshecha*, 132v. The location of the *juego de cañas* is vague in the poem, somewhere between the Algarbe and Andalusia, but he seems to allude to Cádiz when he mentions the resistance to Protestants, quite probably referring to the English assault on this city in 1596.

16 Méndez de Vasconcelos, *Liga deshecha*, 133r.

17 On the propaganda campaign against Enrique IV of Castile, see Weissberger, *Isabel Rules*, 75–6.

18 Enríquez del Castillo, *Crónica*, 108, 113, and 120.

19 Guillén de Ávila, *Panegírico*, 7r.

20 Romero Abao, "Las fiestas de Sevilla," 158.

21 Fernández de Oviedo, *Libro de la cámara real*, 122–3.

22 Padilla, *Crónica*, 45.

23 Bermúdez de Pedraza, *Historia eclesiástica*, 198r.

24 Galíndez Carvajal, "Anales breves," 557.

25 Lalaing, "Voyage," 1:185–6 and 1:194; and the anonymous "Voyage que l'archiduc Philippe fait pour aller en Espagne," 2:612 and 2:621–2. Ramón de Cardona, Fernando of Aragon's stableman, took charge of Philip's training (Padilla, *Crónica*, 87).

26 Domínguez Casas argues that this painting was made by the Flemish artist Jacob van Laethem, *Arte y etiqueta*, 129–30.

27 Watanabe-O'Kelly, "The Early Modern Festival Book," 7. Useful compilations and catalogs of Spanish festival books can be found in Pérez

y Gómez's collection *Relaciones poéticas*; Alenda y Mira, *Relaciones*; Simón Díaz, *Relaciones breves*; and García Bernal, *El fasto público*, 636–61.

28 Girón, *Crónica*, 108–9. For other games of canes with the presence of Charles V, see Vital, "Premier voyage," 3:248–50; Sandoval, *Historia*, 1:450, 2: 249–50, and 2:568; Rodríguez Villa, *El emperador*, 72, 193, 199, 359, and 407; Layna Serrano, *Historia de Guadalajara*, 3:102; Fernández de Oviedo, *Relación*, 415–16; Lange, "Die tagebuchartigen Aufseichnungen," 421–2; Gómez-Salvago Sánchez, *Fastos*, 152; Santa Cruz, *Crónica*, 2:283 and 4:204; Crane, *Johannes Secundus*, 24; Girón, *Crónica*, 141; and Vargas, *Recibimiento*, 56 and 84–6.

29 For this game of canes, see Santa Cruz, *Crónica*, 4:22; and Rodríguez Villa, *El emperador*, 902. For the historical context of Vermeyen's painting, see Horn, *Jan Cornelisz Vermeyen*, 1:25. A different version of this painting, probably from Vermeyen's workshop, is located at the Palais St Vaast in Arras (Horn, *Jan Cornelisz Vermeyen*, 1:83n253).

30 On the use of black clothing, see Colomer, "El negro y la imagen real."

31 *Códice de trajes*, BNE RES/285. Mezquita Mesa dates this manuscript c. 1547, "El *Códice de trajes*," 18. In spite of her rigorous analysis of the manuscript, Mezquita Mesa mistakenly identifies this image with a North African soldier, 24.

32 March, *Niñez y juventud*, 2:402.

33 Fernández de Oviedo, *Libro de la cámara real*, 150–2.

34 Calvete de Estrella, *El felicíssimo viaje*, 203–4; and the anonymous *Relación del camino y buen viaje*, 64v.

35 Santa Cruz, *Crónica*, 4:269–71 and 5:87; Alenda y Mira, *Relaciones*, 1:77 and 1:98; Báez de Sepúlveda, *Relación verdadera*, 158–60; Khevenhüller, *Diario*, 129; Cock, *Relación*, 35, 60–1 and 78–80; Uhagón, *Relaciones históricas*, 228; and Lhermite, *Le passetemps*, 1:155. To celebrate the establishment of the court in Madrid, Philip II ordered the council of Madrid to organize one team for the game of canes in which he would himself participate, AVM, Libro de Acuerdos 14, 16 June 1561, 43v.

36 *Ordenanzas para el buen régimen*, 199.

37 Sancho de Sopranis, *Juegos*, 26–7. I will discuss these laws in more detail in chapter 2.

38 Sánchez Coello describes a similar portrait of the Infant Don Diego dressed in blue, holding an *adarga* in one hand and reeds in the other, Moreno Villa, "Documentos," 261–2. Breuer-Hermann suggests that this second painting, now lost, probably followed the same pattern as the one at the Monastery of Las Descalzas Reales, "Alonso Sánchez Coello," 26. On Sánchez Coello's

painting, see also Bernis, *El traje y los tipos*, 328n353; and López Poza, "Emblemática aplicada," 435.

39 On the influence that these women held over Philip III and how they affected court politics, see Sánchez, *The Empress, the Queen, and the Nun*.

40 For the game in 1595, see, Lhermite, *Le passetemps*, 1:256–7. For the game of 1599, see *Libro de noticias particulares*, 236–51.

41 Lhermite, *Le passetemps*, 1:256–7.

42 "con librea encarnada azul y blanca / capellar y marlota el cuerpo adorna / y la cabeza con bonete turco / de toca tunezi blanca cercado / con manga encarrusada el braço diestro / de quien pende una toca plateada / sereno el uello rostro el cuerpo tiesso / clauadas las rodillas con la silla / rasgando el açicate el cuero duro / de la manchada hijada del cauallo / una caña en la mano blandeando / con que apunta al contrario la herida / y muestra mil destrezas de la lança / ciento y quarenta moros ban siguiendo / de dos en dos el uello jouen diestro / christiano el coraçon y Moro el traje," "Relación a la fiesta que la mañana de San Juan hizo S. A. del Principe nuestro señor, año 1595" (BNE Ms.18644/32, 8r).

43 Gauna, *Relación*, 2:640–50.

44 "Relación de las fiestas que ubo en el casamiento de el excelentísimo señor Duque de Bragança con la excelentísima señora doña Ana de Velasco" (BNE Ms 3826, 1r–20v, 6v and 11r).

45 Khevenhüller, *Diario*, 600–1.

46 *Relación de lo sucedido en la ciudad de Valladolid*, 145–52.

47 Alenda y Mira, *Relaciones*, 1:168; and Quevedo, *Epistolario completo*, 23–4.

48 Herrera, *Translacion*, 38r; López de Zárate, *Obras*, 1:138; and Fernández de Caso, *Discurso*, 14r–16v; On the use of Moorish clothing in this game of canes, see also García García, "Las fiestas de Lerma," 232–3. For an analysis of the ideological stances of this festival, see Marchante-Aragón, "The King," 101–3.

49 Arce, Fiestas reales, 64.

50 For Philip IV's participation in the game of canes held on 21 August 1623, see Simón Díaz, *Relaciones breves*, 241–7; and Soto y Aguilar, *Jornada*, 87. A general analysis on the use of clothing for this festival is Miller, "Dress to Impress," 27–49. The Museo de Historia de Madrid has recently restored a similar composition which is also attributed to Juan de la Corte.

51 In the Portuguese realm, we can still find the lavish festivals held for the wedding between João II of Bragança (later João IV after his proclamation as King of Portugal in 1640) and Luisa de Guzmán in Vila Viçosa in 1633, Cadornega, *Descrição*, 44–5; and Ferreira Figueiroa, *Epitome*, 37r–38v.

52 Elliott and Peña, *Memoriales*, 2:81.

53 López de José, "Sobre el modo," 222.

54 López Párraga, *Elogio*, 14 and 23; Simón Díaz, *Relaciones breves*, 509–13, 512; and Mallea, *Granada festiva*, 22v–25r.

55 As shown in the introduction, the last tailoring book to mention the making of Moorish clothing for the game of canes was Martín de Andújar's *Geometría y trazas pertenecientes al oficio de sastres* (1640), 37. There is no reference to Moorish clothing in the next known tailoring book, Juan de Albayceta's *Geometría y trazas* (1720). The game of canes outlived the use of Moorish clothing well into the eighteenth century. Yet, as Amigo Vázquez shows, a game of canes played in 1783 in Valladolid was perceived as anachronistic ("Imágenes de la Ilustración," 387–8).

56 Tapia y Salcedo, *Ejercicios*, 35–8.

57 "En los juegos de cañas se solia usar, que la mitad saliessen vestidos de Christianos, y la otra mitad de Moros, con todos los requisitos de su trage" (Tapia y Salcedo, *Ejercicios*, 35).

58 Río Barredo, *Madrid*, 161–2.

59 Watanabe-O'Kelly, "Tournaments in Europe," 624.

60 *Naissance*, 356–7.

61 Fuchs, *Exotic Nation*, 11–30, 88.

62 Deloria, *Playing Indian*, 10–37.

63 Fuchs, *Exotic Nation*, 94–102.

2 Moorish Clothing and Nobility

1 Lalaing, "Voyage," 186; Sandoval, *Historia*, 2:249; Vargas, *Recibimiento*, 84; and "Relación a la fiesta que la mañana de San Juan hizo S. A. del Principe nuestro señor, año 1595" (BNE Ms.18644/32, 8r).

2 García Bernal, "La oligarquía sevillana"; and Ramos Sosa, "Fiestas reales sevillanas."

3 Pascual Molina, *Fiesta y poder*; and Amigo Vázquez, *¡A la plaza!*.

4 Festival books and other sources document the celebrations of magnificent games of canes in Toledo, Díez del Corral Garnica, *Arquitectura y mecenazgo*, 220–34. Unfortunately, most of the sixteenth-century municipal proceedings are no longer extant; and it seems that the emphasis of local historiography on the Corpus Christi has eclipsed the study of civil festivals in Toledo.

5 Moraleja Pinilla, *Historia de Medina del Campo*, 249–59; Viforcos Marinas, *La Asunción y el Corpus*, 77–83; Viforcos Marinas, *El León barroco*, 93–6; Lope Toledo, "Logroño"; Merino Álvarez, *La sociedad abulense*, 165–8; Ibáñez Pérez, *Arquitectura civil*, 52–8; and Guerra Sancho, "1605, ha nacido un

príncipe," 34–5; and Guerra Sancho, "Toros en la ciudad de Arévalo" (I am thankful to the author for sharing a copy of this work).

6 Córcoles Jiménez, *La villa de Albacete*, 517–20; Porras Arboledas, "Fiestas y diversiones en Ocaña"; López Gayarre, *Historia*, 238; and Mejía Asensio, "Fiesta en Guadalajara," 128–31.

7 Sancho de Sopranis, *Juegos*; Peláez del Rosal and Rivas Carmona, *Priego de Córdoba*, 101–02; Martín Rosales, "Pervivencias," 528–9; Martín Rosales, "El ocio," 351–77; Aponte Marín, *Gobierno municipal* [complementary CD], 346–47 and 488–527; Aponte Marín, "Juegos de cañas," 25; Cruz Cabrera, *Patrimonio arquitectónico*, 34–5; Araujo Miguélez, *Utrera*, 19–36; Morales Talero, *Anales de la ciudad de Arjona*, 126–7. Different from Andalusia, the kingdom of Granada was considered a separate administrative entity comprising Almería, Málaga, and Granada. In chapter 7 I will deal with the games of canes held in the Kingdom of Granada before the uprising of the Alpujarras in 1568. For the game of canes in the Kingdom of Granada after the 1570s, see Sánchez Ramos, "Fiestas," 453–70; Castillo Fernández, "La tradición taurina"; Conejo Ramilo, *Historia de Archidona*, 253–4 and 496; and Villena Jurado, *Málaga*, 148–52.

8 López, "Fiestas y conmemoraciones," 664–6; Ismael Velo Pensado, *La vida municipal*, 348–50; and Sobrado Correa, *La ciudad de Lugo*, 271–2.

9 Capel Sánchez, *La vida lúdica*, 271–5; and Fernández García, *Historias de Caravaca*, 43–5 and 56–8.

10 Hinojosa Montalvo, "Torneos y justas"; Monteagudo Robles, *El espectáculo del poder*, 38–41, 52, and 93–101; and Ramos Forqués, *La tauromaquia en Elche*, 5.

11 Mateos Royo, "La ciudad con el rey."

12 I have found evidence only for their celebration in Barcelona. (Durán i Sanpere, *Barcelona*, 2:171–259).

13 Pereda, *La arquitectura elocuente*, 114–17. See also Cruz Rodríguez, who traces many references to the game of canes in Salamanca during this period ("Salamanca histórico-cultural," 304–6).

14 Domínguez Ortiz, *Las clases privilegiadas*, 25–9; and Dewald, *The European Nobility*, 22–5.

15 For approaches exploring the transient nature of nobility, see, for the Kingdom of Castile, Soria Mesa, *La nobleza*, 37; Crawford, *The Fight for Status*, 3; and Hernández, "Ayuntamientos urbanos," 101–3. Lee also explores the anxieties about social mobility in genealogical and literary texts (*The Anxiety of Sameness*, 23–98).

16 Bennassar, *Histoire de la tauromachie*, 14–16. Watanabe-O'Kelly also follows Bennasar's observation ("Tournaments in Europe," 623).

17 Horn, *Jan Cornelisz Vermeyen*, 1:26–7.
18 I have analysed those municipal proceedings in which the town council financed the Moorish liveries for the riders of the game of canes, and have not included other municipal proceedings from towns such as Chinchón, Baeza, Alcalá la Real, and Jaén, in which my perusal of their archives for the period 1560–1610 (along with the previous work of local historians) showed that, even when games of canes were regularly held, the town council did not make significant contributions to the festivals, the cost of which were defrayed by aristocratic brotherhoods, wealthy patrons, or participants themselves.
19 Sancho de Sopranis, *Juegos*, 36. References to specific cases can be found in Delgado Barrado and López Arandia, *Poderosos y privilegiados*, 182; Larios Martín, *Nobiliario de Segovia*; and Fernández Salmador and Ferrero Maeso, *Pleitos de hidalguía*, 1:61, 216, 245, 400; 2:496–7; and 3:25. The Royal Chancery of Valladolid (to which all nobility litigations of northern Castile were referred) explicitly recognized participation in game of canes as a "positive act" showing noble status, Fernández de Ayala Aulestia, *Práctica*, 16v. The Royal Chancery of Granada did not single out the game of canes so explicitly, but also recognized participation in certain public acts as proof of nobility (López Nevot, *Práctica*, 474).
20 *El pasajero*, 2:571–2.
21 Rodríguez Marín, *Nuevo documentos cervantinos*, 88, 90, 142, and 148.
22 Drelichman, "Sons of Something," 610. Mosácula María analyses how rich cloth merchants in Segovia entered nobility as a way to control the city council, and how the game of canes was one of the means they used to cement their social promotion (*Los regidores*, 106–8).
23 Cátedra, *Nobleza y lectura*, 579.
24 Palacio Real, II/2121–56, II/2128–246, II/2125–161, II/2138–36, II/2139–104, II/2145–7, II/2154–101. García García, when analyzing these and other similar letters held at the Real Biblioteca de la Historia, suggests that these requests were made during the period in which the court was temporarily moved from Madrid to Valladolid (1601–6), as many nobles did not have the time nor the means to take all their belongings with them, "Las fiestas de corte," 45. While this explanation is plausible, many of these requests are from different periods, which indicates that in some cases they might come from individuals whose legal status as nobles did not correspond with the economic means they were supposed to have – or from individuals who might indeed have a horse, but not one appropriate for the game of canes.
25 For instance, in Alcalá la Real (Jaén), when asked to hold a game of canes in 1601, councilmen complained that many *caballeros* had sold their horses

because they were not using them, Archivo Municipal de Alcalá la Real, Libro de Actas A–13, 14 August 1601. In Priego de Córdoba, one festival was postponed because it coincided with another festival in the nearby city of Granada and therefore they would not be able to borrow the horses from there, as they usually did (AMPC, Actas del Cabildo 1582–8, Legajo 4, Libro 1, 18 August 1586, 206v).

26 Ribero, *Espejo*, 34–5.

27 Ruiz, *A King Travels*, 217.

28 See Aguilar, *Tractado*, 39r; Vargas Machuca, *Teórica y exercicios*, 223–4; Bañuelos y de la Cerda, *Libro de la jineta*, 73; Chacón, *Tractado*, 38; Oleza, *Exercicio militar*, 40v; and Gallego, *Tratado*, 41v.

29 On the projects of creating local militias controled by the monarchy during the sixteenth and seventeenth centuries, see Jiménez Estrella, "Las milicias en Castilla," 84–92.

30 For the responses from the *regidores* in 1562, see AGS, Consejo de Castilla, Leg. 2260. See also González Fuertes and González Fuertes, "La reforma"; Centenero de Arce and Díaz Serrano, "La reconstrucción"; Centenero de Arce, *De repúblicas urbanas*, 61–6; Contreras Gay, "Fuentes"; Hellwege, *Zur Geschichte*; and Ruiz Ibáñez, *Las dos caras de Jano*, 229–32.

31 Some brotherhoods were created based upon this decree, such as the brotherhood of Saint James in Santiago de Compostela, founded in 1564, Pérez Costanti, *Notas viejas galicianas*, 3:129–35. Aristocratic brotherhoods existed before the 1560s. For instance, a brotherhood in Talavera de la Reina had already mandated the celebration of games of canes in 1536, *Ordenanzas de la hermandad de Nuestra Señora del Prado*, 10–12. I am thankful to Rafael Gómez Díaz, from the Archivo Municipal de Talavera de la Reina, for providing me with a copy of this publication.

32 AGS, Cámara de Castilla, Diversos, 25, 1.

33 José Luis Martín analyses and reproduces responses to the 1572 decree from Ávila and its surroundings in "Cofradías de Caballeros." The response from Betanzos can be found in Núñez-Varela y Lendoiro and Rivadulla Porta in *Historia documentada*, 2:235–7 and 2:241–2. In Medina de Rioseco, the brotherhood of Saint John the Baptist, which included the requirement to play games of canes, was founded in 1574. García Chico, *Documentos*, 28–9. In other cases, the attempt to found such aristocratic brotherhoods failed because of the opposition from town councils (Sobaler Seco, "La cofradía").

34 El sueño caballeresco, 96–110.

35 For both edicts, see *Recopilación de las leyes*, 3v–5r.

36 AGS, Cámara de Castilla, Diversos, 25, 1.

37 For the importance of jousts in early modern Iberia, see Fallows, *Jousting*.
38 Luis Zapata, writing towards the end of the sixteenth century, confirms the lowest occurrences of jousts, although, within the same passage, he also undermines the assumption that they marked a clear class difference, as he notes that the horses and armours for the jousts could be borrowed or rented, *Miscelánea*, 162. On Zapata, see Cátedra, "Fiestas caballerescas," 93 and 103.
39 Fallows, *Jousting*, 309.
40 "Pragmática de Felipe II sobre declaración de trajes," AGS, Cámara de Castilla, Diversos 1, 11.
41 *Premática de los vestidos*, 85r–85v; and *Pragmática y nueva orden*, 3r–3v.
42 Early modern equestrian treatises are usually known as *libros de la gineta* because most of them (but not all) deal with this equestrian style. For an overview of this genre, see Balenchana, "Introducción," xvii–lxv. For the sartorial instructions in Iberian equestrian treatises, see Puddu, "Toros y cañas," 823–4n35.
43 Aguilar, *Tractado*, 39v.
44 Fernández de Andrada, *De la naturaleza del caballo*, 134v. This instruction is reproduced verbatim in his next book on the same subject, *Libro de la Gineta de España* (1599), 161r.
45 Dávila Puertocarrero, *Discurso*, 56–7.
46 Ramírez de Haro, *Tratado*, 83r.
47 Oleza, *Exercicio militar*, 41v. Although this work remained in manuscript, it was intended for print, since it includes the publication licence, dated in 1604.
48 Gallego, *Tratado*, 40v.
49 Examples include Pedro Camacho's manuscript *Tratado de la gineta* (1567), partially reproduced in Toro Buiza, *Noticias de los juegos de cañas*, 35; Suárez de Peralta, *Tratado*, 48; Céspedes y Velasco, *Tratado*, n.p.; and Fernández de Andrada, *Nuevos discursos*, 3:9v. Other manuals, while they do not address the use of Moorish clothing explicitly, seem to prefer it when they recommend wearing long vests and the use of *capuz cerrado* [hood] or *bonete* [beret] instead of *gorras* [hats], such as Chacón, *Tractado*, 25 and 28; and Ruiz de Villegas, *Tratado*, 115–16. Vargas Machuca says that his treatise does not deal with how to wear *marlotas* and turbans because of the subjective aspect of fashion, but he seems to take the use of Moorish clothing as a given (*Teórica y exercicios*, 231).
50 See, for instance, Aguilar, *Tractado*, iii r and 85r. This justification can also be found in works defending traditional military practices, such as Barrantes Maldonado, *Diálogo*, 81–2. As Fallows notes, the alleged military

efficacy of the *gineta* riding style was likely a marketing strategy (*Jousting*, 292–309).

51   *Actas de las Cortes de Castilla*, 324–5.

52   Fernández Duro, *Memorias históricas*, 2:539.

53   *Capítulos de reformación*, 12. On the series of sumptuary laws and their enforcement between 1619 and 1623, see Kennedy, "Certain Phases." This decree alludes to Philip III's sumptuary law of 1611 as the most immediate precedent, but obviates that the previous law explicitly allowed an exception for the *marlotas* of the game of canes. The sumptuary restrictions were temporarily suspended this same year of 1623 to celebrate one of the most exuberant festivals held to mark the arrival of the Prince of Wales (Kennedy, "Certain Phases," 95–6).

54   The causes for the decline of the game of canes were doubtless complex. For instance, Carrasco Urgoiti argues that the increasing participation of commoners in the seventeenth century entailed the consequent disaffection of the nobility for these kinds of equestrian performances as a sign of distinction (*El moro retador*, 62–4). Yet commoners had been pushing to be admitted to these equestrian exercises since at least the sixteenth century. What could have changed in the seventeenth century is the perception of this intrusion, which could be a symptom rather than the cause of the decline.

55   As we have seen, Gregorio Tapia y Salcedo's *Exercicios de la gineta* (1643) already refers to the use of Moorish clothing as past, *Ejercicios*, 35–8. Further, subsequent Castilian equestrian treatises do not mention the use of Moorish dress, such as Antonio Luis Ribero's *El espejo del cavallero en ambas sillas* (Madrid: n.p., 1671) and Bruno Joseph de Morla Melgarejo's *Libro nuevo bueltas de escaramuza, de gala, a la gineta* (1737). Andrés Dávila y Heredia still instructs riders to dress as Moors in his *Palestra particular de los exercicios del caballo* (1674), 54v. However, this passage, like many others in this barely original work, is taken directly from Pedro de Aguilar's *Tractado de la gineta* (1572). The blatant way in which Dávila y Heredia plagiarizes a work written a century before him makes one suspect that he is feigning authority, making it difficult to accept as accurate his description of how the game of canes was performed by the 1670s, since he is using the exact words that described games of canes in the mid to late sixteenth century. The use of Moorish dress for the games of canes – or at least the memory of its use – lingered a little bit longer in Portuguese equestrian books. Francisco Pinto Pacheco's *Tratado da cavalaria da gineta* (1670), like Tapia y Salcedo, conceptualized a sartorial opposition between two teams when he suggested that "sera muito ayroso hauer duas quadrillas, hũa à Portugueza e outra à Mourisca" [it will be very gallant to

have two teams, one in the Portuguese style and the other in the Moorish style] (*Tratado*, 165). Antonio Galvam de Andrade's *Arte da cavallaria de gineta e estardiota* (1678) still mandated that the best way to perform the game of canes was to dress up as Moors (*Arte da cavallaria*, 207). Yet Andrade must have been quite elderly in 1678, and his description was probably a remembrance of how he organized the equestrian games for the wedding of João IV of Portugal in Vila Viçosa in 1633. In fact, in spite of his remark about Moorish clothing, he only gives instructions on how to wear the cape (*Arte da cavallaria*, 179–83).

56 There is indeed a significant gap in the editorial history of tailoring books, since the next known one is Juan de Albayceta's *Geometría y trazas* (1720), which does not include any reference to Moorish clothing and further confirms that it was progressively abandoned by the second half of the seventeenth century.

57 Sánchez Ramos, "Fiestas," 467–8; and Viforcos Marinas, *La Asunción y el Corpus*, 66.

58 Viforcos Marinas's chart of León festivals shows that the games of canes disappeared from urban ceremonies after the 1620s (*El León barroco*, 93–6). In the case of Guadalajara, Mejía Asensio attributes the decline in the second half of the seventeenth century to the local nobility's migration to Madrid ("Fiesta en Guadalajara," 128–9). Amigo Vázquez notes the difficulties of having the nobility participate in equestrian performances in Valladolid in the second half of the seventeenth century (*¡A la plaza!*, 248–60).

59 For the presence of Moorish clothing in the inventories of monarchs and nobles, see González Hurtebise, "Inventario," 179 and 188; Bernis, *El traje y los tipos*, 472; Braamcamp "Inventário"; and Rojo Vega, *El Siglo de Oro*, 26 and 270.

60 Gaspar Mercader himself describes the *marlota* of his alter ego Fideno in the pastoral romance *El prado de Valencia*, 141. His description is confirmed by other festival descriptions (Gauna, *Relación*, 1:392).

61 *Renaissance Clothing*, 5.

62 Sandoval, *Historia*, 2:249.

63 Fernández Duro, *Memorias históricas*, 2:279.

64 *Colección de documentos inéditos*, 46–7. It is not clear whether we should add 463 *ducados* for the materials that the tailor Castillo lists as already received, which would raise the total to 861 *ducados*. On this game of canes, see Pascual Molina, *Fiesta y poder*, 374–5.

65 *Colección de documentos inéditos*, 52–3. Compare to the case of Santiago de Compostela in 1566, whose municipal council paid 158 ducados to the embroiderer who made 11 liveries for the game of canes (or 14 *ducados*

per rider). See Arquivo Histórico da Universidade de Santiago de Compostela, Fondo Municipal de Santiago, libro de libranzas, 1550–66, 214v.

66 Simón Díaz, *Relaciones breves*, 7. Indeed, this festival book also recounts how some of the *marlotas* had to be made of damask because they could not find enough silk in the area, which reveals how the availability of resources conditioned the clothing used in the game of canes.

67 Herrera, *Translacion*, 38r.

68 Covarrubias, *Tesoro*, 296.

69 "Carta de Francisco Zapata a Diego Sarmiento de Acuña" (n.p.: n.d.). Palacio Real II/2116–158. The letter is not dated, but it is probably from the end of the sixteenth century or the beginning of the seventeenth.

70 "Carta de Martín Valero Franqueza a Diego Sarmiento de Acuña," Palacio Real II/2127–158.

71 These instructions are reproduced in Pedro Núñez de Avendaño, *De exequendis mandatis regum Hispaniae* (1564), 4v and 6v.

72 Núñez de Avendaño, *De exequendis*, 167v–168r; and García de Saavedra, *De expensis*, 195r–v. For a similar ecclesiastical criticism of the expenses made for festivals, see Jesús María, *Epistolario espiritual*, 86–9.

73 For instance, in Guadalajara in 1546, 1559, 1560, and 1571, Layna Serrano, *Historia de Guadalajara*, 3:462–3, 3:468–9, and 3:475–7; Mejía Asensio, "Fiesta en Guadalajara," 128–31; in Valladolid in 1592, AMV, Libros de Actas, 20 June 1592, 85r–85v; and in Seville in 1599, Tenorio y Cerero, *Noticia*, 8 and 59.

74 Gómez-Salvago Sánchez, *Fastos*, 200.

75 AVM, Secretaría, 2.56.45, which is partially transcribed as an appendix by Benito Ruano, "Recepción madrileña," 95–8. See also Cayetano Martín and Flores Guerrero, "Nuevas aportaciones," 395–7. There is also a very detailed itemization of the expenses made in the festivals, AVM, Contaduría, 1.317.1. Adding all the quantities referring to the liveries of the game of canes, I count a total of almost 6,000 *ducados*, which is similar to the estimate offered in an anonymous description of the festival suggesting that this game cost about 6,500 *ducados*, *Libro de noticias particulares*, 251n2. This is already an exorbitant figure, but still substantially lower than the 15,973 *ducados* shown in the general report. Such a huge gap may suggest that councilmen were tempted to do some kind of creative accounting during the festivals. Similar percentages were spent in clothing to celebrate the victory of Lepanto in Seville in 1575, García Bernal, "La oligarquía sevillana," 357–8; and to celebrate Philip III's entry in Valladolid in 1600, Cabeza Rodríguez, Torremocha Hernández, and Martín de la Guardia, "Fiesta y política," 83. For a general estimate of the financial burden of

festivals for the municipal budget in early modern Seville, see Martínez Ruiz, *Finanzas municipales*, 145–6.

76 AMT, caja 2258. When Philip III requested budgetary moderation, the council of Toledo agreed to not include gold in the damask liveries, as they had initally planned – yet did not renounce distribution of silk liveries.

77 "Eram as librés de setim bordado e forro de telilha as marlotas, ou vaqueiros … As ordinarias eram falsas, mas alguns senhores as mandaram fazer de tella e prata fina, que valiam muyto dinheiro" (Pinheiro da Veiga, *Fastigimia*, 126).

78 Moya Pinedo, *Corregidores*, 183. To this amount, we should probably add the 99 *ducados* listed for freight from Toledo, although it is not clear in the document whether this expense is for all the materials for the festival or only for the fabrics of the game of canes.

79 Another detailed budget for twelve sets of livery for a game of canes celebrated in Valladolid in 1606 reveals a similar figure. The costs for Moorish livery for the participants amounted to 674 *ducados*, or 52 *ducados* per livery – the total figure would be lower than that, since the budget also includes the clothing for trumpeters, "Expedientes de festejos 1600–1609," AMV, CH 97–9, 161r–1v. To celebrate the birth of Philip IV in 1605, the town council of Mula (Murcia) paid about 30 *ducados* for the damask of each livery – to which we should add smaller amounts listed separately for the accessories and for tailoring the clothing, AMMu, Libro de Actas Capitulares 1599–1610, 13 June 1605, 239v–240r. For the same event, the city council of Cartagena allotted 50 *ducados* for each rider of the game of canes, AMC, Libro de Actas Capitulares 1601–1605, 7 May 1605, 299r; and the city of Murcia gave about 27 *ducados* to the participants in a game of canes for Saint John (in addition to the silk textiles which were already distributed in March) (AMM, Libro de Actas 222, 1 March 1605, 243v–4r).

80 One shortcut to explore the conversion between past and present prices is to look at the price of gold. Since one *ducado* was equivalent to 3.5 grams of gold, and since, as of 10 April 2016, one gram of gold cost $40, we could arrive at the equivalence of $140 per *ducado*. Since each of the 32 Moorish liveries for the 1604 festival in Cuenca cost 37 *ducados*, we can calculate the figure of $5,180 for each Moorish outfit. Many historians would object to such a calculation for very good reasons: first because of the enormous fluctuations of the price of gold then and now, and second because prices of commodities are only meaningful when compared to salaries and the cost of living within a specific time period. Yet, taken with care, this calculation might be useful to offer an approximate estimate for the modern reader.

81 Zofío Llorente, *Gremios y artesanos*, 455–8.

82 Figures for prices and salaries are taken from Hamilton, *American Treasure*, 370 and 400.

83 For the *encamisada*, see AVM, Libro de Acuerdos 18, 25 August 1570, 446v–447r; for the game of canes, see Libro de Acuerdos 18, 26 August 1570, 447r–447v, 28 August 1570, 449v–450r, and Libro de Acuerdos 19, 24 November, 28v; and for the *alcancías*, see Libro de Acuerdos 19, 30 October 1570, 2r–2v; 21 November 1570, 21v–22v. For a thorough analysis of these preparations, see Cruz Valdovinos, "La entrada," 425–30.

84 AVM, Libro de Acuerdos 19, 8 November 1970, 10r.

85 Ibid., 21 November 1570, 21v–2v; and 24 November 1570, 28v.

86 Cruz Valdovinos, "La entrada," 428–9. As he points out, it is unclear whether the game of canes took place or not, since there is no register of any reimbursement being made. I am inclined to think that the game of canes did not take place, based on Juan López de Hoyos's description of the festivals, which mentions only the *encamisada* and the *juego de alcancías* (*Real apparato*, 12r–12v and 250r–251r).

87 AMAv, Libro de Actas Consistoriales de 1600, 25 May 1600–21 June 1600, 117r–159r. On this celebration, see also Merino Álvarez, *La sociedad abulense*, 167–8.

88 AMAv, Libro de Actas Consistoriales de 1600, 18 July 1600, 177v–179v.

89 This for instance is what happened in Úbeda in 1563, Real Chancillería de Granada 2057–3, 28r–60v; in Baeza in 1590, Cruz Cabrera, *Patrimonio arquitectónico*, 34–5; and in Jaén in 1593, Jaén, "Papeles viejos," 108.

90 AMA, Libro de Acuerdos 1583–1590, 13 July 1585, 158r.

91 Ibid., 18 July 1587, 305r.

92 Around the same years, the city of Cartagena ordered the purchase of some bulls and commissioned some of its councilmen to organize a game of canes, AMC, Libro de Actas Capitulares, 1585–1588, 5 July 1586, 32r. The usual misunderstanding about defraying the cost of the game of canes soon arose, so that the next month the city had to clarify that, even when its council had ordered the celebration, it was under the assumption that the cost would fall on the nobility (2 August 1586, 41v).

93 AMMR, Caja 64, carpeta 606, 31 August 1584.

94 AMMR, Caja 65, carpeta 609, 28 July 1587.

95 Goy Diz, *A actividade artística*, 2:309–10.

96 Ibid., 2:312. It seems that some monarchs such as Manuel I of Portugal also had a stock of Moorish clothing that they would lend to participants in games of canes at court (Góis, *Chrónica*, 4:199).

97 AMPC, Actas del Cabildo 1582–1588, Legajo 4, Libro 4, 10 October 1601, 189v. Similarly, for the entry of Philip II in Medina del Campo in 1592, the

council paid 50 *ducados* to help defray the cost, even if participants did not justify how they spent this amount, AMMC, H–Caja 162, carpeta 2685, Libros del Mayordomo 1591–1592, item 136. The corresponding municipal proceedings in which sets of livery were offered do not reveal how many riders were supposed to participate in this game of canes, but if there were at least a dozen riders, the final figure per set could not be higher than the case of Priego de Córdoba, AMMC, H–caja 527, Libro de Acuerdos 1590–1593, 26 May 1592, 290r, and 9 June 1592, 300r–v.

98 AMV, 20–30 August 1600, 135r–44r. Something similar happened about the same time in nearby Medina del Campo, in which the *quadrilleros* were offered 36 *ducados* for each rider in their teams, but were explicitly told the next day that they would need to return the difference if they ended up having four riders in their teams instead of six (AMMC, H–Caja 545, Libro de Acuerdos 1601–1603, 20–1 June 1600, 66v–67v and 70r–v).

99 Archivo Municipal de Santa Fe (Granada), Libro del Cabildo, 9 June–1 July 1579, 32r–3v.

100 ARChV, Registro de Ejecutorias, caja 1323, 10.

101 Cervera Vera, *San Vitorino*, 20–2; Guerra Sancho, *San Vitorino*, 15–17. One reason that is not mentioned in the document but might have influenced the opposition of the people of Arévalo is that the 1609 festival showed an extraordinary hike in the budget for the Moorish livery. According to a lawsuit between several tailors in Valladolid, the nobles in Arévalo had organized another game of canes only two years earlier in which they paid 1,200 *ducados* for the same number of 24 liveries (ARChV, Pleitos Civiles, Pérez Alonso (F), Caja 1584.0002, 3r).

102 Archivo Municipal de Leganés, Documentos de San Nicasio 3. This document is partially transcribed by Alonso Resalt and Sánchez, *San Nicasio*, 45–6. The accounting books of the Brotherhood of Saint Nicasius do not show any expenses for games of canes, Archivo Municipal de Leganés, Libro de cuentas de la Cofradía de San Nicasio, 1601–1700. This absence suggests that bullfights and games of canes were funded by the municipality of Leganés, as was often the case – unfortunately, the municipal proceedings for this period are no longer extant.

103 "muchos dias antes las dichas ropas estan condenadas y aplicadas para vasquiñas de las mugeres de los regidores" [many days before the aforementioned clothing are condemned and promised to be turned to skirts for the wives of the government officers] (Castillo de Bovadilla, *Política*, 2:1034–5).

104 "puedese hazer una vasquiña desta marlota," Alcega, *Libro de geometría*, 62v.

105 "puede servir la marlota para una vasquiña falseando las sacaduras de las sisas hilvanandolas hazia dentro y no çurrandolas," Freyle, *Geometría y*

traça, 20r. The patterns for *marlotas* included in the other two seventeenth-century tailoring books by Francisco de la Rocha Burguen (1618) and Martín de Andújar (1640) do not indicate how to transform them into a different garment.

106 "trocar o vender ropas" (Rosal, *Diccionario etimológico*, 443).

107 Jones and Stallybrass, *Renaissance Clothing*, 33.

108 On the trade of second-hand clothing in the late medieval and early modern period, see Allerston, "Reconstructing"; and García Marsilla, "Avec les vêtements."

109 The logical consequence of this progression is that the "alquiladores de hatos" [clothing lenders] began to be called "alquiladores de libreas" [livery lenders] by the second half of the seventeenth century (Agulló y Cobos, "'Cornejos' y 'Peris'," 186).

110 Sánchez Ramos, "Fiestas," 463–4.

3 Unlawful Moorishness

1 "Pude casar mi hija / con un hombre que ha estado / para un juego de cañas convidado" (Quevedo, *Teatro completo*, 470).

2 "en la que solo pueden ser cofrades los que conocidamente lo son [nobles], porque obligan a jugar las cañas" (Larios Martín, *Nobiliario*, 1:231).

3 "antes de mil años espero verle jugar cañas por el nacimiento de algún príncipe" (Vélez de Guevara, *El diablo Cojuelo*, 26).

4 "a tiempo que se celebraban fiestas de toros aquel día y juego de cañas, acto positivo que más excelentemente ejecutan los caballeros de aquella ciudad" (Vélez de Guevara, *El diablo Cojuelo*, 65).

5 Scholars traditionally assume that these ballads were composed in the fourteenth and fifteenth centuries – although there is only scant evidence before they were compiled in the sixteenth century. For interpretations on their original political and ideological context, see MacKay, "The Ballad and the Frontier"; Correa, *Los romances fronterizos*; and Yiacoup, *Frontier Memory*. The success of these compositions in the sixteenth century is visible through their inclusion in musical compilations (Quinn, *The Moor and the Novel*, 31–53).

6 Alemán, *Guzmán de Alfarache*, 1:214–60. For a recent English translation of both Alemán's text and *El Abencerraje*, see Fuchs, Brewer-García, and Ilika, "*El Abencerraje*".

7 The term "Maurophilia" was first coined by Georges Cirot in a series of articles analyzing the figure of the Moor in early modern Spanish

literature, "La maurophilie littéraire." For the interpretation of *El Abencerraje* as a glorification of Christian victory over Islam, see Guillén, *Literature as System*, 193n39; Burshatin, "Power"; Quinn, *The Moor and the Novel*, 55–67; and Lee, *The Anxiety of Sameness*, 184–90. For those scholars who find in the Moorish tale a nostalgic representation of the Islamic period, see, among others, Carrasco Urgoiti, *The Moorish Novel*, 60–72; Avilés, "Los suspiros del *Abencerraje*," 470–1; and Fuchs, *Exotic Nation*, 36–45.

8 Equestrian Moorish performances with a well-developed narrative element can be found in a festival held in Valladolid in 1527, Ruiz García and Valverde Ogallar, "Relación," 188–90; and in the weddings of Duke of Bragança Teodósio II and Ana de Velasco in Vila Viçosa in 1603, "Rellaçao da entrada da señora Duquesa em Villaviçosa e festas que lhe fiseraon," AHN–Nobleza, Toledo, Frías Caja 115–D39. There is also a manuscript of a Spanish translation of the latter, "Relación de las fiestas que ubo en el casamiento de el excelentísimo señor Duque de Bragança con la excelentísima señora doña Ana de Velasco," BNE Ms 3826, 1r–20v. Ferrer Valls transcribes some passages of the Spanish translation (*Nobleza y espectáculo teatral*, 225–33).

9 "vieron venir por donde ellos iban un gentil moro en un caballo ruano; él era grande de cuerpo y hermoso de rostro y parescía muy bien a caballo. Traía vestida una marlota de carmesí y un albornoz de damasco del mismo color, todo bordado de oro y plata. Traía el brazo derecho regazado y labrada en él una hermosa dama y en la mano una gruesa y hermosa lanza de dos hierros. Traía una darga y cimitarra, y en la cabeza una toca tunecí que, dándole muchas vueltas por ella, le servía de hermosura y defensa de su persona. En este hábito venía el moro mostrando gentil continente," *El Abencerraje*, 134–6. Trans. Fuchs, Brewer-García, and Ilika, "*El Abencerraje*," 29.

10 "transportados en verle, erraron poco de dejarle pasar." *El Abencerraje*, 136. Trans. Fuchs, Brewer-García, and Ilika, "*El Abencerraje*," 29.

11 For a general overview of the sartorial aspect in the Moorish ballads, see García Valdecasas, *El género morisco*, 82–5; and Correa, *Los romances fronterizos*, 1:140–7.

12 "vestido de una marlota / medio azul, medio encarnada, / efectos que causa el moro / en la bella mora Guala: / el capellar amarillo, / que es color desesperada; / azul el turbante y toca / por unos celos que trata" (Ruiz Lagos, *Moriscos*, 137).

13 "... se quita / la marlota que llevaba / de verde, morado y blanco / en amarillo aforrada, / y dice: sirva el aforro / por ser color que me cuadra. / Las verdes plumas no quiero, / pues se perdió mi esperanza / ... / La toca

morada dejo, / porque aunque amor no me falta, / podrá ser que halle otro / que pueda mejor gozarla" (Ruiz Lagos, *Moriscos*, 125–6).

14 Martínez Ruiz has thoroughly catalogued all the instances where clothing is mentioned in Pérez de Hita's work, "La indumentaria." He acknowledges in passing, citing Blanchard-Demouge, that Pérez de Hita's sartorial descriptions are based on Moorish festivals held by Christians, "La indumentaria," 56. Yet Martínez Ruiz downplays this evidence in order to maintain that Pérez de Hita's work describes the actual clothing of the Moriscos in sixteenth-century Granada, "La indumentaria," 61–2. Notwithstanding his valuable study of the Morisco inventories of the Archivo de la Alhambra, I disagree with his main thesis, as I will further address in chapter 7.

15 See, for instance, the ballads "Tanta Zaida y Adalifa" and "Ah mis señores poetas" (Ruiz Lagos, *Moriscos*, 162 and 166).

16 Ibid., 166.

17 Lasso de la Vega, *Manojuelo de romances*, 28–31.

18 Carrasco Urgoiti, "Vituperio"; García Valdecasas, "Decadencia"; and Colonge, "Reflets littéraires," 139–47.

19 Sánchez Jiménez, "La batalla del romancero," 179–81.

20 Guillén, *Literature as System*, 193n39.

21 My emphasis on how class struggle is encoded in Moorish clothing should not be understood to argue that Moorish fictions had absolutely no bearing on the debates about the Moriscos. Representation is not an either/or question, as it has been usually framed in debates about literary maurophilia and maurophobia. Even as I argue that Moorish fictions were an indirect way to negotiate the distribution of power among Old Christians across social lines, it is not my intention to dismiss their explicitly xenophobic content, deployed by the satirical ballads. It is undeniable that the selection of this rhetoric echoed the stigmatization of the Moriscos as it was found in political and religious discourses and practices. I will explore this in chapter 8.

22 "aquel yegüero llorón, / aquel jumental jinete, / natural de do nació, / de yegüeros descendiente, / hombres que se proveen ellos, / sin que los provean los reyes" (Góngora, *Romances*, 232).

23 See Orozco Díaz, *Lope y Góngora*, 31–9; and Jammes, *La obra poética*, 121–6.

24 Jammes, *La obra poética*, 122, followed by Carreño in his edition of the poem already cited. Neither Jammes nor Carreño explain what would be so obvious in this scatological allusion.

25 "otra quadrilla de seis / moros de mediana talla / qu'apenas tenian cauallos / ni aun enpuñan çimitarras ... / Aunque de remiendos yban /

no pareçia mal su gala / que no s'esperaua tanto / de los que tan poco
alcançan" (BNE Ms.18644/32, 1v).

26 "Los que no tienen dinero / alli estan / y entre nosotros no estan. / Alli
estan los caualleros / haciendo al amor mil fieros / con mas plumas
que dineros ... / despues de aber almorçado / es verdad / a sus casas
se an tornado / y el bestido desnudado / por tanto no le gastar" (BNE
Ms.18644/32, 2v–3r).

27 Torres, "Toros y cañas," 354–8.

28 "fiados los tafetanes, / alquilados los cauallos / y prestados los boçales"
(Torres, "Toros y cañas," 358).

29 "las marlotas son vasquiñas / que a sus mugeres les hazen: / de los capellares,
bandas, / y cuellos de los turbantes" (Torres, "Toros y cañas," 355).

30 "Regidores vestidos de codicia / con ropas de brocado, seda y lana, /
reciben nuestra Reina soberana, / haciéndola mil fiestas de avaricia,"
reproduced in Benito Ruano, "Recepción madrileña," 86.

31 "a costa del labrador / vista paño, y rompa seda" (*Romancero general*, 387r).

32 "salgan a jugar cañas / vestidos de mil maneras, / ni que traygan
alquiladas / en sus zambras las libreas" (*Romancero general*, 388r).

33 "No ha quedado hebilleta / de cuantos hatos tenía / y no es cantidad
pequeña. / Allá me los tienen todos / esos señores Poetas, / con que
componen más Moros / que la ardiente Libia lleva" [I don't even have
a little bucket left from all the costumes I had, and it was not a small
quantity. Those mister poets took them all, and with them they make more
Moors than there are in the burning Libya] (Lasso de la Vega, *Manojuelo*,
364–5).

34 "¿Quién compra dieciséis moros / que han quedado de unas cañas?"
(Lasso de la Vega, *Manojuelo*, 101).

35 "las marlotas venderé / de damasco azul y plata / ... a un hombre que
alquila hatos / el Corpus para las danzas, / venderé toca y turbante, / los
datilados y manga" (Lasso de la Vega, *Manojuelo*, 102).

36 "Hasta que les ponga el día / en las manos dos azadas, / escabaránme
las viñas / regaránme huerta y granja / y venderlos he a galera / cuando
monedas no haya" (Lasso de la Vega, *Manojuelo*, 103). The image of
the Moriscos as an impoverished group is in itself another stereotype
(Childers, "Disappearing Moriscos," 58–9).

37 The first instance of the interpretation of anti-Moorish ballads as directed
against Moriscos can be found in the first part of Jerónimo Alcalá Yáñez's
Alonso, mozo de muchos amos (1624), in which the main character says
that his master used to write Moorish ballads until Philip III decreed the
expulsion, and he then started writing pastoral poetry instead, *Alonso*, 319.

Alcalá Yáñez is clearly paraphrasing the anti-Moorish ballads "Ah mis
señores poetas" and "Toquen apriesa a rebato," which proposed pastoral
as an alternative to Moorish themes, Ruiz Lagos, *Moriscos*, 168 and 184.
On this debate, see Irigoyen-García, *The Spanish Arcadia*, 22–4. Yet Alcalá
Yáñez confuses different times and therefore alters the correlation between
literary fashions and historical events, as the ballads recommending
the cultivation of the pastoral themes as an alternative to the literary
celebration of gallant Moors were composed at least a decade before the
expulsion.

38 Savariego de Santana, *Libro de la Iberiada*, 2v. I am grateful to Miguel
Martínez for pointing out this rare epic poem.

39 "multitud de moros o secta" (Covarrubias, *Tesoro*, 815).

40 See Milhou, "Desemitización," 44–50; and Milhou, "Fronteras, puentes
y barreras"; Stallaert, *Etnogénesis y etnicidad*, 65–9; and Perceval, *Todos
son uno*, 46. Fuchs has taken up Milhou's contribution, complicating the
concept of cultural cleansing of everything Moorish. She shows that it
was not a uniform social strategy and that in many instances recognized
Moorish cultural practices were openly embraced as signs of aristocratic,
local, or even national identity (*Exotic Nation*, 11–30).

41 "teniendo por grandeza y gallardía vestirse a la morisca con marlota,
capellar y toca, y regozijar en aquel hábito las ciudades y corte
representando ... un tropel Morisco" (Núñez de Velasco, *Diálogos*, 377).

42 "Jineta y cañas son contagio moro; / restitúyanse justas y torneos, / ... /
Suceda a la marlota la coraza" [The *jineta* riding style and the game of
canes are a Moorish contagion; let's restore fights and tournaments ... May
the cuirasse replace the *marlota*] (Quevedo, *Poesía original completa*, 135–6).

43 In a previous article I cited Núñez de Velasco's opinion as representative
of this line of thought calling for cultural cleansing, "'Poco os falta para
moros'," 357. However, as I expanded my research, I realized that he
and the other authors analysed here are rather isolated voices that are
meaningful only within larger social debates not necessarily related to the
Moriscos. On the confrontation between commoners and nobles regarding
warfare, see Miguel Martínez, *Frontlines*, 54–85.

44 On the social implications of the promotion of the game of canes as an
alternative to the joust, see Fallows, *Jousting*, 309.

45 See the anonymous *Espejo de la consciencia*, liv r.; and Jesús María,
Epistolario espiritual, 86–9. Many other religious treatises refer to the game
of canes approvingly, such as Bartolomé de Medina's *Breve instrucción de
cómo se ha de administrar el Sacramento de la penitencia* (1579), 150r; Pedro
de Valderrama's *Exercicios espirituales para todas las festividades de los santos*

(1608), 195; and Fray Ángel Manrique's *Sanctoral Cisterciense, hecho de varios discursos* (1613), 231v. The only explicit criticism is that of Fray Pedro Simón, who in 1626 condemned the practice of Spaniards of "vestirse en sus juegos de cañas libreas de aquella abominable nacion de Moros: cosa bien digna de perpetuo destierro de todos los terminos Christianos" [dressing in the livery of those execrable Muslims for their games of canes, which is something that deserves eternal exile from Christian lands], *Primera parte de las noticias historiales*, 37. However, in spite of the bitterness of this denunciation, his goal was not to propose the eradication of garb associated with Islam, but to prove that clothing is not a reliable indicator of the ethnic origin of a people.

46 See Pedro de Covarrubias, *Remedio de jugadores*, xxi v; Alcocer, *Tratado del juego*, 289–94; and Guzmán, *Los bienes del honesto trabajo*, 197–8 and 436–7. Only Francisco de Luque Faxardo criticizes the game of canes, but the dialogue form of this treatise presents it as an irony rather than serious criticism, *Fiel desengaño contra la ociosidad y los juegos* (1603), 144v. Here it should be noted that in Spanish *juego* means both "game" (both board games and sport) and "gambling," which explains why both topics are often treated together.

47 On moralists' opinions on clothing in early modern Spain, see Puerta Escribano, *Historia del gremio*, 170–8; and Rodríguez Cacho, "Pecar en el vestir."

48 Indeed, games of canes were often organized to celebrate religious festivities, such as the transfer of the alleged remains of Saint Secundus of Abula in Ávila (1594), Cianca, *Historia*, 321–2; the transfer of the remains of Fray Bartolomeu dos Mártires to Viana do Castelo (1609), Cacegas, *Vida*, 262; the beatification of Saint Luis Beltrán in Valencia (1609), Gómez, *Los sermones y fiestas*, 225–32; the beatification of Saint Teresa of Ávila in 1614, Amigo Vázquez, *¡A la plaza!*, 438–40; or the acceptance of the Immaculate Conception of the Virgin in Alcalá de Henares in 1617, "Relación de las famosas fiestas."

49 Nirenberg proposes a similar interpretation of the strategical use of Anti-Judaism in early modern Spain (*Anti-Judaism*, 217–45).

50 Even though the "moro gracioso" is a tag more often applied to Old Christian commoners trying to dress in gallant Moorish clothing, it has been analysed only in relation to a certain theatrical stereotypization of the Moriscos, since it is often conflated with the similar albeit different type of the "morisco gracioso," which I will analyse in chapter 6. At best, it is mentioned as one of the many instances in which characters "a lo gracioso" offer a parodic contrast to noble characters (Gómez, *La figura del donaire*, 70–2).

51 *Los cautivos de Argel*, 255; *La desdichada Estefanía*, 56; *La doncella Teodor*, 312; and *La octava maravilla*, 174v.

52 Vélez de Guevara, *Don Pedro Miago*, 161.

53 *Las quinas de Portugal*, 586; and *El cobarde más valiente*, 434.

54 *El conde de Saldaña*, 1:79–95, 91; and *La manga de Sarracino*, 8r.

55 The 1680 manuscript describes the commoner Cosme as "morillo baharí," *La luna africana*, Biblioteca Nacional de España Ms. 15.540, 1680. 3:12v. The meaning of the term *baharí* is unclear. According to the early modern lexicographer Diego de Guadix, *baharí* means "maritime," *Recopilación*, 371. Thus this play was probably associating the unlawful use of Moorish clothing with seamen, who had a poor social reputation. The eighteenth-century imprints of *La mejor luna africana* describe Cosme with the most common term of "Moro ridículo" (*La mejor luna africana*, 33).

56 Profeti "Il manoscritto autografo," 249. In this case, the reference to the "moro gracioso" appears only in a 1664 print version attributed to Francisco de Rojas, but not in the original manuscript by Juan Pérez de Montalbán from the 1630s.

57 "las sábanas de la cama / y el bonete de mi tío / con que duerme cuando hay frío, / y aqueste... ¿cómo se llama? / ... ciegayernos u almaizar, / frazada u ... ¿Qué es? ... quesicosa / que a mi figura espantosa / le sirve de capellar. / Esta adarga y esta lanza / que en cas de mi amo he cogido / hoy de molde me ha venido" (Vélez de Guevara, *Don Pedro Miago*, 161).

58 "Yo pienso que me he vestido al reves" (Cubillo de Aragón, *La manga de Sarracino*, 8).

59 "no es algarabía / aquello, sino gallego, / y bonete de disfraces, / árbol de muchos injertos" (Ruiz Lagos, *Moriscos*, 18).

60 "Héteme aquí convertido / en morabito de Orense, / engerto un gallego en moro." (Tirso de Molina, *Las quinas de Portugal*, 579).

4 Lope's Moors: Self-Fashioning and Resentment

1 See, among others, Mas, *Les Turcs*, 1:387–91 and 2:7–147; Márquez Villanueva, *Moros, moriscos y turcos*, 187–214; Case, *Lope and Islam*.

2 Moreno Mendoza, "En hábito de comediante," 152. In addition to commercial theatre, we should consider as well the less scriptural urban ballets included in the celebrations of Corpus Christi. For instance, Jean Sentaurens documents the celebration of many urban ballets inspired in so-called Moorish literature in Seville at least from 1576 to 1652 (*Séville et le théâtre*, 2:788–9, 2:794–5, and 2:1286).

3 Sánchez de Badajoz, *Farsas*, 233–59.

4 Muñoz, *Mencía de Mendoza*, 156–60.

5 Sentaurens, *Séville et le théâtre*, 2:1196. Sentaurens also cites the description of another ballet named *La manga de Sarracino*, which was performed in 1646 and specifies that the Moors should act as if they were playing canes, *Séville et le théâtre*, 2:794–5. Urban ballets imitating the game of canes are also documented for Segovia in 1611, Flecniakoska, "Les fêtes du Corpus," 230–1; for Madrid in 1570, 1595, 1599, and 1649, Sánchez Cano, "Dances"; and García García, "Máscaras," 50–1; for Burgos in 1615, Miguel Gallo, *Teatro y parateatro*, 158; and for Tordesillas in 1605, Rojo Vega, *Fiestas y comedias*, 90.

6 The stage directions indicate "luego comienzan los instrumentos y entra el juego de cañas" [then the instruments play and the game of canes enters the stage]. After that, the characters praise the Moorish clothing allegedly worn by the participants, Villacastín, *Triunpho de la fortuna*, 62v. On this passage, see García Soriano, *El teatro universitario*, 326; and Asenjo, *La tragedia de San Hermenegildo*, 1:34.

7 Tárrega, El prado de Valencia, 140–3.

8 "En verme en tales hazañas, / … / llevo puesto en mis entrañas / o que soy Moro de Argel, / o que voy a jugar a cañas," Tárrega, *El prado de Valencia*, 175. For a more thorough analysis of the Moorish impersonation in Tárrega's play, Irigoyen-García, "'Poco os falta'," 355–69.

9 "para que nos traiga a costa / de trabajos y dinero, / marlotas, mantos y tocas / de moros de berbería, / que en Valencia todavía / las hay propias y no pocas" (Tárrega, *El prado de Valencia*, 165).

10 While in *El prado de Valencia* the use of Moorish clothing becomes self-reflexive (but also elusive), Tárrega included the game of canes in other plays as well. *Las suertes trocadas y torneo venturoso* begins with the long description of a game of canes in an unnamed city (1:380–441). *La enemiga favorable* (published in 1616) begins with the sounds and music of the game of canes being played off stage, and immediately afterwards the main characters appear "vestidos de juego de cañas, con capellares y marlotas amarillas, azicates, lanças, y adargas" [dressed for the game of canes, with *capellares* and yellow *marlotas*, spurs, lances, and *adargas*] (1:576–7).

11 Canet Vallés, "Introducción," 53–8; and García Santo-Tomás, *La creación del Fénix*, 93–108.

12 Case, *Lope and Islam*, 183–5. For the analysis of Lope's plays with Muslim characters, see also Mas, *Les Turcs*, 387–91; Carrasco Urgoiti, *Vidas fronterizas*, 179–92; and Carrasco Urgoiti, *El moro retador*, 279–313. Morley and Tyler identify more than 300 "Moorish" characters in Lope's oeuvre, *Los nombres de personajes*, 2:606–10.

13 In some plays there are references to characters dressing for the game of canes (without clarifying whether they are dressing as Moors or not), such as *El príncipe perfecto, primera parte* (1618), 472; and *La vitoria de la honra* (1635), 119.

14 Presotto, "Vestir y desvestir"; Carrascón, "Disfraz y técnica teatral"; and Higashi, "La construcción escénica."

15 Wilder, "Lope, Pinedo," 22. As Jones and Stallybrass note for the case of early modern England, "Costumes were prior to any particular play. The stock from a previous production could shape both the subject matter and the number of plays that might be necessary to recoup the financial outlay" (*Renaissance Clothing*, 196).

16 Davis, "Introducción," 16–17.

17 On Lope's sojourns in Toledo, see San Román, *Lope de Vega*, ix–xxi. On the importance of Toledo for the manufacture of silk textiles, see Nombela, *Auge y decadencia*, 284–303; and Santos Vaquero, *La industria textil*, 41–78.

18 San Román, *Lope de Vega*, lxxxvii–cviii.

19 San Román published several documents showing Gaspar de Porres's intense clothing trading activity (ibid., 46–214).

20 See Fernández Martín, *Comediantes*, 22 and 32; Esquerdo, "Indumentaria"; Pérez Pastor, "Nuevos datos," 370–1; and García Gómez, *Vida teatral*, 100 and 103.

21 García Gómez, *Vida teatral*, 188.

22 García García, "El alquiler de hatos," 51–3; "Los hatos de actores," 183–8; "El alquilador de hatos," 704n28 and 706–8; San Román, *Lope de Vega*, 65, 96, 108, and 116; Agulló y Cobos, "'Cornejos' y 'Peris'," 183–5; and Rojo Vega, *Fiestas y comedias*, 261–4.

23 We find these transactions for Berja in 1622, Sánchez Ramos, "Fiestas," 463–4; and for Madrid in 1633, "'Cornejos' y 'Peris,'" 196–7. García García also states that the *alquiladores de hatos* provided their costumes for the game of canes, but he does not give any concrete example, "El alquiler de hatos," 54 and 57. Such transactions between clothing lenders and the organizers of games of canes account for only those performances in which municipal councils with tight budgets could not afford to give away Moorish clothing as "livery" in its original sense.

24 Jones and Stallybrass, *Renaissance Clothing*, 175–206.

25 García García, "Los hatos de actores," 173.

26 By my count, there were at least 8 *marlotas*, 12 *capellares*, 7 *sayos vaqueros*, and 5 *mantos de mora* (AHPM, protocolo 2559, 676r–712v).

27 One *capellar*, 2 sleeves, and one *jubón* are so qualified (AHPM, 2559, 689v–90r, 702v and 703v). There is no indication why some Moorish garments

are identified as related to the game of canes whereas others are not. The inventory of the clothing that lender Miguel de Fonseca made in 1592 in Valladolid lists 8 "marlotas de juego de cañas" (AHPV, Protocolo 759, 232v).

28 AHPM, 2559, 713r–65v.
29 AHPM, 6897, 115v. Partially reproduced by Agulló y Cobos ("'Cornejos' y 'Peris'," 197).
30 Lasso de la Vega, *Manojuelo*, 364–5.
31 Ibid., 101–2.
32 "No había en aquel tiempo tramoyas, ni desafíos de moros y cristianos," Cervantes, *Teatro completo*, 8. Agustín de Rojas Villandrando, in his *El viaje entretenido* (1603), also locates the introduction of battles between Muslims and Christians in the theatre of the 1580s, *El viaje entretenido*, 152. On how these authors tried to construct a specific story of the development of Spanish theatre, see Burningham, *Radical Theatricality*, 173–7.
33 See, among others, Matas Caballero, "Luis Vélez de Guevara," 322; García Valdés, "Comedias"; and Carrasco Urgoiti, *El moro retador*.
34 Vélez de Guevara, *Don Pedro Miago*, 174.
35 "MINGO. ¿Juegan moros y cristianos / con un mismo traje? / BERRUECO. Yo, Mingo, sospecho que sí, / y que las parejas son / un moro con un cristiano" (ibid., 194).
36 The stage directions instruct: "Sale toda la compañía, de juego de cañas" [The entire troupe appears dressed for the game of canes] (ibid., 199).
37 On the need to restage a play when there is a heavy investment in clothing, see Jones and Stallybrass, *Renaissance Clothing*, 196.
38 I cite from the *suelta* at the Universitätsbibliothek Freiburg, which has no date on the title-page and is dated circa 1650 in their catalogue. There is also an eighteenth-century inprint at the British Library, which is the one usually cited by the scarce bibliography on this work. On *La manga de Sarracino*, see Whitaker, *The Dramatic Works*, 62–5. Otero Mondéjar discovered that Cubillo de Aragón was of Morisco origin, as he made a successful case for staying in Granada during the expulsion of 1609 by claiming that his ancestors were noble Moriscos from Aragón who had been Christians for centuries ("Álvaro Cubillo de Aragón").
39 Schaeffer, *Geschichte*, 2:97–9. On the traces of Cubillo de Aragón's dramatic activity in the 1620s and 1630s see Whitaker, *The Dramatic Works*, 14–16. Sentaurens registers a ballet called *La manga de Sarracino* staged in Seville in 1646, *Seville et le théatre*, 2:794. The title seems to indicate that this ballet was inspired by Cubillo de Aragón's play, which would have been written before that date.

40 "En el cuarto de Comares, / la hermosa Galiana, / con estudio y con destreza, / labraba una rica manga / para el fuerte Sarracino, / que por ella juega cañas," Ruiz Lagos, *Moriscos*, 154. The story of this ballad was amplified in the first part of Ginés Pérez de Hita's *Guerras civiles de Granada* (1595), 85–7. While both the anonymous ballad and Pérez de Hita's version locate the story in Granada, Cubillo de Aragón's *La manga de Sarracino* is set in Toledo, as Lope de Vega did in his play *Los palacios de Galiana*.

41 The *Diccionario de Autoridades* (1726–39) states that the right sleeve worn in the game of canes was called *Sarracena* (*Diccionario de la lengua castellana*, 2:128). Because of the authority traditionally granted to the Real Academia Española, this information has been widely disseminated in subsequent scholarship. If this definition were correct, it would mean that the title of *La manga de Sarracino* would be redundant, since both *manga* and *sarracena* would actually refer to the sleeve for the game of canes. Yet I have not been able to find any occurrence of the term *sarracena* with the meaning of Moorish sleeve in the works I have surveyed; it thus seems that this would be a late semantic evolution and that the name *sarracena* was given to the sleeve after the name of the fictitious character, thanks to the influence of these poets and dramatists writing on the story of Galiana and Sarracino.

42 Cubillo de Aragón, *La manga*, 11v.

43 On this play, see Carrasco Urgoiti, *El moro retador*, 245–76.

44 *La luna africana*, BNE, Ms. 15.540, 1:9v–16v. I cite this manuscript copy dated 1680, which restarts foliation for each act. There are also many eighteenth-century reprints of this play, retitled *La mejor luna africana* and still staged as late as 1798. For the play and its potential reference to an actual festival held at court, see Carrasco Urgoiti, *El moro retador*, 255–6 and 267–9.

45 La luna africana, 3:12v.

46 On the concern about actors wearing luxurious garments that were the object of sumptuary laws, see García García, "Los hatos de actores," 178–9. In 1615, actors were allowed to wear luxurious garments with the condition that they refrained from doing so off stage (Varey and Shergold, *Teatros y comedias*, 56).

47 On the dissemination of Lope's Moorish ballads, see Alvar, *El romancero*, 103–22.

48 For biographical readings of these poems, see Goyri de Menéndez Pidal, "Los romances"; Carreño, *El romancero lírico*, 55–116; and García Valdecasas, *El género morisco*, 28–34 and 41–8. For an assessment of the criteria for determining the attribution of these ballads, see Sánchez Jiménez, "Introducción," 23–36.

49 Goyri de Menéndez Pidal, "Los romances," 407.
50 Ruiz Lagos, *Moriscos*, 69–70.
51 Ibid., 83–4.
52 "él mismo se trae la adarga, / en quien un Fénix parece, / que en vivas llamas se abrasa / y en cenizas se resuelve," Ruiz Lagos, *Moriscos*, 87. Lope's middle name was Félix, and he often referred to himself as Phoenix.
53 "Por la plaza de Sanlúcar / galán paseando viene / el animoso Gazul, / de blanco, morado y verde. / Quiérese partir el Moro / a jugar cañas a Gelves, / que hace fiestas el Alcaide / por las treguas de los Reyes" (Ruiz Lagos, *Moriscos*, 76).
54 García Reidy, *Las musas rameras*, 217–42; and Wright, *Pilgrimage*, 16–23.
55 Greenblatt, *Renaissance Self-Fashioning*, 4.
56 On these parodies, see Carrasco Urgoiti, "Vituperio," 116–22; and García Valdecasas, "Decadencia," 137–51.
57 Márquez Villanueva, "Lope infamado de morisco," 160–72.
58 I must agree here with Sánchez Jiménez's criticism of Márquez Villanueva's reading, "La batalla," 179–81. I disagree however with the former's conclusion that it is merely a literary exchange: even if poets merely use the language of xenophobia to mock each other and not to make a conscious intervention in the political debate about the Moriscos, we cannot simply conclude that the selection of this language lacks ideological undertones.
59 "Mas como el vestir de pluma / tan poco o nada les cuesta, / de palabra y pluma arrojan / costura que el viento lleva," Lasso de la Vega, *Manojuelo*, 366–7. Lasso de la Vega is playing with the ambiguity of Spanish *pluma*, which means both "quill" and "feather," as feathers were an essential element of Moorish clothing at the beginning of the seventeenth century.
60 "El que a Adalifes y Azarques / sacó costosas libreas, / saque para sí un bonete / y verá lo que le cuesta" (Ruiz Lagos, *Moriscos*, 184).
61 "No lleva por la marlota / bordadas cifras, ni letras / en el campo de la adarga ... / porque es el moro idiota, / y no ha tenido poeta / de los sastres de este tiempo, / cuyas plumas son tijeras" (ibid., 176).
62 "Váyase con Dios Gazul, / lleve el diablo a Celindaja, / y vuelvan esas marlotas / a quien se las dio prestadas" (ibid., 165). On the allusions to Lope in this poem and its attribution to Luis de Góngora, see Orozco Díaz, *Lope y Góngora*, 48–52.
63 On this ballad, see Fuchs, *Exotic Nation*, 84–7; and Orozco Díaz, *Lope y Góngora*, 52–8. Carrasco Urgoiti suggests that it was composed within the circle of Pedro de Padilla, who may have been a Morisco and was one of the first compilers and composers of Moorish ballads ("Vituperio," 132–4).

64 "Si este triste maldiciente / de vestidos tiene falta, / podréisle dar porque calle / vuestras marlotas de gracia, / y entienda el mísero pobre / que son blasones de España, / ganados a fuego y sangre, / no (como él dice) prestadas" (Ruiz Lagos, *Moriscos*, 170–1).

65 On the interrelation between Moorish ballads and theatre in Lope's earlier plays, see Carrasco Urgoiti, *El moro retador*, 123–56, and Gallo, "Le maschere."

66 "para ser lozano / un cristiano hidalgo, es llano / que ha de tener algo moro" (Vega, *El hijo de Reduán*, 88).

67 Case, *Lope and Islam*, 186–7.

68 Castillejo, *Las cuatrocientas comedias*, 41.

69 Regarding the interruption in the composition of Moorish ballads at the beginning of the seventeenth century, Carrasco Urgoiti also observes that, in contrast, courtly Moorishness continued in full swing in spite of the expulsion ("Vituperio," 137).

70 For Lope's self-fashioning at court, see García Reidy, *Las musas rameras*, 255–8 and Wright, *Pilgrimage*. For an overview of the treatment of the game of canes in Lope's ouevre, see Cornejo, "La funcionalidad." Yet Cornejo focuses on the representation of bullfights and does not try to identify any kind of evolution in Lope's representation of the game of canes.

71 Entrambasaguas, *Lope de Vega*, 29–30n22. As usual, this festival book includes a description of a game of canes (Vega, *Relación de las fiestas que la imperial ciudad de Toledo hizo*, 11r–14r).

72 Vega, *La burgalesa de Lerma*, 41–3; *Lo que pasa en una tarde*, 55–60; and *No son todos ruiseñores*, 147–8.

73 Quevedo, *Epistolario*, 23.

74 Bershas, "Lope de Vega"; Atienza, "La (re)conquista"; Pedraza Jiménez, "Lope"; and Vélez-Sainz, *El Parnaso*, 166–76.

75 See Morel-Fatio, "Les origines," 44–53. On the use of the coat of arms of the Carpio, Lope's own invention, see McCready, *La heráldica*, 196–201. Pamp interprets Lope's desire to be recognized as noble as a way to cover for a possible *converso* origin, *Lope de Vega*, 19–27.

76 Gauna, *Relación*, 1:176–7.

77 Wright's interpretation of this episode is that Lope did obtain some kind of favour, since, no matter the circumstances, he was able to address the monarch in person, *Pilgrimage*, 60–2. I agree with Vélez-Sainz, who on the contrary argues that this ridiculous appearance is telling of Lope's poor reputation at court (*El Parnaso*, 177). Indeed, it is also significant that we know of this episode only through Gauna's description, while Lope never mentioned his address to Philip III, not even in his own poetic description of the 1599 festivals in Valencia.

78 On Lope de Vega's authorship, see Kossoff, *"Los cautivos de Argel."*

79 "morisco del Reino de Valencia, en su hábito, como ellos andan" (Vega, *Los cautivos de Argel*, 223).

80 "Salgan todos los Moros que pudieren en procesion, y detrás, si puede ser a caballo, y si no a pie; aquel Francisco morisco, muy galán, de moro" (Vega, *Los cautivos de Argel*, 235).

81 "Hale hecho allí el Marqués / fiestas, Rey de Argel, tan grandes / que se han visto desde aquí; / y no es mucho que el mar pasen, / que los fuegos del castillo, / del mar, dando en los cristales / los mostraba como espejo, / que muestra la propia imagen" (Vega, *Los cautivos de Argel*, 259).

82 On the game of canes in 1599 Valencia, see Gauna, *Relación*, 2:640–50.

83 "Y advierte que las libreas / no eran invención morisca, / sino cristiana y moderna, / marlotas, y capellares, / capas y vaqueros eran" (Vega, *La burgalesa de Lerma*, 43).

84 "El juego de cañas es de vaqueros y capas sin oro; dizen que con aderezos de monte, plateados los jaezes sobre cuero de las colores; la nouedad me agrada; de lo demas no entiendo" (Vega, *Epistolario*, 3:127).

85 Bernis, *El traje y los tipos*, 59–62.

86 Morley and Bruerton, *Cronología*, 321–2. Case argues that it should be closer to 1613, since the sympathetic view of the literary Moor found in the play would be surprising after the expulsion of the Moriscos (*Lope and Islam*, 66).

87 "Sus golillas, sus vestidos / y sus cabellos rizados; / sus manos blancas, que apenas, / que por no verlas lastimadas, / los puños de las espadas / tocaron de afeites llenas" (Vega, *La envidia de la nobleza*, 17).

88 Kirschner and Clavero, *Mito e historia*, 201–2; and Cartagena Calderón, *Masculinidades*, 106. I wonder whether the allusion to the *golilla* should not make us reconsider the date of composition proposed by Morley and Bruerton, since this garment was introduced by Philip IV in 1623, according to Anderson ("The Golilla").

89 "sacar un turco un cuello de cristiano," Vega, *Arte nuevo*, 151. On sartorial anachronisms on stage, and their possible intentional uses, see Ruano de la Haza, "El vestuario," 55–9.

90 Ruiz Lagos, *Moriscos*, 18.

91 "Eso es cosa para moros, / muy vieja y cansada ya. / En tiempo del moro Muza / ... era cosa / de gusto; ya es enfadosa, / con turbante o caperuza," Vega, *Amor secreto*, 411. For the equivalence between Lope and Fabio in this play, see Trambaioli, "Lope de Vega," 29–30.

92 "Sólo asegurarte puedo / que esta obstentación y gasto / no ha sido por cuenta suya, / sino a costa de sus amos. / No ayas miedo que alguacil /

llebe dézima en mil años / de execución que les haga / por tantas telas y rasos, / ni que se quexe oficial / de las echuras de tantos / vestidos," Vega, *Lo que pasa en una tarde*, 60. As Cornejo shows, Lope was probably present at those festivals ("Lope de Vega").

93 Fray Juan de Jesús María criticized the game of canes, among many other aspects, because many participants would face insurmountable debts (*Epistolario*, 88).

94 "Sus hopalandas traía y su turbante, y como era Moreno, alto y bien puesto de bigotes, veníale el hábito como nacido" (Vega, *La desdicha por la honra*, 210). On the sources Lope used to compose this novella, see Bataillon, *"La desdicha por la honra."*

95 "Representó Felisardo únicamente, y viéndose en su verdadero traje lloraba lágrimas verdaderas, enternecido de justas memorias y arrepentido de injustas ofensas" (Vega, *La desdicha por la honra*, 212).

96 "yo no entiendo de caracoles, sino de sonetos" (Vega, *Epistolario*, 4:128).

97 Aristocratic writers, by contrast, figured prominently in the game of canes, especially in the kingdom of Valencia. Guillén de Castro is mentioned as one of the participants for a game of canes held in Valencia in 1590 (Tárrega, *El prado de Valencia*, 142). There are also many references to the participation of Gaspar Mercader in several games of canes (Gauna, *Relación*, 1:392); Aguilar, *Fiestas nupciales*, 98; and Aguilar, *Fiestas que la ciudad*, 168–9. Mercader even refers to himself playing canes in his pastoral romance *El prado de Valencia*, 141.

98 One case of a professional writer whose social position conditions his relation to Moorishness is Gaspar Aguilar. As I will show in chapter 6, his blatantly Islamophobic work may be closely related to his ambivalent social status.

5 Policing Moriscos in Sixteenth-Century Granada

1 For compilations of these legal documents, see Gallego y Burín and Gámir Sandoval, *Los moriscos*; Ayala, *Sínodo*; López Martín, *Don Pedro Guerrero*; Pérez de Heredia y Valle, *El concilio provincial*; Ladero Quesada, *Los mudéjares*; Boronat y Barrachina, *Los moriscos*; and Carrasco Manchado, *De la convivencia*, 223–401. Some of these documents have been translated to English by Fuchs, Brewer-García, and Ilika, *"The Abencerraje,"* 112–24. A short but very thorough summary of the sartorial legislation concerning Moriscos can be found in Benítez Sánchez-Blanco, "Carlos V."

2 I borrow this concept from Martínez Bermejo, who applies it to early modern sumptuary legislation in general and not specifically to the Moriscos ("Beyond Luxury," 97–8).

3 "los moriscos siguieron empleando muchas prendas de sus trajes hasta
el momento mismo de su expulsión definitiva en el año 1609" (Gallego y
Burín and Gámir Sandoval, *Los moriscos*, 62).

4 "Le Morisque … par son vêtement, était en relation avec tout un passé
glorieux, et aussi avec ses frères maghrébins. C'était pour lui un des signes
d'identité auquel il était très attaché" (Cardaillac, "Le Vêtement," 26).

5 "En contraste con el traje cristiano, sometido a una moda cambiante y en
continua transformación de la Baja Edad Media, el de los musulmanes se
caracteriza por su estabilidad. Podían pasar siglos sin que cambiasen la
forma de sus vestidos" (Bernis, *El traje y los tipos*, 461). Astor Landete takes
an even more extreme approach, as she describes the clothing of medieval
mudéjares in Valencia by using sources referring to Muslims in very
different places and historical periods, *Valencia*, 66–9. Conversely, other
scholars have tried to trace the possible influence that Moriscos might
have had on North African clothing, such as Albarracín de Martínez Ruiz,
Vestido y adorno, 21–35; and Gozalbes Busto, "Lo andaluz."

6 *Renaissance Clothing*, 7. For a critique of "Islamic fashion" as an immutable
concept, see also Moors, "'Islamic Fashion'," 177–80.

7 As Tueller observes, when dealing with Morisco religious and cultural
practices, royal decrees always referred to a stereotypical Morisco and
disregarded temporal changes and regional diversity (*Good and Faithful
Christians*, 53 and 57). For an analysis of the stereotype of the Moriscos in
early modern Spain, see also Perceval, *Todos son uno*.

8 "Por quanto los moros deste reyno de Granada no pueden traer cauallos …
permitimos que … puedan traer ropas de seda segund que lo han
acostumbrado" (*Libro de las bulas y pragmáticas*, 2:266r).

9 The 1499 decree alludes to the surrender treaty of Granada for the prohibition
of Muslims riding horses. However, there seems to be something inaccurate
in this reference, since the treaties of Guadix, Almería, and Granada explicitly
stated that Muslims would be allowed to keep their horses (Ladero Quesada,
Los mudéjares, 133, 138, and 174). We must therefore assume that the Catholic
monarchs issued an amendment between 1492 and 1499 to the capitulations
prohibiting the use of horses to the Muslim inhabitants of Granada, but such
a document (if it ever existed) is no longer extant.

10 *Libro de las bulas y pragmáticas*, 2:269v–72r. On the case of Asturias, see
Carracedo Falagán, "La regulación jurídica," 59.

11 I have only seen this law cited by López de Coca Castañer, from whom I
take the reference ("La seda," 50).

12 Coleman, *Creating*, 63.

13 "para que vuestra conversaçion sea syn escandalo a los christianos de
naçion y non piensen que aun teneys la seta de Mahomad en el coraçon

es menester que vos conformeys en todo y por todo a la buena y honesta conversaçion de los buenos y honestos christianos y christianas en vestir y calçar y afeytar," reproduced in Ladero Quesada, *Los mudéjares*, 295. Also in Rodríguez de Diego and Marchena Ruiz, *Los moriscos*, 64.

14 Castro, "El tratado," 42. See also Johnston, "Hernando de Talavera."

15 "que hasta que ayan rasgado las ropas que agora tienen non sean obligados a traer otras" (Ladero Quesada, *Los mudéjares*, 275).

16 "como los otros cristianos de nuestros reinos, porque no aia diferencia de los cristianos biejos" (Ladero Quesada, *Los mudéjares*, 317). According to Domínguez Ortiz and Vincent, similar edicts were also issued for Baza and Huéscar (*Historia*, 20).

17 "no pudiesen hacer nuevamente ninguna ropa morisca ni traer más de las que al presente tenían hechas" (Gallego y Burín and Gámir Sandoval, *Los moriscos*, 174). Also reproduced in *Cedulario del reino de Granada*, 72–3. The decree was issued under the name of Juana I of Castile, but as the document acknowledged, the order came from Fernando II of Aragon, who was the regent of Castile between 1507 and 1516.

18 Gallego y Burín and Gámir Sandoval, *Los moriscos*, 175.

19 "que los dichos sastres pueden hacer y cortar capuces de sayas de jirones e de cuatro cuartas para hombres, y jubones a la castellana y calzas para hombres, y ropones, que ellos dicen cotas, y toda ropa de hombres, excepto marlotas; e que no corten ni hagan ropa alguna para mujeres a la morisca" (Gallego y Burín and Gámir Sandoval, *Los moriscos*, 175).

20 *Cedulario del reino de Granada*, 187–8. The term *converso* quite likely refers here to converts from Judaism, not to Moriscos. Yet, when a new decree on 29 July 1513 alludes to the previous one, it replaces *conversos* from Jewish origin by *mudéjares* (which in this context likely refers to the Moriscos in the rest of the Kingdom of Castile) (Gallego y Burín and Gámir Sandoval, *Los moriscos*, 177); (*Cedulario del reino de Granada*, 177–9).

21 In 1541, one ordinance for the tailors of Granada required Morisco tailors to be examined before they were allowed to make clothing in the Castilian manner, complaining that they were already doing it without the proper licence. The same ordinance also gives instructions on how to make clothing *a la morisca*, without addressing Moriscos in particular (*Ordenanzas que los muy ilustres*, 148r).

22 "mantos de paño y descubiertas las caras, según que andan las cristianas viejas" (Gallego y Burín and Gámir Sandoval, *Los moriscos*, 178).

23 Martínez Medina, "El gran retablo mayor," 97–8 and 108.

24 Gallego y Burín and Gámir Sandoval, *Los moriscos*, 179; *Cedulario del reino de Granada*, 293–4.

25 "el abito, todas las mujeres lo traen castellano, y quien otra cosa a dicho no dixo verdad" (López de Mendoza, *Correspondencia*, 2:514–15).

26 Ibid., 2:534. Even if all those decrees were signed under the name of Juana I of Castile, the Count of Tendilla addressed his responses directly to Fernando II of Aragon as regent for Castile.

27 Ibid., 2:535.

28 Jiménez Estrella critiques the traditional image of the Mendozas as the moderate faction towards the Moriscos, emphasizing that they had an economic and political interest in placing themselves as the mediators between the Moriscos and the monarchy (*Poder*, 177).

29 López de Mendoza, *Escribir y gobernar*, 53–4. This and all subsequent references to this correspondence come from the CD transcriptions.

30 Ibid., 574–5. See also 814.

31 Ibid., 737.

32 Ibid., 110.

33 Pérez García and Fernández Chaves analyse how the pressure on the Morisco cultural practices over the period 1511–15 was tightly related to the negotiation of their fiscal status, *Las élites moriscas*, 23–6. They reproduce in an appendix the letter by Fernando of Aragon, 166–9.

34 López de Mendoza, *Escribir y gobernar*, 157, 737, and 838.

35 "¿Qué cosa, es, señor, mandar su alteza quitar los vestidos moriscos? ... Pues nosotros, señor, en España hasta la venida del rey don Enrrique el bastardo, ¿qué ábito ... trayamos syno el morisco...? ¿dexavan los reyes de ser christianos y santos por esto? No, ¡por Dios!" (López de Mendoza, *Escribir y gobernar*, 195–6).

36 Gallego y Burin and Gámir Sandoval, *Los moriscos*, 198–205.

37 Ibid., 202–3.

38 Alonso Santa Cruz's *Crónica del emperador Carlos V* (c. 1550–2) states that in 1527 Charles V mandated "que todas las moriscas y moriscos se vistiesen como cristianos" [that all Moriscas and Moriscos dress like Christians] (*Crónica*, 2:247). Santa Cruz manipulated the letter of the decree by including a reference to Morisco men absent in Charles V's decree. This apparently minor variant construes male Moriscos visually as if they were in fact dressing as "Moors." This distortion was disseminated throughout subsequent historiographical works, such as Prudencio de Sandoval's *Vida y hechos del emperador Carlos V* (1615), which uses exactly the same words (*Historia*, 2:173).

39 Most sixteenth-century discourses commenting on Morisco customs only refer to clothing when they deal with women. This delimitation applies as well to other parts of the Iberian Peninsula. An agreement between

the Moriscos of Valencia and Charles V made in 1528 also recognized that the issue of Morisco clothing had more to do with Morisco women than men (Boronat y Barrachina, *Los moriscos*, 1:423). For a critique of how Morisco women have been construed as more "traditional" and always attached to the preservation of so-called Morisco culture, see Birriel Salcedo, "Mujeres," 494–5. As García Pedraza suggests, there is a certain methodological inaccuracy in analysing Morisca clothing without conducting a parallel analysis of Old Christian women's wardrobes ("Entre la media luna y la cruz," 64). The issue of female veiling reappeared during the early modern period in several cities in Spain and colonial Latin America in contexts in which the Islamic legacy was not part of the debate (Bass and Wunder, "The Veiled Ladies," and Coleman, *Creating*, 63). Perry suggests that the use of the veil may have constituted a means of empowerment for Morisco women (*The Handless Maiden*, 7–9).

40 Núñez Muley, "The Original Memorial," 211–12. See also Barrios Aguilera, *La convivencia negada*, 260.

41 Navagero, *Il viaggio*, 25v. A similar description of Morisco women can be found in a letter written by Juan Negro, Navagero's secretary, on 8 June 1526 (Cicogna, *Della vita*, 340).

42 A full discussion of how Weiditz and subsequent European costume books might have overemphasized the exoticness of Morisco women is beyond the scope of this book. Suffice it to say here that, while these and similar images are reproduced by almost any scholar dealing with the Moriscos, some caution is needed when using them as visual proof of Morisco sartorial practices. There is no evidence that Weiditz actually visited Granada and it is more plausible to suspect that he was relying either on prototypes or descriptions made by others (Hampe, "Introduction," 21–3). For an analysis of the ideology underlying sixteenth-century costume books, see Defert, "Un genre ethnographique," 25–41. Even if Weiditz's drawings were an accurate description of Granada in the 1520s, they cannot be used to illustrate how Morisco women dressed several decades later, as has often been the case in the scholarship.

43 Ayala, *Sínodo*, 63v.

44 "y lo que mas es de doler, algunas Christianas Viejas en nuestro Obispado casadas con estos nueuamente conuertidos auer dexado su traje antiguo y tomado el de las moriscas" [that which is more painful, is that some Old Christian women in our bishopric, married to these newly converted, have abandoned their old dress and have taken that of the Moriscas] (Ayala, *Sínodo*, 63v).

45 "assi varones, como mugeres … no sean osados a traer vestiduras ni
   habitos moriscos, specialmente se quiten las sauanas, marlotas y el atauio
   de las cabeças, y se pongan mantos y sayas y tocas a modo de Christianas"
   (ibid., 63v).
46 Pérez de Heredia y Valle, *El concilio provincial*, 40–51.
47 Ibid., 67–9.
48 "requieran de doctrinas … ansi mismo a los christianos viejos que truxeren
   habito de christianos nueuos" (ibid., 263).
49 "se les podría mandar que los que de nueuo se casasen se vistiesen como
   cristianos viejos, y que las demás que anduviesen en hábito morisco
   ellos o sus mujeres, o criados por el tiempo que les durasen las ropas ya
   hechas, por muy principales y caballeros que sean, no fuesen regidores
   ni alguaciles, ni gozasen de privilegio de armas, ni de hidalguía, y fuesen
   llamados por padrón en las iglesias a misa y doctrina, para convidarlos por
   este camino a que dejen el hábito, antes que se les gasten las ropas" (López
   Martín, *Don Pedro Guerrero*, 128). This letter is also reproduced in Marín
   Ocete, "El Concilio provincial," 155–60. While Marín Ocete does not date
   it, López Martín gives 10 December 1565, which seems to be correct, since
   there is another copy of the same letter at IVDJ, Altamira, envío 1, tomo
   3, exp. 32, which has the same date. It is, however, strange that Philip II's
   response is dated 24 Oct. 1565, since this one should necessarily come after
   Pedro Guerreo's letter (Marín Ocete, "El Concilio provincial," 160).
50 "lo que se proueia en la congregaçion del año de XXVI y en la del año de
   XXXVIIII y lo que demas desto esta ordenado por pracmaticas y çedulas
   y otras prouisiones particulares, y juntamente lo que en vuestra carta se
   propone y apunta" (Marín Ocete, "El Concilio provincial," 162; and López
   Martín, *Don Pedro Guerrero*, 119).
51 Mármol Carvajal, *Historia*, 114–16.
52 López de Mendoza, "Mémoire," 17.
53 MS. Add. 28704, British Library, 13v and 15r. This letter suggests that the
   prohibition of Morisco clothing was issued in August 1566. Yet no scholar
   seems to have located the original order of the decree – and I had no
   luck in my own perusal of AGS, Registro General del Sello, August 1566.
   This decree has been dated traditionally on 17 November 1566, after the
   compilation of laws made in 1567, but this is probably a confusion with the
   date of the germane prohibition on the Arabic language, which is indeed
   dated 17 Nov. 1566, as reproduced by Rodríguez de Diego and Marchena
   Ruiz, *Los moriscos*, 89–90; and Castillo Fernández, as an appendix to his
   edition of Mármol Carvajal, *Historia*, 735–7.

54 AZ, Altamira, 158–2, n.f.

55 Mármol Carvajal, *Historia*, 120.

56 *Pregmáticas y provisiones de S. M. el Rey don Philippe nuestro señor, sobre la lengua y vestidos, y otras cosas que an de hazer los naturales deste Reyno de Granada* (Granada: Hugo de Mena, 1567). The decrees were included shortly afterwards in a legal compilation made in 1567 (Recopilación de las leyes, 152r–3r). This second version of the decree, which is the basis of subsequent legal compilations, contains only the extracts of the prohibitions, but not the legal and historical justification that preceded each of them in the version printed by Hugo de Mena. I find it striking that, in spite of the centrality of this decree in Morisco scholarship, no scholar ever seems to have consulted the original version until recently.

57 *Pregmáticas y provisiones*, [2r]. Yet Mármol Carvajal, probably following Philip II's letters, states that the Junta of Madrid was looking at Charles V laws from 1526, *Historia*, 116. His opinion is followed by modern historians such as Caro Baroja, *Los moriscos*, 157.

58 "ningunos de los dichos nueuamente conuertidos del dicho reyno de Granada, ni descendientes dellos, no puedan hazer ni cortar de nueuo almalafas ni marlotas, ni otras calças ni vestidos, de las que usauan y trayan en tiempo de moros, y que los vestidos que de nuevo hizieren sean conforme a los que traen las christianas viejas, conuiene a saber, mantos y sayas," *Pregmáticas y provisiones*, 2r–v. While this decree prohibits "that clothing that they used to wear in the time of the Moors," the short version of the decree included a misleading rubric that is not in the original: "Que los moriscos no traygan vestidos de moros, sino que se conformen en los trajes con los christianos viejos" [That the Moriscos should not wear clothing of Moors, but that they should conform in clothing with Old Christians], *Recopilación de las leyes*, 152v.

59 For instance, a letter sent to Rome from the Jesuit mission in El Albaicín in November 1567 reported that the laws prohibited the clothing of the Morisco women, Griffin, "'Un muro invisible'," 145. As we have seen, Núñez Muley claimed that Morisco men were already dressing in the Castilian way, "The Original Memorial," 212. Brianda Pérez, Fernando de Válor's wife, deposed that the Moriscos who were conspiring with Válor in 1567 "le paresçían en su traje y ábito, por andar bestidos de negro y bien tratados, ser gente de bien y rrica" [it seemed to her that they were respected and rich people, since they were well dressed in black]. In contrast, she also reported that some of the Moriscas present in the same room were wearing *marlotas* and other adornments (Rodríguez de Diego and Marchena Ruiz, *Los moriscos*, 95–7). It is unclear, however, whether the

Moriscas present at Fernando de Válor's coronation were wearing *marlotas* because this was their habitual clothing or, more likely, because they were wearing ceremonial clothing for the occasion.

60 "Cuanto al hábito, se mandó que no se hiciesen de nuevo marlotas, almalafas, calzas, ni otra suerte de vestido de los que se usaban en tiempo de moros; y que todo lo que se cortase e hiciese, fuese a uso de cristianos" (Mármol Carvajal, *Historia*, 117). With minor modifications, all the English translations from Francisco Núñez Muley come from Barletta's translation, *A Memorandum*, 105.

61 Even Gallego y Burín and Gámir Sandoval, who made available many of the original legal documentation on the Moriscos of Granada, were content to offer only Mármol Carvajal's summary of Philip II's decree (*Los moriscos*, 273–4).

62 "las dichas almalafas y marlotas *y otros vestidos* hechos que fueren de seda o tuuieren alguna guarnicion de qualquier seda, las puedan traer y trayan por un año tan solamente, y las que no fueren de seda ni tuuieren guarnicion, por dos años" (*Pregmáticas y provisiones*, 2v).

63 The decree on clothing is therefore equivalent to that of the prohibition of owning black slaves and carrying weapons, which, as Vincent notes, were intended to impose on the Moriscos a "process of social regression" ("La mobilité sociale," 56–9).

64 "los nuestros subditos y naturales de nuestros Reynos puedan traer todo género de seda en ropa" (*Premática de los vestidos*, 3v–4r).

65 For instance, see the decrees of 1465 and 1475 in Carrasco Manchado, *De la convivencia*, 209 and 212–13. Medieval legislation, even if no longer enforced, was widely remembered in the early modern period. Alfonso X's *Las siete partidas* was edited in 1491 by Alonso Díaz de Montalvo, and again in 1555 by Gregorio López, with several reprints in both cases.

66 On inquisitorial *inhabilitación* see Dedieu, "Herejía," 139–56.

67 Feliciano Chaves points out in passing that "sumptuary legislations helped control the Moriscos' access to luxury and to curb the prosperity of the merchant class, which relied on the production of 'illegal' cloth and clothing for their economic success" (*Mudejarismo*, 147n34). Zayas also notes this issue, but attributes it to the luxurious silk textiles being "a source of pride and nostalgia" [fuente de orgullo y añoranza] (*Los moriscos*, 113n119).

68 On how the differential taxation actually treated the Moriscos as heretics, see Galán Sánchez, "'Herejes consentidos'," and "El dinero del rey."

69 Indeed, in spite of the participation of the Moriscos in the initial stages of silk manufacturing, by the 1560s most of the tailors in the cities of Malaga

and Granada were Old Christians. According to López de Coca Castañer, only in Almería were there still Morisco tailors ("La seda," 40–1).

70 "Habiéndose acabado de imprimir la nueva premática, el presidente don Pedro de Deza ... mandó que se pregonase en la ciudad de Granada y en las otras de aquel reino el primero día del mes de enero del año del Señor mil quinientos sesenta y siete. Este día se juntaron los alcaldes del crimen de la Real Chancillería y el corregidor con todas las justicias de la ciudad y con gran solemnidad de atabales, trompetas, sacabuches, ministriles y dulzainas la pregonaron en las plazas y lugares públicos de la ciudad y de su Albayzín" (Mármol Carvajal, *Historia*, 122).

71 Castillo Fernández, *Entre Granada y el Magreb*, 70–9.

72 "los moriscos sienten tanto que anden las moriscas los rostros descubiertos que dan grandissima priessa a berles vestidos a la castellana y las moriscas se huelgan con el nueuo habito" [the Moriscos so resent that the Moriscas should go about with their faces uncovered that they are pressing their women to see them dressed in the Castilian manner, and the Moriscas rejoice with their new clothing] (AZ, Altamira 158–2). In another letter from 6 January 1567, Deza reports that, because of the sudden demand for clothing in the Castilian manner, merchants increased their prices and Moriscos decried the abuse (IVDJ, Altamira, envío 1, tomo 2, exp. 197).

73 AZ, Altamira 158–2, n.f.

74 Mármol Carvajal, *Historia*, 135.

75 In a cursory perusal of several municipal proceedings in the provinces of Granada, Málaga, and Almería for January 1567, I did not encounter any mention to the decree. I could find only one slim proof of the application of the decree: In March 1567, the Inquisitors of Granada complained to the Supreme Council of the Inquisition because one of their agents had been seized by the Royal representative in Granada for wearing prohibited *calzas* [hose], and the Inquisitors in Granada conferred with tailors to refute that such garment were against the "pragmática de los trajes" (AHN, Inq, leg. 2.603/195). Pérez de Colosía Rodríguez and Gil Sanjuan (from whom I have taken this reference) interpret that the document refers to Philip II's prohibition of Morisco customs ("Málaga y la Inquisición," 11). If their interpretation were correct, this incident would reveal that the decree was being enforced before the deadline set by Philip II, and would also indicate that its implementation was arbitrary, since even between two Christian institutions there was no consensus on the categorization of what garments should count as "Morisco." Yet, when the letters allude to the "pragmática de los trajes," it is also plausible to interpret that they refer to the general sumptuary laws, and not to Philip II's specific decree for the Moriscos. Indeed, the real political issue in the discussion is not

clothing (which is mentioned only once), but the question of whether the Inquisition's agents could carry certain weapons, namely daggers (AHN, Inq, leg. 2.603/95, 196 and 198).

76 On Núñez Muley, see, among others, Fuchs, *Mimesis and Empire*, 102–4; Barletta, "Introduction"; Harvey, *Muslims of Spain*, 213; Cardaillac, "Le Vêtement," 23; Feliciano Chaves, *Mudejarismo*, 156–7; Matthew Carr, *Blood and Faith*, 134–5; Carrasco Manchado, *De la convivencia*, 79–80; Vincent, *El río morisco*, 93–7; and Kimmel, *Parables of Coercion*, 36–40.

77 There is no study on what Moriscos thought about sartorial practices. It seems that, in contrast to Christian sources, the Moriscos themselves did not grant as much importance to clothing as is generally assumed. While Núñez Muley's noble status may explain his emphasis on the sartorial issue, we should wonder whether a Morisco commoner, even a crypto-Muslim one, would give as much weight to clothing.

78 "en las cosas ricas no se da liçençia para más de un año" (Núñez Muley, "The Original Memorial," 214).

79 Núñez Muley, "The Original Memorial," 202.

80 APAG, L–187–96. This document was discovered by Castillo Fernández, "Las estructuras sociales," 214; he also reproduces it as an appendix in his edition of Mármol Carvajal, *Historia*, 745–7.

81 Castillo, "Sumario e recopilación," 43.

82 Harvey, *Muslims of Spain*, 209.

83 On 3 February 1569, Pedro de Deza wrote to Diego de Espinosa to report a rumour according to which the Marquis of Mondéjar had supported the uprising with the Morisco elite, so he could place himself as a mediator between them and the monarch (IVDJ, Altamira, envío 1, tomo 2, exp. 196). Deza also observed that, even if he did not give credence to the rumour (to the spread of which he nonetheless contributes), most Moriscos were not really concerned about the application of the decrees.

84 Mármol Carvajal, *Historia*, 123–30.

85 "Mirad por Dios, quanto es menos dañoso mudar lengua y habito, pues ni la boz Morisca os hazia Moros, ni desnudais el coraçon con el vestido" (Fuenmayor, *Vida y hechos*, 84r).

86 Pérez de Hita, *La guerra de los moriscos*, 14.

87 "Mándanos dejar nuestro hábito, y vestir el castellano. Vístense entre ellos los tudescos de una manera, los franceses de otra, los griegos de otra, los frailes de otra, los mozos de otra, y de otra los viejos: cada nación, cada profesión y cada estado usa su manera de vestido, y todos son cristianos; y nosotros moros, porque vestimos a la morisca, como si trajésemos la ley en el vestido, y no en el corazón" (Hurtado de Mendoza, *Guerra de Granada*, 117).

88 Harvey, *Muslims of Spain*, 214.
89 Bleda, *Corónica*, 660–1.
90 Ibid., 670–1.
91 Martínez Bermejo, "Beyond Luxury," 103.
92 "La voluntad de terminar de una vez para siempre con toda una estructura social, con toda una cultura, era clara y no había nada que hacer ante ella. Nada, salvo la guerra," Caro Baroja, *Los moriscos*, 160. Similar statements can be found in Domínguez Ortiz and Vincent, *Historia*, 33.
93 For a thorough overview of early modern historiographical works dealing with the War of the Alpujarras, see Castillo Fernández, "La guerra de los moriscos"; Castillo Fernández, *Entre Granada y el Magreb*, 273–96; and Kimmel, *Parables of Coercion*, 117–46. In chapter 8, I analyse how the War of the Alpujarras was imagined in seventeenth-century literary works.
94 Zagorin, *Rebels and Rulers*, 2:13.
95 On the political confrontation between the Chancery of Granada and the Mendozas, see Caro Baroja, *Los moriscos*, 149–60; Jiménez Estrella, *Poder*, 136–62; and Pérez, "'Letrados' et seigneurs," 235–44.
96 Rodríguez de Ardila, "Historia de los Condes de Tendilla," 94. A similar historiographical interpretation is found in Ibáñez de Segovia, *Historia*, 370v.
97 Benítez Sánchez-Blanco, *Heroicas decisiones*, 200.
98 On the Inquisitorial action against the Moriscos in sixteenth-century Granada, see García Fuentes, *La Inquisición en Granada*; and García Ivars, *La represión*, 177–90.
99 Garrad, "La industria sedera," 90–8. See also López de Coca Castañer, "La seda," 56.
100 Cara Barrionuevo, "La ganadería," 207.
101 Castillo Fernández, "La asimilación," 347–8 and 354; and "Las estructuras sociales," 226–30. Similarly, Vincent points to the introduction of a new tax in June 1568 (*Andalucía*, 113–16).
102 There were only a few honourable exceptions to such an interpretation, such as the Castilian ambassador in France, Francés de Álava, who stated that the main reason behind the uprising was the social and political repression against the Moriscos, and criticized what he saw as distorted public opinion: "la mayor parte de las personas con quien yo platiqué y oí platicar desta materia en Granada atribuían la obstinación de los moriscos al permitirles el hábito morisco a sus mujeres y algunas ceremonias moriscas" [most of the people with whom I spoked and heard talk about

this issue of Granada attributed the resistance of the Moriscos to allowing them to use the Morisco dress for their women and some Morisco ceremonies] (Paz, *Archivo General de Simancas*, 684–5). Similarly, Esteban del Rincón, when describing the uprising of the Moriscos in Baza, states that the lament about Philip II's decrees was the excuse for the rebellion, rather than the cause (IVDJ, Altamira, envío 1, tomo 6, exp. 186).

103 "cuando se generalizó la sublevación debió de haber una especie de restauración del traje musulmán" (Caro Baroja, *Los moriscos*, 138). Caro Baroja's book was first published in 1957.

104 "tenemos noticia de que la sublevación de los moriscos fue acompañada de una especie de restauración del traje musulmán" (Martínez Ruiz, "La indumentaria," 18). Similar assertions are found in Arié, "Acerca del traje," 139; Barrios Aguilera, *La convivencia negada*, 260; and Carrasco, *Deportados*, 75.

105 Neither scholar cites Hurtado de Mendoza's *Guerra de Granada*, in which there is scarcely any reference to clothing. They also do not cite Pérez de Hita's second part of the *Guerras civiles de Granada* (published 1619), quite arguably because his rendition of the uprising deals with Moorish dress in a very complex way that precludes using his text to defend the myth of the Morisco sartorial revival. In Pérez de Hita, scenes of confusion, in which Old Christians and Moriscos are indistinguishable from one another, are common (*La guerra de los moriscos*, 21, 62, 68, 125, and 130–1). The difficulty of clearly distinguishing between both sides in armed confrontations is also confirmed by Vázquez Rengifo (*Grandezas*, 375). When talking about Abenfarax's attempt to incite the Albaicín to revolt, Pérez de Hita does not mention that they were dressed as Turks (as Mármol Carvajal did) (*La guerra de los moriscos*, 19–20). Instead, Pérez de Hita alludes in other passages to how, inversely, Christian soldiers dressed as Turks to trick the Moriscos (*La guerra de los moriscos*, 100–1 and 122–3). The only episode that would account for some sort of cultural revival is the description of the festivals held by the Moriscos in Purchena during the rebellion in the Alpujarras (*La guerra de los moriscos*, 154–7). Yet this passage is too fanciful to be taken as historically reliable information, and, as Carrasco Urgoiti points out, it is but a pale echo of the gallant Moorish ceremonies that Pérez de Hita himself had crafted in the first part of the *Guerras civiles* (1595) (*Los moriscos*, 84–7).

106 "si sus propios vestidos no le acusaran, porque ... devisaron los que le buscaban el cafetán de grana que llevaba vestido y el turbante blanco de la cabeza" (Mármol Carvajal, *Historia*, 689).

107 "andaba Aben Humeya vistoso delante de todos en un caballo blanco con
    una aljuba de grana vestida y un turbante turquesco en la cabeza" (ibid.,
    502).
108 According to a report on the meeting to negotiate the surrender of the
    Moriscos, El Habaquí came with 300 soldiers dressed in the Turkish style,
    cited by Castillo Fernández in his edition of Mármol Carvajal, *Historia*,
    608n230.
109 AZ, Altamira 158–105.
110 Mármol Carvajal, *Historia*, 131. Bernis defines the *faldellín* as a purely
    Christian garment, but her analysis also suggests that there were possible
    affinities between the *faldellín* and the *almalafa* (*El traje y los tipos*, 211–3,
    and 488).
111 Mármol Carvajal, *Historia*, 412.
112 "on est bien forcé de voir dans l'attitude du comte de l'inconscience ou de
    la provocation" (Joseph Pérez, "'Letrados' et seigneurs," 240).
113 Harris, *Aztecs*, 209.
114 "hizo que todos los compañeros dejasen los sombreros y monteras que
    llevaban y se pusiesen bonetes colorados a la turquesca, y sus toquillas
    blancas encima, para que pareciesen turcos" (Mármol Carvajal, *Historia*, 190).
115 Many authors do not refer at all to Abenfarax disguising his men as
    Turks during his attempt to incite the Albaicín to revolt, e.g., López de
    Mendoza, "Mémoire," 19–20; Fuenmayor, *Vida y hechos*, 86r–7r; Pérez de
    Hita, *La guerra de los moriscos*, 19–20; Rodríguez de Ardila, "Historia,"
    95–6; Vincent, "Les jesuites chroniqueurs," 441–2 and 444; and Barrios
    Aguilera, "La guerra de los moriscos," 417. Hurtado de Mendoza says
    only that Abenfarax and his men came with musical instruments and
    that the Count of Tendilla was scandalized by the Morisco music (*Guerra
    de Granada*, 128–30). Of all of the accounts on Abenfarax's uprising, only
    one anonymous report believed that there were actual Turkish and North
    African soldiers among the revolters (AZ, Altamira 158–5).
116 "moros vestidos ... como moros" (Mármol Carvajal, *Historia*, 193).

6 Searching for the Iberian Moorish Morisco

1 Núñez Muley, "The Original Memorial," 211, trans. Barletta, *A
  Memorandum*, 70.
2 Otero Mondéjar, "La reconstrucción," 81.
3 Carrasco Manchado, *De la convivencia*, 317–27. Caro Baroja claims that
  this 1572 edict refers to clothing, but he is actually interpolating that issue

based on his expectations (*Los moriscos*, 206). We can still find isolated voices requesting the implementation of the edict, such as Luis Hurtado de Toledo, who recommended in 1576 that the decree on language and clothing be applied to the Moriscos deported to Toledo ("Memorial," 512).

4 Carrasco, *Deportados*, 120–4; Conte Cazcarro, *Los moriscos*, 321–8; Lasmarías Ponz, "Cultura material," 231–6; García-Arenal, *Inquisición y moriscos*, 75; Dedieu, "Les Morisques," 496; and Fernández Chaves and Pérez García, *En los márgenes*, 55. Sáez, in his study of how the bishopric of Toledo dealt with the Moriscos from Granada, shows that there was some concern about the use of Arabic and other cultural practices, but does not mention clothing as one of them ("Los moriscos").

5 Something similar happens with all the signs that Inquisitors sought as proof of heresy, as Root notes: "The relation of heresy to deviant customs seems to have been worked out from case to case at the local level by the Inquisition's lawyers, rather than by the theologians at higher levels of the Church" ("Speaking Christian," 126). As Ruiz Ibáñez shows, the definition of who was considered a Morisco during the expulsion was an ad-hoc process which most often depended on individual social standing ("'Sin tratar de otros'").

6 "Speaking Christian," 130.

7 Tueller, *Good and Faithful Christians*, 9–10.

8 Ibid., 43. Similarly, García-Arenal notes that "[e]n un morisco, todo lo que a un cristiano viejo le parece inhabitual e insólito es 'ceremonia de moros'" [regarding Moriscos, everything that looks unusual and unheard-of is considered "Moorish ritual"] (*Inquisición y moriscos*, 66).

9 Bernis compiles a few references to sartorial diversity, especially in northern Castile, but as she points out, the information on regional particularities is scant, since popular classes were rarely considered an object worthy of description (*La indumentaria española*, 49–50). On the Basque country, see Juaristi, *Vestigios de Babel*, 88–99; on Aragon, see Soláns Soteras, *La moda*, 170–6.

10 "el ábito y traxe y calçado no se puede dezir de moros ... Puédese dezir ques traxe del rreyno y prouinçia, como en todos los rreynos de Castilla y los otros rreynos y prouinçias tienen los traxes diferentes unos de otros, y todos cristianos; y ansí el dicho áuito y traxe deste rreyno es muy diferente de los traxes de los moros de aliende y Berbería ... de manera que no se puede afundar ni dezir que el traxe de los nueuamente conuertidos es traxe de moros" (Núñez Muley, "The Original Memorial," 211, trans. Barletta, *A Memorandum*, 70).

11 "Los Moriscos de la Andaluzia les tengo por muy ricos y que en el traje y lengua se nos parecen mucho mas que los de el reyno de Valencia" (Lapeyre, *Geografía*, 182n26).

12 Carrasco, "*Limpieza*," 292.

13 "sus tratos, vestidos, testamentos y toda horden de vibir son de cristianos viejos" (Guardia y López, "La mitad de oficios," 57). A 1594 report from the Inquisition of Murcia also holds that the Moriscos in this area were not different from Old Christians (Blázquez Miguel, *El tribunal*, 118).

14 Otero Mondéjar, "La reconstrucción," 297.

15 "que siendo como son jornaleros cortadores de carne e personas baxas e serviles, contra lo dispuesto por leyes y pregmaticas traen rropas de seda" (AGS, CRC 371, exp. 22, "Gerónimo García, alguacil mayor de Lorca, contra Diego de Viamonte, carnicero, y consortes, moriscos, por tener ropas de seda y oro que no les son permitidas por ley" (1583), 1r).

16 "demas de ser cortadas … conforme a el abito de que usan los cristianos viejos y gente principal desta ciudad estan cortadas conforme a lo dispuesto por las prematicas reales de su Magestad" (4r).

17 "porque la parte contraria confiesa que las ropas … son de las que usa la gente principal desta ciudad, las quales por decretos destos reynos estan prohibidas a la parte contraria por ser mujer y nuera de carnicero que es mas vil oficio de quantas ay en el mundo, demas por ser el dicho Diego de Viamonte y la dicha María Muñoz moriscos de los que se reuelaron contra Dios y contra la Magestad Real y por el mismo caso quedaron ynabiles para vestir ropas de seda e de todos los demas vestidos onrosos sin espresa liçencia de su Magestad" (6r).

18 "quanto a el traje y vestidos de los dichos moriscos del Reyno de Granada solamente esta dispuesto por leyes e prematicas de su Magestad que en todo usen de los dichos vestidos conforme a el trage e uso de los cristianos viejos y que no vistan rropas cortadas a la morisca" (7r). Jiménez also points out that their wedding closely followed Christian ritual.

19 8r–v.

20 *Pregmáticas y provisiones*, [2r–v]; and *Recopilación de las leyes*, 152r–3r.

21 9r and 12r–15v.

22 18r–26v.

23 27v.

24 On the Moriscos of Lorca, see Guerrero Arjona, *Lorca*, 161–213; and Jiménez Alcázar, "Moriscos en Lorca."

25 35r.

26 Guerra de Lorca, *Cathecheses*, 23r–33v. For an English translation, see Busic, "Saving the Lost Sheep," 304–31.

27 I cite using Busic's translation, "Saving the Lost Sheep," 313 and 317.

28 Ferrero Hernández, "*De habitv*," 267.

29 "por quanto nos consta por uista de oxos que las mugeres de la dicha uilla andan con uestidos e traxes al modo del de las mugeres aráuigas y aunque por nos les a sido reprehendido en el púlpito y en otras partes e puesto penas que no traygan los dichos vestidos sino que en ello se conformen con los vestidos que traen las demás mugeres de los demás lugares de este prioratto convecinos a la dicha uilla de Magaçela, e porque no es raçón que semexantes ávitos aya memoria de ellos ni se ussen a onde tanto se aborrecen la memoria de ellos. Por tanto mandamos que ninguna muger de la dicha uilla de qualquier estado e calidad que sea, … trayga ningún vestido de los antiguos sino que los traygan como las demás mugeres de los lugares convecinos" (Miranda Díaz, *Reprobación*, 214).

30 Ibid., 221–6.

31 "traer el áuito más corto o más largo es uso de estas tierras, y no rrito ni cerimonia por donde hallará vuestra merced que todas las mugeres de los ombres ricos y principales de la dicha villa traen las sayas y uestidos largos e conplidos como quien lo puede hacer, e que las mugeres de los probres que los traygan más cortos no es de marauillar porque no pueden más, pues sabe vuestra merced que la xente pobre de la dicha villa es muy más pobre que de otro ningún lugar porque no ay ofizio ninguno de qué ganar el xornalero" (ibid., 204).

32 Ibid., 231.

33 Ibid., 112–17. In spite of a lack of evidence, Miranda Díaz suggests that the Consejo de Órdenes would have sided with the Prior of Magacela.

34 The conflict is replicated in nearby Hornachos, by far the largest Morisco community in Castile, where the curate Diego de Cuenca informed the Inquisition about the alleged crypto-Islamic practices of the Moriscos, including the Moriscas' sartorial differences as well (Mayorga Huertas, *Los moriscos*, 66).

35 On the Moriscos of Murcia, see Flores Arroyuelo, *Los últimos moriscos*; and García Avilés, *Los moriscos*.

36 Vilar, *Los moriscos*, 36.

37 Molina Templado, "Acerca de la expulsión," 96.

38 Fray Juan de Pereda's report is reproduced in its entirety by González Castaño, "El informe."

39 González Castaño, "El informe," 230.

40 "si … en el traxe y abito son pareçidos a los otros moriscos o tenidos por differentes dellos" (ibid., 234).

41 "ninguno ha vestido a lo morisco" (ibid., 224).

42 Ibid., 224.

43 Ibid., 233.

44 "vistiendo cassi a nuestro modo" (Rojas, *Relaciones*, 21v–22r). Barceló
and Labarta, in their study of clothing in Morisco notary documents and
dowries, list all the sartorial terminology used, but do not extrapolate any
conclusions from it, and it is therefore hard to determine whether the use
of Arabic terms is specific to the Moriscos or whether it is the same as their
Old Christian counterparts; they only note quite the contrary, that *marlotas*
appear only once in their documents, while they are ubiquitous in Old
Christian documents ("Indumentaria," 53). On the sartorial assimilation of
the Moriscos of Valencia in the early modern period, see García Marsilla,
"Diferencia e integración," 341–51.

45 "por quanto los dichos moros tienen bestidos moriscos los quales son
differentes de los bestidos de los christianos, señaladamente en lo de
las mugeres, a las quales seria muy grave averlo de mudar" (Boronat y
Barrachina, *Los moriscos*, 1:423).

46 Benítez Sánchez-Blanco, "Un plan," 142.

47 "Un plan," 134–5.

48 "se devria mandar que no huviese christiano nueuo sastre, y que los viejos
no pudiesen cortar ropa que no fuese a nuestro uso, y si pareçiese quitar
los vestidos, señalando algun breue termino, seria lo mejor. Aunque en
esto no pareçe que ay mucho en que reparar por no ser de las cosas en que
ellos ponen su fuerça" (British Library, MS Egerton 1511, 129r–v). Ciscar
Pallarés cites a different version of this statement in which Ribera uses
"fe" (faith) instead of "fuerça" (resistance) ("Los moriscos," 173). Similarly,
in 1587, Martín de Salvatierra, bishop of Segorve, wrote to Phillip II that
there was no use making the Moriscos abandon their clothing, since the
Moriscos in Castile and Aragon continued to be Muslims in spite of being
no different from the Old Christians in their dress (Boronat y Barrachina,
Los moriscos, 1:629).

49 Ehlers, *Between Christians and Moriscos*, 106–50; and Benítez Sánchez-
Blanco, *Heroicas decisiones*, 334.

50 "el habito moriego en los hombres no esta usado, a lo menos como
antiguamente solia, sino que andan vestidos al modo de los naturales del
Reyno de Valencia, salvo que algo de los sayos y capas diferencian por
traer los sayos en çierta forma y mas largos de faldamentos y las capas assi
mismo, pero esto sera facil de remediarse con advertir a los sastres que
oviere en los lugares de nuevos convertidos que no diferençien el trage y
habito dellos de los de los cristianos viejos, y que las mugeres assi mismo
usan muy pocas del habito moriego y en muy pocas cosas, y con que se les

quitasen algunas aljurias que se suelen poner y alhenar las uñas y señalar los braços y no ponerse tocas leonadas quedaria remediado" (British Library, Ms. Egerton 1511, 110r). See also García Cárcel, "La inquisición," 411.

51 "tenían el hábito muy poco diferenciado de lo que usan en el Reino, sino que se avisase a los sastres que no les hiciesen vestidos al uso moriego sino al traje y hábito que en el Reino se usa" (Martínez Millán, "Las facciones cortesanas," 195).

52 British Library, Ms. Egerton 1511, 280r–6r.

53 "el Regente de la cancillería de Valencia hizo relación ... que, en el obispado de Orihuela, había muchas mujeres que traían almalafas cortas y calzas enroscadas y otras cosas del hábito moriego, ... se ha resuelto ... que a los que traxeren el dicho hábito, se les debía quitar por ser tan conocido traje de moros. Y entiéndese que sólo en el obispado de Orihuela traen el dicho hábito" (Martínez Millán, "Las facciones cortesanas," 195).

54 On the Moriscos of Orihuela, see Benítez Sánchez-Blanco, "Entre el optimismo y la decepción"; and Martínez Valls, "Los moriscos."

55 Carrasco Rodríguez, "La ciudad de Orihuela," 81–91; Riera, *Rentas eclesiásticas*, 26–8 and 73–4; Benítez Sánchez-Blanco, "Entre el optimismo y la decepción," 75–6.

56 "Ordenaciones de Esteban de Almeida," AGS, Patronato Eclesiástico, legajo 156 (n.f.). As usual, this document omits that Old Christians also consumed clothing *a la morisca*, and thus faced the Moriscos with a model of sartorial decency, even if it framed it as a cultural confrontation. On Almeida's ordinances, see Riera, *Rentas eclesiásticas*, 46.

57 Vilar, "Las 'ordinaciones'," 396.

58 "el quitarles el vestido es cosa muy fácil y muy esencial para que se olviden desde luego de sus bárbaras costumbres y ansí convendría quitar luego que en las bodas no llevassen de casa de sus padres ropa a la morisca con la ceremonia y solemnidad que la llevan ni menos que en las cartas nupciales expresassen ropas o joyas al trage morisco, ni en los testamentos dexassen legados de ropas con el nombre y trage dicho" (Boronat y Barrachina, *Los moriscos*, 1:653). Later in 1595, Esteve prohibited the Moriscas from wearing certain coloured shoes in Novelda (Doménech Belda, "Los moriscos," 81); and in nearby Monòver (Poveda, *Visites*, 54). While we may tend to read this prohibition as a repression of Morisco traditional customs, this is probably, as in many other cases, a moralizing instruction based on local sumptuary concerns – indeed, if the wearing of coloured shoes was a Morisco sartorial particularity, it is striking not to find it in any other source referring to their alleged sartorial practices.

59 Boronat y Barrachina, *Los moriscos*, 1:654–5.

60 Ibid., 2:18. Philip III disregarded Esteve's preocupation with this issue (Zayas, *Los moriscos*, 380).

61 The Moriscos of Coix claimed, however, that they would be allowed to keep their traditional clothing at home if they could not meet the deadline to modify them (Archivo Histórico de Orihuela, PN–613, Protocolo Salvador Boivia, 28 March 1600 (n.f.)). Ojeda Nieto provides a partial transcription of this document ("Visiones," 29). There is also a very similar document from Elche, dated 5 March 1600 (Navarro Belmonte, Serra Jaén, and Álvarez Fortes, *Moriscos*, 156–7).

62 Martínez Valls, "Los moriscos," 262 and 265.

63 "todos los lugares de los Christianos nueuos renunciaron a todas las ropas y joyas hechas a la Morisca, obligandose con aucto ante notarios publicos de conformarse en todo y por todo con el honesto traje de vestir de los Christianos viejos" (ACA, CA, legajo 699, expediente 24/18). This document is also cited in Ciscar Pallarés, "Notas," 229; and Benítez Sánchez-Blanco, "Entre el optimismo y la decepción," 98. Balaguer states that he holds a copy of the notarized document, which he unfortunately does not reproduce, nor does he make explicit what towns were included.

64 "han inventado y inventan cada dia nuevos trajes, no del todo conformes a los antiguos, pero muy differentes del uso de los Christianos viejos, particularmente las mugeres, procurando en todo lo que pueden differenciarse en el modo de vestir de las Christianas viejas" (ACA, CA, legajo 699, expediente 24/18).

65 Carrasco Rodríguez, "La ciudad de Orihuela," 258.

66 Nirenberg, *Communities of Violence*, 6.

7 Moriscos Performing as Moors

1 Martínez Ruiz, "La indumentaria." In addition to this article, he published many of the documents on which he based his research in his *Inventarios de bienes moriscos*. For a similar approach in the case of Almería, see Segura del Pino, "Solidaridad," 257.

2 Aranda Doncel has looked at wedding contracts from the Moriscos deported from Granada in Córdoba (*Los moriscos*, 261). In their study of Morisco clothing in early modern Valencia, Barceló and Labarta are careful to state that theirs is a limited linguistic analysis of the terminology used in Morisco documents ("Indumentaria," 50).

3 Indeed, as Aranda Doncel acknowledges, the wedding contracts that he analyses only reflect the transactions made by a minority of wealthy

Moriscos (*Los moriscos*, 258). Moreno Díaz del Campo does compare the wardrobes of Moriscos and Old Christians, but attributes the presence of garments labelled *a la morisca* in the inventories of the latter to the cultural influence of the former ("El hogar morisco," 111–12).

4 APAG, L-79-24. Fernández Chaves and Pérez García analyse how the inventories of Old Christians in Seville reflect their pillaging of the belongings of the rebellious Moriscos in Granada (*En los márgenes*, 73–6). For an example of how Old Christian soldiers profited from the miserable state of the Moriscos by buying their *marlotas* and *almaizares* at very low prices during their deportation, see Arribas, "Deportación," 43.

5 Fonseca, *Relación*, 117–18. Lomas Cortés analyses the registers of the goods taken by the Moriscos during their deportation and concludes that there was no sartorial difference with Old Christians, at least in Castile ("Aixovar," 12–18).

6 Rublack, *Dressing Up*, 211.

7 As Jones and Stallybrass point out, in the early modern period clothing was very often used to store wealth before the establishment of banks (*Renaissance Clothing*, 26–32). See also Rublack, *Dressing Up*, 5–6. Such a use is confirmed by the report of Juan of Austria's spy, Alonso Xabalí, who tells that, when the Moriscos tried to buy wheat from Morocco during the uprising of the Alpujarras, they used *marlotas* as an exchange good (AZ, Altamira 158-105).

8 "no se habla en los vestidos de sus bodas y plazeres, porque aquellos vestidos tiénenlos guardados para los tales dichos, y los hereda en tres o quatro herençias para gozarse y aprobecharse dellos para aquellos tiempos o para quando de neçeçidad los vienen a vender o empeñar" (Núñez Muley, "The Original Memorial," 211, trans. Barletta, *A Memorandum*, 70).

9 Boronat y Barrachina, *Los moriscos*, 1:653.

10 Cardaillac, "La Vêtement," 27. The 1565 Church Council of Granada recommended not to provide a funeral for Moriscos if they were not dressed in the Castilian manner (Pérez de Heredia y Valle, *El concilio provincial*, 428). For the use of Morisco clothing in weddings, see also Martínez Ruiz, "La indumentaria," 119.

11 "sobre todo amicissimos (y assi tenian comunmente gaytas, sonajas, adufes) de baylas, danças ..., y de todos los entretenimientos bestiales en que con descompuesto bullicio y griteria, suelen yr los moços villanos vozinglando por las calles. Vanagloriauanse de baylones ... y del canto, y corredores de toros, y de otros hechos semejantes de gañanes" (Aznar Cardona, *Expulsión justificada*, 2:34v).

12 This is true even if there were also courtly versions of bullfights. See for instance, Campos Cañizares, *El toreo caballeresco*. For instance, in

1563 Úbeda, Fernando de Bustillo agreed to have bullfights only on the condition that there was also a game of canes, because, as he reportedly said, "los toros solos tiene por cosa de aldeanos" [he considers having only bullfights to be very peasant-like] (Real Chancillería de Granada, 2057–3, 39r).

13 "y todos estos juegos tan diversos unos de los otros los ordenó el Reyecillo por no tener orden de correr toros ni tener cavallos y aderezos para juego de cañas" (Pérez de Hita, *La guerra de los moriscos*, 154). On this passage, see Carrasco Urgoiti, *Los moriscos*, 84–7; and Quinn, *The Moor and the Novel*, 93–7.

14 On the *zambra*, see Gallego y Burín and Gámir Sandoval, *Los moriscos*, 88–98; Fernández Manzano, *De las melodías*, 55–8 and 153–63; and Ramos López, *La música*, 49–54.

15 Fernández Manzano, *De las melodías*, 56–7 and 158–60. The earliest documented prohibition of *zambras* was that of Fernando de Toledo, Duke of Alba, in 1514, as he tried to ban it in Huéscar and Castilléjar, Fernández Manzano, *De las melodías*, 153. This seems, however, to be an isolated and local prohibition.

16 Ayala, *Sínodo*, 91v. On the Inquisitorial attempts to persecute the *zambras* in the early 1560s, see Colosía Rodríguez and Gil Sanjuan, "Málaga," 59–60.

17 *Pregmáticas y provisiones*, 3r–v. In this case, Philip II's decree very closely replicates the recommendation issued by the archbishop of Granada in 1565, López Martín, *Don Pedro Guerrero*, 130. The prohibition was reinstated in a subsequent decree in 1572, Carrasco Manchado, *De la convivencia*, 326. Núñez Muley complained in his memorandum to the monarch that the *zambras* were not related to the practice of Islam ("The Original Memorial," 214–16).

18 García Fuentes, *La Inquisición en Granada*, 142–3, 166, and 183–4; for persecutions against the *zambra* in La Mancha, see García-Arenal, *Inquisición y moriscos*, 77–8; and Moreno Díaz del Campo, *Los moriscos*, 309. The *zambras* were also prohibited by the 1586 Synod of Seville (Fernández Chaves and Pérez García, *En los márgenes*, 352).

19 See Fernández Manzano, *De las melodías*, 151–2, 158, and 160–1; for Huéscar, see Girón Pascual, "Mercaderes milaneses," 71. Núñez Muley also says that the archbishop Hernando de Talavera included *zambras* in the Christian liturgy in 1502 ("The Original Memorial," 215).

20 See Sentaurens, *Seville et le théâtre*, 2:1286; Aranda Doncel, "Las danzas," 186–7; Tapia Sánchez, *La comunidad morisca*, 277; Santamaría Conde, "Sobre la vida," 27–9; Sánchez Moltó, "Fiestas," 190; and López Megías and Ortiz López, *Almansa*, 79. I have also found similar cases in Almagro in 1573,

AMA, Libro de Acuerdos 1573–1582, 16 May 1573, 31v; Arévalo (Ávila), AMAre, Libro de Acuerdos, 30 April 1591; and Talavera de la Reina, AMTR, Libros de Acuerdos 16, 9 June 1595; and Libros de Acuerdos 19, 13 June 1603, 204v. I am grateful to César Pacheco and Yolanda Moreno for pointing out the case of Talavera de la Reina, which they analyse in detail in a forthcoming article ("La comunidad morisca en Talavera"). In 1596 the Moriscos of Lorca were commissioned to organize a dance for the Corpus Christi, but as they were rehearsing publicly, someone complained and the town council wrote the bishop of Cartagena asking for his approval (Guerrero Arjona, *Lorca*, 188).

21 "una dança de mas aparato [y] vistosa ynbençion que ser pueda" (AMV, Libros de Actas, 18 June 1600, 68r).

22 Tristán García, "Las fiestas oficiales," 396–7; and Castillo Fernández, "La tradición taurina," 162.

23 AMMz, Libro de Actas Capiturales, 21 August 1572, 363r. On this celebration, see Guillén Riquelme, *Un siglo*, 194–208. The arrival of the Moriscos was accompanied by a letter from Enrique de Rocafull, lord of Albatera, who seems to consider the Morisco band as his own property (AMMz, sección 1, leg. 109, exp. 3). This document has already been cited by Guillén Riquelme (although he dates it in 1570) (*Un siglo*, 204n327). I am grateful to Magdalena Campillo, from the Archivo Municipal de Mazarrón, for providing me with a copy. On the Moriscos of Albatera, see Serna Hernández, who refers to the Morisco musicians of Albatera performing in several festivals near Orihuela in the 1570s (*Mudéjares*, 20). It seems that the *zambra* was common in Mazarrón. In 1566, the council proposed bringing a *zambra* performance without specifying from where (AMMz, Libro de Actas Capitulares, 1 September 1566, 72r).

24 AMMu, Libro de Actas Capitulares 1599–1610, 22 October 1601, 51r. These *zambreros* were again the Moriscos of Albatera.

25 Pérez de Hita, *Guerras civiles*, 36, 115, 145, and 151.

26 Ruiz Lagos, *Moriscos*, 164.

27 Lasso de la Vega, *Manojuelo*, 130.

28 AMB, legajo 90, "Pleito entre Baza y su villa de Cúllar con el Marqués de los Vélez." I am grateful to Javier Castillo Fernández for pointing to this reference and for providing me with a transcription.

29 "cuarenta moriscos a pie en hábito de moros, con sonajas y panderetes y un carro con música de violones y otros instrumentos, con lo cual fue a Palacio, y en la plaza adelante hicieron la zambra al modo morisco, que paresció muy bien a muchos" (Cabrera de Córdoba, *Relaciones*, 114). Luis Hurtado de Mendoza, IV Marquis of Mondéjar and V Count of

Tendilla, died in Valladolid in 1604; he was the same who, as Mayor of the Alhambra since 1561, organized several Moorish performances in Granada before the uprising of the Alpujarras (as analysed below). One wonders whether, while in Valladolid, the count reencountered some of the Moriscos from Granada with whom he had organized Moorish festivals forty years earlier.

30 Joly, "Voyage," 525–6.

31 González Hernández, *Moros y cristianos*, 219.

32 Sanz Ayán finds in the *zambreros* of Granada one of the first signs of professionalization of performers in the Iberian Peninsula ("Felipe II," 57–8). Sentaurens documentas several ballets named after the *zambra*, *Seville et le théâtre*, 2:1224. There is no indication that the participants were Moriscos, which suggests that by then the *zambra* (or a certain version of it) was commonly performed by Old Christian musicians. For instance, in 1599, Portuguese, Flemish, and Italian merchants performed a *zambra* to celebrate Margarita of Austria's entry in Madrid (*Libro de noticias particulares*, 228); see also Sánchez Cano, "Dances," 150.

33 Inversely, and probably because music and dance were the only instances in which the Moriscos' participation in Iberian Moorishness was relatively accepted and even in some cases promoted, these performances were stigmatized as improper forms of Moorishness for Old Christians. In the very rare cases in which Old Christians were accused of passing as "Moors" it was because they did so while engaging in dancing in the company of Moriscos. This was the case of the Old Christian Cristóbal Duarte Ballester, who was accused by the Inquisition of having engaged in Islamic ceremonies and of having dressed as a Moor and danced the *zambra* with the Moriscos. See Surtz, "Crimes of the Tongue"; and Surtz, "Maurofilia y maurofobia."

34 See Gómez Vozmediano, *Mudéjares*, 40; Moreno Díaz del Campo, *Los moriscos*, 54–5; Tapia Sánchez, *La comunidad morisca*, 283; and Ruiz Ibáñez, *Las dos caras de Jano*, 223. Vincent points out that in 1591 the Moriscos were ordered to serve in the army as sappers ("Los moriscos granadinos," 174–7).

35 Horn, *Jan Cornelisz Vermeyen*, 1:26. Similarly, in 1526 the *caballeros de cuantía* of Écija welcomed Charles V dressed in Moorish garb (Gómez-Salvago Sánchez, *Fastos*, 193); and in 1569 the council of Córdoba ordered the *caballeros de cuantía* to show up in colourful clothing with *marlotas* and *capellares* to perform a military muster to welcome Philip II (Archivo Municipal de Córdoba, AH 01.06.01, exp. 11, 10 December 1569, 8v).

36 On the interrelation between festivals and military exhibitions, see
   González Hernández, *Moros y cristianos*, 31–6.
37 "estaban ya tan encendidos los unos y los otros ... que si assí no se atajara,
   no pudiera dexar de parar en veras" (Gómez de Castro, *Recibimiento*, 80).
   There is an alternative short description of the same royal entry written
   by Francisco del Campo which is equally inconclusive (*El muy sumptuoso
   y real recebimiento*, n.d). According to Francisco del Campo, two days later,
   Philip II requested that they repeat the mock battle so he and his men
   could participate in it.
38 Horozco, *Relaciones históricas*, 192–4.
39 Rodríguez de Ardila, "Historia," 112–13.
40 "En amaneziendo, se rrepresentaron los dos canpos, y pasando don
   Luis en su cavallo enpezaron los moriscos a entrar por los dos puentes,
   llebando mangas de arcabuzeros, y enpezaron a trabar su escaramuza tan
   braua y reñida como si de veras fuera, haziendose muertos de un cabo
   y de otro muchos dellos. Y abiendo un rato que esto andaba ... enpezo la
   cavalleria a entrar por los puertos, y el brauo don Luis delante dellos ...
   y trabandose la escaramuza, se vinieron a juntar todos quatroçientos
   de a caballo, cossa que jamas se a bisto en aquella ciudad, y de tan gran
   reguzijo que a todos tenia suspensos; y assi duro gran rato la escaramuza
   de a pie y de a cavallo" (Rodríguez de Ardila, "Historia," 113–14).
41 Rodríguez Ardila's description has been read (in my opinion, erroneously)
   through the confrontational celebrations of *moros y cristianos* (Flores
   Arroyuelo, *De la aventura*, 128–30; and Harris *Aztecs*, 207–8). These
   scholars do not take into account that the text does not reveal any religious
   resolution and that all the participants seem to be wearing Moorish
   clothing. While this is the only extant account of a mock battle in the
   1560s in the city of Granada, there is indirect evidence that the Count
   of Tendilla regularly organized similar military performances in which
   the participants dressed as Moors. When some soldiers were prosecuted
   for not having participated in the *escaramuza* [skirmish] for the festival
   of Saint John in 1565, they alleged in their defence that they had already
   purchased Moorish clothing, but that they were not able to participate due
   to unforeseen circumstances (APAG, L–88–14 and L–124–62).
42 The council ordered "que los vecinos de Banamaurel, Çujar y Canyles
   vengan en orden e trayan cañas y varas largas puestos hierros de papel a
   manera de lanças y trayan su capitan y alferez con vandera e sus añafiles
   e trompetillas" [that the inhabitants of Benamaurel, Zújar and Caniles
   come in order carrying canes and long reeds, with spearheads made out of

paper as if they were lances, and bring their captain and lieutenant with their flags and musical instruments] (AMB, Libro de Actas del Cabildo, 6 April 1525). This passage is also partially transcribed by Francisco Tristán García, who notes that these villages were inhabited almost exclusively by Moriscos ("Benamaurel," 94n75).

43 AMB, Libro de Actas del Cabildo, 25 April 1556. A description of the festival included in a later session confirms the participation of the inhabitants of Benamaurel, Zújar, and Caniles as part of the infantry (AMB, Libro de Actas del Cabildo, 3 May 1556).

44 AGS, Consejo de Castilla, legajo 2260 (n.f.). Explicit mentions of the Moriscos appear for Hornachos, 121r; Vera, 186v; Baza, Almería, and Guadix, 196r; Vélez-Málaga, 214r; and Ronda, 297v. See also González Fuertes and González Fuertes, "La reforma," 134–7.

45 As Mármol Carvajal adds, the next day the Christian soldiers found a bag of red berets that they assumed were intended to be distributed among the Moriscos of El Albaicín (*Historia*, 194).

46 Bermúdez de Pedraza follows Mármol Carvajal but rephrases Abenfarax's passing in a very significant way: "dexando … las monteras y sombreros, tomaron bonetes colorados con toquillas blancas para representar el papel de turcos" [taking off … their headdresses and hats, they took red berets with white turbans to perform the role of Turks] (*Historia eclesiástica*, 242r). With the selection of the verb *representar* [to perform a role] Bermúdez de Pedraza underlines the theatricality of attempting to pass as Turks.

47 In his poetic rendition of the uprising of the Alpujarras, Juan Rufo makes the inhabitant of the Albaicín reply to Abenfarax's order to revolt: "No andeys en vano, aqui haziendo alarde, / hermanos, que venis pocos y tarde" [Don't come in vain bragging off, my brothers, since you are too few and come late] (*La Austriada*, 35r). Rufo's use of the word *alarde*, while not conclusive, might indicate that his contemporaries read Abenfarax's act within the context of Iberian military musters. This was not the only occasion during the uprising in which the Moriscos dressed as Turks. Mármol de Carvajal also refers tangentially to how in May 1569, the Moriscos of Canillas (Málaga) joined the uprising and "por bravosidad se pusieron todos los mancebos y gandules las mangas de las marlotas de las moriscas en las cabezas y tocas blancas alderredor para parecer turcos" [out of bravery, the young males and the rebels put the sleeves of Moriscas' *marlotas* on their heads with white headresses to look like Turks] (Mármol Carvajal, *Historia*, 440). Vázquez Rengifo, even if he presents himself as a witness of many of the events he describes in the area of Vélez-Málaga, reproduces Mármol Carvajal almost verbatim (*Grandezas*, 241). In this

second case, Mármol Carvajal emphasizes that the intention of the passing was to show *bravosidad*, and not to trick anybody into believing that they were real Turks.

48 AMPC, Actas del Cabildo 1582–1588, Legajo 4, Libro 1, 1 August 1586, 203v. A subsequent session confirms this proposal, and two people were commissioned to each organize the Christian and the Moorish squads, 8 August 1586, 206r.

49 "agan lista de la jente de a caballo, así de caballería como de contías y otros caballeros que tengan caballos … para que salgan a la morisca todos los más que pudieren con lanzas y adargas. Y porque serán algunos jente nueba se manda que, tomada la raçón de los que salen, se agan otras tantas lanças de caña con los yerros contraechos plateados … y asimismo que tomen consigo a … otros cristianos nuevos del barrio para que bistan en ábito de moriscas, con sus almalafas bien puestas, cuarenta muchachas todas bien adereçadas con otros treinta muchachos de ocho a diez años, y estos an de salir a la morisca" (AMPC, Actas del Cabildo 1582–1588, Legajo 4, Libro 1, 25 August 1586, 210r–v). Durán Alcalá provides a partial (and not entirely accurate) transcription of this passage ("IV Centenario," 10). Cobo Calmaestra merely conceives of this festival as yet another instance of *moros y cristianos*, obviating that the *zuiza* finally mandated that all the participants dress *a la morisca* ("Aproximación," 14).

50 Two years later, the council organized a night equestrian exercise in which half of the twenty riders were told to dress *a la morisca* while the other half would dress with "sus libreas" (AMPC, Actas del Cabildo 1582–1588, Legajo 4, Libro 1, 21 March 1588, 321v–322r). This seems to be what was often called an *encamisada*, a kind of night masque in which riders would dress up and march through the town with large candles. Yet it is uncertain what kind of sartorial opposition the council is trying to inspire, whether this is some sort of *moros y cristianos* or whether they mean that some participants would receive livery from municipal funds while others would need to procure their own.

51 Peláez del Rosal and Rivas Carmona, *Priego de Córdoba*, 113–14, n89. Manuel Peláez del Rosal has informed me that this case will be further analysed in his forthcoming *Los moriscos de la villa de Priego de Córdoba*.

52 AGS, Consejo de Castilla, libro 370, 332v and 343v.

53 Ibid., libro 372, 19r. According to Hellwege, from whom I have taken these two references, this document actually prohibits the Moriscos from being enlisted as *caballeros de cuantía* (*Zur Geschichte*, 3–4, n7).

54 AHN, Órdenes Militares, Archivo Histórico de Toledo, 36658, "Proceso causado a pedimento del licenciado don Pedro Cortés." For a thorough

analysis of this lawsuit, see Childers, "Manzanares"; and Gómez Vozmediano, *Mudéjares*, 130–1. Several portions of this document have been transcribed by Childers, "Manzanares," 307–9; Gómez Vozmediano, *Mudéjares*, 224–6; and Moreno Díaz del Campo, *Los moriscos*, 549–55.

55 "tocando unas dulzaynas al modo morisco y con el tambor haçiendo muestras de algazara e rregoçijo, leuantando los braços hacia arriua y haçiendo muestras y señales de moros" (AHN, OOMM, AHT, 36658, 9v–10r). Only one of the witnesses describes the music using the term *zambras*, 21r.

56 Gómez Vozmediano, *Mudéjares*, 130.

57 Childers, "Manzanares," 289n3 and 294–5.

58 AHN, OOMM, AHT, 36658, 11v and 22r.

59 Gutiérrez de Villegas's exact words are "en esta prouinçia son usadissimas estas zuizas con los mismos del Reyno" [in this province these *zuizas* are extremely commonly held including the same [people] from the Kingdom] (ibid., 67v). Childers infers that Gutiérrez de Villegas refers to the Moriscos deported from the kingdom of Granada in 1570 ("Manzanares," 294). While his reading is entirely plausible, it is also possible to interpret it to mean that Gutiérrez de Villegas was referring to the *mudéjares* of the Kingdom of Castile, and more specifically to those Moriscos who had converted to Christianity long before in the territories of the Order of Calatrava and Almagro and had the privilege of carrying weapons because of their degree of assimilation.

60 Childers, "Manzanares," 294.

61 Naturally, because of the currency that Moorishness had in early modern Iberian society, Moriscos tried to capitalize on it to defend their own place. For instance, in 1584, one impoverished Morisco youngster claimed to be from the same lineage as the literary character Jarifa (Childers, "Review," 129).

62 Moreno Díaz del Campo, *Los moriscos*, 314–16. Indeed, it is not by chance that, as Childers has shown, the same Moriscos who led the *zuiza* in Manzanares were litigating to be recognized as Old Christians and not as Moriscos ("Manzanares," 301–4).

63 Calero Palacios, *Ciudad*, 64; Tristán García, "Las fiestas oficiales," 396–402; Ybáñez Worboys, "Fiestas"; Archivo Municipal de Vera, Actas Capitulares, 27 August 1566; Archivo Municipal de Antequera, Libro de Actas Capitulares, Lb–1599, 19 July 1562, 204r; Cruz Cabrera and Escañuela Cuenca, *El Cabildo de Motril*, 193 and 360.

64 Pérez Boyero, *Moriscos y cristianos*, 366.

65 AMG, Actas de Cabildo 3, 2 October 1517, 181v; Actas de Cabildo 6, 21 June 1566 through 28 June 1566, 223v–245r; and Actas de Cabildo 9,

August 1566 through 8 September 1566, 293r–327r. Indirect evidence that games of canes were regularly held in sixteenth-century Granada is the repairing of the Campo del Príncipe in 1513 to make it suitable for running bulls and playing canes (AMG, Actas de Cabildo 2, 5 Jul 1513, 67r). Unfortunately, the municipal proceedings between 1522 and 1566 are no longer extant.

66 Münzer, *Itinerarium*, 64.

67 Bermúdez de Pedraza, *Historia eclesiástica*, 198r.

68 Lange, "Die tagebuchartigen Aufseichnungen," 421–2. Juan Negro also describes a Moorish equestrian spectacle (Cicogna, *Della vita*, 340). For a thorough analysis of Charles V's entry, see Gómez-Salvago Sánchez, *Fastos*, 97–103.

69 "Los cristianos que vinieron ... a raíz de su conquista ... no tuvieron que aprenderlo, lo conocían y practicaban tan bien como los moros" (Tapia Garrido, *Historia general*, 7:366).

70 On the Nasrid aristocracy, see Soria Mesa, "De la conquista"; and Peinado Santaella, *Aristócratas nazaríes*.

71 Libro de las bulas y pragmáticas, 2:266r.

72 Fournel-Guérin, "Fiestas profanas," 630–1. Carrasco Urgoiti reproduces one letter addressed to Philip II and one report alluding to the same events (*El problema morisco*, 117 and 148).

73 Cardaillac, "Le Vêtement," 24; and Colás Latorre, "Los moriscos aragoneses," 153.

74 Calvete de Estrella, *El felicíssimo viaje*, 76. Fernández Chaves suggests that Juan de Granada would have felt out of place in this Moorish performance ("Entre la gracia y la justicia," 28).

75 28 June 1566, AMG, Actas de Cabildo 6, 244v. On the Zegrí family and their integration into Granadan society, see García Pedraza, "La asimilación," 40–6.

76 On the social ascent of wealthy Moriscos to nobility in the kingdom of Granada, see Castillo Fernández, "Las estructuras sociales," 201–5; and Galán Sánchez, "The Muslim Population," 71–89. For the social climbing of the Moriscos who remained in Spain after the expulsion, see Soria Mesa, *Los últimos moriscos*.

8 Moriscos as Theatrical Bodies

1 Ruiz Lagos, *Moriscos*, 178–81.

2 Ibid., 191.

3 Ibid., 198–9.

4 Ibid., 176.

5 Ibid., 182 and 189.

6 "Viene Arbolán todo el día / de cavar cien aranzadas, / por un puñado de harina / y una tarja horadada: / viene el otro delincuente / y sácale a la mañana / a la jineta vestido / de verde y flores de plata ... / Hace Muza sus buñuelos; / dice el otro, aparta, aparta, / que entra el valeroso Muza / cuadrillero de unas cañas" (Ruiz Lagos, *Moriscos*, 167–8).

7 "ridiculos en su traje, yendo vestidos por la mayor parte, con greguesquillos ligeros de lienço, o de otra cosa valadi al modo de Marineros, y con ropillas de poco valor, y mal compuestos adrede, y las mugeres de la misma suerte, con un corpezito de color, y una saya sola, de forraje amarillo, verde, o azul, andando en todos tiempos ligeras y desembaraçadas, con poca ropa, casi en camissa," Aznar Cardona, *Expulsión justificada*, 2:32v–3r. Martínez-Góngora reads these passages as a way to dispel the ghost of the economic competition between Old Christians and Moriscos ("El vestido," 509).

8 Villalmanzo Cameno, "La colección pictórica," 58. For similar interpretations, see also Bernis, *El traje y los tipos*, 486–7; and Lee, *The Anxiety of Sameness*, 153–6. This reading is probably reliable, since the men in the lower section of the painting are dressed in a very similar manner to other figures clearly identified as Old Christians – yet we should not totally discard that some of these "noble Christian" figures wearing black might actually represent wealthy Moriscos.

9 Aznar Cardona, while describing them as a miserable people heading to their exile, singled out several rich Moriscas dressed with lavish clothing and jewelry, *Expulsión justificada*, 2:5v–6r. The anonymous ballad "Gran revuelta hay en España," published as a chap book in the wake of the expulsion, claimed that the reason for their banishment was not their alleged apostasy, but their sartorial practices of wearing silk and brocades, which threatened the codification of social difference: "Era ya tanta su pompa / y triunfo demasiado, / que por ellos no conocen / el caballero y hidalgo" [Their splendour and ostentation was so excessive that because of them the gentleman and the *hidalgo* can no longer be known], Ruiz Lagos, *Moriscos*, 218. The anonymous author of the ballad conceives of the Morisco that assimilated into the higher ranks of Iberian society as more threatening for the fiction of social identity than the unassimilable one. Thus the lack of stability of sartorial signs is attributed exclusively to Moriscos, as if this were not in fact a larger social phenomenon in most early modern societies.

10 "con los calzones de estameña rotos; / los sayos de un color que pardo ha sido ... / ricas togas rozagantes" (Aguilar, *Expulsión*, 176–7). That the

Moriscos appearing in the third act of Aguilar's play *El gran patriarcha don Juan de Ribera* are characterized as labourers and the stage directions do not say anything about their clothing supports the interpretation that they were construed as commoners, as proposed here.

11 In her article on Gaspar Aguilar's sartorial characterization of the Moriscos, Martínez-Góngora analyses the passages in which they are construed as miserably dressed bodies, but omits the other passages in which the Moriscos are imagined in relation to Moorish clothing ("El vestido," 497–500).

12 "Quédense atrás los miserables daños / que padeció de España el suelo hermoso …. / Y el mal que resultó de los engaños / del padre de la Cava cauteloso, / por cuyos pensamientos arrogantes / España vio marlotas y turbantes," Aguilar, *Expulsión*, 346.

13 "Y así por la divina providencia / se fue de las Ideas de la gente, / de los Moros la plática, el lenguaje, / la traición, la crueldad, el talle, el traje" (Aguilar, *Expulsión*, 324).

14 "se prueban las marlotas y turbantes: / como algunos mancebos, inclinados / a ser y parecer representantes, / que antes de la comedia, van vestidos / de los trajes que tienen prevenidos," Aguilar, *Expulsión*, 183. In a later passage, he also describes some Moriscas in Aragon revealing their true sartorial and religious allegiances during the expulsion when "[d]espués que de Aragón las han echado / mudaron de costumbres y de trajes, / pues de sus corazones expelida / está la Cristiandad aunque fingida" [after they have been expelled from Aragon, they changed their costumes and clothing, since their fake Christianity has been expelled from their hearts] (*Expulsión*, 341).

15 Another epic poem on the expulsion, Juan Méndez de Vasconcelos's *Liga deshecha por la expulsión de los Moriscos* (1612), also presents the potential rebellion of the Moriscos as a sartorial revival: "turbantes sueltan, ponense galanes" [they loosen their turbans and adorn themselves] (*Liga deshecha*, 51r).

16 Ruiz Lagos, "Introducción," in Aguilar, *Expulsión*, 56–7.

17 Aguilar, *Fiestas nupciales*, 73–8 and 92–103; and Aguilar, *Fiestas que la ciudad*, 166–77. For the game of canes held in Valencia for the beatification of Fray Luis Beltrán, see also Gómez, *Los sermones*, 225–32.

18 On the particular social position of Gaspar Aguilar within the literary circles in Valencia and how this may be reflected in his work, see Sirera, "Mercaderes," 355–6.

19 Guadalajara y Xavier, *Memorable expulsión*, 83v.

20 Aznar Cardona, *Expulsión justificada*, 2:137v.

21 Or, as Dadson puts it, "the Moriscos could not win in this dialectical struggle: if they did not speak Castilian and persisted in dressing in an Arab style, they were deemed to be unassimilable; if they did speak the language and dressed like any other Christian, then they were potential spies, a fifth column bent on helping the enemies of the Crown," *Tolerance and Coexistence*, 114.

22 On the representation of the Morisco in the sixteenth-century theatre, see Surtz, "La imagen"; Garrot Zambrana, "Hacia la configuración"; Belloni, "La evolución"; and Colonge, "Reflets," 147–57. On Moorish jargon on stage, see Sloman, "The Phonology"; Case, "The Significance"; Santos Domínguez, "El lenguaje teatral"; and Congosto Martín, "La lengua."

23 *Farsa del sacramento*; Sánchez de Badajoz, *Recopilación en metro*, 463–8; Hurtado de Toledo and Carvajal, *Cortes*, 57v; and Rueda, *Las cuatro comedias*, 147–51.

24 Case, Lope and Islam, 9.

25 Vega, *Los cautivos*, 223 and 235.

26 Vélez de Guevara, "Baile de los moriscos," 231.

27 "otro coro de musicos, vestidos de Moros, turbantes, marlotas, y capellares, y dos dançarines en el mismo habito, de tabies, velillos, y bordados, con muchas plumas, y bandas, vizarros, y costosos; con ellos dos Moras, tambien adereçadas luzidamente a lo Africano; baylauan los quatro la çambra," Herrera, *Translación*, 49r. The translation of this passage, with slight adaptations, is taken from Marchante-Aragón, "The King," 113.

28 Marchante-Aragón, "The King," 116–18. I have also followed this tack elsewhere, Irigoyen-García, *The Spanish Arcadia*, 102–3.

29 Herrera, *Translación*, 38r.

30 "Moro ridiculo (por el vestido, figura personal, y lenguaje aljamiado de su voz)," Herrera, *Translación*, 49v; Marchante-Aragón, "The King," 98.

31 Morley and Bruerton, *Cronología*, 430.

32 Ibid., 85.

33 González Barrera, "Estudio," in Vega, *La doncella Teodor*, 30–1.

34 Morley and Bruerton, *Cronología*, 88.

35 As Case notes, even though the Morisco appears frequently as a jester and low figure, the expression "moro gracioso" applied to them is only found in two plays by Lope, "El morisco gracioso," 789–90.

36 Pelorson, "Recherches," 12–18 and 38. See Irigoyen-García, "'Ni chivato ni carnero'." Even though the Morisco appears frequently in the *comedia* and there are several plays representing the uprising of the Alpujarras, as we will see in the next section, there is almost no play representing the expulsion – hence the importance of this piece. Pedraza Jiménez,

when tracing the few references to the expulsion, notes that it had a very limited impact on theatre ("La expulsion," 197), but does not consider *Los moriscos de Hornachos* nor Aguilar's *El gran patriarcha don Juan de Ribera*. On Aguilar's play, see Figueroa, who also suggests that the lack of theatrical representations of the expulsion is caused by the difficulties of presenting a morally conflicting issue, "La expulsión."

37 "Sentaos, direos una letra; / aunque hecha por christianos, / es de gusto y alegria, / y puede regocijaros / porque es de la reyna mora / que en Almeria tiene estado" [Take a seat, and I will tell you a ballad that, though written by Christians, is very pleasant and cheerful, and may delight us, because it deals with the Moorish Queen of Almería] (Bourland, "Los moriscos de Hornachos," 1:563).

38 Castillo Fernández, "La guerra de los moriscos," 700–1.

39 On the dramatic representation of the uprising of the Alpujarras, see Símini, "La rebelión."

40 Pérez de Hita states that his second part of the *Guerras civiles de Granada* was finished by 1597 (even if it was not published until 1619), *La guerra de los moriscos*, 353. Hurtado de Mendoza's text was probably composed between 1571 and 1575 and circulated widely in manuscript form, Blanco-González, "Introducción," 82. Mármol Carvajal must have finished a preliminary version by 1572, when he first tried to publish it (but could not until 1600), Puglisi, "Escritura y ambición," 146; and Castillo Fernández, *Entre Granada y el Magreb*, 106–7 and 304–6.

41 A full analysis of how the Moriscos of Granada have been visually "Moorified" in subsequent historiography is beyond the scope of the present study.

42 Antolínez de Burgos, *Historia eclesiástica*, 253–5.

43 Cabrillana also notes the incongruity in the clothing of the male Moriscos in Heylan's engraving, but he also believes that the sartorial representation of the Moriscas is in turn "realistic," without interrogating how the alleged "realism" of an image of events that took place more than fifty years before Heylan's time cannot have been created from the actual observation of reality, but from the elaboration of an already existing iconographic tradition ("Imágenes," 69).

44 There are certainly some precedents in urban ballets. For the feast of Corpus Christi in Guadalajara in 1571, one ballet with four Christians and four Moors staged the uprising of the Alpujarras – precisely as Granada's exiled Moriscos were settling there (Layna Serrano, *Historia de Guadalajara*, 3:474).

45 "los vestidos eran bonísimos, porque capellares, marlotas y turbantes en casa los teníamos" (Alcalá Yáñez, *Alonso*, 716).

46 According to Spratlin, *Juan Latino* was composed between 1610 and 1621, *Juan Latino*, 206. As Panford notes, the play could have been composed as late as 1626, "La figura del negro," 77. On this play, see also Ivory, "*Juan Latino*"; and Fra Molinero, *La imagen de los negros*, 125–62.

47 "que no traigan almalafas, / ni marlotas, ni vestido / que no sea a nuestra usanza. / Y para gastar sus ropas, / se dan dos años, y mandan / a las señoras moriscas, / que no se cubran las caras," Jiménez de Enciso, *El encubierto*, 175.

48 "¡Mandarnos que la lengua en que nacimos / mudemos en tres años, y dexemos / los vestidos y trajes que vestimos, / cosa inhumana es! ... / ... La pobre gente, / ¿cómo puede comprar vestidos nuevos? / o ¿por qué de los suyos mal se siente? / Los egipcios, armenios y suevios / Cristianos son, y visten este traje" (Jiménez de Enciso, *El encubierto*, 213).

49 "si hubo un chico Rey que el Reino diese, / habrá un grande Válor que lo restaure," Jiménez de Enciso, *El encubierto*, 215. The term "el rey chico" refers to the last king of Nasrid Granada, Abu 'abd Allah Muhammad XI, known in Castilian as Boabdil El Chico. On the representation of this figure, and the emasculation implicit in this epithet, see Cartagena Calderón, *Masculinidades*, 78–87.

50 "con una fuente, y en ella todo el vestido de moro famoso, y un turbante con una corona y una toca grande y un cetro" (Jiménez de Enciso, *El encubierto*, 229).

51 All quotations from this play come from Erik Coenen's edition. The play has been traditionally dated circa 1633; Coenen shows that this date has been mistakenly attributed based on confusion with a different play by Juan Pérez de Montalbán and that the first reference to its representation dates from 1659 (although he concedes that the play was quite probably composed much earlier than that), "Introducción," 48. Bayo, citing the same sources used by Coenen, still argues that the play was probably composed in the 1630s by comparing it with other plays by Calderón and the circulation of his works, "Problemas contextuales," 79–81. Devos argues that the title of the play should be *El Tuzaní de la Alpujarra o amor después de la muerte*, "El título." On the different versions of this play and the ideological significance of its variants, see Ruiz Lagos, "Introducción," 54–69.

52 Cruz, "Making War," 17–18.

53 Parker, *The Mind and Art*, 318–20. Wilson has suggested that, since the date of the play is uncertain, it might allude to the rebellions of Portugal and Catalonia in 1640 ("Si África llora," 420).

54 Carrasco, "Contra la guerra," 133–7; Bayo, "Problemas contextuales," 85–8; and Olsen, "'Ley ser," 74–5. On the Moriscos who stayed or returned after the expulsion, see Dadson, "Official Rhetoric"; and Soria Mesa, *Los últimos moriscos*.

55 Case, "Honor," 64–5.

56 García Soormally, "El cuerpo"; Sieber, "El monstruo," 740; and Walzer, "Los moriscos."

57 "Salen todos los Moriscos … vestidos a lo morisco, casaquillas y calzoncillos, y las Moriscas jubones blancos" (Calderón de la Barca, *Amar*, 79).

58 Devos, "Calderón's Ambiguity," 114–15. While I find Devos's interpretation suggestive, another possibility is that the terminology of Moorish clothing had evolved by the 1630s. The *calzones*, which Devos ascribes to the representation of black slaves, are found in the characterization of gallant Moors as well – for instance, in one ballet held in Seville in 1639 (Sentaurens, *Seville et le théâtre*, 2:1183).

59 "Las condiciones, pues, eran / algunas de las pasadas / y otras nuevas, que venían / escritas con más instancia, / en razón de que ninguno / de la nación africana / … pudiese / tener fiestas, hacer zambras, / vestir sedas, verse en baños, / ni oírse en alguna casa / hablar en su algarabía, / sino en lengua castellana" (Calderón de la Barca, *Amar*, 82–93).

60 Coenen also points out that Calderón takes the information about the prohibitions from Mármol Carvajal ("Las fuentes," 476–8).

61 "Coronado, pues, el Válor, / la primer cosa que ordena / fue, por oponerse en todo / a las pregmáticas nuestras … / que ninguno se llamara / nombre cristiano, ni hiciera / ceremonia de cristiano … / que ninguno hablar pudiese, / sino en arábiga lengua, / vestir sino traje moro, / ni guardar sino la secta / de Mahoma" (Calderón de la Barca, *Amar*, 121–2).

62 Pérez de Hita, *La guerra de los moriscos*, 324–39.

63 "me puse este trage de Christiano; por que lo soy" (Pérez de Hita, *La guerra de los moriscos*, 336).

64 Calderón de la Barca, *Amar*, 132.

65 "¿Cómo puede ser, / si vienes tan disfrazado, / conocerte? Y pues mudado / el traje los dos traemos, / pasar entre ellos podemos, / sin sospecha averiguada, / por cristianos, pues en nada / ya moriscos parecemos" (Calderón de la Barca, *Amar*, 172).

66 "Tú, que bien el lengua hablar, … / tú, que español parecer, / seguro poder pasar; / mé, que no sé pronunciar, … / mé, que este traje no he usado, / ¿cómo escosar el castigo?" Calderón de la Barca, *Amar*, 172–3. My

translation to English cannot convey that Alcuzcuz is speaking a debased version of Spanish.

67 As Olsen states, although she focuses on culinary aspects instead of the sartorial element, "Alcuzcuz can safely bring his ethnic difference into dialogue with the pleasures of Spanish culture and allow a public to face in good humor their real anxieties over religious and cultural assimilation" ("Ser ley," 68).

68 Greer, "The Politics of Memory," 126.

69 González de Cunedo, *A un traidor*, 84v. On this play, see Luca, "Una comedia olvidada."

70 Ibid., 106r.

71 Ibid., 86r.

72 The only extant copy of this play is a *suelta* located at the Real Biblioteca, VIII/17152(5).

73 Fajardo y Acevedo, *Comedias*, 186.

74 Ibid., 177.

75 Ibid., 149. For the date and circumstances of the play's composition, see Símini, "La rebelión," 227–30.

76 "os ha puesto con la pragmática a todos yugo pesado y grossero" (Fajardo y Acevedo, *Comedias*, 158).

77 "aviendo contravenido / a lo tratado y dispuesto, / nos hazen negar la ley / del profeta verdadero, / que dexemos nuestro trage, / la lengua de los abuelos, / nuestras zambras y júbilos" (ibid., 156).

78 "querer mudarnos los trages / es tirar a empobrecernos, / porque más de tres millones / valen los adornos nuestros. / Quatrocientas mil personas / que han de vestirse de nuevo, / ¿qué nos costará?" (ibid.).

79 Ibid., 157.

80 "con turbantes a lo turco / vengan, que si descubiertos / fueren de algún accidente, / la sospecha hará más riesgo, / creyendo que el gran Señor / favorece nuestro intento" (ibid., 158).

81 Mármol Carvajal, *Historia*, 191–2.

82 "haziendo, por mayor befa, / de los frontales vestidos" (Fajardo y Acevedo, *Comedias*, 171).

83 "rompiendo los Ornamentos, y vestiduras Sagradas, vistiendoselas por mofa, y escarnio," Escolano Ledesma, *Memorial*, 3. A literary precedent for this image can be found in Lupercio Leonardo de Argensola's historical play *Isabela* (c. 1581), in which Muslims repress Christians in twelfth-century Saragossa by desecrating their churches and relics and transforming them into garments for equestrian performances (*Tragedias*, 191).

84 "de almaizares y turbantes / haremos tapetes ricos" (Fajardo y Acevedo, *Comedias*, 184).
85 Ibid., 180–1.
86 Ibid., 189.

Conclusions

1 Fallows, *Jousting*, 297–8.
2 On the higher proportion of *hidalgos* in northern Spain, see Soria Mesa, *La nobleza*, 43.
3 Marín, "Fiestas caballerescas," 113; her opinion is also followed by Fallows, *Jousting*, 289.
4 Durán i Sanpere, *Barcelona*, 2:171–259.
5 On Charles V's entry see Libre de la benauenturada vinguda. For Oleza, see Exercicio militar, 12r.
6 On the presence of the game of canes in colonial Latin America, see López Cantos, *Juegos*, 173–83; Harris, *Aztecs*, 122–69; Flores Hernández, "La *jineta indiana*," 650; and Rappaport, "Buena sangre," 43–4.
7 Fuchs, *Exotic Nation*, 96–102.
8 Guarino, *Representing*, 86–91.
9 Bernis, "Échanges."

Works Cited

Archival Sources

ACA: Archivo de la Corona de Aragón
AGS: Archivo General de Simancas*
AHN: Archivo Histórico Nacional*
AHN-Nobleza: Archivo Histórico Nacional. Sección Nobleza*
AHPM: Archivo Histórico de Protocolos de Madrid
AHPV: Archivo Histórico Provincial de Valladolid
AMA: Archivo Municipal de Almagro (Ciudad Real)
AMAre: Archivo Municipal de Arévalo (Ávila)
AMAv: Archivo Municipal de Ávila
AMB: Archivo Municipal de Baza (Granada)
AMG: Archivo Municipal de Granada***
AMC: Archivo Municipal de Cartagena (Murcia)**
AMM: Archivo Municipal de Murcia**
AMMC: Archivo Municipal de Medina del Campo (Valladolid)
AMMR: Archivo Municipal de Medina de Rioseco (Valladolid)
AMMu: Archivo Municipal de Mula (Murcia)**
AMMz: Archivo Municipal de Mazarrón (Murcia)**
AMPC: Archivo Municipal de Priego de Córdoba (Córdoba)
AMT: Archivo Municipal de Toledo
AMTR: Archivo Municipal de Talavera de la Reina
AMV: Archivo Municipal de Valladolid***
APAG: Archivo del Patronato de la Alhambra y Generalife (Granada)
ARChV: Archivo de la Real Chancillería de Valladolid*
AVM: Archivo de Villa de Madrid
AZ: Archivo Biblioteca Francisco Zabálburu (Madrid)

IVDJ: Instituto Valencia de Don Juan (Madrid)
BNE: Biblioteca Nacional de España***

* Some of the documents from these archives are available at Portal de Archivos Españoles: pares.mcu.es.
** All the municipal proceedings from the archives of Murcia are available at Proyecto Carmesí: Archivos Históricos de la Región de Murcia: http://www.regmurcia.com/servlet/s.Sl?METHOD=FRMSENCILLA&sit=c,373,m,139,ser v,Carmesi.
*** Some of the documents from these archives are available at their respective websites.

Works Cited

Abencerraje (Novela y romancero), El. Ed. Francisco López Estrada. Madrid: Cátedra, 1997.

Actas de las Cortes de Castilla. Vol. 34. Madrid: Congreso de los Diputados, 1911.

Aguilar, Gaspar. *Expulsión de los moros de España*. Ed. Manuel Ruiz Lagos. Alcalá de Guadaira: Guadalmena, 1999.

– *Fiestas nupciales que la ciudad y reino de Valencia han hecho al casamiento del rey don Felipe III con doña Margarita de Austria (Valencia, 1599)*. Ed. facsímile Antonio Pérez y Gómez. Cieza: "la fonte que mana y corre," 1975.

– *Fiestas que la ciudad de Valencia hizo con motivo de la beatificación del Santo Fr. Luis Bertrán*. Ed. Francisco Carreres y Vallo. Valencia: Antonio López, 1914.

– *El gran patriarcha don Juan de Ribera*. In *Norte de la poesía española*. Ed. Aurelio Mey. Valencia: Felipe Mey, 1616. n.p.

Aguilar, Pedro de. *Tractado de la cavalleria de la gineta*. 1572. Ed. facsimile. Seville: Extramuros, 2007.

Agulló y Cobos, Mercedes. "'Cornejos' y 'Peris' en el Madrid de los siglos de oro (alquiladores de trajes para representaciones teatrales)." In *Cuatro siglos de teatro en Madrid*. Eds. Andrés Peláez and Fernanda Andura. Madrid: Consorcio Madrid Capital Europea de la Cultura, 1992. 181–200.

Albarracín de Martínez Ruiz, Joaquina. *Vestido y adorno de la mujer musulmana de Ŷebala (Marruecos)*. Madrid: Centro Superior de Investigaciones Científicas, 1964.

Albayceta, Juan de. *Geometría y trazas*. Zaragoza: Francisco Revilla, 1720.

Alcalá Yáñez, Jerónimo. *Alonso, mozo de muchos amos (primera y segunda parte)*. Ed. Miguel Donoso Rodríguez. Madrid: Iberoamericana, 2005.

Alcega, Juan de. *Libro de geometria, pratica, y traça*. Madrid: Guillermo Drouy, 1580.

Alcocer, Francisco. *Tratado del juego.* Salamanca: Andrea de Portomariis, 1569.

Alemán, Mateo. *Guzmán de Alfarache.* Ed. José María Micó. 2 vols. Madrid: Cátedra, 1997.

Alenda y Mira, Jenaro. *Relaciones de solemnidades y fiestas públicas de España.* 2 vols. Madrid: Rivadeneyra, 1903.

Allerston, Patricia. "Reconstructing the Second-Hand Clothes Trade in Sixteenth- and Seventeenth-Century Venice." *Costume* 33.1 (1999): 46–56.

Alonso Resalt, Juan, and José María Sánchez. *San Nicasio, un patrón para Leganés.* Leganés: Ayuntamiento de Leganés, 2000.

Alvar, Manuel. *El romancero: Tradicionalidad y pervivencia.* Barcelona: Planeta, 1970.

Álvarez-Ossorio Alvariño, Antonio. "Rango y apariencia. El decoro y la quiebra de la distinción en Castilla (ss. XVI–XVIII)." *Revista de Historia Moderna* 17 (1998–9): 263–78.

Amigo Vázquez, Lourdes. *¡A la plaza! Regocijos taurinos en el Valladolid de los siglos XVII y XVIII.* Seville: Universidad de Sevilla, 2010.

– "Imágenes de la Ilustración: Las fiestas vallisoletanas en honor de Carlos IV (1789–1790)." In *Ocio y vida cotidiana en el mundo hispánico en la Edad Moderna.* Ed. Francisco Núñez Roldán. Seville: Universidad de Sevilla, 2007. 367–89.

Anderson, Ruth Matilda. "The Golilla: A Spanish Collar of the 17th Century." *Waffe und Kostumkunde* 11 (1969): 1–19.

– *Hispanic Costume 1480–1530.* New York: Hispanic Society of America, 1979.

Andrade, Antonio Galvam de. *Arte da cavallaria de gineta e estardiota.* Lisboa: Joam da Costa, 1678.

Andújar, Martín de. *Geometría y trazas pertenecientes al oficio de sastres.* Madrid: Alonso Pérez, 1640.

Antolínez de Burgos, Justino. *Historia eclesiástica de Granada.* Ed. Manuel Sotomayor. Granada: Universidad de Granada, 1996.

Aponte Marín, Ángel. *Gobierno municipal, élites y monarquía en Jaén durante el reinado de Felipe III (1598–1621).* Jaén: Universidad de Jaén, 2010. [includes complementary CD]

– "Juegos de cañas en el Jaén Barroco." *Diario Jaén* 18-6-1989: 25.

Aranda Doncel, Juan. "Las danzas de las fiestas del Corpus en Córdoba durante los siglos XVI y XVII: Aspectos folklóricos, económicos y sociales." *Boletín de la Real Academia de Córdoba* 98 (1978): 173–94.

– *Los moriscos en tierras de Córdoba.* Córdoba: Monte de Piedad y Caja de Ahorros de Córdoba, 1984.

Araujo Miguélez, Antonio. *Utrera y sus antiguas fiestas de toros.* Utrera: Ayuntamiento de Utrera, 1999.

Arce, Francisco de. *Fiestas reales en Lisboa*. Ed. Antonio Pérez Gómez. Valencia: "la fonte que mana y corre," 1956.

Argensola, Lupercio Leonardo. *Tragedias*. Ed. Luigi Giuliani. Zaragoza: Prensas Universitarias de Zaragoza, 2009.

Arias Dávila Puertocarrero, Juan. *Discurso … para estar a la gineta con gracia y hermosura*. Sanz Egaña 1–66.

Arié, Rachel. "Acerca del traje musulmán en España desde la caída de Granada hasta la expulsión de los moriscos." In *Études sur la civilisation de l'Espagne musulmane*. Leiden: Brill, 1990. 121–41.

Arribas, María Soledad. "Deportación de los moriscos de Torres a la ciudad de Valladolid en 1572. Fuentes documentales." *Sumuntan* 1 (1991): 35–46.

Asenjo, Julio. *La tragedia de San Hermenegildo y otras obras del teatro español de colegio*. 2 vols. Valencia: Universitat de València, 1995.

Astor Landete, Marisa. *Valencia en los siglos XIV y XV: Indumentaria e imagen*. Valencia: Ajuntament de València, 1999.

Atienza, Belén. "La (re)conquista de un valido: Lope de Vega, el Duque de Lerma y los godos." *Anuario Lope de Vega* 6 (2000): 39–49.

Avilés, Luis F. "Los suspiros del *Abencerraje*." *Hispanic Review* 71.4 (2003): 453–72.

Ayala, Martín de. *Sínodo de la diócesis de Guadix y Baza*. Ed. facsimile Carlos Asenjo Sedano. Granada: Universidad de Granada, 1994.

Aznar Cardona, Pedro. *Expulsión justificada de los Moriscos Españoles*. Huesca: Pedro Cabarte, 1612.

Báez de Sepúlveda, Jorge. *Relación verdadera del recibimiento que hizo la ciudad de Segovia a la magestad de la reyna nuestra señora doña Anna de Austria*. Eds. Sagrario López Poza and Begoña Canosa Hermida. Segovia: Fundación Juan de Borbón, 1998.

Balenchana, Juan Antonio de. "Introducción." Bañuelos y de la Cerda v–lxxi.

Bañuelos y de la Cerda, Luis. *Libro de la jineta y descendencia de los caballos Guzmanes*. Ed. Juan Antonio de Balenchana. Madrid: Sucesores de Rivadeneyra, 1877.

Barbour, Nevill. "The Significance of the Word *Maurus*, with its Derivatives *Moro* and *Moor*, and of Other Terms Used by Medieval Writers in Latin to Describe the Inhabitants of Medieval Spain." In *Actas do IV Congresso de Estudos Árabes e Islâmicos*. Leiden: Brill, 1971. 253–66.

Barceló, Carmen, and Ana Labarta. "Indumentaria morisca valenciana." *Sharq Al-Andalus* 2 (1985): 49–73.

Barletta, Vincent. "Introduction." Núñez Muley, *A Memorandum* 1–54.

Barrantes Maldonado, Pedro. *Diálogo entre Pedro Barrantes Maldonado y un cauallero estrangero que cuenta el saco que los turcos hizieron en Gibraltar en 1540*. Ed. José López Romero. [n.p.]: Espuela de Plata, 2009.

Barrios Aguilera, Manuel. *La convivencia negada. Historia de los moriscos del reino de Granada*. Comares: Granada, 2007.

– "La guerra de los moriscos de Granada en el *Sumario de Prohezas y casos de guerra* de Juan de Arquellada." *Chronica Nova* 22 (1995): 407–28.

Barrios Aguilera, Manuel, and Ángel Galán Sánchez, eds. *La historia del reino de Granada a debate: Viejos y nuevos temas. Perspectivas de estudio*. Málaga: Diputación de Málaga, 2004.

Bass, Laura R., and Amanda Wunder. "The Veiled Ladies of the Early Modern Spanish World: Seduction and Scandal in Seville, Madrid, and Lima." *Hispanic Review* 77.1 (2009): 97–144.

Bataillon, Marcel. "*La desdicha por la honra*: Génesis y sentido de una novela de Lope." *Nueva Revista de Filología Hispánica* 1.1 (1947): 13–42.

Bayo, Juan Carlos. "Problemas contextuales en torno a *Amar después de la muerte* o *El tuzaní de la Alpujarra*." In *Calderón y el pensamiento ideológico y cultural de su época*. Eds. Manfred Tietz and Gero Arnscheidt. Stuttgart: Franz Steiner Verlag, 2008. 70–93.

Belloni, Benedetta. "La evolución de la figura del morisco en el teatro español del Siglo de Oro." In *"Scripta manent." Actas del I Congreso Internacional Jóvenes Investigadores Siglo de Oro (JISO 2011)*. Eds. Carlos Mata Induráin and A. J. Sáez. Pamplona: Universidad de Navarra, 2012. 34–46.

Bennassar, Bartolomé. *Histoire de la tauromachie: Une société du spectacle*. Paris: Desjonquères, 1993.

Benítez Sánchez-Blanco, Rafael. "Carlos V y los moriscos granadinos." In *Historia de la Inquisición en España y América I*. Eds. Joaquín Pérez Villanueva and Bartolomé Escandell Bonet. Madrid: Centro de Estudios Inquisitoriales, 1984. 474–87.

– "Entre el optimismo y la decepción: la evangelización de los moriscos de la diócesis de Orihuela." In *Modernitas: Estudios en homenaje al profesor Baudillo Barreiro Mallón*. Ed. Manuel-Reyes García Hurtado. A Coruña: Universidade da Coruña, 2008. 75–109.

– *Heroicas decisiones: La monarquía católica y los moriscos valencianos*. Valencia: Institució Alfons El Magnànim, 2001.

– "Un plan para la aculturación de los moriscos valencianos: 'Les ordinacions' de Ramírez de Haro (1540)." Cardaillac, *Les Morisques*. 125–57.

Benito, Ana I. "La ubicua presencia del moro: Maurofilia y maurofobia literaria como productos de consumo cristiano." In *Disobedient Practices: Textual Multiplicity in Medieval and Golden Age*. Eds. Belén Bistué and Anne Roberts. Newark, DE: Juan de la Cuesta, 2015. 103–28.

Benito Ruano, Eloy. "Recepción madrileña de la reina Margarita de Austria." *Anales del Instituto de Estudios Madrileños* 1 (1966): 85–98.

Bermúdez de Pedraza, Francisco. *Historia eclesiástica, principios y progressos de la ciudad y religión cathólica en Granada*. Granada: Imprental Real, 1638.

Bernis, Carmen. *El traje y los tipos sociales en* El Quijote. Madrid: El Viso, 2001.

– *Trajes y modas en la España de los Reyes Católicos*. 2 vols. Madrid: Centro Superior de Investigaciones Científicas, 1978–9.

– "Échanges pendant la Renaissance entre les modes espagnoles et les modes de l'Europe centrale et orientale (hongroise, albanaise et turque)." In *Évolution générale et développement régionaux en histoire de l'art*. Ed. György Rózsa. 3 vols. Budapest: Akadémiai Kiadó, 1972. 1: 705–13.

– *Indumentaria española en tiempos de Carlos V*. Madrid: Instituto Diego Velázquez, 1962.

– "Modas moriscas en la sociedad cristiana del siglo XV y principios del XVI." *Boletín de la Real Academia de la Historia* 144 (1959): 199–236.

– *Indumentaria medieval española*. Madrid: Instituto Diego Velázquez, 1956.

– "La moda en la España de Felipe II a través del retrato de corte." Saavedra 65–111.

Bershas, Henry N. "Lope de Vega and the Post of Royal Chronicler." *Hispanic Review* 31.2 (1963): 109–17.

Birriel Salcedo, Margarita. "Mujeres del reino de Granada: Historia y género." Barrios Aguilera and Galán Sánchez 485–501.

Blancas, Jerónimo de. *Coronaciones de los sereníssimos Reyes de Aragón*. Ed. Juan Francisco Andrés de Uztárroz. Zaragoza: Diego Dormer, 1641.

Blanco-González, Bernardo. "Introducción." Hurtado de Mendoza 7–86.

Blanes Andrés, Roberto. *Valencia y el Magreb: Las relaciones comerciales marítimas (1600–1703)*. Barcelona: Bellaterra, 2010.

Blázquez Miguel, Juan. *El tribunal de la Inquisición en Murcia*. Murcia: Real Academia Alfonso X el Sabio, 1986.

Bleda, Jaime. *Corónica de los moros de España*. Valencia: Patricio Mey, 1618.

Boronat y Barrachina, Pascual. *Los moriscos españoles y su expulsión*. 2 vols. Valencia: Francisco Vives y Mora, 1901.

Boucharb, Ahmed. *Os pseudo-mouriscos de Portugal no séc. XVI: Estudo de uma especificidade a partir das fontes inquisitoriais*. Trans. Maria Filomena Lopes de Barros. Lisboa: Hugin, 2004.

Bourdieu, Pierre. *Distinction: A Social Critique of the Judgement of Taste*. Trans. Richard Nice. Cambridge, MA: Harvard UP, 1984.

Bourland, C.B., ed. "Los moriscos de Hornachos." *Modern Philology* 1 (1903–1904): 547–62; 2 (1904–1905): 77–96.

Braamcamp, Anselmo. "Inventário da Guarda-roupa de D. Manuel." *Archivo Historico Português* 2 (1904): 381–417.

Brann, Ross. "The Moors?" *Medieval Encounters* 15 (2009): 307–18.

Breuer-Hermann, Stephanie. "Alonso Sánchez Coello: vida y obra." Saavedra 13–35.

Brisset Martín, Demetrio E. "Fiestas hispanas de moros y cristianos." In *Actas de las Primeras Jornadas de Religiosidad Popular: Almería, 1996*. Eds. Valeriano Sánchez Ramos and José Ruiz Fernández. Almería: Instituto de Estudios Almerienses, 1997. 361–80.

Burningham, Bruce R. *Radical Theatricality: Jongleuresque Performance on the Early Spanish Stage*. West Lafayette, IN: Purdue UP, 2007.

Burshatin, Israel. "Power, Discourse and Metaphor in the *Abencerraje*." *MLN* 99 (1984): 195–213.

Busic, Jason David. "Saving the Lost Sheep: Mission and Culture in Pedro Guerra de Lorca's *Catecheses mystagogicae pro aduenis ex secta Mahometanada: Ad Parochos, & Potestates* (1586)." Diss. Ohio State U, 2009.

Cabeza Rodríguez, Antonio, Margarita Torremocha Hernández, and Ricardo M. Martín de la Guardia. "Fiesta y política en Valladolid. La entrada de Felipe III en el año 1600." *Investigaciones Históricas: Época Moderna y Contemporánea* 16 (1996): 77–87.

Cabrera de Córdoba, Luis. *Relaciones de las cosas sucedidas en la corte de España, desde 1599 hasta 1614*. Madrid: J. Martín Alegría, 1857.

Cabrillana, Nicolás. "Imágenes de moriscos: Del simbolismo al realismo (1519–1650)." In *Actes du VIIIe Symposium International d'Études Morisques sur Images des morisques dans la litterature et les arts*. Ed. Abdeljelil Temimi. Zaghouan: Fondation Temimi, 1999. 65–82.

Cacegas, Luís. *Vida de Dom Frei Bertolameu dos Martires da Ordem dos Pregadores*. Viana: Nicolao Carvalho, 1609.

Cadornega, António de Oliveira de. *Descrição de Vila Viçosa*. Ed. Heitor Gomes Teixeira. Lisboa: Impresa Nacional-Casa da Moeda, 1983.

Calderón de la Barca, Pedro. *Amar después de la muerte*. Ed. Erik Coenen. Madrid: Cátedra, 2008.

– [attributed]. *El rollo de Ézija*. N.p.: n.e., c. 1672. Real Biblioteca (Madrid). VIII/17152(5).

Calero Palacios, María del Carmen. *Ciudad, memoria y escritura: Los libros de actas capitulares del cabildo de Almuñécar (1552–1582)*. Granada: Universidad de Granada, 2010.

Calvete de Estrella, Juan Cristóbal. *El felicíssimo viaje del muy alto y muy poderoso don Phelippe*. Ed. Paloma Cuenca. Madrid: Sociedad Estatal para la Conmemoración de los Centenarios de Felipe II y Carlos V, 2001.

Campo, Francisco del. *El muy sumptuoso y real recebimiento que la imperial ciudad de Toledo hizo a la entrada de la serenissima Reyna nuestra Señora doña Isabel de la Paz*. Seville: Sebastián Trujillo, [1560].

Campos Cañizares, José. *El toreo caballeresco en la época de Felipe IV: Técnicas y significado socio–cultural*. Seville: Fundación Real Maestranza de Caballería de Sevilla, 2007.

Cancionero de obras de burlas provocantes a risa. Eds. Pablo Jauralde Pou and Juan Alfredo Bellón Cazabán. Madrid: Akal, 1974.

Cancionero de Juan Alfonso de Baena. Eds. Brian Dutton and Joaquín González Cuenca. Madrid: Visor, 1993.

Canet Vallés, José Luis. "Introducción." Tárrega, *El prado de Valencia* 11–78.

Capel Sánchez, Juan José. *La vida lúdica en la Murcia bajomedieval*. Murcia: Real Academia Alfonso X el Sabio, 2000.

Capítulos de reformación que su Magestad se sirue de mandar guardar por esta ley, para el gouierno del Reyno. Madrid: Tomas Junti, 1623.

Cara Barrionuevo, Lorenzo. "La ganadería de la ciudad de Granada y la Alpujarra en la primera mitad del siglo XVI." Barrios Aguilera and Galán Sánchez 179–208.

Cardaillac, Louis. "Le Vêtement des morisques." In *Signes et marques du convers: Espagne, XVème–XVIème siècles*. Ed. Haïm-Vidal Sephiha. Aix-en-Provence: Université de Provence, 1993. 15–30.

– ed. *Les Morisques et leur temps*. Centre National de la Recherche Scientifique, 1983.

Caro Baroja, Julio. *Los moriscos del reino de Granada*. Madrid: Istmo, 2000.

Carr, Matthew. *Blood and Faith: The Purging of Muslim Spain*. New York: New Press, 2009.

Carracedo Falagán, Carmen. "La regulación jurídica de la indumentaria femenina en Castilla durante la Edad Moderna." *Revista Jurídica de Asturias* 15 (1992): 57–76.

Carrasco, Rafael [Raphaël]. *"Limpieza* à Grenade dans la seconde moitié du XVIe siècle." In *La pureté de sang en Espagne: Du lignage à la "race"*. Eds. Raphaël Carrasco, Annie Molinié, and Béatrice Perez. Paris: Presses de l'Université Paris-Sorbonne, 2011. 279–304.

– *Deportados en nombre de Dios. La expulsión de los moriscos: Cuarto centenario de una ignominia*. Barcelona: Destino, 2009.

– "Contra la guerra: Calderón y los moriscos de las Alpujarras." In *Guerra y paz en la comedia española*. Eds. Felipe B. Pedraza Jiménez, Rafael González Cañal and Elena E. Marcello. Almagro: Universidad de Castilla-La Mancha, 2007. 127–55.

Carrasco Manchado, Ana Isabel. *De la convivencia a la exclusión. Imágenes legislativas de mudéjares y moriscos. Siglos XIII–XVII*. Madrid: Sílex, 2012.

Carrasco Rodríguez, Antonio. "La ciudad de Orihuela y el pleito del obispado en la edad moderna." Diss. Universidad de Alicante, 2001.

Carrasco Urgoiti, María Soledad. *Los moriscos y Ginés Pérez de Hita*. Barcelona: Bellaterra, 2006.

– *Vidas fronterizas en las letras españolas*. Barcelona: Bellaterra, 2005.

– "Apuntes sobre el calificativo 'morisco' y algunos textos que lo ilustran." In *Averroes dialogado y otros momentos literarios y sociales de la interacción cristiano-musulmana en España e Italia*. Ed. André Stoll. Kassel: Reichenberger, 1998. 187–209.

– *El moro retador y el moro amigo (estudios sobre fiestas y comedias de moros y cristianos)*. Granada: Universidad de Granada, 1996.

– *The Moorish Novel*. Boston: Twayne, 1976.

– *El problema morisco en Aragón al comienzo del reinado de Felipe II*. Chapel Hill: University of North Carolina, 1969.

– "Vituperio y parodia del romance morisco en el romancero nuevo." Fonquerne and Esteban 115–38.

Carrascón, Guillermo. "Disfraz y técnica teatral en el primer Lope." *Edad de Oro* 16 (1997): 121–36.

Carreño, Antonio. *El romancero lírico de Lope de Vega*. Madrid: Gredos, 1979.

Cartagena Calderón, José R. *Masculinidades en obras: El drama de la hombría en la España imperial*. Newark, DE: Juan de la Cuesta, 2008.

Cascão, João. *Uma jornada ao Alentejo e ao Algarve: A alteração das linhas de força da política nacional*. Ed. Francisco de Sales Loureiro. Lisbon: Horizonte, 1984.

Case, Thomas E. *Lope and Islam*. Newark, DE: Juan de la Cuesta, 1993.

– "Honor, Justice, and Historical Circumstance in *Amar después de la muerte*." *Bulletin of the Comediantes* 36.1 (1984): 55–69.

– "The Significance of Morisco Speech in Lope's Plays." *Hispania* 65.4 (1982): 594–600.

– "El morisco gracioso en el teatro de Lope." In *Lope de Vega y los orígenes del teatro español*. Ed. Manuel Criado de Val. Madrid: Edi-6, 1981. 785–90.

Castillejo, David. *Las cuatrocientas comedias de Lope: Catálogo crítico*. Madrid: Ediciones de Arte y Bibliofilia, 1984.

Castillo, Alonso del. "Sumario e recopilación de todo lo romançado por mí, el licenciado Alonso del Castillo." In *Memorial histórico español: Colección de documentos, opúsculos y antigüedades*. Ed. Pascual de Gayangos. Vol. 3. Madrid: Real Academia de la Historia, 1852. 1–164.

Castillo de Bovadilla, Jerónimo. *Política para regidores y señores de vassallos*. 2 vols. Madrid: Luis Sánchez, 1597.

Castillo Fernández, Javier. *Entre Granada y el Magreb: Vida y obra del cronista Luis del Mármol Carvajal (1524–1600)*. Granada: Universidad de Granada, 2016.

– "Las estructuras sociales." In *Historia del reino de Granada II: Época morisca y repoblación (1502–1630)*. Ed. Manuel Barrios Aguilera. Granada: Universidad de Granada, 2000. 180–230.

– "La tradición taurina en el noreste de la provincia de Granada." *Demófilo* 25 (1998): 153–63.

– "La asimilación de los moriscos granadinos: Un modelo de análisis." In *Disidencias y exilios en la España moderna*. Eds. Antonio Mestre Sanchís and Enrique Giménez López. Alicante: Universidad de Alicante, 1997. 347–61.

– "La guerra de los moriscos granadinos en la historiografía de la época (1570–1627)." Barrios Aguilera and Galán Sánchez. 677–703.

Castro, Teresa de. "El tratado sobre el vestir, calzar y comer del arzobispo Hernando de Talavera." *Espacio, Tiempo y Forma, Serie III, Historia Medieval* 14 (2001): 11–92.

Cátedra, Pedro M. *El sueño caballeresco. De la caballería de papel al sueño real de don Quijote*. Madrid: Abada, 2007.

– *Nobleza y lectura en tiempos de Felipe II: La biblioteca de don Alonso Osorio, Marqués de Astorga*. Valladolid: Junta de Castilla y León, 2002.

– "Fiestas caballerescas en tiempos de Carlos V." In *La fiesta en la Europa de Carlos V*. Madrid: Sociedad Estatal para la Celebración de los Centenarios de Felipe II y Carlos V, 2000. 93–117.

Catlos, Brian A. *Muslims of Medieval Latin Christendom c. 1050–1614*. Cambridge: Cambridge UP, 2014.

Cayetano Martín, Carmen, and Pilar Flores Guerrero. "Nuevas aportaciones al recibimiento en Madrid de la reina doña Margarita de Austria (24 de octubre de 1599)." *Anales del Instituto de Estudios Madrileños* 25 (1988): 387–400.

Cedulario del reino de Granada (1511–1514). Eds. Pedro José Arroyal Espigares, Esther Cruces Blanco and María Teresa Martín Palma. Málaga: Universidad de Málaga, 2008.

Centenero de Arce, Domingo. *De repúblicas urbanas a ciudades nobles: Un análisis de la evolución y desarrollo del republicanismo castellano (1550–1621)*. Madrid: Biblioteca Nueva, 2012.

Centenero de Arce, Domingo, and Ana Díaz Serrano. "La reconstrucción de una identidad hidalga: los caballeros de cuantía de la ciudad de Murcia durante los siglos XVI y XVII." In *Las élites en la época moderna: La monarquía española*. Eds. Enrique Soria Mesa, Juan Jesús Bravo Caro, and José Miguel Delgado Barrado. 4 vols. Córdoba: Universidad de Córdoba, 2009. 4: 95–106.

Cervantes Saavedra, Miguel de. *Teatro completo*. Eds. Florencio Sevilla Arroyo and Antonio Rey Hazas. Barcelona: Planeta, 1987.

Cervera Vera, Luis. *San Vitorino, patrón de Arévalo*. Arévalo: Boletín de El Terral, 1983.

Céspedes y Velasco, Francisco de. *Tratado de la gineta*. Lisboa: Luis Estupiñán, 1609.

Chacón, Hernán. *Tractado de la cauallería de la gineta*. Ed. Noel Fallows. Exeter: U of Exeter P, 1999.

Childers, William. "Disappearing Moriscos." In *Cross-Cultural History and the Domestication of Otherness*. Eds. Michal Jan Rozbicki and George O. Ndege. New York: Palgrave, 2012. 51–64.

– "Review of *Exotic Nation: Maurophilia and the Construction of Early Modern Spain*." *Calíope: Journal of the Society of Renaissance and Baroque Hispanic Society* 16.2 (2010): 127–31.

– "Manzanares 1600: Moriscos from Granada Organize a Festival of 'Moors and Christians.'" In *The Conversos and Moriscos in Late Medieval Spain and Beyond. 1. Departures and Change*. Ed. Kevin Ingram. Leiden: Brill, 2009. 287–310.

Cianca, Antonio de. *Historia de la vida, invencion, milagros y traslacion de San Segundo, primero obispo de Ávila*. Ed. Jesús Arribas. Ávila: Institución "Gran Duque de Alba," 1993.

Cicogna, Emanuele Antonio. *Della vita e delle opere di Andrea Navagero*. Venezia: Tipografia Andreola, 1855.

Cirot, Georges. "La maurophilie littéraire en Espagne au XVIe siècle." *Bulletin Hispanique* 40.2 (1938): 150–7; 40.3 (1938): 281–96; 40.4 (1938): 433–47; 41.1 (1939): 65–85; 41.4 (1939): 345–51; 42.3 (1940): 213–27; 43.3–4 (1940): 265–89; 44.2–4 (1942): 96–102; and 46.1 (1944): 5–25.

Ciscar Pallarés, Eugenio. "Los moriscos de Valencia." In *La expulsión de los moriscos*. Ed. Antonio Moliner Prada. Barcelona: Nabla, 2009. 147–77.

– "Notas sobre la predicación e instrucción de los moriscos en Valencia a principios del siglo XVI." *Estudis: Revista de Historia Moderna* 15 (1989): 205–44.

Clare, Lucien. "Les deux façons de monter à cheval en Espagne et au Portugal pendant le siècle d'Or." In *Des Chevaux et des hommes: Équitation et société*. Ed. Jean-Pierre Digard. Avignon: Caracole, 1988. 73–83.

Cobo Calmaestra, Rafael. "Aproximación al problema morisco en Priego de Córdoba (1486–1611)." *Legajos* 1 (1998): 7–18.

Cock, Henrique. *Relación del viaje hecho por Felipe II, en 1585, a Zaragoza, Barcelona y Valencia*. Ed. Alfredo Morel-Fatio and Antonio Rodríguez Villa. Madrid: Sucesores de Rivadeneyra, 1876.

Coenen, Erik. "Las fuentes de *Amar después de la muerte*." *Revista de Literatura* 69.138 (2007): 467–85.

Colás Latorre, Gregorio. "Los moriscos aragoneses: Una definición más allá de la religión y la política." *Sharq Al-Andalus* 12 (1995): 147–61.

Colección de documentos inéditos para la historia de España. Vol. 27. Madrid: Viuda de Calero, 1855.

Coleman, David. *Creating Christian Granada: Society and Religious Culture in an Old-World Frontier City, 1492–1600*. Ithaca: Cornell UP, 2003.

Colomer, José Luis. "El negro y la imagen real." Colomer and Descalzo 1: 77–111.

Colomer, José Luis, and Amalia Descalzo, eds. *Vestir a la española en las cortes europeas (siglos XVI y XVII)*. 2 vols. Madrid: Centro de Estudios Europa Hispánica, 2014.

Colonge, Chantal. "Reflets littéraires de la question morisque entre la guerre des Alpujarras et l'expulsion (1571–1610)." *Boletín de la Real Academia de Buenas Letras de Barcelona* 33 (1969–1970): 137–243.

Conejo Ramilo, Ricardo. *Historia de Archidona*. Granada: Anel, 1973.

Congosto Martín, Yolanda. "La lengua de los moriscos en los tratados gramaticales, en las obras lexicográficas y en la literatura de los siglos de oro." In *Caminos actuales de la historiografía lingüística: Actas del V Congreso Internacional de la Sociedad Española de Historiografía Lingüística*. Ed. Antonio Roldán Pérez. 2 vols. Murcia: Universidad de Murcia, 2006. 1: 375–87.

Constable, Olivia Remie. *Trade and Traders in Muslim Spain: The Commercial Realignment of the Iberian Peninsula, 900–1500*. Cambridge: Cambridge UP, 1994.

Conte Cazcarro, Ángel. *Los moriscos de la ciudad de Huesca. Una convivencia rota*. Huesca, Instituto de Estudios Altoaragoneses, 2009.

Contreras Gay, José. "Fuentes para el estudio sociológico de la caballería de cuantía de Andalucía. La caballería de cuantía de Córdoba antes de su desaparición en 1619." *Chronica Nova* 15 (1986–7): 27–73.

Córcoles Jiménez, María Pilar. *La villa de Albacete en la primera mitad del siglo XVII: Estructura y funcionamiento de la administración municipal*. Albacete: Instituto de Estudios Albacetenses, 2008.

Córdoba de la Llave, Ricardo. "Algunas consideraciones sobre el legado tecnológico andalusí en la Córdoba cristiana." *Acta Historica et Archaeologica Medieavalia* 18 (1997): 335–75.

Cortés Hernández, Susana, and Estrella Ocaña Rodríguez. "Manuscrito de sastrería." In *La moda española en el Siglo de Oro: Museo de Santa Cruz, Toledo. 25 de marzo-14 de junio de 2015*. Toledo: Junta de Castilla-La Mancha, 2015. 357.

Cornejo, Manuel. "La funcionalidad de los juegos de toros y cañas en el teatro de Lope de Vega." In *Actas del XVI Congreso de la Asociación Internacional de*

Hispanistas: Nuevos caminos del hispanismo. Eds. Pierre Civil and Françoise Crémoux. Madrid: Iberoamericana, 2010. Complementary CD-ROM, n.p.

– "Lope de Vega y las fiestas de Lerma de 1617. La teatralización de 'las fiestas de Castilla en *Lo que pasa en una tarde.*" *Mélanges de la Casa de Velázquez* 37.1 (2007): 179–98.

Correa, Pedro. *Los romances fronterizos.* 2 vols. Granada: Universidad de Granada, 1999.

Covarrubias, Pedro de. *Remedio de jugadores.* Salamanca: Juan de Junta, 1543.

Covarrubias, Sebastián de. *Tesoro de la lengua castellana o española.* Ed. Martín de Riquer. Barcelona: Alta Fulla, 2003.

Crane, Dougall. *Johannes Secundus: His Life, Work, and Influence on English Literature.* Leipzig: Bernhard Tauchnitz, 1931.

Crawford, Michael J. *The Fight for Status and Privilege in Late Medieval and Early Modern Castile, 1465–1598.* University Park, PA: Pennsylvania State UP, 2014.

Crespo, Hugo Miguel. "Trajar as aparências, vestir para ser: O testemunho da pragmática de 1609." In *O luxo na região do Porto ao tempo do Filipe II de Portugal (1610).* Ed. Gonçalo de Vasconcelos e Sousa. Porto: Universidade Católica, 2012. 93–148.

Crónica de Juan II de Castilla. Ed. Juan de Mata Carriazo y Arroquia. Madrid: Real Academia de la Historia, 1982.

Cruz, Anne J. "Making War, Not Love: The Contest of Cultural Difference and the Honor Code in Calderón's *Amar después de la muerte.*" *Calíope* 6.1–2 (2000): 17–33.

Cruz Cabrera, José Policarpo. *Patrimonio arquitectónico y urbano en Baeza (siglos XVI–XVIII): Aristocracia urbana y conmemoración pública.* Granada: Universidad de Granada, 1999.

Cruz Cabrera, José Policarpo, and Encarnación Escañuela Cuenca. *El Cabildo de Motril en el siglo XVI. Catálogo de Actas (1537–1587).* Motril: Ayuntamiento de Motril, 1997.

Cruz Rodríguez, Javier. "Salamanca histórico-cultural en la transición del siglo XVI al XVII: Música y otros elementos en la visita que realizó Felipe III en el año 1600." PhD diss, Universidad de Salamanca, 2011.

Cruz Valdovinos, José Manuel. "La entrada de la reina Ana en Madrid en 1570: estudio documental." *Anales del Instituto de Estudios Madrileños* 28 (1990): 413–51.

Cubillo de Aragón, Álvaro. *El conde de Saldaña, primera parte.* In *Dramáticos posteriores a Lope de Vega.* Ed. Ramón de Mesonero Romanos. 2 vols. Madrid: Rivadeneyra, 1858. 1: 79–95.

– *La manga de Sarracino, y buen término de amor.* n.p.: n.d. (18th c.). British Library.

– *La manga de Sarracino.* N.p.: n.d. (c. 1650). Universitätsbibliothek Freiburg, E1032, n-13.

Dadson, Trevor J. *Tolerance and Coexistence in Early Modern Spain: Old Christians and Moriscos in the Campo de Calatrava.* Woodbridge: Tamesis, 2014.

– "Official Rhetoric versus Local Reality: Propaganda and the Expulsion of the Moriscos." Pym 1–24.

– *Los moriscos de Villarrubia de los Ojos (siglos XV–XVIII): Historia de una minoría asimilada, expulsada y reintegrada.* Madrid: Iberoamericana, 2007.

Dávila y Heredia, Andrés. *Palestra particular de los exercicios del cauallo.* Valencia: Benito Macé, 1674.

Davis, Charles. "Introducción: Lope de Vega en el Archivo Histórico de Protocolos de Madrid." In *27 documentos de Lope de Vega Carpio en el Archivo Histórico de Protocolos de Madrid.* Madrid: Comunidad de Madrid, 2004. 13–52.

Dedieu, Jean-Pierre. "Herejía y limpieza de sangre: La inhabilitación de los herejes y de sus descendientes en España en los primeros tiempos de la Inquisición." In *Inquisición y sociedad.* Ed. Ángel de Prado Moura. Valladolid: Universidad de Valladolid, 1999. 139–56.

– "Les Morisques de Daimiel et l'Inquisition (1502–1612)." Cardaillac, *Les Morisques* 495–522.

Defert, Daniel. "Un genre ethnographique profane a XVIe: Les livres d'habits (essai d'ethno-iconographie)." *Histoires de l'Anthropologie (XVIe–XIXe siècles).* Ed. Britta Rupp-Eisenreich. Paris: Klincksieck, 1984. 25–41.

Delgado Barrado, José Miguel, and María Amparo López Arandia. *Poderosos y privilegiados: Los Caballeros de Santiago de Jaén (siglos XVI–XVIII).* Madrid: Centro Superior de Investigaciones Científicas, 2009.

Deloria, Philip J. *Playing Indian.* New Haven, CT: Yale UP, 1998.

Devaney, Thomas. *Enemies in the Plaza: Urban Spectacle and the End of Spanish Frontier Culture, 1460–1492.* Philadelphia: U of Pennsylvania P, 2015.

Devos, Brent W. "Calderón's Ambiguity with respect to the Moriscos in *El Tuzaní de la Alpujarra.*" *Anuario Calderoniano* 2 (2009): 111–27.

– "El título de *El Tuzaní de la Alpujarra* o *Amor después de la muerte,* de Pedro Calderón de la Barca." *Revista Canadiense de Estudios Hispánicos* 32.3 (2008): 523–7.

Dewald, Jonathan. *The European Nobility, 1400–1800.* Cambridge: Cambridge UP, 1999.

Díaz-Mas, Paloma, ed. *Romancero.* Barcelona: Crítica, 2001.

Díaz Rodríguez, Antonio J. "Sotanas a la morisca y casullas a la chinesca: El gusto por lo exótico entre los eclesiásticos cordobeses (1556–1621)." *Investigaciones Históricas* 30 (2010): 31–48.

Diccionario de la lengua castellana. 6 vols. Madrid: Real Academia Española, 1726–39.

Díez del Corral Garnica, Rosario. *Arquitectura y mecenazgo. La imagen de Toledo en el Renacimiento.* Madrid: Alianza, 1987.

Doménech Belda, Carolina. "Los moriscos y nuestros antepasados." *Betania* 44 (1996): 79–83.

Domínguez Casas, Rafael. *Arte y etiqueta de los Reyes Católicos: Artistas, residencias, jardines y bosques.* Madrid: Alpuerto, 1993.

Domínguez Ortiz, Antonio. *Las clases privilegiadas en la España del antiguo régimen.* Madrid: Istmo, 1993.

Domínguez Ortiz, Antonio, and Bernard Vincent. *Historia de los moriscos. Vida y tragedia de una minoría.* Madrid: Revista de Occidente, 1979.

Drelichman, Mauricio. "Sons of Something: Taxes, Lawsuits, and Local Political Control in Sixteenth-Century Castile." *The Journal of Economic History* 67.3 (2007): 608–42.

Duarte, Dom [King Duarte I of Portugal]. *Livro da ensinança de bem cavalgar toda sela.* Ed. Joseph M. Piel. Lisboa: Bertrand, 1944.

Durán Alcalá, Francisco. "IV Centenario de la Fuente del Rey." *Adarve* 269 (15 July 1987): 8–10.

Durán i Sanpere, Agustí. *Barcelona i la seva història.* 3 vols. Barcelona: 1973.

Echevarría Arsuaga, Ana. *Caballeros en la frontera. La guardia morisca de los reyes de Castilla (1410–1467).* Madrid: UNED, 2006.

Ehlers, Benjamin. *Between Christians and Moriscos: Juan de Ribera and Religious Reform in Valencia, 1568–1614.* Baltimore: Johns Hopkins UP, 2006.

Elliott, John H., and José F. de la Peña. *Memoriales y cartas del conde-duque de Olivares.* 2 vols. Madrid: Alfaguara, 1978–1980.

Enríquez del Castillo, Diego. *Crónica del Rey don Enrique el cuarto.* In *Crónicas de los reyes de Castilla.* Ed. Cayetano Rosell. Vol. 3. Biblioteca de Autores Españoles 70. Madrid: Rivadeneyra, 1878. 97–222.

Entrambasaguas, Joaquín de. *Lope de Vega en las justas poéticas toledanas de 1605 y 1608.* Madrid: Centro Superior de Investigaciones Científicas, 1969.

Escolano Ledesma, Diego. *Memorial a la reina Nuestra Señora acerca de las muertes que en odio de la fe y Religión Christiana dieron los Moriscos reuelados a los Christianos viejos (y algunos nuevos) residentes en las Alpuxarras deste Reyno de Granada, en el leuantamiento del año 1568.* Granada: Baltasar de Bolibar, 1671.

Espejo de la consciencia. Medina del Campo: Alexo de Herrera, 1552.

Esquerdo, Vicenta. "Indumentaria con la que los cómicos representaban en el siglo XVII." *Boletín de la Real Academia Española* 58.215 (1978): 447–544.

Étienvre, Jean-Pierre. *Márgenes literarios del juego: Una poética del naipe, siglos XVI–XVIII*. London: Tamesis, 1990.

Fajardo y Acevedo, Antonio. *Comedias*. Ed. Diego Símini. Lecce: Adriatica, 2000.

Fallows, Noel. *Jousting in Medieval and Renaissance Iberia*. Woodbridge: Boydell Press, 2010.

Farsa del sacramento llamada de los lenguajes. In *Colección de autos, farsas y coloquios del siglo XVI*. Ed. Léo Rouanet. 4 vols. Barcelona: L'Avenç, 1901. 3: 331–5.

Feliciano Chaves, María Judith. "Muslim Shrouds for Christian Kings? A Reassessment of Andalusi Textiles in Thirtheenth-Century Castilian Life and Ritual." In *Under the Influence: Questioning the Comparative in Medieval Castile*. Eds. Cynthia Robinson and Leyla Rouhi. Leiden: Brill, 2005. 101–31.

– "Mudejarismo in its Colonial Context: Iberian Cultural Display, Viceregal Luxury Consumption, and the Negotiation of Identities in Sixteenth-Century New Spain." Diss. U of Pennsylvania, 2004.

Fernández Chaves, Manuel F. "Entre la gracia y la justicia del Rey. El linaje real de los Infantes de Granada ante la rebelión y el castigo de los Moriscos." *Ámbitos* 22 (2009): 23–34.

Fernández Chaves, Manuel F., and Rafael M. Pérez García. *En los márgenes de la ciudad de Dios. Moriscos en Sevilla*. Valencia: Universitat de València, 2009.

Fernández de Andrada, Pedro. *Nuevos discursos de la gineta de la gineta de España, sobre el uso del cabeçón*. Seville: Alonso Rodríguez Gamarra, 1616.

– *Libro de la gineta de España*. Seville: Alonso de la Barrera, 1599.

– *De la naturaleza del caballo*. Seville: Fernando Díaz, 1580.

Fernández de Ayala Aulestia, Manuel. *Práctica y formulario de la Chancillería de Valladolid*. Valladolid: Joseph de Rueda, 1667.

Fernández de Caso, Francisco. *Discurso en que se refieren las solenidades, y fiestas, con que el excelentissimo Duque celebro en su villa de Lerma, la Dedicacion de la Iglesia Colegial, y translaciones de los Conuentos que ha edificado allí*. n.p.: n.d. [c. 1617–18].

Fernández de Oviedo, Gonzalo. *Libro de la cámara real del príncipe don Juan, oficios de su casa y servicio ordinario*. Ed. Santiago Fabregat Barrios. Valencia: Universitat de València, 2006.

– *Relación de lo sucedido al rey Francisco I de Francia*. In *Colección de documentos inéditos para la historia de España*. Vol. 38. Madrid: viuda de Calero, 1861. 404–550.

Fernández Duro, Cesáreo. *Memorias históricas de la ciudad de Zamora, su provincia y obispado*. 4 vols. Madrid: Sucesores de Rivadeneyra, 1882–3.

Fernández García, Francisco. *Historias de Caravaca*. Caravaca: Ayuntamiento de Caravaca, 2015.

Fernández Manzano, Reynaldo. *De las melodías del reino nazarí a las estructuras musicales cristianas*. Granada: Diputación de Granada, 1985.

Fernández Martín, Luis. *Comediantes, esclavos y moriscos en Valladolid, siglos XVI y XVII*. Valladolid: Universidad de Valladolid, 1988.

Fernández-Puertas, Antonio. "Vestimenta de Abū 'Abd Allāh Muḥammad, Boabdil: Rīḥiyya, Juff, Mallūta, 'Imāna." In *En el epílogo del islam andalusí: la Granada del siglo XV*. Ed. Celia del Moral. Granada: Universidad de Granada, 2002. 399–477.

Fernández Salmador, Ana Isabel, and Concepción Ferrero Maeso. *Pleitos de hidalguía que se conservan en el Archivo de la Real Chancillería de Valladolid (extracto de sus expedientes). Siglo XVII. Reinado de Felipe III*. 3 vols. Madrid: Ediciones Hidalguía, 2012.

Ferreira Figueiroa, Diogo. *Epitome das festas que se fizeram no cazamento do serenissimo Principe Dom Ião, deste nome segundo … com a Excellentissima senhora Dona Luisa Francisca de Guzmão*. Evora: Manuel Carvalho, 1633.

Ferrer Valls, Teresa. *Nobleza y espectáculo teatral (1535–1622)*. Valencia: Universitat de València, 1993.

Ferrero Hernández, Cándida. "*De habitv et lingva relegandis*: Los ritos de los moriscos según Pedro Guerra de Lorca." In *Ritus infidelivm: Miradas interconfesionales sobre las prácticas religiosas en la edad media*. Eds. José Martínez Gázquez and John Victor Tolan. Madrid: Casa de Velázquez, 2013. 261–73.

Figueroa, Melissa. "La expulsión de los moriscos en *El gran patriarca don Juan de Ribera*, de Gaspar Aguilar: Un festejo a medias." *Bulletin of the Comediantes* 66.2 (2014): 27–44.

Flecniakoska, Jean-Louis. "Les fêtes du Corpus à Ségovie (1594–1636). Documents inédits (suite et fin)." *Bulletin Hispanique* 56.3 (1954): 225–48.

Flores Arroyuelo, Francisco J. *De la aventura al teatro y la fiesta. Moros y cristianos*. Murcia: Nausícaä, 2003.

– *Los últimos moriscos (Valle de Ricote, 1614)*. Murcia: Real Academia Alfonso X el Sabio, 1989.

Flores Hernández, Benjamín. "La *jineta indiana* en los textos de Juan Suárez de Peralta y Bernardo de Vargas Machuca." *Anuario de Estudios Americanos* 54.2 (1997): 639–64.

Fonquerne, Yves-René, and Alfonso Esteban, eds. *Culturas populares. Diferencias, divergencias, conflictos*. Madrid: Universidad Complutense, 1986.

Fonseca, Damián. *Relación de la expulsión de los moriscos del reino de Valencia*. Valencia: Sociedad Valenciana de Bibliófilos, 1878.

Fournel-Guérin, Jacqueline. "Fiestas profanas y diversiones de la comunidad morisca aragonesa." *Nueva Revista de Filología Hispánica* 30.2 (1981): 630–7.

Fra Molinero, Baltasar. *La imagen de los negros en el teatro del Siglo de Oro.* Madrid: Siglo XXI, 1995.

Freyle, Diego de. *Geometría y traça para el oficio de los sastres.* Seville: Fernando Díaz, 1588.

Fuchs, Barbara. *Exotic Nation: Maurophilia and the Construction of Early Modern Spain.* Philadelphia: U of Pennsylvania P, 2008.

– "The Spanish Race." In *Rereading the Black Legend. The Discourses of Religious and Racial Difference in the Renaissance Empires.* Eds. Margaret R. Greer, Walter D. Mignolo, and Maureen Quilligan. Chicago: U of Chicago P, 2007. 88–98.

– *Passing for Spain: Cervantes and the Fictions of Identity.* Urbana: U of Illinois P, 2003.

– *Mimesis and Empire.* Cambridge: Cambridge UP, 2001.

Fuchs, Barbara, Larissa Brewer-García, and Aaron J. Ilika, eds. and trans. *"El Abencerraje" and "Ozmín y Daraja": Two Sixteenth-Century Novellas from Spain.* Philadelphia: U of Pennsylvania P, 2014.

Fuenmayor, Antonio de. *Vida y hechos de Pio V.* Madrid: Luis Sánchez, 1595.

Gachard, Louis-Prosper, ed. *Collection des voyages des Souverains des Pays Bas.* 4 vols. Bruxelles: F. Hayez, 1874–82.

Galán Sánchez, Ángel. "El dinero del rey y la 'ley de la comunidad': Pacto político y contrato fiscal en el Reino de Granada tras la conquista." In *Avant le contrat social: Le contrat politique dans l'Occident médiéval, XIIIe–XVe siècle.* Ed. François Foronda .Paris: Publications de la Sorbonne, 2011. 653–83.

– "The Muslim Population of the Christian Kingdom of Granada: Urban Oligarchies and Rural Communities." In *Oligarchy and Patronage in Late Medieval Spanish Society.* Ed. María Asenjo-González. Turnhout: Brepols, 2009. 71–89.

– "'Herejes consentidos': La justificación de una fiscalidad diferencial en el Reino de Granada." *Historia. Instituciones. Documentos* 33 (2006): 173–209.

Galíndez Carvajal, Lorenzo. "Anales breves del reinado de los Reyes Católicos." In *Crónicas de los reyes de Castilla.* Vol. 3. Biblioteca de Autores Españoles 70. Madrid: Atlas, 1953. 533–65.

Gallego, Pedro. *Tratado da gineta, ordenado das respostas que hum caualeiro de muita experiencia deu a 24 perguntas.* Lisbon: Pedro Craesbeeck, 1629.

Gallego y Burín, Antonio, and Alfonso Gámir Sandoval. *Los moriscos del reino de Granada según el sínodo de Guadix de 1554.* Ed. Darío Cabanelas Rodríguez. Granada: Universidad de Granada, 1968.

Gallo, Antonella. "Le maschere del moro di Granada: dal 'romancero' alle 'comedias de moros y cristianos' del primo Lope de Vega." In *La maschera e l'altro*. Ed. Maria Grazia Profeti. Florence: Alinea, 2005. 197–222.

García-Arenal, Mercedes. *Inquisición y moriscos. Los procesos del Tribunal de Cuenca*. Madrid: Siglo XXI, 1983.

García Avilés, José María. *Los moriscos del Valle de Ricote*. Alicante: Universidad de Alicante, 2007.

García Bernal, José Jaime. "La oligarquía sevillana y las fiestas caballerescas en el ápice del imperio fiipino (1571–1584)." In *Estudios de historia moderna en homenaje al profesor Antonio García-Baquero*. Ed. León Carlos Álvarez y Santaló. Seville: Universidad de Sevilla, 2009. 349–64.

– *El fasto público en la España de los Austrias*. Seville: Universidad de Sevilla, 2006.

García Cárcel, Ricardo. "La inquisición y los moriscos valencianos: Anatomía de una represión." In *Actas de las Jornadas de Cultura Árabe e Islámica (1978)*. Madrid: Instituto Hispano-Árabe de la Cultura, 1981. 401–17.

García Chico, Esteban. *Documentos para la historia de Medina de Rioseco*. Valladolid: Imprenta Castellana, 1947.

García de Saavedra, Juan. *De expensis et meliorationibus*. Alcalá de Henares: Antonio Sánchez de Leyva, 1578.

García Fuentes, José María. *La Inquisición en Granada en el siglo XVI: Fuentes para su estudio*. Granada: Diputación Provincial de Granada, 1981.

García García, Bernardo José. "Máscaras en el vestuario de representación (1561–1606). Hatos de comediantes, contratación de fiestas y alquiler de accesorios." In *Máscaras y juegos de identidad en el teatro español del Siglo de Oro*. Ed. María Luisa Lobato. Madrid: Visor, 2011. 36–57.

– "Las fiestas de corte en los espacios del valido: La privanza del duque de Lerma." In *La fiesta cortesana en la época de los Austrias*. Eds. María Luisa Lobato and Bernardo J. García García. Valladolid: Junta de Castilla y León, 2003. 35–77.

– "Los hatos de actores y compañías." *Cuadernos de Teatro Clásico* 13–14 (2000): 165–90.

– "El alquilador de hatos Luis de Monzón y el negocio teatral madrileño a comienzos del Seiscientos." In *La burguesía española en la edad moderna*. Ed. Luis Miguel Enciso Recio. 3 vols. Valladolid: Universidad de Valladolid, 1996. 2: 695–706.

– "El alquiler de hatos de comedia y danzas en Madrid a principios del s. XVII." *Cuadernos de Historia Moderna* 10 (1989–1990): 43–64.

– "Las fiestas de Lerma de 1617. Una relación apócrifa y otros testimonios." García García and Lobato 203–45.

García García, Bernardo J., and María Luisa Lobato, eds. *Dramaturgia festiva y cultura nobiliaria en el Siglo de Oro*. Madrid: Iberoamericana: 2007.

García Gómez, Ángel María. *Vida teatral en Córdoba (1602–1694): Autores de comedias, representantes y arrendadores. Estudio y documentos*. Woodbridge: Tamesis, 2008.

García Ivars, Flora. *La represión en el tribunal inquisitorial de Granada, 1550–1819*. Madrid: Akal, 1991.

García Marsilla, Juan Vicente. "Avec les vêtements des autres: Le marché du textile d'occasion dans la Valence médiévale." In *Objets sous contrainte: Circulation des objets et valeur des choses au Moyen Âge*. Eds. Laurent Feller and Ana Rodríguez. Paris: Publications de la Sorbonne, 2013. 124–43.

– "Diferencia e integración. Las formas de la vida cotidiana entre los mudéjares y moriscos valencianos." In *Entre tierra y fe. Los musulmanes en el reino cristiano de Valencia (1238–1609)*. Ed. Norberto Piqueras Sánchez. Valencia: Universitat de València, 2009. 341–62.

García Pedraza, Amalia. "Entre la media luna y la cruz: Las mujeres moriscas." In *Las mujeres y la ciudad de Granada en el siglo XVI*. Granada: Concejalía de la Mujer, 2000. 55–67.

– "La asimilación del morisco don Gonzalo Fernández el Zegrí: Edición y análisis de su testamento." *Al-Qantara* 16.1 (1995): 39–58.

García Reidy, Alejandro. *Las musas rameras: Oficio dramático y conciencia profesional en Lope de Vega*. Madrid: Iberoamericana / Vervuert, 2013.

García Santo-Tomás, Enrique. *La creación del Fénix: Recepción crítica y formación canónica del teatro de Lope de Vega*. Madrid: Gredos, 2000.

García Soormally, Mina. "El cuerpo sin marca en *El Tuzaní de la Alpujarra*." *Bulletin of the Comediantes* 64.1 (2012): 111–29.

García Soriano, Justo. *El teatro universitario y humanístico en España*. Toledo: Talleres Tipográficos de R. Gómez, 1945.

García Valdecasas, Amelia. "Decadencia y disolución del Romancero morisco." *Boletín de la Real Academia Española* 69 (1989): 131–58.

– *El género morisco en las fuentes del "Romancero general"*. Valencia: Diputación de Valencia, 1987.

García Valdés, Celsa Carmen. "Comedias de moros y cristianos en el teatro de Tirso de Molina." In *El ingenio cómico de Tirso de Molina: Actas del II Congreso Internacional*. Eds. Ignacio Arellano, Blanca Oteiza, and Miguel Zugasti. Madrid: Instituto de Estudios Tirsianos, 1998. 121–38.

Garrad, Kenneth. "La industria sedera granadina en el siglo XVI y su conexión con el levantamiento de las Alpujarras (1568–1571)." *Miscelánea de Estudios Árabes y Hebraicos* 5 (1956): 73–98.

Garrot Zambrana, Juan Carlos. "Hacia la configuración del 'musulmán' en el teatro prelopesco." In *Edad de Oro Cantabrigense: Actas del VII Congreso de la Asociación Internacional Siglo de Oro.* Eds. Anthony Close and Sandra María Fernández Vales. Vigo: Asociación Internacional Siglo de Oro, 2006. 293–8.

Gauna, Felipe de. *Relación de las fiestas celebradas en Valencia con motivo del casamiento de Felipe III.* Ed. Salvador Carreres Zacarés. 2 vols. Valencia: Acción Bibliográfica Valenciana, 1926.

Girón, Pedro. *Crónica del emperador Carlos V.* Ed. Juan Sánchez Montes. Madrid: Centro Superior de Investigaciones Científicas, 1964.

Girón Pascual, Rafael María. "Mercaderes milaneses y regidores de Huéscar en el siglo XVI: Los Cernúsculo." In *Campesinos, nobles y mercaderes: Huéscar y el Reino de Granada en los siglos XVI y XVII.* Ed. Juan Pablo Díaz López. Huéscar: Ayuntamiento de Huéscar, 2005. 51–74.

Góis, Damião de. *Chrónica do felicíssimo rei D. Manuel.* 4 vols. Eds. Joaquim Martins Teixeira de Carvalho and David Lopes. Coimbra: Universidade de Coimbra, 1926.

Gómez, Jesús. *La figura del donaire o el gracioso en las comedias de Lope de Vega.* Seville: Alfar, 2006.

Gómez, Vicente. *Los sermones y fiestas que la ciudad de Valencia hizo por la Beatificación del glorioso padre San Luys Bertrán.* Valencia: Juan Chrysostomo Garriz, 1609.

Gómez de Castro, Alvar. *Recibimiento que la imperial ciudad de Toledo hizo a la magestad de la reina nuestra señora doña Isabel.* Ed. Carlota Fernández Travieso. A Coruña: SIELAE, 2007.

Gómez-Salvago Sánchez, Mónica. *Fastos de una boda real en la Sevilla del quinientos (Estudio y documentos).* Seville: Universidad de Sevilla, 1998.

Gómez Vozmediano, Miguel Fernando. *Mudéjares y moriscos en el Campo de Calatrava. Reductos de convivencia, tiempos de intolerancia (siglos XV–XVII).* Ciudad Real: Diputación Provincial de Ciudad Real, 2000.

Góngora, Luis de. *Romances.* Ed. Antonio Carreño. Madrid: Cátedra, 2000.

González Alcantud, José Antonio. *Lo moro. Las lógicas de la derrota y la formación del estereotipo islámico.* Barcelona: Anthropos, 2002.

González Arce, José Damián. *Apariencia y poder: La legislación suntuaria castellana en los siglos XIII y XVI.* Jaén: Universidad de Jaén, 1998.

González Castaño, Juan. "El informe de fray Juan de Pereda sobre los mudéjares murcianos en vísperas de la expulsión, año 1612." *Áreas* 14 (1992): 219–35.

González de Cunedo, Miguel. *A un traidor dos alevosos.* In *Parte tercera de comedias de los mejores ingenios de España.* Madrid: Melchor Sánchez, 1653. 84r–106v.

González Fuertes, Ángela Rosario, and Manuel Amador González Fuertes. "La reforma de los caballeros de cuantía de 1562: Un intento fracasado de crear una milicia ciudadana." In *Madrid, Felipe II y las ciudades de la monarquía.* Ed. Enrique Martínez Ruiz. Madrid: Actas, 2000. 1: 129–41.

González Hurtebise, Eduardo. "Inventario de los bienes muebles de Alfonso V de Aragón como infante y como rey (1412–1424)." *Anuari de l'Institut d'Estudis Catalans* 1 (1907): 148–88.

Goy Diz, Ana. *A actividade artística en Santiago, 1600–1648.* 2 vols. Santiago de Compostela: Concello da Cultura Galega, 1998.

Goyri de Menéndez Pidal, María. "Los romances de Gazul." *Nueva Revista de Filología Hispánica* 7.3–4 (1953): 403–16.

Gozalbes Busto, Guillermo. "Lo andaluz en la indumentaria marroquí (contribución al estudio de la historia de Marruecos)." *Boletín de la Asociación Española de Orientalistas* 14.1 (1978): 143–53.

González Hernández, Miguel-Ángel. *Moros y cristianos: Del alarde medieval a las fiestas reales barrocas (ss. XV–XVIII).* Monforte del Cid: Ayuntamiento de Monforte del Cid, 1999.

Greenblatt, Stephen. *Renaissance Self-Fashioning: From More to Shakespeare.* Chicago: U of Chicago P, 1980.

Greer, Margaret R. "The Politics of Memory in *El Tuzaní de la Alpujarra.*" Pym 113–30.

Griffin, Nigel. "'Un muro invisible': Moriscos and Cristianos Viejos in Granada." In *Mediaeval and Renaissance Studies on Spain and Portugal in Honour of P. E. Russell.* Eds. F.W. Hodcroft, D.G. Pattison, R.D.F. Pring-Mill and R.W. Truman. Oxford: Society for the Study of Mediaeval Languages and Literature, 1981. 133–54.

Guadalajara y Xavier, Marcos de. *Memorable expulsión y justísimo destierro de los moriscos de España.* Pamplona: Nicolás de Assiayn, 1613.

Guadix, Diego de. *Recopilación de algunos nombres arábigos que los árabes pusieron a algunas ciudades y otras muchas cosas.* Eds. Elena Bajo Pérez and Felipe Maíllo Salgado. Gijón: Trea, 2005.

Guardia y López, Luis de la. "La mitad de oficios en concejos. Madridejos y otros casos, entre el Medievo y la Edad Moderna." *Espacio, Tiempo y Forma, Serie III, Historia Medieval* 20 (2007): 43–95.

Guarino, Gabriel. *Representing the King's Splendour: Communicatin and Reception of Symbolic Forms of Power in Viceregal Naples.* Manchester: Manchester UP, 2010.

Guerra de Lorca, Pedro. *Cathecheses mystagogicae pro aduenis ex secta Mahometana.* Madrid: Pedro Madrigal, 1586.

Guerra Sancho, Ricardo. "1605, ha nacido un príncipe: Regocijos de juegos de cañas y toros." *Diario de Ávila* 3 July 2013 (Extra Ferias y Fiestas de Arévalo): 34–5.

– *San Vitorino Mártir (1610–2010)*. Arévalo: Ayuntamiento de Arévalo, 2011.

– "Toros en la ciudad de Arévalo: Tradición de los festejos populares documentado desde el siglo XV." Unpublished manuscript.

Guerrero Arjona, Melchor. *Lorca. De ciudad de frontera a ciudad moderna. Transformaciones políticas, sociales y económicas (1550–1598)*. Murcia: Real Academia Alfonso X El Sabio, 2005.

Guillén, Claudio. *Literature as System: Essays Toward the Theory of Literary History*. Princeton: Princeton UP, 1971.

Guillén de Ávila, Diego. *Panegírico a la reina doña Isabel*. Ed. facsimile. Madrid: Real Academia Española, 1951.

Guillén Riquelme, Mariano C. *Un siglo en la historia de Mazarrón: De la fundación de las Casas de los Alumbres a la concesión del privilegio de villazgo, 1462–1572*. Murcia: Real Academia Alfonso X el Sabio, 2001.

Guzmán, Pedro de. *Los bienes del honesto trabajo y daños de la ociosidad*. Madrid: Imprenta Real, 1614.

Hamilton, Earl J. *American Treasure and the Price Revolution in Spain, 1501–1650*. New York: Octagon, 1965.

Hampe, Theodor. "Introduction." In Christoph Weiditz. *Authentic Everyday Dress of the Renaissance: All 154 Plates from the "Trachtenbuch"*. New York: Dover, 1994. 5–61.

Harris, Max. *Aztecs, Moors, and Christians: Festivals of Reconquest in Mexico and Spain*. Austin: U of Texas P, 2000.

Harvey, L.P. *Muslims of Spain, 1500 to 1614*. Chicago: U of Chicago P, 2005.

Hellwege, Johann. *Zur Geschichte der spanischen Reitermilizen. Die Caballería de Cuantía unter Philipp II. und Philipp III. (1562–1619)*. Wiesbaden: Franz Steiner Verlag, 1972.

Hernández, Mauro. "Ayuntamientos urbanos, trampolines sociales. Reflexiones sobre las oligarquías locales en la Castilla moderna." *Mélanges de la Casa de Velázquez* 34.2 (2004): 91–114.

Herrera, Pedro de. *Translacion del Santissimo Sacramento a la iglesia colegial de San Pedro de la villa de Lerma, con la solenidad y fiestas, que tuuo para celebrarla el Excellentissimo Señor don Francisco Gomez de Sandoual y Roxas*. Madrid: Juan de la Cuesta, 1618.

Hersch, Philip, Angus MacKay, and Geraldine MacKendrick. "The Semiology of Dress in Late Medieval and Early Modern Spain." *Razo: Cahiers du Centre d'Études Médiévales de Nice* 7 (1987): 95–110.

Higashi, Alejandro. "La construcción escénica del disfraz en la comedia palatina temprana de Lope." *Nueva Revista de Filología Hispánica* 53.1 (2005): 31–65.

Hinojosa Montalvo, José. "Torneos y justas en la Valencia foral." *Medievalismo* 23 (2013): 209–40.

Horn, Hendrik J. *Jan Cornelisz Vermeyen, Painter of Charles V, and his Conquest of Tunis: Paintings, Etchings, Drawings, Cartoons, and Tapestries.* 2 vols. Doornspijk: Davaco, 1989.

Horozco, Sebastián de. *Relaciones históricas toledanas.* Ed. Jack Weiner. Toledo: Instituto Provincial de Investigaciones y Estudios Toledanos, 1981.

Hurtado de Mendoza, Diego. *Guerra de Granada.* Ed. Bernardo Blanco-González. Madrid: Castalia, 1970.

Hurtado de Toledo, Luis. "Memorial de algunas cosas notables que tiene la imperial ciudad de Toledo." In *Relaciones de los pueblos de España ordenadas por Felipe II. Reino de Toledo. Tercera parte.* Eds. Carmelo Viñas and Ramón Paz. Madrid: Centro Superior de Investigaciones Científicas, 1963. 481–576.

Hurtado de Toledo, Luis, and Michael de Carvajal. *Cortes de casto amor y Cortes de la muerte.* Ed. facsimile Antonio Rodríguez-Moñino. Valencia: Bonaire, 1964.

Ibáñez de Segovia, Gaspar. *Historia de la Casa de Mendoza.* Ms. BN MSS/3315.

Ibáñez Pérez, Alberto C. *Arquitectura civil del siglo XVI en Burgos.* Burgos: Caja de Ahorros de Burgos, 1977.

Irigoyen-García, Javier. "'Ni chivato ni carnero': La construcción de la diferencia étnica en la comedia *Los moriscos de Hornachos.*" *Bulletin of Spanish Studies* 91.8 (2014): 1159–74.

– "The Game of Canes between the Lusus Troiae and the Albanian Stradioti: Defining Moorish and Classical in the Early Modern Spanish Mediterranean." In *Mediterranean Identities in the Premodern Era: Islands, Entrepôts, Empires.* Eds. Kathryn L. Reyerson and John Watkins. Burlington: Ashgate, 2013. 231–47.

– *The Spanish Arcadia: Sheep Herding, Pastoral Discourse, and Ethnicity in Early Modern Spain.* Toronto: U of Toronto P, 2013.

– "'Poco os falta para moros, pues tanto lo parecéis': Impersonating the Moor in the Spanish Mediterranean." *Journal of Spanish Cultural Studies* 12.3 (2011): 355–69.

Ivory, Annette. "*Juan Latino*: The Struggle of Blacks, Jews, and Moors in Golden Age Spain." *Hispania* 62.4 (1979): 613–18.

Jaén, Pedro de. "Papeles viejos." *Senda de los huertos* 34 (1994): 105–10.

Jammes, Robert. *La obra poética de don Luis de Góngora y Argote.* Madrid: Castalia, 1987.

Jesús María, Fray Juan de. *Epistolario espiritual para personas de diferentes estados*. Uclés: Domingo de la Iglesia, 1624.

Jiménez Alcázar, Juan Francisco. "Moriscos en Lorca. Del asentamiento a la expulsión (1571–1610)." *Áreas* 14 (1992): 115–40.

Jiménez de Enciso, Diego. *El encubierto y Juan Latino*. Ed. Eduardo Juliá Martínez. Madrid: Real Academia Española, 1951.

Jiménez Estrella, Antonio. "Las milicias en Castilla: Evolución y proyección social de un sistema de defensa alternativo al ejército de los Austrias." In *Las milicias del rey de España. Sociedad, política e identidad en las Monarquías Ibéricas*. Ed. José Javier Ruiz Ibáñez. Madrid: Fondo de Cultura Económica, 2009. 72–103.

– *Poder, ejército y gobierno en el siglo XVI: La capitanía general del reino de Granada y sus agentes*. Granada: Universidad de Granada, 2004.

Johnston, Mark D. "Hernando de Talavera on Conduct: Cultural Hegemony in Post-Conquest Granada." *Confluencia* 30.3 (2015): 11–22.

Joly, Barthélemy. "Voyage en Espagne (1603–1604)." Ed. Louis Barrau-Dihigo. *Revue Hispanique* 20 (1909): 459–618.

Jones, Ann Rosalind, and Peter Stallybrass. *Renaissance Clothing and the Materials of Memory*. Cambridge: Cambridge UP, 2000.

Juaristi, Jon. *Vestigios de Babel: Para una arqueología de los nacionalismos españoles*. Madrid: Siglo XXI, 1992.

Kennedy, Ruth Lee. "Certain Phases of the Sumptuary Decrees of 1623 and their Relation to Tirso's Theatre." *Hispanic Review* 10.2 (1942): 91–115.

Khevenhüller, Hans. *Diario de Hans Khevenhüller, embajador imperial en la corte de Felipe II*. Ed. Félix Labrador Arroyo. Madrid: Sociedad Estatal para la Conmemoración de los Centenarios de Felipe II y Carlos V, 2001.

Kimmel, Seth. *Parables of Coercion: Conversion and Knowledge at the End of Islamic Spain*. Chicago: U of Chicago P, 2015.

Kirschner, Teresa J., and Dolores Clavero. *Mito e historia en el teatro de Lope de Vega*. Alicante: Universidad de Alicante, 2007.

Kossoff, Ruth H. "*Los cautivos de Argel*, comedia auténtica de Lope de Vega." In *Homenaje a William L. Fichter*. Eds. A. David Kossoff and José Amor y Vázquez. Madrid: Castalia, 1971. 387–97.

Ladero Quesada, Miguel Ángel. *Los mudéjares de Castilla en tiempos de Isabel I*. Valladolid: Instituto Isabel la Católica, 1969.

Lalaing, Antoine de. "Voyage de Philippe le Beau en Espagne, en 1501." Gachard 1: 120–340.

Lange, Johannes. "Die tagebuchartigen Aufseichnungen des pfälzischen Hofarztes Dr. Johannes Lange über seine Reise nach Granada im Jahre 1526." Ed. Adolf Hasenclever. *Archiv für Kulturgeschichte* 4 (1907): 385–439.

Lapeyre, Henri. *Geografía de la España morisca.* Trans. Luis C. Rodríguez García. Valencia: Diputación Provincial de Valencia, 1986.

Larios Martín, Jesús. *Nobiliario de Segovia.* 5 vols. Segovia: Instituto Diego de Colmenares, 1956.

Lasmarías Ponz, Israel. "Cultura material de los moriscos aragoneses: Vestido y apariencia." In *Los moriscos en los señoríos aragoneses: Actas de las terceras Jornadas del Proyecto Archivo Ducal de Híjar - Archivo abierto.* Ed. María José Casaus Ballester. Teruel: Centro de Estudios Mudéjares, 2013. 211–44.

Lasso de la Vega, Gabriel. *Manojuelo de romances.* Ed. Eugenio Mele and Ángel González Palencia. Madrid: Saeta, 1942.

Layna Serrano, Francisco. *Historia de Guadalajara y sus Mendozas en los siglos XV y XVI.* 4 vols. Madrid: Aldus, 1942.

Lee, Christina H. *The Anxiety of Sameness in Early Modern Spain.* Manchester: Manchester UP, 2016.

Lhermite, Jehan. *Le passetemps de Jehan Lhermite.* 2 vols. Eds. Charles Ruelens, Émile Ouverleaux and Jules Jean Petit. Antwerpen: J.-E. Buschmann, 1890–6.

Libre de la benauenturada vinguda del Emperador y Rey don Carlos en la sua ciutat de Mallorque. Ed. facsimile. Palma de Mallorca: Mossèn Alcover, 1973.

Libro de las bulas y pragmáticas de los Reyes Católicos. Eds. Alfonso García-Gallo and Miguel Ángel Pérez de la Canal. 2 vols. Madrid: Instituto de España, 1973.

Libro de noticias particulares, así de nacimientos de príncipes, como entrada de reyes. Eds. Francisco J. Marín, Teresa Prieto, and Juan Carlos Zofío. Madrid: Ayuntamiento de Madrid, 2005.

Livro dos regimentos dos officiaes mecanicos da mui nobre e sempre leal cidade de Lixboa (1572). Ed. Vergílio Correia. Coimbra: Universidade de Coimbra, 1926.

Llompart i Moragues, Gabriel. "Imágenes de una cultura caballeresca (a propósito de un ciclo de pinturas de fiestas nobiliarias en Palma de Mallorca)." In *El linaje del Emperador: Iglesia de la Preciosa Sangre. Centro de Exposiciones San Jorge, Cáceres, del 24 de octubre de 2000 al 7 de enero de 2001.* Ed. Javier Portús. [Cáceres]: Sociedad Estatal para la Conmemoración de los Centenarios de Felipe II y Carlos V, 2001. 159–69.

– "Festes i devocions santjoanistes." In *L'Orde de Malta, Mallorca i la Mediterrània: Exposició realitzada pel Sobirà Orde de Malta, Delegació de Balears, i el Consell de Mallorca.* Palma: Sobirà Orde de Malta; Consell de Mallorca, 2000. 93–106.

Lomas Cortés, Manuel. "Aixovar, diners i contraban. L'equipatge dels moriscs expulsats segons els registres de béns de Castella." *Recerques. Història, Economia, Cultura* 61 (2010): 5–24.

Lope Toledo, José María. "Logroño en el siglo XVI: Toros y cañas." *Berceo* 68 (1963): 257–78.

Lopes de Barros, Maria Filomena. *Tempos e espaços de mouros: A minoria muçulmana no reino português (séculos XII–XV)*. Braga: Fundação Calouste Gulbenkian, 2007.

– "Body, Baths, and Cloth: Muslim and Christian Perceptions in Medieval Portugal." *Portuguese Studies* 21 (2005): 1–12.

López, Roberto J. "Fiestas y conmemoraciones regias en Galicia durante el reinado de Felipe II." In *El reino de Galicia en la monarquía de Felipe II*. Ed. Antonio Eiras Roel. Santiago de Compostela: Xunta de Galicia, 1998. 651–71.

López-Baralt, Luce. "La estética del cuerpo entre los moriscos del siglo XVI, o de cómo la minoría perseguida pierde el rostro." In *Le corps dans la société espagnole des XVie et XVIIe siècles*. Ed. Augustin Redondo. Paris: Publication de la Sorbonne, 1990. 335–48.

López Cantos, Ángel. *Juegos, fiestas y diversiones en la América española*. Madrid: MAPFRE, 1992.

López de Coca Castañer, José Enrique. "La seda en el reino de Granada (siglos XV y XVI)." In *España y Portugal en las rutas de la seda: Diez siglos de producción y comercio entre Oriente y Occidente*. Barcelona: Universitat de Barcelona, 1996. 33–57.

López de Hoyos, Juan. *Real apparato, y sumptuoso recebimiento con que Madrid ... rescibio a la Serenissima reyna D. Ana de Austria*. Ed. facsimile. Madrid: Ábaco, 1976.

López de José, Alicia. "Sobre el modo en que los caballeros han de galantear a las damas y entrar en Palacio y en el aposento de la Reina." In *La década de oro en la comedia española, 1630–1640: Actas de las XIX Jornadas de Teatro Clásico, Almagro, 9, 10 y 11 de julio de 1996*. Almagro: Universidad de Castilla-La Mancha, 1997. 213–28.

López de Mendoza, Íñigo [Count of Tendilla]. *Escribir y gobernar: El último registro de correspondencia del conde de Tendilla (1513–1515)*. Eds. María Amparo Moreno Trujillo, María José Osorio Pérez, and Juan María de la Obra Sierra. Includes supplementary CD with transcriptions. Granada: Universidad de Granada, 2007.

– *Correspondencia del conde de Tendilla, 1508–1513*. Ed. Emilio Meneses García. 2 vols. Madrid: Real Academia de la Historia, 1973–4.

– "Mémoire presenté au roi Philippe II par Íñigo López de Mendoza." In *L'Espagne au XVIe et au XVIIe siècle. Documents historiques et littéraires*. Ed. Alfred Morel-Fatio. Heilbronn: Henninger, 1878. 1–96.

López de Zárate, Francisco. *Obras varias de Francisco López de Zárate*. Ed. José Simón Díaz. 2 vols. Madrid: Centro Superior de Investigaciones Científicas, 1947.

López Gayarre, Pedro Antonio. *Historia documental del urbanismo en Talavera (1450–1700)*. Talavera de la Reina: Ayuntamiento de Talavera de la Reina, 2011.

López Martín, Juan. *Don Pedro Guerrero: Epistolario y documentación*. Roma: Instituto Español de Historia Eclesiástica, 1974.

López Megías, Francisco R., and María Jesús Ortiz López. *Almansa y los reyes de España (Siglos XVI al XXI)*. La Alberca: Diego Moreno Micol, 2012.

López Nevot, José Antonio. *Práctica de la Real Chancillería de Granada*. Granada: Comares, 2005.

López Párraga, Francisco. *Elogio heroico de las solemnes fiestas Reales, de Toros y juegos de Cañas, que la muy noble Ciudad de Sevilla, y su Senado, hizieron al felicissimo nacimiento de Baltazar, Principe de Castilla*. Jerez de la Frontera: Hernando Rey, 1630.

López Poza, Sagrario. "Emblemática aplicada y artificios de la cultura visual en los juegos caballerescos del Siglo de Oro." In *Cultura oral, visual y escrita en la España de los Siglos de Oro*. Eds. Inmaculada Osuna and Eva Llergo. Madrid: Visor, 2010. 413–62.

Luca, Chiara de. "Una comedia olvidada sobre la rebelión de las Alpujarras." *Quaderni, Università degli Studi di Lecce, Dipartimento di Lingue e Letterature Straniere* 21 (1999): 27–47.

La luna africana [c. 1680]. BNE Ms/15.540.

Luque Faxardo, Francisco de. *Fiel desengaño contra la ociosidad y los juegos*. Madrid: Miguel Serrano de Vargas, 1603.

MacKay, Angus. "The Ballad and the Frontier in Late Medieval Spain." *Bulletin of Hispanic Studies* 53 (1976): 15–33.

Maíllo Salgado, Felipe. "Jinete, jineta y sus derivados. Contribución al estudio del medievo español y al de su léxico." *Studia Philologica Salmanticiensia* 6 (1981): 105–17.

Mallea, Salvador de. *Granada festiva en el Real nacimiento del Sereníssimo Príncipe Don Felipe Próspero*. Granada: Baltasar de Bolibar, 1658.

Manrique, Ángel. *Sanctoral Cisterciense, hecho de varios discursos*. Barcelona: Hieronymo Margarit, 1613.

Maranges i Prat, Isidra. *La indumentària civil catalana (segles XIII–XV)*. Barcelona: Institut d'Estudis Catalans, 1991.

March, José M. *Niñez y juventud de Felipe II: Documentos inéditos sobre su educación civil, literaria y religiosa y su iniciación en el gobierno (1527–1547)*. 2 vols. Madrid: Ministerio de Asuntos Exteriores, 1941–2.

Marchante-Aragón, Lucas A. "The King, the Nation and the Moor: Imperial Spectacle and the Rejection of Hybridity in *The Masque of the Expulsion of the Moriscos*." *Journal for Early Modern Cultural Studies* 8.1 (2008): 98–133.

Marchi, Francesco de. *Narratione particolare delle gran feste e trionfi fatti in Portogallo et in Fiandra nello sposalitio dell'Illustrissimo et Eccellentissimo Signore, il Signor Alessandro Farnesse, Prencipe di Parma e Piacenza, e la Serenissima Donna Maria di Portogallo (1566).* In Giuseppe Bertini. *Le nozze di Alessandro Farnese: Feste alle corti di Lisbona e Bruxelles.* Milano: Skira, 1997. 77–132.

Marín, Manuela. "Signos visuales de la identidad andalusí." In *Tejer y vestir: De la antigüedad al islam.* Ed. Manuela Marín. Madrid: Centro Superior de Investigaciones Científicas, 2001. 137–80.

Marín, María Carmen. "Fiestas caballerescas aragonesas en la Edad Moderna." In *Fiestas públicas en Aragón en la Edad Moderna.* Ed. Eliseo Serrano Martín. Zaragoza: Diputación General de Aragón, 1995. 109–18.

Marín Ocete, Antonio. "El Concilio provincial de Granada en 1565." *Archivo Teológico Granadino* 25 (1962): 23–178.

Mármol Carvajal, Luis del. *Primera parte de la descripción general de África.* 2 vols. Granada: René Rabut, 1573.

– *Historia del rebelión y castigo de los moriscos del reino de Granada.* Ed. Javier Castillo Fernández. Granada: Universidad de Granada, 2015.

Márquez Villanueva, Francisco. *Moros, moriscos y turcos de Cervantes.* Barcelona: Bellaterra, 2010.

– *El problema morisco (desde otras laderas).* Madrid: Libertarias, 1991.

– "Lope infamado de morisco: *La villana de Getafe*." *Anuario de Letras* 21 (1983): 147–82.

Martín, José Luis. "Cofradías de Caballeros en la Castilla del quinientos: El caso de Ávila." *Espacio, Tiempo y Forma, Serie IV, Historia Moderna* 7 (1994): 409–34.

Martín Rosales, Francisco. "Pervivencias del concepto de frontera en Alcalá la Real en el AMAR." In *II Estudios de frontera: Actividad y vida en la frontera, congreso celebrado en Alcalá la Real 19–22 de noviembre de 1997.* Ed. Francisco Toro Ceballos and José Rodríguez Molina. Jaén: Diputación Provincial de Jaén, 1998. 528–9.

– "El ocio en la Alcalá del siglo XVI y XVII." *El Toro de Caña* 1 (1996): 331–93.

Martínez, Miguel. *Frontlines: Soldiers' Writing in the Early Modern Hispanic World.* Philadelphia: U of Pennsylvania P, 2016.

Martínez Bermejo, Saúl. "Beyond Luxury: Sumptuary Legislation in 17th-Century Castile." *Making, Using and Resisting the Law in European History.* Eds. Günther Lottes, Eero Medijainen and Jón Viðar Sigurðson. Pisa: Plus-Pisa UP, 2008. 93–108.

Martínez-Góngora, Mar. "El vestido del morisco como signo de la diferencia en la *Expulsión de los moros de España*, de Gaspar de Aguilar." *Revista Canadiense de Estudios Hispánicos* 34.3 (2010): 497–515.

– "El discurso africanista del Renacimiento en *La primera parte de la descripción general de África* de Luis del Mármol Carvajal." *Hispanic Review* 77.2 (2009): 171–95.

Martínez Medina, F. Javier. "El gran retablo mayor." In *El libro de la Capilla Real*. Ed. José Manuel Pita Andrade. Granada: Miguel Sánchez, 1994. 97–111.

Martínez Millán, José. "Las facciones cortesanas ante la expulsión de los moriscos." *Chrónica Nova* 36 (2010): 143–96.

Martínez Ruiz, Juan. *Inventarios de bienes moriscos del reino de Granada (siglo XVI)*. Madrid: Centro Superior de Investigaciones Científicas, 1972.

– "La indumentaria de los moriscos, según Pérez de Hita y los documentos de la Alhambra." *Cuadernos de la Alhambra* 3 (1967): 55–124.

Martínez Ruiz, José Ignacio. *Finanzas municipales y crédito público en la España moderna: La hacienda de la ciudad de Sevilla, 1528–1768*. Seville: Ayuntamiento de Sevilla, 1992.

Martínez Valls, Joaquín. "Los moriscos de la diócesis de Orihuela a finales del siglo XVI y legislación particular canónica sobre los mismos." *Anales de la Universidad de Alicante. Facultad de Derecho* 1 (1982): 243–72.

Mas, Albert. *Les Turcs dans la littérature espagnole du siècle d'or*. 2 vols. Paris: Centre de Recherches Hispaniques, 1967.

Matas Caballero, Juan. "Luis Vélez de Guevara y las comedias de moros." In *Espacio, tiempo y género en la comedia española: Actas de las II Jornadas de teatro clásico. Toledo, 14,15 y 16 de noviembre de 2003*. Eds. Felipe B. Pedraza Jiménez, Rafael González Cañal, and Gemma Gómez Rubio. Almagro: Universidad de Castilla-La Mancha, 2005. 319–40.

Mateos Royo, José Antonio. "La ciudad con el rey: Municipio, monarquía y ritual cívico en Zaragoza bajo Felipe III (1598–1621)." *Pedralbes* 21 (2001): 137–64.

Mayorga Huertas, Fermín. *Los moriscos de Hornachos crucificados y coronados de espinas*. Madrid: Cultiva Comunicación, 2009.

McCready, Warren T. *La heráldica en las obras de Lope de Vega y sus contemporáneos*. Toronto: Warren T. McCready, 1962.

Medina, Bartolomé de. *Breve instrucción de cómo se ha de administrar el Sacramento*. Salamanca: Mathias Gast, 1579.

Mejía Asensio, Ángel. "Fiesta en Guadalajara (siglos XVI–XVIII)." *Cuadernos de Etnología de Guadalajara* 30–31 (1998–9): 67–140.

La mejor luna africana. Valencia: Joseph de Orga, 1764.

Méndez de Vasconcelos, Juan. *Liga deshecha por la expulsión de los Moriscos de los Reynos de España*. Madrid: Alonso Martín, 1612.

Mendía, Felisa. "Libros españoles de sastrería de los siglos XVI a XVIII." *Revista Bibliográfica y Documental* 3.1–4 (1949): 93–140.

Meneses, Manuel de. *Chrónica do muito alto e muito esclarecido príncipe D. Sebastião*. Lisboa: Officina Ferreyriana, 1730.

Mercader, Gaspar. *El prado de Valencia*. Ed. Henri Mérimée. Toulouse: Edouard Privat, 1907.

Merino Álvarez, Abelardo. *La sociedad abulense durante el siglo XVI. La nobleza*. Madrid: Real Academia de la Historia, 1926.

Mesía de la Cerda. *Fiestas de toros y cañas celebradas en la ciudad de Córdoba el año de 1651, con una advertencia para el juego de las cañas, y un discurso de la caballería del torear*. Ed. Manuel Pérez de Guzmán y Boza. Seville: E. Rasco, 1887.

Mezquita Mesa, Teresa. "El *Códice de trajes* de la Biblioteca Nacional de España." *Goya* 346 (2014): 16–41.

Miguel Gallo, Ignacio Javier de. *Teatro y parateatro en las fiestas religiosas y civiles de Burgos (1550–1752): Estudio y documentos*. Burgos: Ayuntamiento de Burgos, 1994.

Milhou, Alain. "Fronteras, puentes y barreras. Identidad hispano–cristiana y rechazo de lo semítico (siglos XV–XVII)." *Cahiers du CRIAR* 18–19 (1998–9): 167–209.

– "Desemitización y europeización en la cultura española desde la época de los Reyes Católicos hasta la expulsión de los moriscos." *La cultura del Renaixement: Homenatge al pare Miquel Batllori*. Ed. Manuel Fernández Álvarez. Bellaterra: Universitat Autónoma de Barcelona, 1993. 35–60.

Miller, Lesley Ellis. "Dress to Impress: Prince Charles Plays Madrid, March–September 1623." In *The Spanish Match: Prince Charles's Journey to Madrid, 1623*. Ed. Alexander Samson. Burlington: Ashgate, 2006. 27–49.

– "Aspects of Men's Dress in Spain, 1600–1636: Courtly Developments and Popular Problems." MA Thesis. Courtauld Institute of Art, University of London, 1982.

Miranda Díaz, Bartolomé. *Reprobación y persecución de las costumbres moriscas: El caso de Magacela (Badajoz)*. Magacela: Ayuntamiento de Magacela, 2005.

Molina, Tirso de [Gabriel Téllez]. *El cobarde más valiente*. In *Comedias de Tirso de Molina. Vol. 2*. Ed. Emilio Cotarelo y Mori. Madrid: Bailly Bailliere, 1907. 416–37.

– *Las quinas de Portugal*. In *Comedias de Tirso de Molina. Vol. 2*. Ed. Emilio Cotarelo y Mori. Madrid: Bailly Bailliere, 1907. 568–90.

Molina Templado, José David. "Acerca de la expulsión mudéjar del Valle en 1613." In *Seminario internacional Valle de Ricote: 400 aniversario del primer bando de expulsión de los moriscos, 1609–2009*. Eds. María Cruz Gómez

Molina and José Miguel Abad González. Abarán: Consorcio Turístico Mancomunidad Valle de Ricote, 2010. 95–104.

Monteagudo Robledo, María Pilar. *El espectáculo del poder. Fiestas reales en la Valencia moderna*. Valencia: Ajuntament de València, 1995.

Moors, Annelies. "'Islamic Fashion' in Europe: Religious Conviction, Aesthetic Style, and Creative Consumption." *Encounters* 1.1 (2009): 175–201.

Moraleja Pinilla, Gerardo. *Historia de Medina del Campo*. Medina del Campo: Manuel Mateo Fernández, 1971.

Morales Talero, Santiago de. *Anales de la ciudad de Arjona*. Arjona: Ayuntamiento de Arjona, 1965.

Morel-Fatio, Alfred. "Les origines de Lope de Vega." *Bulletin Hispanique* 7 (1905): 38–53.

Moreno Díaz del Campo, Francisco J. "El hogar morisco: Familia, transmisión patrimonial y cauce de asimilación." *Al Kurras: Cuadernos de Estudios Mudéjares y Moriscos* 1.1 (2015): 97–119.

– *Los moriscos de la Mancha: Sociedad, ecconomía y modos de vida de una minoría en la Castilla moderna*. Madrid: Consejo Superior de Investigaciones Científicas, 2009.

Moreno Mendoza, Arsenio. "En hábito de comediante. El vestido en la pintura y el teatro en el Siglo de Oro español." *Goya* 312 (2006): 143–54.

Moreno Moreno, María Yolanda. "Los mudéjares de Talavera de la Reina en la baja Edad Media," PhD diss. Universidad Nacional de Educación a Distancia, 2015.

Moreno Villa, José. "Documentos sobre pintores recogidos en el Archivo de Palacio." *Archivo Español de Arte y Arqueología* 12.36 (1936): 261–8.

Morla Melgarejo, Bruno Joseph. *Libro nuevo bueltas de escaramuza, de gala, a la gineta*. ed. facsímile. Seville: Extramuros, 2012.

Morley, S. Griswold, and Courtney Bruerton. *Cronología de las comedias de Lope de Vega*. Trans. María Rosa Cartes. Madrid: Gredos, 1968.

Morley, S. Griswold, and Richard W. Tyler. *Los nombres de personajes en las comedias de Lope de Vega: Estudio de onomatología*. 2 vols. Valencia: Castalia, 1961.

Mosácula María, Francisco Javier. *Los regidores de la ciudad de Segovia, 1556–1665: Análisis socioeconómico de una oligarquía urbana*. Valladolid: Universidad de Valladolid, 2006.

Moya Pinedo, Jesús. *Corregidores y regidores de la ciudad de Cuenca desde 1.400 a 1.850*. Cuenca: León Sánchez, 1977.

Münzer, Hieronymus. *Itinerarium Hispanicum Hieronymi Monetarii, 1494–1495*. Ed. Ludwig Pfandl. *Revue Hispanique* 48 (1920): 1–179.

Muñoz, Ferran. *Mencía de Mendoza y la viuda de Mateo Flecha*. Valencia: Institució Alfons El Magnànim, 2001.

Navagero, Andrea. *Il viaggio fatto in Spagna, et in Francia*. Vinegia: Domenico Farri, 1563.

Navarro Belmonte, Carmel, Joaquim Serra Jaén, and Ana Maria Álvarez Fortes, eds. *Moriscos del sude Valencià: Memòria d'un poble olvidat*. Elx: Ajuntament d'Elx, 2009.

Nirenberg, David. *Anti-Judaism: The Western Tradition*. New York: W.W. Norton, 2013.

– *Communities of Violence: Persecution of Minorities in the Middle Ages*. Princeton: Princeton UP, 1996.

Nombela, José María. *Auge y decadencia en la España de los Austrias. La manufactura textil de Toledo en el siglo XVI*. Toledo: Ayuntamiento de Toledo, 2003.

Núñez de Avendaño, Pedro. *De exequendis mandatis regum Hispaniae*. Salamanca: Juan Cánovas, 1564.

Núñez de Velasco, Francisco. *Diálogos de contención entre la milicia y la ciencia*. Ed. Antonio Espino López. Madrid: Ministerio de Defensa, 2008.

Núñez Muley, Francisco. *A Memorandum for the President of the Royal Audiencia and Chancery Court of the City and Kingdom of Granada*. Trans. Vincent Barletta. Chicago: U of Chicago P, 2007.

– "The Original Memorial of Don Francisco Núñez Muley." Ed. Kenneth Garrad. *Atlante* 2 (1954): 199–226.

Núñez-Varela y Lendoiro, José Raimundo, and José Enrique Rivadulla Porta. *Historia documentada de Betanzos de los Caballeros*. 2 vols. Betanzos: Caja de Ahorros de Galicia, 1984.

Ojeda Nieto, José. "Visiones sobre los moriscos del obispado-gobernación de Orihuela en tiempos de la expulsión." In *III Congreso de Estudios del Vinalopó: La comunidad morisca en el Valle del Vinalopó*. Ed. Gabriel Segura Herrero. Petrer: Centro de Estudios Locales del Vinalopó, 2009. 25–37.

Oleza, Jaume de. *Exercicio militar en el qual se contienen muchos documentos y primores, assi de la Brida como de la Gineta*. 1604. Arxiu Municipal de Can Bordils (Palma de Mallorca) Ms 52.

Olsen, Margaret M. "'Ley ser, morir el más feo?': Calderón's *Morisco Gracioso* Teases out Spain's Violence." *Bulletin of the Comediantes* 62.2 (2010): 63–78.

Ordenanzas del concejo de Alcalá la Real (Siglos XV y XVI). Ed. María Teresa Murcia Cano. Alcalá la Real: Ayuntamiento de Alcalá la Real, 2011.

Ordenanzas de la hermandad de Nuestra Señora del Prado, años 1536, 1850, 1926 y 1973. Talavera de la Reina: Ayuntamiento de Talavera de la Reina, 1991.

Ordenanzas para el buen régimen y gobierno de la muy noble, muy leal e imperial ciudad de Toledo. Ed. Antonio Martín Gamero. Toledo: José de Cea, 1858.

Ordenanzas que los muy ilustres y magníficos señores de Granada mandaron guardar para la buena gouernación de su república. Granada: Francisco de Ochoa, 1672.

Orozco Díaz, Emilio. *Lope y Góngora frente a frente.* Madrid: Gredos, 1973.

Otero Mondéjar, Santiago. "Álvaro Cubillo de Aragón, poeta morisco del Siglo de Oro. Entorno familiar y aportaciones documentales." *Il Confronto Letterario* 58 (2012): 235–61.

– "La reconstrucción de una comunidad. Los moriscos en los reinos de Córdoba y Jaén (ss. XVI–XVII)." Diss. Universidad de Córdoba, 2012.

Pacheco, César, and Yolanda Moreno. "La comunidad morisca en Talavera: Los repartidos del Reino de Granada (1570–1609)." *Cuaderna: Revista de Estudios Humanísticos de Talavera y su Entorno* 21 (2015–16, in press).

Padilla, Lorenzo de. *Crónica de Felipe I, llamado el Hermoso.* Eds. Miguel Salvá and Pedro Sainz de Baranda. Madrid: Viuda de Calero, 1846.

Pamp, Diane J. *Lope de Vega ante el problema de la limpieza de sangre.* Northampton: Smith College, 1968.

Panford, Moses E. "La figura del negro en cuatro comedias barrocas." PhD diss. Temple University, 1993.

Pardo Molero, Juan Francisco. *La guerra de Espadán (1526): Una cruzada en la Valencia del renacimiento.* Segorbe: Ayuntamiento de Segorbe, 2000.

Parker, Alexander A. *The Mind and Art of Calderón: Essays on the Comedias.* Ed. Deborah Kong. Cambridge: Cambridge UP, 1998.

Pascual Molina, Jesús F. *Fiesta y poder: La corte en Valladolid (1502–1559).* Valladolid: Universidad de Valladolid, 2013.

Paz, Julián. *Archivo General de Simancas. Catálogo IV. Secretaría de Estado (capitulaciones con Francia y negociaciones diplomáticas de los embajadores de España en aquella corte), Vol. 1.* Madrid: Junta para la Ampliación de Estudios e Investigaciones Científicas, 1914.

Pedraza Jiménez, Felipe B. "La expulsion de los moriscos en el teatro áureo: Los ecos de un silencio." In *Textos sin fronteras. Literatura y sociedad II.* Eds. Hala Awaad and Mariela Insúa. Pamplona: Universidad de Pamplona, 2010. 179–200.

– "Lope, Lerma y su duque a través del epistolario y varias comedias." García García and Lobato 269–89.

Peinado Santaella, Rafael G. *Aristócratas nazaríes y principales castellanos.* Málaga: Diputación de Málaga, 2008.

Peláez del Rosal, Manuel, and Jesús Rivas Carmona. *Priego de Córdoba: Guía histórica y artística de la ciudad.* Salamanca: Ayuntamiento de Priego, 1980.

Pelorson, Jean-Marc. "Recherches sur la 'comedia' 'Los moriscos de Hornachos.'" *Bulletin Hispanique* 74.1–2 (1972): 5–42.

Peraita, Carmen. "'Como una casa portatil': Cultura del tapado y políticas del anonimato en el espacio urbano del siglo XVII." Colomer and Descalzo 1: 291–318.

Perceval, José María. *Todos son uno: Arquetipos, xenofobia y racismo. La imagen del morisco en la Monarquía Española durante los siglos XVI y XVII.* Almería: Instituto de Estudios Almerienses, 1997.

Pereda, Felipe. *La arquitectura elocuente: El edificio de la universidad de Salamanca bajo el reinado de Carlos V.* Madrid: Sociedad Estatal para la Conmemoración de los Centenarios de Felipe II y Carlos V, 2000.

Pereira, Carlos. *Naissance et renaissance de l'équitation portugaise: Du XVe au XVIIIe siècle d'après l'étude des textes fondateurs.* Paris: L'Harmattan, 2010.

Pérez, Joseph. "'Letrados' et seigneurs." Cardaillac, *Les Morisques* 235–44.

Pérez Boyero, Enrique. *Moriscos y cristianos en los señoríos del reino de Granada (1490–1568).* Granada: Universidad de Granada, 1997.

Pérez Costanti, Pablo. *Notas viejas galicianas.* 3 vols. Vigo: Sindicatos Católicos, 1925–6.

Pérez de Colosía Rodríguez, María Isabel, and Joaquín Gil Sanjuan. "Málaga y la Inquisición (1550–1600)." *Jábega* 38 (1982): 3–100.

Pérez de Heredia y Valle, Ignacio. *El concilio provincial de Granada en 1565. Edición crítica del malogrado concilio del arzobispo Guerrero.* Roma: Instituto Español de Historia Eclesiástica, 1990.

Pérez de Hita, Ginés. *La guerra de los moriscos (segunda parte de las* Guerras civiles de Granada*).* Ed. Paula Blanchard-Demouge. Ed. facsimile Joaquín Gil Sanjuán. Granada: Universidad de Granada, 1998.

– *Guerras civiles de Granada. Primera parte.* Ed. Shasta M. Bryant. Newark, DE: Juan de la Cuesta, 1982.

Pérez García, Rafael M., and Manuel F. Fernández Chaves. *Las élites moriscas entre Granada y el Reino de Sevilla. Rebelión, castigo y supervivencias.* Seville: Universidad de Sevilla, 2015.

Pérez Martín, Antonio. "El derecho y el vestido en el antiguo régimen." *Anales de Derecho* 16 (1998): 261–89.

Pérez Pastor, Cristóbal. "Nuevos datos acerca del histrionismo español en los siglos XVI y XVII (segunda serie)." *Bulletin Hispanique* 9.4 (1907): 360–85.

Pérez y Gómez, Antonio, ed. *Relaciones poéticas sobre las fiestas de toros y cañas.* 8 vols. Cieza: "la fonte que mana y corre," 1971–3.

Perry, Mary Elizabeth. *The Handless Maiden: Moriscos and the Politics of Religion in Early Modern Spain.* Princeton: Princeton UP, 2007.

Pinheiro da Veiga, Tomé. *Fastigimia.* Ed. Maria de Lurdes Belchior. Lisbon: Impresa Nacional-Casa da Moeda, 2009.

Pinto Pachecho, Francisco. *Tratado da cavalaria da gineta*. Lisbon: Ioam da Costa, 1670.

Porras Arboledas, Pedro Andrés. "Fiestas y diversiones en Ocaña a comienzos del siglo XVI: *Corpus Christi*, toros, juego de pelota, mancebías, etc." *Cuadernos de Historia del Derecho* extra 2 (2010): 507–67.

Poveda, Rafael. *Visites*. Monòver: Viuda de Manuel Vidal, 1993.

Pragmática y nueva orden, cerca de los vestidos, y trajes, assí de hombres, como de mugeres, y otras cosas, que se mandan guardar. Madrid: Juan de la Cuesta, 1611.

Pregmáticas y provisiones de S. M. el Rey don Philippe nuestro señor, sobre la lengua y vestidos, y otras cosas que an de hazer los naturales deste Reyno de Granada. Granada: Hugo de Mena, 1567.

Premática de los vestidos y trajes: la qual mandó el Rey nuestro señor se publicasse el año de mil y quinientos y sesenta y tres. Madrid: Pedro Madrigal, 1590.

Premática en que se mandan guardar las últimamente publicadas, sobre los tratamientos, y cortesías, y andar en coches, y en traer vestidos, y trajes, y labor de las sedas. Madrid: Juan de la Cuesta, 1611.

Presotto, Marco. "Vestir y desvestir: Apuntes sobre la indumentaria en la dramaturgia del primer Lope de Vega." *Annali di Ca' Foscari* 34.1–2 (1995): 365–83.

Profeti, Maria Grazia. "Storia di O. Sistema della moda e scrittura sulla moda nella Spagna del Secolo d'Oro." In *Identità e metamorfosi del barocco ispanico*. Ed. Giovanna Calabrò. Naples: Guida, 1987. 113–48.

– "Il manoscritto autografo del 'Caballero del Febo' di Juan Pérez de Montalbán." *Miscellanea di Studi Ispanici* 14 (1966–67): 218–309.

Puddu, Raffaele. "'Toros y cañas': I giochi equestri nella Spagna del Secolo d'Oro." *Quaderni Storici* 117.3 (2004): 807–29.

Puerta Escribano, Ruth de la. *La segunda piel. Historia del traje en España (del siglo XVI al XIX)*. Valencia: Generalitat Valenciana, 2006.

– "Los tratados del arte del vestir en la España moderna." *Archivo Español de Arte* 293 (2001): 45–65.

– "Reyes, moda y legislación jurídica en la España moderna" *Ars Longa* 9–10 (2000): 65–72.

– *Historia del gremio de sastres y modistas de Valencia del siglo XIII al siglo XX*. Valencia: Ayuntamiento de Valencia, 1997.

– "Las leyes suntuarias y la restricción del lujo en el vestir." Colomer and Descalzo 1: 209–31.

Puglisi, Anthony M. "Escritura y ambición: La *Historia del rebelión y castigo de los moriscos* de Luis del Mármol Carvajal." *Investigaciones Históricas* 28 (2008): 141–56.

Pym, Richard J., ed. *Rhetoric and Reality in Early Modern Spain*. London: Tamesis, 2006.

Quevedo, Francisco de. *Teatro completo*. Eds. Ignacio Arellano and Celsa Carmen García Valdés. Madrid: Cátedra, 2011.

– *Poesía original completa*. Ed. José Manuel Blecua. Barcelona: Planeta, 1999.

– *Epistolario completo de Francisco de Quevedo-Villegas*. Ed. Luis Astrana Marín. Madrid: Reus, 1946.

Quinn, Mary B. *The Moor and the Novel: Narrating Absence in Early Modern Spain*. New York: Palgrave, 2013.

Ramírez de Haro, Diego. *Tratado de la brida y gineta, y de las caballerías que en entrambas sillas se hacen y enseñan a los caballos, y de las formas de torear a pie y a caballo*. BNE Ms/9432.

Ramos Forqués, Alejandro. *La tauromaquia en Elche*. Elche: Imprenta Lepanto, 1980.

Ramos López, Pilar. *La música en la catedral de Granada en la primera mitad del siglo XVII: Diego de Pontac*. 2 vols. Granada: Diputación Provincial de Granada, 1994.

Ramos Sosa, Rafael. "Fiestas reales sevillanas en el imperio (1500–1550)." In *Premios Ciudad de Sevilla de Investigación 1986*. Seville: Ayuntamiento de Sevilla, 1988. 163–238.

Rappaport, Joanne. "Buena sangre y hábitos españoles: repensando a Alonso de Silva y Diego de Torres." *Anuario Colombiano de Historia Social y de la Cultura* 39.1 (2012): 19–48.

Recopilación de las leyes destos reynos hecha por mandado … de Felipe II. Segunda parte de las leyes del reyno. Alcalá de Henares: Andrés de Angulo, 1567.

Recopilación de las ordenanzas del Concejo de Jerez de la Frontera, siglos XV–XVI. Eds. María Antonia Carmona Ruiz and Emilio Martín Gutiérrez. Cádiz: Universidad de Cádiz, 2010.

Recopilación de las ordenanzas de la muy noble y muy leal cibdad de Sevilla. Eds. Víctor Pérez Escolano and Fernando Villanueva Sandino. Seville: Gráficas del Sur, 1975.

Redondo, Augustin."La religion populaire espagnole au XVIe siècle: un terrain d'affrontement?" Fonquerne and Esteban 329–69.

"Relación de las famosas fiestas que se hizieron en la Universidad de Alcalá de Henares." In *Fuentes para la historia de Madrid y su provincia. Tomo I: Textos impresos de los siglos XVI y XVII*. Ed. José Simón Díaz. Madrid: Instituto de Estudios Madrileños, 1964. 175–7.

"Relación de las fiestas que ubo en el casamiento de el excelentísimo señor Duque de Bragança con la excelentísima señora doña Ana de Velasco." BNE Ms/3826, 1r–20v.

Relación de lo sucedido en la ciudad de Valladolid desde el punto del felicíssimo nacimiento don Felipe Domínico Víctor. Ed. Patricia Marín Cepeda. Valladolid: Fundación Instituto Castellano y Leonés de la Lengua, 2005.

Relación de los hechos del muy magnífico e más virtuoso señor, el señor don Miguel Lucas, muy digno condestable de Castilla. Eds. Juan Cuevas Mata, Juan del Arco Moya and José del Arco Moya. Jaén: Universidad de Jaén, 2001.

Relación del camino y buen viaje que hizo el Principe de España Don Phelipe nuestro señor, año de … 1548 … que passo de España en Italia, y fue por Alemania hasta Flandres. n.e.: n.p., 1551.

Resende, Garcia de. *Livro das obras de Garcia de Resende.* Ed. Evelina Verdelho. Lisboa: Fundação Calouste Gulbenkian, 1994.

Ribero, Antonio Luis. *El espejo del cavallero en ambas sillas.* Madrid: n.p., 1671.

Ricard, Robert. "Espagnol et portugais 'marlota': Recherches sur le vocabulaire du vêtement hispano-mauresque." *Bulletin Hispanique* 53.2 (1951): 131–56.

Riera, Juan. *Rentas eclesiásticas, moriscos y penitenciados (Los obispos de Cartagena y Orihuela a mediados del siglo XVI).* Valladolid: Universidad de Valladolid, 1984.

Río Barredo, María José del. *Madrid, urbs regia: La capital ceremonial de la Monarquía Católica.* Madrid: Marcial Pons, 2000.

Ríos Saloma, Martín F. *La Reconquista. Una construcción historiográfica (siglos XVI–XIX).* Madrid: Marcial Pons, 2011.

Rocha Burguen, Francisco de la. *Geometría y traça perteneciente al oficio de sastres.* Valencia: Patricio Mey, 1618.

Rodríguez de Ardila, Gabriel. "Historia de los Condes de Tendilla." Ed. Raymond Foulché-Delbosc. *Revue Hispanique* 31 (1914): 63–131.

Rodríguez Cacho, Lina. "Pecar en el vestir: Del púlpito a la sátira." *Edad de Oro* 8 (1989): 193–205.

Rodríguez de Diego, Julia Teresa, and Eduardo J. Marchena Ruiz. *Los moriscos españoles trasterrados.* Madrid: Ministerio de Cultura, 2009.

Rodríguez Marín, Francisco. *Nuevo documentos cervantinos.* Madrid: Real Academia Española, 1914.

– *Luis Barahona de Soto: Estudio biográfico, bibliográfico y crítico.* Madrid: Real Academia Española, 1903.

Rodríguez Villa, Antonio. *El emperador Carlos V y su corte según las cartas de don Martín de Salinas, embajador del infante don Fernando (1522–1539).* Madrid: Real Academia de la Historia, 1903.

Rojas, Juan Luis de. *Relaciones de algunos sucesos postreros de Berbería, salida de los Moriscos de España y entrega de Larache.* Lisbon: Jorge Rodriguez, 1613.

Rojas Villandrando, Agustín. *El viaje entretenido.* Ed. Jaen Pierre Ressot. Madrid: Castalia, 1972.

Rojo Vega, Anastasio. *Fiestas y comedias en Valladolid. Siglos XVI–XVII.* Valladolid: Ayuntamiento de Valladolid, 1999.

– *El Siglo de Oro. Inventario de una época.* Valladolid: Junta de Castilla y León, 1996.

Romancero general, en que se contienen todos los romances que andan impressos. Ed. Francisco López. Madrid: Juan de la Cuesta, 1604.

Romero Abao, Antonio del Rocío. "Las fiestas de Sevilla en el siglo XV." In *Las fiestas de Sevilla en el siglo XV y otros estudios*. Ed. José Sánchez Herrero. Madrid: Deimos, 1991. 12–178.

Root, Deborah. "Speaking Christian: Orthodoxy and Difference in Sixteenth-Century Spain." *Representations* 23 (1988): 119–32.

Rosal, Francisco del. *Diccionario etimológico. Alfabeto primero de Origen y Etimología de todos los vocablos originales de la Lengua Castellana*. Ed. Enríquez Gómez Aguado. Madrid: Centro Superior de Investigaciones Científicas, 1992.

Ruano de la Haza, José María. "El vestuario en el teatro de corral." *Cuadernos de Teatro Clásico* 13–14 (2000): 43–62.

Rublack, Ulinka. *Dressing Up: Cultural Identity in Renaissance Europe*. Oxford: Oxford UP, 2010.

Rueda, Lope de. *Las cuatro comedias*. Ed. Alfredo Hermenegildo. Madrid: Cátedra, 2001.

Rufo, Juan. *La Austriada*. Madrid: Alonso Gómez, 1584.

Ruiz, Teófilo F. *A King Travels: Festive Traditions in Late Medieval and Early Modern Spain*. Princeton: Princeton UP, 2012.

Ruiz de Villegas, Hernán. *Tratado de caualleria a la gineta (1569–1572)*. Ed. Valentín Moreno Gallego. Madrid: Unión de Bibliófilos Taurinos, 2012.

Ruiz García, Elisa, and Pedro Valverde Ogallar. "Relación de las fiestas caballerescas de Valladolid de 1527: Un documento inédito." *Emblemata* 9 (2003): 127–94.

Ruiz Ibáñez, José Javier. "'Sin tratar de otros'. Expulsión y permanencia de los mudéjares del Reino de Murcia." *Murgetana* 131 (2014): 289–302.

– *Las dos caras de Jano: Monarquía, ciudad e individuo. Murcia, 1588–1648*. Murcia: Universidad de Murcia, 1995.

Ruiz Lagos, Manuel. *Moriscos. De los romances del gozo al exilio*. Seville: Guadalmena, 2001.

– "Introducción." In Pedro Calderón de la Barca. *El Tuzaní de la Alpujarra*. Seville: Guadalmena, 1998. 11–80.

Rumeu de Armas, Antonio. *Cádiz, metrópoli del comercio con África en los siglos XV y XVI*. Cádiz: Caja de Ahorros de Cádiz, 1976.

Saavedra, Santiago, ed. *Alonso Sánchez Coello y el retrato en la corte de Felipe II*. Madrid: Museo del Prado, 1990.

Sáez, Ricardo. "Los moriscos en el arzobispado de Toledo a finales del siglo XVI." In *Homenaje a don Ignacio Gallego Peñalver*. Toledo: Seminario Conciliar, 1984. 61–72.

Sagovia, Baltasar. *Llibre de geometria del offici de sastres*. Barcelona: Esteve, 1617.

Salvà i Ballester, Adolf. *Bosqueig històric i bibliogràfic de les festes de moros i cristians*. Alicante: Instituto de Estudios Alicantinos, 1958.

Salvador Esteban, Emilia. "Datos sobre el comercio con el norte de África en la Valencia del siglo XVI." In *Primer Congreso de Historia del País Valenciano*. 4 vols. Valencia: Universidad de Valencia, 1976. 3: 119–24.

Sánchez, Magdalena. *The Empress, the Queen, and the Nun: Women and Power at the Court of Philip III of Spain*. Baltimore: Johns Hopkins UP, 1998.

Sánchez Cano, David. "Dances for the Royal Festivities in Madrid in the Sixteenth and Seventeenth Centuries." *Dance Research* 23.2 (2005): 123–52.

Sánchez de Badajoz, Diego. *Farsas*. Ed. Miguel Ángel Pérez Priego. Madrid: Cátedra, 1985.

– *Recopilación en metro*. Ed. Frida Weber de Kurlat. Buenos Aires: Universidad de Buenos Aires, 1968.

Sánchez Jiménez, Antonio. "Introducción." Lope de Vega. *Romances de juventud*. Ed. Antonio Sánchez Jiménez. Madrid: Cátedra, 2015. 9–156.

– "La batalla del romancero: Lope de Vega, los romances moriscos y *La villana de Getafe*." *Anuario Lope de Vega* 20 (2014): 160–86.

Sánchez Moltó, Manuel Vicente. "Fiestas del recibimiento de las reliquias de San Félix de Alcalá (1607)." *Anales Complutenses* 19 (2007): 159–97.

Sánchez Ramos, Valeriano. "Fiestas de toros y cañas en Berja (primer cuarto del siglo XVII). Notas para el estudio de la fiesta barroca." In *Actas del III Congreso de Folclore Andaluz*. Almería: Centro de Documentación Musical de Andalucía, 1990. 453–70.

Sancho de Sopranis, Hipólito. *Juegos de toros y cañas en Jerez de la Frontera*. Jerez: Centro de Estudios Jerezanos, 1960.

Sandoval, Prudencio de. *Historia de la vida y hechos del emperador Carlos V*. Ed. Carlos Seco Serrano. 3 vols. Biblioteca de Autores Españoles 80–2. Madrid: Atlas, 1955–6.

San Román, Francisco de. *Lope de Vega, los cómicos toledanos y el poeta sastre: Serie de documentos inéditos de los años de 1590 a 1615*. Madrid: Imprenta Góngora, 1935.

Santa Cruz, Alonso de. *Crónica del emperador Carlos V*. Eds. Ricardo Beltrán y Rózpide and Antonio Blázquez y Delgado-Aguilera. 5 vols. Madrid: Real Academia de la Historia, 1920–5.

Santamaría Conde, Alfonso. "Sobre la vida de los moriscos granadinos deportados en la villa de Albacete." *Al-Basit: Revista de Estudios Albacetenses* 18 (1986): 5–32.

Santos Domínguez, Luis Antonio. "El lenguaje teatral del morisco." *Boletín de la Biblioteca de Menéndez Pelayo* 63 (1987): 5–16.

Santos Vaquero, Ángel. *La industria textil sedera de Toledo*. Cuenca: Universidad de Castilla-La Mancha, 2010.

Sanz Ayán, Carmen. "Felipe II y los orígenes del teatro barroco." *Cuadernos de Historia Moderna* 23 (1999): 47–78.

Sanz Egaña, Cesáreo. *Tres libros de la gineta de los siglos XVI y XVII*. Madrid: Sociedad de Bibliófilos Españoles, 1951.

Savariego de Santana, Gaspar. *Libro de la Iberiada de los hechos de Scipion Africano en estas partes de España*. Valladolid: Luis Sánchez, 1603.

Schaeffer, Adolf. *Geschichte des spanischen Nationaldramas*. 2 vols. Leipzig: F.A. Brockhaus, 1890.

Segura del Pino, Dolores. "Solidaridad y signos de identidad de la población morisca de Almería." *Sharq Al-Andalus* 14–15 (1997–1998): 245–61.

Sentaurens, Jena. *Séville et le théâtre: De la fin du Moyen Âge à la fin du XVIIe siècle*. 2 vols. Bordeaux: Presses Universitaires de Bordeaux, 1984.

Serna Hernández, Joaquín. *Mudéjares, cristianos y moriscos de Albatera*. Albatera: Ayuntamiento de Albatera, 2002.

Sieber, Diane. "El monstruo en su laberinto: Cristianos en las Alpujarras de *Amar después de la muerte*." In *Actas del XIII Congreso de la Asociación Internacional de Hispanistas*. Eds. Florencio Sevilla Arroyo and Carlos Alvar Ezquerra. 4 vols. Madrid: Castalia, 2000. 1: 740–6.

– "The Frontier Ballad and Spanish Golden Age Historiography: Recontextualizing the *Guerras civiles de Granada*." *Hispanic Review* 65.3 (1997): 291–306.

Símini, Diego. "La rebelión de las Alpujarras en tres comedias del Siglo de Oro (Calderón, Fajardo, Cunedo)." *Jornadas de Teatro del Siglo de Oro XXI–XXIII*. Ed. Antonio Serrano. Almería: Instituto de Estudios Almerienses, 2007. 221–31.

Simón Díaz, José. *Relaciones breves de actos públicos celebrados en Madrid de 1541 a 1650*. Madrid: Instituto de Estudios Madrileños, 1982.

Simón, Pedro. *Primera parte de las noticias historiales de las conquistas de tierra firme en las Indias Occidentales*. Cuenca: Domingo de la Iglesia, 1626.

Sirera, Josep Lluís. "Mercaderes, campesinos y jornaleros en el teatro de Gaspar Aguilar." In *Modelos de vida en la España del Siglo de Oro. Vol. 1: El noble y el trabajador*. Eds. Ignacio Arellano and Marc Vitse. Madrid: Iberoamericana, 2004. 353–65.

Sloman, Albert E. "The Phonology of Moorish Jargon in the Works of Early Spanish Dramatists and Lope de Vega." *Modern Language Review* 44 (1949): 207–17.

Sobaler Seco, María Ángeles. "La cofradía de nobles caballeros de Santiago de Soria (1572): Un intento frustrado de corporativismo nobiliar." *Investigaciones Históricas: Época Moderna y Contemporánea* 12 (1992): 9–30.

Sobrado Correa, Hortensio. *La ciudad de Lugo en el Antiguo Régimen. Siglos XVI–XIX*. Lugo: Diputación Provincial de Lugo, 2001.

Soláns Soteras, María Soledad. *La moda en la sociedad aragonesa del siglo XVI*. Zaragoza: Institución "Fernando el Católico," 2009.

Soria Mesa, Enrique. *Los últimos moriscos. Pervivencias de la población de origen islámico en el reino de Granada (siglos XVII–XVIII)*. Valencia: Universitat de València, 2014.

– *La nobleza en la España moderna*. Madrid: Marcial Pons, 2007.

– "De la conquista a la asimilación. La integración de la aristocracia nazarí en la oligarquía granadina. Siglos XV–XVII." *Áreas* 14 (1992): 49–64.

Soto y Aguilar, Diego de. *Jornada madrileña del Príncipe de Gales: Fiestas de toros y cañas en su honor*. Ed. Diego Ruiz Morales. Madrid: Unión de Bibliófilos Taurinos, 1967.

Sousa Congosto, Francisco de. *Introducción a la historia de la indumentaria en España*. Madrid: Istmo, 2007.

Spratlin, Valaurez B. *Juan Latino, Slave and Humanist*. New York: Spinner Press, 1938.

Stallaert, Christiane. *Etnogénesis y etnicidad. Una aproximación histórica-antropológica al casticismo*. Barcelona: Proyecto A, 1998.

Suárez de Figueroa, Cristóbal. *El pasajero*. Ed. María Isabel López Bascuñana. 2 vols. Barcelona: Promociones y Publicaciones Universitarias, 1998.

– *Plaza universal de todas las ciencias y artes*. Madrid: Luis Sánchez, 1615.

Suárez de Peralta, Juan. *Tratado de la jineta y de la brida*. Ed. José Álvarez del Villar. México D. F.: [n.p.], 1950.

Suárez Montañés, Diego. *Historia del maestre último que fue de Montesa y de su hermano don Felipe de Borja*. Eds. Beatriz Alonso Acero and Miguel Ángel de Bunes Ibarra. Valencia: Institució Alfons el Magnànim, 2004.

Surtz, Ronald E. "Crimes of the Tongue: The Inquisitorial Trials of Cristóbal Duarte Ballester." *Medieval Encounters* 12.3 (2006): 519–32.

– "Maurofilia y maurofobia en los procesos inquisitoriales de Cristóbal Duarte Ballester." In *Mélanges Luce López-Baralt*. Ed. Abdeljelil Temimi. 2 vols. Zaghouan: Fondation Temimi, 2001. 2: 711–21.

– "La imagen del moro en el teatro peninsular del siglo XVI." In *Actes du VIIe Symposium International d'Études Morisques*. Ed. Abdeljelil Temimi. Zaghouan: Fondation Temimi, 1999. 251–60.

Szmolka Clares, José. "Estudio." *Epistolario del conde de Tendilla (1504–1506)*. Eds. María Amparo Moreno Trujillo and María José Osorio Pérez. 2 vols. Granada: Universidad de Granada, 1996. 1: xv–cxxxvi.

Tapia Sánchez, Serafín de. "Los moriscos de Castilla la Vieja, ¿una identidad en proceso de disolución?" *Sharq Al-Andalus* 12 (1995): 179–95.

– *La comunidad morisca de Ávila*. Salamanca: Universidad de Salamanca, 1991.

Tapia Garrido, José Ángel. *Historia general de Almería y su provincia*. 14 vols. Almería: Monte de Piedad y Caja de Ahorros de Almería, 1989.

Tapia y Salcedo, Gregorio de. *Ejercicios de la gineta al príncipe nuestro señor Baltasar Carlos*. Ed. facsimile. Madrid: Turner, 1980.

Tárrega, Francisco Agustín. *El prado de Valencia*. Ed. José Luis Canet Vallés. London: Tamesis, 1985.

– *La enemiga favorable*. In *Poetas dramáticos valencianos*. Ed. Eduardo Juliá Martínez. 2 vols. Madrid: Revista de Archivos, 1929. 1: 576–621.

– *Las suertes trocadas, y torneo venturoso*. In *Poetas dramáticos valencianos*. Ed. Eduardo Juliá Martínez. 2 vols. Madrid: Revista de Archivos, 1929. 1: 380–441.

Tejeda Fernández, Margarita. *Glosario de términos de la indumentaria regia y cortesana en España (siglos XVII y XVIII)*. Málaga: Universidad de Málaga, 2006.

Tenorio y Cerero, Nicolás. *Noticia de las fiestas en honor de la Marquesa de Denia hechas por la ciudad de Sevilla en el año de 1599*. Seville: C. de Torres, 1896.

Toro Buiza, Luis. *Noticias de los juegos de cañas reales tomadas de nuestros libros de gineta*. Seville: Imprenta Municipal, 1944.

Toro Ceballos, Francisco. *El discurso genealógico de Sancho de Aranda*. Alcalá la Real: Centro de Estudios Históricos "Carmen Juan Lovera," 1993.

Torres, José María. "Toros y cañas." *Revista de Valencia* 1 (1880–1881): 349–58.

Trambaioli, Marcella. "Lope de Vega y la casa de Moncada." *Criticón* 106 (2009): 5–44.

Tristán García, Francisco. "Benamaurel, villa de la jurisdicción bastetana. De la época nazarí a la morisca (1436–1567)." *Péndulo: Papeles de Bastitania* 8 (2007): 71–98.

– "Las fiestas oficiales en la Baza del siglo XVI." In *Iglesia y sociedad en el reino de Granada (ss. XVI–XVIII)*. Eds. Miguel Luis López-Guadalupe Muñoz, Antonio Lara Ramos, and Antonio Luis Cortés Peña. Granada: Universidad de Granada, 2003. 389–410.

Tueller, James B. *Good and Faithful Christians: Moriscos and Catholicism in Early Modern Spain*. New Orleans: UP of the South, 2002.

Uhagón, Franciso R. de. *Relaciones históricas de los siglos XVI y XVII*. Madrid: Sociedad de Bibliófilos Españoles, 1896.

Valderrama, Pedro. *Exercicios espirituales para todas las festividades de los santos*. Madrid: Alonso Martín, 1608.

Varey, J.E., and N.D. Shergold. *Teatros y comedias en Madrid: 1600–1650*. London: Tamesis, 1971.

Vargas Machuca, Bernardo de. *Teórica y exercicios de la gineta*. Sanz Egaña 113–270.

Vargas, [Maestro]. *Recibimiento que se hizo en Salamanca a la Princesa doña María de Portugal, viniendo a casarse con el Príncipe don Felipe II.* Ed. Jacobo Sanz Hermida. Salamanca: Velociraptor, 2001.

Vázquez Rengifo, Juan. *Grandezas de la ciudad de Vélez y hechos notables de sus naturales.* Eds. Joaquín Novella Román and Ángel Pérez Pascual. Vélez-Málaga: Ayuntamiento de Vélez-Málaga, 1998.

Vega, Lope de. *La doncella Teodor.* Ed. Julián González Barrera. Kassel: Reichenberger, 2008.

– *Arte nuevo de hacer comedias.* Ed. Enrique García Santo-Tomás. Madrid: Cátedra, 2006.

– *Fiestas de Denia.* Ed. Maria Grazia Profeti. Firenze: Alinea, 2004.

– *La desdicha por la honra.* In *Novelas a Marcia Leonarda.* Ed. Antonio Carreño. Madrid: Cátedra, 2002. 179–231.

– *Novelas a Marcia Leonarda.* Ed. Antonio Carreño. Madrid: Cátedra, 2002.

– "Descripción de la Tapada." In *Obras poéticas.* Ed. José Manuel Blecua. Barcelona: Planeta, 1983. 704–25.

– *La vitoria de la honra.* In *Las ferias de Madrid y La vitoria de la honra.* Ed. Alva V. Ebersole. Valencia: Hispanófila, 1977.

– *No son todos ruiseñores.* In *Obras de Lope de Vega.* Vol. 32. Ed. Marcelino Menéndez Pelayo. Biblioteca de Autores Españoles 249. Madrid: Atlas, 1972. 137–84.

– *Lo que pasa en una tarde.* Ed. Richard Angelo Picerno. Chapel Hill: U of North Carolina P, 1971.

– *La desdichada Estefanía.* Ed. J.H. Arjona. Valencia: Castalia, 1967.

– *Epistolario de Lope de Vega Carpio.* Ed. Agustín G. de Amezúa. 4 vols. Madrid: Real Academia Española, 1935–43.

– *Amor secreto hasta celos.* In *Obras de Lope de Vega.* Vol. 3. Ed. Emilio Cotarelo y Mori. Madrid: Real Academia Española, 1917. 390–421.

– *La burgalesa de Lerma.* In *Obras de Lope de Vega: Obras dramáticas.* Vol. 4. Ed. Emilio Cotarelo y Mori. Madrid: Real Academia Española, 1917. 30–73.

– *Los cautivos de Argel.* In *Obras de Lope de Vega: Obras dramáticas.* Vol. 4. Ed. Emilio Cotarelo y Mori. Madrid: Real Academia Española, 1917. 223–60.

– *Los palacios de Galiana.* In *Obras de Lope de Vega.* Vol. 13. Ed. Marcelino Menéndez Pelayo. Madrid: Sucesores de Rivadeneyra, 1902. 161–202.

– *La envidia de la nobleza.* In *Obras de Lope de Vega.* Vol. 11. Ed. Marcelino Menéndez Pelayo. Madrid: Real Academia Española, 1900. 3–38.

– *El hijo de Reduán.* In *Obras de Lope de Vega.* Vol. 11. Ed. Marcelino Menéndez Pelayo. Madrid: Real Academia Española, 1900. 87–124.

– *El príncipe perfecto, primera parte.* In *Obras de Lope de Vega.* Vol. 10. Madrid: Real Academia Española, 1899. 447–87.

– *La octava maravilla*. In *Décima parte de las comedias de Lope de Vega Carpio*. Madrid: Juan de la Cuesta, 1618. 151v–176v.

– ed. *Relación de las fiestas que la imperial ciudad de Toledo hizo al nacimiento del Príncipe N. S. Felipe IIII*. n.p.: n.e., 1605.

Vélez de Guevara, Luis. *Don Pedro Miago*. Eds. William R. Manson and C. George Peale. Newark, DE: Juan de la Cuesta, 2005.

– "Baile de los moriscos." In *Teatro breve*. Ed. Héctor Uráiz Tortajada. Madrid: Iberoamericana, 2002. 231–5.

– *El diablo Cojuelo*. Ed. Ramón Valdés. Barcelona: Crítica, 1999.

Vélez-Sainz, Julio. *El Parnaso español: Canon, mecenazgo y propaganda en la poesía del Siglo de Oro*. Madrid: Visor, 2006.

Velo Pensado, Ismael. *La vida municipal de A Coruña en el siglo XVI*. A Coruña: Diputación Provincial de A Coruña, 1992.

Viforcos Marinas, María Isabel. *La Asunción y el Corpus, de fiestas señeras a fiestas olvidadas*. León: Universidad de León, 1994.

– *El León barroco. Los regocijos taurinos*. León: Universidad de León, 1992.

Vilar, Juan Bautista. *Los moriscos del reino de Murcia y obispado de Orihuela*. Murcia: Real Academia Alfonso X el Sabio, 1992.

– "Las 'ordinaciones' del Obispo Tomás Dassio, un intento de asimilación de los Moriscos de la diócesis de Orihuela." Cardaillac, *Les Morisques* 383–410.

Villacastín, Tomás de. *Triunpho de la fortuna*. Real Academia de la Historia. Ms 9-2566. 45v–69r.

Villalmanzo Cameno, Jesús. "La colección pictórica sobre la expulsión de los moriscos." In *La expulsión de los moriscos del reino de Valencia*. Valencia: Fundación Bancaja, 1997. 34–68.

Villalobos, Simón de. *Modo de pelear a la gineta*. Sanz Egaña 67–112.

Villena Jurado, José. *Málaga en los albores del siglo XVII desde la documentación municipal*. Málaga: Diputación Provincial de Málaga, 1994.

Vincent, Bernard. "Los moriscos granadinos y la monarquía (1570–1609)." In *Ciudades en conflicto (siglos XVI–XVIII)*. Eds. José I. Fortea and Juan E. Gelabert. Valladolid: Junta de Castilla y León, 2008. 163–79.

– "La mobilité sociale." In *La movilidad social en la España del Antiguo Régimen*. Eds. Inés Gómez González and Miguel Luis López-Guadalupe Muñoz. Granada: Comares, 2007. 49–60.

– *El río morisco*. Trans. Antonio Luis Cortés Peña. Valencia: Universitat de València, 2006.

– "Carlos V en Granada." *Carlos V. Europeísmo y universalidad*. Eds. Juan Luis Castellano and Francisco Sánchez-Montes González. 5 vols. Madrid: Sociedad Estatal para la Conmemoración de los Centenarios de Felipe II y Carlos V, 2001. 1: 283–90.

– "Les jesuites chroniqueurs. Récits de la guerre des Alpujarras." *Chronica Nova* 22 (1995): 429–66.

– *Andalucía en la Edad Moderna: Economía y sociedad*. Granada: Diputación Provincial de Granada, 1985.

– "¿Qué aspecto físico tenían los moriscos?" *Andalucía moderna: Actas II Coloquio Historia de Andalucía*. 2 vols. Córdoba: Monte de Piedad y Caja de Ahorros de Córdoba, 1983. 2: 335–40.

Vital, Laurent. "Premier voyage de Charles-Quint en Espagne, de 1517 à 1518." Gachard 1–303.

"Voyage que l'archiduc Philippe fait pour aller en Espagne." In *Die Handschriften der K. K. Hofbibliothek in Wien*. Ed. Joseph Chmel. 2 vols. Viena: Carl Gerold, 1840–1841. 2: 554–655.

Walzer, Hannaa'. "Los moriscos de *Amar después de la muerte*." In *Ayer y hoy de Calderón*. Eds. Jesús Pérez-Magallón and José María Ruano de la Haza. Madrid: Castalia, 2002. 134–45.

Watanabe-O'Kelly, Helen. "The Early Modern Festival Book: Function and Form." In *Europa Triumphans: Court and Civic Festivals in Early Modern Europe*. Ed. J.-R. Mulryne, Helen Watanabe-O'Kelly and Margaret Shewring. 2 vols. Aldershot: Ashgate, 2004. 1: 3–17.

– "Tournaments in Europe." In *Spectaculum Europaeum: Theatre and Spectacle in Europe (1580–1750)*. Eds. Pierre Béhar and Watanabe-O'Kelly. Wiesbaden: Harrassowitz Verlag, 1999. 595–720.

Weiditz, Christoph. *Authentic Everyday Dress of the Renaissance: All 154 Plates from the* Trachtenbuch. Ed. Theodor Hampe. New York: Dover, 1994.

Weissberger, Barbara F. *Isabel Rules: Constructing Queenship, Wielding Power*. Minneapolis: U of Minnesota P, 2004.

Whitaker, Shirley B. *The Dramatic Works of Álvaro Cubillo de Aragón*. Chapel Hill: University of North Carolina, 1975.

Wilder, Thornton. "Lope, Pinedo, Some Child-Actors, and a Lion." *Romance Philology* 7.1 (1953): 19–25.

Wilson, Margaret. "'Si África llora, España no ríe': A Study of Calderón's *Amar después de la muerte* in Relation to its Source." *Bulletin of Hispanic Studies* 61.3 (1984): 419–25.

Wright, Elizabeth R. *Pilgrimage to Patronage: Lope de Vega and the Court of Philip III, 1598–1621*. Lewisburg, PA: Bucknell UP, 2001.

Ybáñez Worboys, Pilar. "Fiestas representativas de la política beligerante de Carlos I." *Baetica: Estudios de Arte, Geografía e Historia* 20 (1998): 415–26.

Yiacoup, Şizen. *Frontier Memory: Cultural Conflict and Exchange in the* Romancero fronterizo. London: Modern Humanities Research Association, 2013.

Zagorin, Perez. *Rebels and Rulers, 1500–1600.* 2 vols. Cambridge: U of Cambridge P, 1982.

Zapata, Luis. *Miscelánea o varia historia.* Ed. Antonio Carrasco González. Llerena: Editores Extremeños, 1999.

Zayas, Rodrigo de. *Los moriscos y el racismo de Estado: Creación, persecución y deportación (1499–1612).* Córdoba: Almuzara, 2006.

Zofío Llorente, Juan Carlos. *Gremios y artesanos en Madrid, 1550–1650. La sociedad del trabajo en una ciudad cortesana preindustrial.* Madrid: Centro Superior de Investigaciones Científicas, 2005.

Index

TORONTO IBERIC

CO-EDITORS: Robert Davidson (Toronto) and Frederick A. de Armas (Chicago)

EDITORIAL BOARD: Josiah Blackmore (Harvard); Marina Brownlee (Princeton); Anthony J. Cascardi (Berkeley); Justin Crumbaugh (Mt Holyoke); Emily Francomano (Georgetown); Jordana Mendelson (NYU); Joan Ramon Resina (Stanford); Enrique Garcia Santo-Tomás (U Michigan); Kathleen Vernon (SUNY Stony Brook)